Introduction

Welcome to the world of case modding. Inside this book you will discover everything you need to know to become a member of this new and exiting aspect of the computer age.

What Is Case Modding?

Computer modification, or *modding*, is the art and science of taking standard computer components and changing them in some way to better suit your needs. You might hear it referred to as "computer modding," "case modding," or usually just "modding," but it's all the same. Just take a computer component or case and change it from its original form and you are now a "modder."

Mods typically come in two varieties: functional and visual. *Overclocking*, or increasing airflow would be a functional mod. A visual mod would include things like painting a case. The best mods include both aspects in a single package.

Modders are all around you every day, without your even realizing it. Every child or adult that takes things apart just to see how they work is showing latent modding skills. Curiosity, challenge, stubbornness—these are all the things that haunt and bless every modder out there.

Modding has a far longer history than most people realize. Many of the people in the community will state that modern modding came about in 1998 with the first published "blowhole" on www.hardforum.com and/or in February of 2000 with the first full-body mod, the "Unreal Case" by John Young III (a.k.a. Ultragooey). But truth be told, there is evidence of case modding far earlier, back before the Internet was accessible to everyone and long before digital cameras were affordable by anyone. Ask questions about the birth of modding on any of modding forums, and you will get heated debates from people who claim they modded their first computer case back in the 1800s or so it seems . . .

But in the end it doesn't matter. Knowing what has come before in the modding community can give you ideas and teach you things, but don't get hung up on it. Take modding for what it is to you. Maybe it means overclocking to squeeze every last ounce of performance from your machine. Maybe it means painting a beautiful picture on the side of your case. Just figure out how you want to express yourself and go for it.

Why You Should Mod

Why even bother with all this modding stuff? What's the reason you'd even want to go through all the pain and trouble? A few rare people will be able to win some contests or have 15 minutes of fame in some magazine from their case mod. Even fewer people will make a living by modding cases. The primary reason for modding a case is a deep desire to be unique.

It doesn't really matter if your case is red or black or silver or any other color. It doesn't matter how fast your computer is. It doesn't matter if it's small or large. The amount of memory or speed of your CPU doesn't matter. What matters is that you like your computer. If it's too slow and won't do what you want it to do, you won't like it. But just as much, if it's ugly to you it won't make you happy either. People spend lots of time customizing their virtual desktops—isn't the outside of computer just as important?

What's in This Book?

The first part of this book is designed to give you an overview of most of the common techniques, tools, and components used in computer modding. Contained within these pages are descriptions of most of the common components used in modern case modding and some pros and cons for each which will allow you to make up your own mind about what you want to use for your case mods. There are also descriptions of tools and techniques that you will want to use. After reading this section, you will have all the knowledge necessary to create your own case mods just like the pros.

In short, the first part of the book covers topics such as:

- How to get started on a mod
- Cooling
- Cable management
- Adding lights
- Cutting
- Creating exterior finishes
- Soldering
- Electronics
- Common mods
- Advanced skills

The second part of this book contains detailed descriptions of some popular mods on the Web. These are not just pictures of the mods or a few simple paragraphs describing what the mods contain. No, these are the stories of how these mods were built step by step, written by the creators themselves. When looking over these creations, you won't be wondering "how can I do that?" because you'll have all the information already.

The mods contained in this book include:

- **Matrimony Mod**—This is a truly inspired mod. Using case modding as the ultimate way to express his love (and his "geek" nature), a case modder turns a PC into a marriage proposal.

- **The Mad Scientist**—Another theme case, this one brings backs images of a scientist's lab with analog gauges and bubbling liquid tubes. This is one case that was built one brick at a time.

- **Picture Frame PC**—This low-powered PC fits entirely into a small picture frame that can be hung on the wall. This is a perfect way to start sneaking mods all around the house without your wife realizing it.

- **Framed 8.0 Custom PC**—A space-saving dream come true, a full PC hanging on the wall. It's almost like the picture frame PC on steroids.

- **miniMAME**—Modern PC games with their difficult controls just not good enough for you? Old arcade games cool, but don't have enough space? How about a small cocktail table arcade game inspired mod? Guaranteed apartment friendly.

- **$3,000 Fish Tank**—A custom-built acrylic cube, lots of water, and a computer. What else can be said, other than "cool!"

- **UFOs Have Landed**—Back to the 50s. The alien invasion continues with this one of a kind case based on "B" movies and a wok.

- **Millennium Falcon PC**—The most famous hunk of junk on the galaxy has a computer placed inside its guts. Based on the popular toy from the *Star Wars* movies.

- **Aircraft Carrier PC**—Another toy meets the twenty-first century. A toy of the aircraft carrier Enterprise has a mini-PC installed inside, along with a custom themed mouse unlike anything you've ever seen.

Finally, there are also two appendices. The first of these additions to the book will give you an introduction to overclocking—the art of running your computer faster than it was designed to run. The second of the appendices includes many useful resources, with everything from great places to buy components to online forums for the free exchange of modding ideas.

How to Use This Book

The first half of this book covers all of the skills and knowledge you will need for most case mods. Read through the first half and familiarize yourself with those items, because simply reading about some of the components out there may give you some great ideas. Beyond that, you can always refer back to sections when the time comes for you to start that piece of your case mod.

It would be nice to say that everything you ever wanted to know about case modding is in this book. But the truth is, new artists are coming up with new ways to mod cases every day. Use the skills, tools, and components described in the first half of the book as a starting point for yourself. Building on these, you may come up with other techniques that no one has thought up yet.

The second half of this book can be used in a number of ways. First, you can use the detailed chapters to recreate any mod there. Perhaps you are a *Star Wars* fan? Then, create a Millennium Falcon PC. Maybe your girlfriend is just as much of a "geek" as you are, and you want to propose to her? Maybe create a case mod to ask that all-important question. Imitation is the highest form of flattery, or so they say. . . .

Or use some of the techniques the modders in part two used to create your own work of modding art. There are a lot of uncommon techniques used in these mods, from controlling multiple LEDs off the hard drive activity LED (see Chapter 9) to using an air pump to make a mad scientist's bubbling experiment come to life (see Chapter 12). Any of these techniques could be exactly what you need to finish off your project.

Finally, use these mods for inspiration. Like one of them, but think you can do better? Maybe you want to change the color one of these mods uses or change the overall size? No matter what you do, if these mods inspire you to create something of your own, then I'm sure the modders who have shared their creations would feel honored.

Conventions Used in This Book

Throughout the book, you'll find highlighted text where I point out cautions, cross-references, and helpful recommendations. Specifically, three types of highlighted pointers appear:

 Gives you valuable information that will help you avoid disaster. Read all of these carefully!

 These are pointers to other areas in the book or on the Internet where you can find more information on the subject at hand.

 A recommendation of best-practice methods and superior products or tools to use.

Companion Web Site

For links, updates, and full color art, please visit this book's companion Web site at
www.wiley.com/compbooks/extremetech.

Conclusion

After reading this book, go out there and create something. Don't say "that can't be done." Say "Why can't that be done?" Use your imagination. Modding knows no constraints, no boundaries. Challenge yourself. Surprise yourself. Surprise everyone.

Personally, I can't wait to see what you can create.

Basic Training

part

Getting Started

The hardest part of computer case modification project is getting started. Because there are so many things to consider and so many tasks to perform, the whole project can seem overwhelming. In reality, it's not that bad. You just have to be logical about the steps involved and everything will come together just fine.

The first three things you should consider when getting started are as follows: How to create a plan, what other options you have besides creating a modification, or "mod," from scratch yourself, and what resources you have available to you. All of these areas are important and can make or break a good case mod.

Creating a Plan

One of the most important aspects to modding anything is to have a plan. It's like driving a car—there is very little chance that you will end up where you want to go unless you know where you want to go.

In general, it's best to come up with a theme for your modifications first, maybe sketching a few designs on paper (or if you are really advanced, using some drafting or computer aided design program). Think about why you want to do this mod and what purpose it serves. Think about how much money you have available for the mod. Think about how it will look when it's done, and if you will really be happy when it's complete.

What's Your Computer For?

The main deciding factor in what type of mod you're going for should be what you most use your computer for. If you simply use your computer for Web surfing and an occasional game of solitaire, you don't need some huge multi-thousand dollar game machine with seven cold cathode lights and twelve fans (yes, such systems do exist). A small desktop computer or small form factor computer will serve the purpose perfectly. If you're a more artistic person, an extreme case mod (such as putting a computer inside a model car or spaceship) could be the perfect thing to put on your desk. If you're less artistic and more conservative, what could be better than a nice wooden humidor PC?

If you're a gamer, a huge case with lots of fans that can withstand the rigors of being brought to LAN party after LAN party is the way to go. Add some lights, a custom paint job with some good logos, and you'll be happy. When trying to squeeze every last drop of performance from that processor and video card, water cooling could be just what the doctor ordered if you're a serious gamer (but more home-bound). In that case, a nice water-cooled rig might be the way to go. What good is a computer with handles when you could have an overclocked monster with five-channel surround sound?

Luckily, there are lots of case mods appropriate for each group. You just have to know what you want. They say that half the fun is getting there, and that's certainly the case with modding.

Considerations

Part of your plan has to include the big considerations every modder must deal with; warranties, a place to work, cost, tools, and where to buy parts are all important aspects to modding that are often ignored until too late in the process. By thinking about these aspects up front, your chance of a successful mod are greatly increased. These may all seem like trivial concerns, but they definitely are not.

How to Void Your Warranty in 10 Easy Steps

The fact is that modding a computer (or part of a computer) will void the warranty. This means that you can never return those parts should they fail, whether or not the mod had anything to do with the failure. Be prepared for this before you mod anything—modding is a one-way process. Never mod anything if you are afraid, for any reason, that you may need to return it or have it replaced.

It is important to realize that 99 percent of all mods do void the warranty on computer parts. It doesn't matter if the mod was responsible for the failure, companies don't want to have to replace parts after some modder has modified them. This isn't inherently evil, it's just good business sense. A modified part can never be fixed and sold again as new, so companies won't deal with returns on modified parts.

Modders have a strange relationship with companies that sell computer parts. On the one hand, modders love to see new products on the market and buy them. And companies love to sell products, of course. On the other hand, modders like to modify the products—it's in their very nature or they wouldn't be called modders. And companies hate to see their products modified, because afterwards the products are often unrecognizable and even potentially dangerous. Companies are afraid of lawsuits and other claims against them. But ironically, those same companies often take the ideas that modders came up with and create new products based on them. They then sell those same products back to other modders!

The products the companies created based on the ideas of the modders may be no better than the mods that were created (and are often worse quality) except they come with a warranty. Wait long enough, and it seems that any fresh idea in the modding community will be a real product with a warranty.

But really, how many times have you actually used a warranty for a computer component?

Your Modding Workshop

One often overlooked aspect to modding is that you have to have an acceptable place to work on your mods or they will never come out right. Ideally, you are looking for a place far away from pets or children where you can do potentially dangerous work without having to be concerned about anyone but yourself.

Some key aspects for a workshop (or workbench) are:

- **Lots of table space**—The more space you have, the easier it will be to mock up something or wait for one piece with glue on it to dry while working on a different piece. It's very important that no one else touch your workbench, or you will find yourself spending many frustrating hours trying to find something that someone else moved (or ruined accidentally).

- **Power for tools and computers**—The more power, the better. Not only should you have enough power plugs, but you should also be aware of how many amps are available on those plugs. Many power tools use quite a bit of power, especially when they're first turned on.

- **Good lighting**—Not only will your eyes thank you, but seeing important details is difficult with poor lighting. When soldering, for example, you will need a lot of light right on the small components you are working on.

- **A comfortable chair**—No one likes to stand for hours on end, so a chair is important. The more comfortable the chair is, the more you will want to mod. If the chair doesn't feel good, your sore back and shoulders will slowly kill your desire to mod.

- **Organizational storage**—Someplace nearby to store your tools and supplies, be it a rack with shelving or even some plastic drawers, will really help. Digging through box after box of tools to look for the specific one you need wastes time. Having everything organized and sorted up front will make life much more pleasant.

One nice area for a mod workshop is a garage. They are generally pretty big, have at least one large door for ventilation (this is especially nice when you need to paint), and a few metal shavings on the floor won't hurt anything. Most family members don't exactly like to hang out in the garage at night, so you will probably have some time to work undisturbed. Throw in a mini-fridge and some drinks, and you are really set!

Preparing a Budget

Unfortunately, cost is one of the major concerns when modding (or doing just about anything in life). That's not to say that modding is expensive. Many great mods are very cheap. Some modders have even made cases entirely of cardboard, and when done well these mods are very nice while costing less than $50. But you should come up with a basic budget for your mod up front.

Include in your costs the basic parts you want and any special tools you may need to purchase because you don't already own them. Mods always run over budget, so plan that into your expenses as well. Incidentals such as glue, compressed air, and paint seem small, but five dollars here and there quickly add up, so it's always good to add some money for those as well.

Don't underestimate the chance that a mod may spiral out of control budget-wise. For example, one time there was a contest for the best low-cost mod. I had the idea about painting a mouse and adding a few LEDs to the exterior of the mouse, along with some simple engravings. The rules for the contest stated a $15 dollar limit. No problem—a cheap mouse can go for under $6, a couple of $2 cans of paint, and a few $1 LEDs. To make a long story short, the first mouse got destroyed when the paint didn't adhere right to the plastic. I bought another mouse, then another, then another as I kept accidentally ruining parts. In the end, the less than $15 dollar mod cost well over $60, and I didn't even win an honorable mention!

Tip The relative cost of incidentals like paint are a larger percentage of the cost when the basic components are cheaper. When modding a mouse, the mouse itself could cost $10, while the cost of paints could be closer to $30. On the same note, when modding a $200 case, the cost of paint could easily be only $35.

Try to figure out the cost of the large components you plan to purchase and add some money for all the incidentals like paint or glue. If any component is particularly challenging to mod, you may want to plan the cost of purchasing two of them into the final budget for your mod. Taking inventory of what supplies you already have on hand before buying any new supplies can help keep the costs down a little—no need to buy more paint or glue if you already have plenty around.

Improper planning for budgets can easily lead to having to stop a mod halfway through due to insufficient funds. Or worse—a fight with your significant other!

Tools

Tools are some of the things that are hard to swallow at first, cost-wise. When working on your very first mod, you may have to purchase a rotary tool such as a Dremel, a drill set, some hole saws, and various rulers. Add that to the cost of the parts for the mod itself, and it's difficult to justify the purchase of a lot of tools. However, the more mods you work on and the more projects you do around the house, the more the relative cost of the tool decreases, and you begin to see the advantages of having them around. Having the right tool for the job makes your projects turn out better and take less time to complete.

Most mods require some basic tools. These tools won't be used for every mod, but they are generic enough that if you plan to mod more than one case they really start to pay for themselves:

- **Rotary tool**—This is the most important tool in any modder's arsenal. This is a small device with replaceable tips for various purposes. You would most often use a cutting disc or a sanding wheel attachment, but there are literally hundreds of attachments available. There are several different manufacturers of these devices, but the most common is the Dremel (see Figure 1-1). These are available at any good hardware store.

- **Drill**—While a rotary tool can be used to drill holes, it is a poor tool for that purpose. A real drill, preferably hand held for modding, is a much easier and more useful tool for making holes. Remember to get a good assortment of drill bits in various sizes. Also,

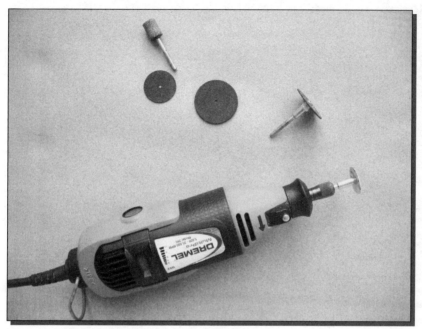

FIGURE **1-1: Dremel rotary tool with a few attachments.**

drills will enable you to purchase hole saws. Hole saws provide a very quick and easy way to make large holes for fans. If possible, get a drill with a keyless chuck (see Figure 1-2), otherwise you will need a special tool (the "key") to change drill bits, which is just one more thing to potentially lose.

- **Soldering iron**—These are covered in greater detail in a Chapter 7, but a soldering iron is essential for making circuits of simply for lengthening wires inside your case. Figure 1-3 shows a wand-style soldering iron.

- **Screwdriver set**—A decent screwdriver set with magnetic replaceable tips (for different size screws) is essential and cheap. Invest in a set and you won't ever regret it.

- **Jewelers' screwdriver set**—Sometimes screws on small circuit boards are much smaller than a standard screwdriver set can work on. In these circumstances, an even smaller set of screwdrivers, often referred to as jewelers' screwdrivers, are needed.

- **Hot glue gun**—These are small gunike devices that take round tubes of semihard glue and melt them, allowing the melted glue to hold items together (see Figure 1-4). These are very useful for holding wires to circuit boards. When using hot glue, the glue tends to spill out over the sides of the parts being connected, so hot glue is best used for parts hidden from view (such as the inside of front panel of a case to hold lights in place. The glue itself can be removed by hand with a little effort, so this tool makes for great flexibility in modding.

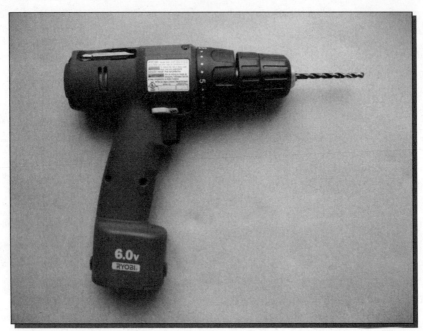

FIGURE 1-2: Electric drill with keyless chuck.

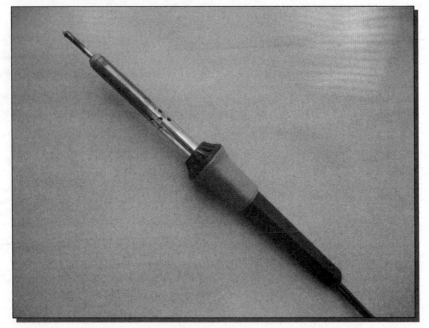

FIGURE 1-3: Wand style soldering iron.

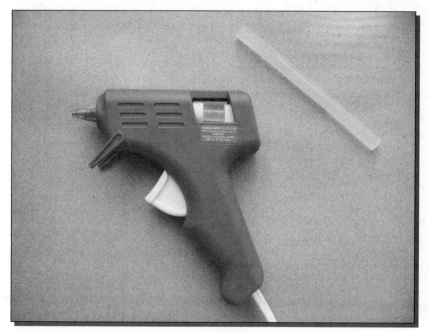

FIGURE **1-4:** Hot glue gun and replacement glue stick.

■ **Various glues**—Every modder should have at least two different types of glue handy: white glue and general purpose epoxy (see Figure 1-5). White glue is great for holding papers or cardboard together, while epoxy is great for high-strength applications.

When planning your mod, keep in mind what tools you think you will need for the project. If you don't have one of the tools you need, remember to factor the cost of the tool into the project budget.

Where to Buy Parts

When it comes to buying parts, there are really only two options: local computer stores and online shops.

If you are lucky, you live near a metropolitan area with several computer superstores. By going there, you can see whatever parts you want in person. You can decide by looking if they seem like good products or if they seem cheaply put together. Before modding any component, you should always test it as it was designed to operate first. If it fails, returning the product is a lot easier if the store is local to you (depending on the store's return policy, of course). You can compare one product to another easily.

On the other hand, the prices in retail outlets will be higher than in online stores. Due to the costs of stocking shelves with products and hiring sales people, few if any retail stores can match the prices of their online counterparts. The selection will also be very limited compared

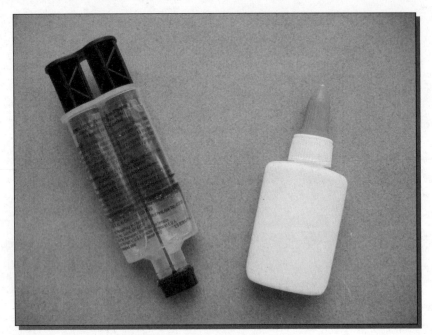

FIGURE 1-5: Epoxy and white glue.

with an online store. You may be able to compare products side by side in a retail store, but don't expect to compare many.

Online stores offer a far wider variety of products, making it far more likely that you will find what you need right away. They also offer, in general, much better prices than retail stores. You can even use online price comparison sites such as www.pricewatch.com or www.pricegrabber.com to find the lowest prices available. Very often, you may not need to pay tax on the products because they come from out of state. Overall, shopping online allows you to get exactly what you want and for a better price.

But there is also a dark side to purchasing online. Some stores are very unreliable and may sell repackaged or used parts as new. Some dealers also do bait and switch, sending products other than what you ordered or defective products on purpose. Also, be aware of the difficulties in returning products to online stores—you have to contact the dealer for an RMA number, package up the product, usually pay the shipping charges yourself, and make sure they get the product back. That's not even including the "restocking" fee that many of them charge, even when it was their mistake in the first place! Finally, even if the dealer does the right thing, the package can sometimes be damaged or lost during shipment.

Tip   You can minimize your risk when shopping online by using a dealer rating Web site such as www.resellerratings.com. Never purchase from a dealer with a bad rating. It's better to pay a few dollars more and be sure that the dealer is on the up and up. Also remember to purchase parts using a credit card rather than a debit card or PayPal because you will have a better chance of disputing a bad charge if something goes wrong.

In the end, you'll probably use both local stores and online stores for what they each do best. When you know exactly what you need (for example, a Pentium 4 processor @ 2.4Ghz), buy from a reputable online dealer and save a few bucks. For something you may need to return (for example, a cheap DVD-ROM drive), buy from a local dealer with a good return policy.

Don't forget all the other stores you have local to you which are literally treasure troves of mod supplies: home improvement stores, auto parts stores, pet stores, used electronics stores, toy stores, department stores, and even pawn shops. All those stores have supplies you might need for great mods. Everything from cheap tubing (pet stores and home improvement stores) to old radios (pawn shops) to children's toilets (department stores) have been used effectively in great computer mods. Don't limit yourself to just computer equipment stores, or you are truly missing out on some of the best sources for supplies.

Motivation

Why are you doing your mod? It's an important question to ask. Many full-scale mods involving a custom case, keyboard, mouse, speakers, and so on, will take months of work to complete. Is the mod you are working on sufficiently interesting to keep you from getting bored of the project halfway through?

Search any of the online forums work-log sections (detailed later on in this chapter), and you will find dozens of work logs that were never finished. Some of the modders ran out of money, but most of them probably got bored because they didn't think about their own motivation.

Try and choose a project that will interest you for a while, something that can hold your interest even when things aren't going well. Make sure your ideas for a modded case are interesting enough that you are willing to spend not only the money but also the hours it takes to complete.

Modding Without the Effort

What can you do if you don't have the time to mod a case, but you want a cool-looking PC just like all those other people out on the net or at your local LAN party? Well, there are several options at varying price levels and with varying time commitments.

Not everyone is up for the late-night planning, the purchasing of power tools, frequent trips to home improvement and electronics stores, and the never-ending application of band-aids to various body parts. Of course, you miss most of the fun as well, but sometimes it's nice to start out slowly by building on something someone else has started.

Boutique Dealers

There are a number of dealers selling computers optimized for gaming or other applications. These systems can be configured somewhat by selecting from a small list of what components they come with, and the systems rigorously tested for performance and compatibility. Dealers that do this, such as Falcon Northwest and Alienware (see Figure 1-6), are usually referred to as boutique dealers.

FIGURE 1-6: Alienware Area 51 system.

For a truly no-fuss but cool-looking computer, companies like these can't be beat. You can customize what components are installed, they come with cool-looking cases (some companies even let you choose a paint job for the case), and work flawlessly. These companies also offer customer support lines to help solve any problems you may encounter after purchasing the system and getting it home. However, these systems are typically expensive and don't really qualify as a "mod" in anyone's eyes. You get a cool computer with support, but anyone with the same amount of money as you can get the exact same thing.

That being said, these are still impressive systems that will amaze most of your friends. Some dealers are even offering custom laser cutting of the side panel with high-intensity lighting installed. This certainly does qualify as a mod, even if you didn't do the work yourself.

Premodified Cases

Moving up in the difficulty scale are premod cases. Over the past couple of years, there have been a growing number of what modders refer to as "premod" cases popping up in stores all over the world. These cases usually include windows, colored fans, colored lights, multiple switches and dials, and so on. As a matter of fact, it has become difficult to find anything but premod cases in many computer stores. The days of the beige box, if not completely over, are numbered.

Most true modders despise these new premod cases because no work went into creating them. Whether a case is truly a rectangular beige box or a green, glowing triangle doesn't matter. In most modders' eyes, a case is not unique if just anyone can buy it. However, a standard beige box has limited upgrade potential without truly "modding" it (i.e., cutting a hole for window or something like that). But a premod case has much more potential. If you mount some colored fans inside the case or add an appliqué (really, just a semitransparent sticker) on the inside of the window it becomes a unique creation, even if it is easily reproducible.

Many of the accessories that are the building blocks of a good mod can be applied to one of these premod cases with a limited skill set. The ability to plug a Molex connector into another Molex connector and maybe screw something in using a screwdriver is all that is needed for many of those accessories. Every one of these add-ons makes the case a little more yours, even if these additions are not really considered "mods" by most other modders.

All of the techniques detailed in this book can be used to modify a premod case as well as any other type of case. The premod case simply becomes the canvas you start from. The more mods done to a premod case, the more it truly becomes your own creation. Subsequently, the more respect that mod will get from the mod community. Anyone trying to show off a premod case with a few simple add-ons such as lighted fans will get laughed off the modding forums online, but the more custom mods that are performed to that case, the more people will take notice.

In the end, it still comes down to what looks good or performs well for you. If you're fine with a premod case that you added a couple of lighted fans to, great. You're the one who has to work with this computer, no one else.

Commissioning a Case

If you have the urge to have something truly unique and have extra funds available, you can contact some of the better-known modders out there to build a case for you. A simple mod, such as a custom fan grill, may cost around $20 or so, while a full custom-themed mod, including all the computer components, could easily cost over $3,000. What services these modders offer will vary greatly along with the general quality of the mod, so this is one of those instances that a good deal of homework is necessary.

Using any of the popular modding sites, get an account and post in the forums that you are looking for someone to do a mod for you. Generally, a number of people will respond with help. There are a few modders out there who are trying to make a business of creating great cases for people. There are even more modders who would be interested in building a case just for the challenge of it (but need someone else to foot the bill for the parts) even if they end up not keeping the case mod themselves. Because a lot of modders tend to be younger, they often have more time than money available to them. Ultimately, having someone provide the money for parts they can mod with will be enough to get them interested, even if in the end all they have are some cool pictures of the case they built and a little pocket change.

Whether you use a "professional" case modder or just someone with time to kill, you will want to see examples of their work. Typically, they should provide Web sites showing those examples. Also, get their phone number and talk to them to get a sense of their work ethic and if you can trust them. It's sad to say, but you would probably want to do some searching online and make sure that you can verify that they have actually built the cases they claim to. Some people are not above claiming credit for other peoples' work. You should also talk about the timeframe for creating the mod and what is included in it. Are they just providing a cool case, or something with all the components such as CPU, motherboard, and other components installed?

Related to timeframe is of course the fun subject—theme. If you are paying all this money for the case, then you probably have some idea in mind of what your new case should look like rather than just letting the modder go wild. If you are a peaceful person who owns dozens of stuffed teddy bears, you may not be looking for a case encrusted with over one hundred skulls and a case window that drips blood. Talk about the subject matter with your modder until you feel the issue is resolved completely.

That being said, commissioning a well-known modder is also a great idea for companies. Several companies have commissioned case mods from people in the community. Both Intel and VIA have commissioned mods, as well as other companies. These mods are a great way to make a splash at a trade show or even simply "wow" visitors in the main lobby. Figure 1-7 shows a sample mod sponsored by VIA Technologies.

FIGURE 1-7: VIA Technologies, Inc., sponsored this mod by supplying the mini-itx motherboard contained within.

Available Resources

As they say, no man is an island, and this holds particularly true for case modders. You don't have to work on a case mod in some dingy garage with no light or no input from anyone. There are quite a few resources available to you to help you plan and create your mod. Use these resources, and your modding experience (not to mention the mod itself) will be much more enjoyable.

Imagineering

The first available resource is your own imagination and knowledge. Imagineering is a term first dreamed up by the folks at Disney. It represents the melding of both imagination and engineering, and there are few terms that better describe case modding. Disney imagineering includes people who are engineers, artists, visionaries, plumbers, and just about every other occupation you could think of. The same is true of great case modding.

Before you start your mod, brainstorm for ideas. It doesn't matter whether you have the tools or talents necessary at this stage. Simply get all the ideas you have down on paper. Then slowly combine all those ideas until you have a good idea what your design should be. Let your imagination run wild. The best mods are things that seem ridiculous to some others, but break the boundaries.

Don't underestimate this step. All the little details of a great mod come from somewhere, and those ideas almost always come from the initial brainstorming sessions. It's 10 times easier to plan something into a mod from the beginning than to add it after the mod is underway.

Help! I've Ruined My Case!

You might find yourself hitting some speed bumps along the path of modding your case, but don't panic. It's very rare that a single error will "ruin" any case mod you're working on. Granted, a single misstep with a power tool can render something nonfunctional, but when viewed as a single piece of a larger mod you can still recover from the problem. Simply change the design of the mod and move on. Modding in general is trying to break free from the mold that someone else has placed on the computer (and consequently, you). The expression "life gives you lemons, so make lemonade" is trite, but sometimes accurate.

One example from personal experience is when I was adding an LCD character display to my first modded computer. I was unable to cut a decent rectangular hole for the LCD module to fit in a 5¼ bay insert. I used up all my spare bay covers and wasn't able to do it. Then, about a week later, I had an idea for a solution. I used a color laser printer at work to print a template I designed in Visio on a piece of clear transparency. It was essentially a black rectangle with a clear center. I cut out the black rectangle and glued it over the LCD panel which was attached to the poorly cut bay insert. The printed part of the transparency hid the unsightly lines from the poor cuts and gave it a very professional look (see Figure 1-8). I've subsequently used that technique several times, each time with great success.

FIGURE 1-8: LCD character display with printed transparency cover.

Another example I read about involved someone who tried an elaborate hard-drive window modification. After putting it all back together, the hard drive didn't function. Only the LEDs he had installed inside worked. But that person went on to use the nonfunctioning hard drive for aesthetics only by using the hard drive (actually two of them) as "eyes" placed on the outside of the mod (the mod had an insect theme to it). I've also heard about people using dead hard drives as speakers by somehow running electricity to the drive motors. I've personally used a magnet salvaged from a dead hard drive to degauss monitors with no separate controls to do that. The important lesson is to learn to adapt to the current situation.

Sometimes you'll make an error that will seem unrepairable for all intents and purposes. Perhaps you might be working on a one-of-kind component you got off eBay or a $700 video card when you suddenly ruin it. That means that you forgot one of the fundamental rules of modding—if you can't afford to break it, don't mod it. As I've mentioned before, manufacturers don't look kindly on the modding of computers and won't honor any warranties if a part has been modded whether or not the mod had anything to do with the failure. Be forewarned. Please note that it's also possible to render parts of your body nonfunctional with power tools, and these errors are harder to recover from. Please remember to use all safety precautions when using tools. Not to sound too error prone or raise my life insurance rates, but I've personally gauged my finger with a screwdriver deep enough to give me a permanent scar, had my soldering iron burn through its own cord and shock me, and temporarily burnt a fingerprint off by grabbing freshly cut (and melted) plastic.

LAN parties

Another source of ideas, solutions, and companionship are at LAN Parties. LAN parties are places where groups of people get together to play video games, eat, and generally have a good time together. Many of these events are sponsored by companies that provide prizes as a form of marketing. Some LAN parties also contain competitions for the best modded case.

The best way to find out about the various LAN parties out there is visiting online forums. Recently, a number of Web sites have gone up where people can post about upcoming LAN parties in their area, plus the larger LAN parties (usually 100+ people) usually have their own Web sites.

Tip

There are a few Web sites that list LAN parties all over the USA and/or the world. A couple of places to start are www.lanparty.com and www.tomshardware.com/game/lanparty .html.

Even if there is no competition for modders, the bigger events will surely entice some of the local modders to come and show off their stuff to the other participants. You can go to the event and look at these mods in person to determine what you like about them and what you don't. Talk to the modders themselves and get ideas from them. If your case is already under construction, take it with you and show it to them, or take some photos to show.

Even a LAN party without any modded cases (hard to imagine, but possible) can still be useful. Remember that all those game players are computer enthusiasts themselves, and you can probably get some good ideas off them as well. Ask questions about what bugs them about their cases or computers. Ask them what they like. Listen and learn.

Online forums

With all the resources available, it's easy to forget the best resource of all—the other modders. The modding forums on various Web sites such as www.hardforums.com, www.gruntville.com, and www.pheaton.com (among others) are the true mother lode of resources. Register for a free account on any of these sites (or countless others), read through some of the threads and start asking any questions that you have. Just try to remember these rules whenever you go to a new forum:

- You are a guest on that Web site and should act as such. The moderators are your hosts, so remember to be nice and not to flame anyone (at least until you're considered a regular).

- Nearly every forum has a FAQ (frequently asked questions) section. Be sure to read through it before posting any questions. FAQs answer a lot of questions as well as stating the rules about what you can and cannot do.

- Do not, under any circumstance, take a picture of your completely stock case (even if it already has lights and such) and post a message about how great it is.

- Never claim credit for someone else's work.

Once you know those rules, the online forums are an incredible source of technical knowledge and help, all for free! People on the forums will offer support, ideas, and sources of cheap equipment and deals. That's not to say that everyone on the Internet is nice—there are some Web sites that are downright hostile to outsiders. But by and large, most modders welcome outsiders and new ideas. Introduce yourself and have some fun!

Wrapping Up

Should you buy a prebuilt computer from a dealer? Maybe you should buy a premod and add some lights? Hmmm . . . maybe you should pay someone to build something great for you? Or maybe you should go all out and try building something great yourself?

If you are into computers at all, you've probably upgraded your computer already. You might have added more memory or replaced a CD-ROM drive with a DVD-ROM drive or replaced your video card with something more powerful. Modding follows many of the same steps as a standard upgrade.

When you decided to upgrade, you had a purpose. You wanted your machine to run more programs at the same time, or you wanted to be able to watch movies on it, or something like that. You had a need, and without even thinking about it, you came up with a plan to fix the problem. Modding is the same—you have a problem and you're looking for a solution. Maybe your computer looks boring, or you feel that it would work better if it had more cooling. You need a plan to successfully solve the problem.

It comes down to what you want to do with your time and money. Many people feel that the best part of modding is being able to show off the work you yourself did. Whether the case turns out like a work of art or looks like a hideous deformed monster, have fun in the process of creating something. Don't be scared off by modding; it *is* fun and not as hard as people think. Throughout the rest of the book, you'll learn everything you need to get a solid footing in the world of computer modding.

Cooling

Today's computers are an amazing collection of microscopic electronic pathways literally pulsing with energy. The speeds at which their processors function has climbed at an amazing rate that was predicted in the 1960s by the cofounder of Intel, Gordon Moore. His prediction, referred to as "Moore's law," says that the number of transistors in an integrated circuit will roughly double every 12 to 18 months. While good news for those who crave more features in their computers, there is a dark cloud that hangs over the advances. That dark cloud is increased heat generation.

Computer chips need to be cooled somehow or they will malfunction. Some chips generate very little heat and need no additional cooling other than the air that surrounds them. Other chips need pieces of metal called heatsinks attached to them to increase the surface area, which in turn helps dissipate heat. Other chips, such as modern CPUs, need not only a heatsink but also some form of active cooling such as a fan or a waterblock attached to them.

How hot is too hot? Well, that depends on a lot of factors. In general, you want everything to be as cool as it possibly can be. The acceptable range of temperatures that processors and other components function correctly at is different for each type of processor or chip, so consult your documentation or the manufacturers' Web sites for that info. As to how you know the temperature, many modern processors and motherboards contain built-in temperature probes that report back to custom utilities designed by the manufacturer. Also, you can buy separate temperature probes that will display the temperature to you—often as part of a fan controller (see the section on fans).

This chapter covers many different methods of cooling and how you can achieve some cool mod effects while solving the cooling problem.

Passive Cooling

By far the simplest cooling method is passive cooling. Passive cooling is the cooling of computer chips without using any electrical mechanism. As stated earlier, some chips operate at low enough temperatures that simply having them open to the air is good enough to cool them. Other chips need something called a heatsink attached to them to help them cool effectively.

A heatsink, quite simply, is a metal structure that attaches to a computer chip to help dissipate heat, or "sink" the heat away. By attaching these structures to the chips, the surface area of the chip essentially increases, and this increases the amount of area that is cooled by the surrounding air. The heatsinks come in various designs and are made from a variety of metals. For example, copper is an excellent metal for transferring heat but is quite heavy. Aluminum is another popular material because it's easy to work with and light, but it isn't as good at transferring heat. Many heatsinks use a combination of both of these metals as an attempt to get the best of both worlds.

The cost of a heatsink varies greatly with the overall design, the materials, and the size of the heatsink. Small, average-performing heatsinks for various chips can often be purchased for less than a dollar, while top-of-the-line CPU coolers can cost upwards of $50. Advanced techniques in heatsink construction such as heatpipes (liquid filled tubes within the heatsink structure that help move heat from one part of the heatsink to another) raise the cost even more.

You can mod the components in your system by adding extra heatsinks to chips that don't have them. One popular mod is to add small aluminum heatsinks to the small memory chips present on modern video cards. By helping to lower the temperature of these chips, you greatly increase the chances that the part will be able to overclock successfully or simply be more stable. By increasing the cooling performance of a chip, you reduce a major limiting factor in the performance of the chip. That's not to say that a better cooled chip will automatically perform better, just that should you manually overclock it, you will have a better chance of success.

Attaching a Heatsink

Attaching a heatsink to computer chips can be accomplished in a few different ways:

- **Thermal tape** (approximately $6)—This special double-sided tape not only attaches two components together but also helps heat pass from one side to the other. Normal tape tends to block heat from passing from one side to the other. This method does the job, but it's not the best solution. Figure 2-1 shows thermal tape applied to heatsinks for BGA RAM.

- **Thermal epoxy** (approximately $8 to $15)—This glue, in addition to attaching two surfaces, also transfers heat well. Thermal epoxy comes as two tubes of material that must be mixed in equal parts and then applied to the surface of the chip in an even manner. Be warned, this epoxy is often electrically conductive, so if any of the glue seeps out between the heatsink and chip and touches the small metal contacts on the chip, the chip is effectively ruined.

- **Thermal compound** (approximately $1 to $18)—This sticky substance transfers heat well, but unlike glue has little to no holding power. When using this, you'll need some sort of mounting bracket to hold the component and heatsink together. Thermal compound, sometimes called thermal paste, usually comes in some type of syringe (see Figure 2-2). Most CPUs are attached using this method.

- **Thermal pad** (free with some heatsinks)—This substance lies somewhere between thermal tape and thermal compound. Similar to thermal compound in function, it generally comes preapplied to heatsinks (see Figure 2-3) for easy attachment to CPUs. Modern Intel retail CPUs come with a fan/heatsink combo that includes a thermal pad.

FIGURE 2-1: Thermal tape applied to heatsinks for BGA RAM.

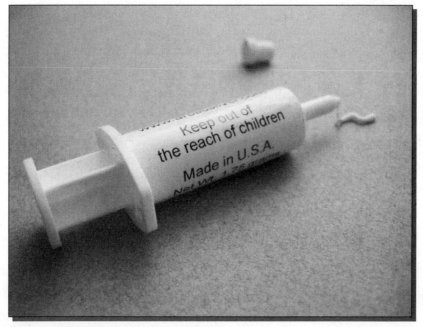

FIGURE 2-2: Thermal compound in a syringe.

FIGURE 2-3: Thermal pad applied to Pentium 4 stock heatsink.

Avoiding Problems

A couple of things need to be said about the use of thermal compound or thermal epoxy. First, use only a couple drops. The idea is that these substances are supposed to fill the microscopic holes between the component and the heatsink only. A small amount evenly spread over the chip is the right way. If there is any leakage out from under the heatsink, you used too much.

Also important is the quality of the substance. Many different manufacturers make these compounds, and not all are created equal. Several compounds have recently been found to be making false claims about their composition and characteristics. Using a high-quality compound will only cost a few dollars more and is worth the investment.

Modding forums and review sites are the best places to get recommendations on the best of the various thermal transfer compounds.

Lapping a Heatsink

All flat surfaces contain irregularities that keep them from being perfectly flat, at least on a microscopic level. This is one of the problems that thermal compound tries to solve. But obviously, the smoother the surface, the less thermal compound needs to be used and the better the heat transfer will be. Lapping is the process of smoothing the surface of the heatsink, usually to a mirror-like finish.

A good-quality heatsink, like those from Zalman, will already have a mirror finish better than that you can produce yourself. However, other heatsinks are often not as professionally done and can use some help. Simply, if the surface of the heatsink that attaches to the chip doesn't act as a mirror, it can be lapped for better heat transfer—often resulting in a 1 or 2 degree Celsius difference in temperature! Be aware that price alone is no indicator of quality, because there are plenty of expensive heatsinks with less than perfectly smooth surfaces.

Wet a sheet of 400-grit wet-or-dry sandpaper and lay it on a flat, smooth surface such as a glass table. Place a small amount of soap on the heatsink and spread it out evenly. Then place the heatsink on the sandpaper, and without using any real pressure downward, move the heatsink up and down on the paper a dozen times. Turn the heatsink 90 degrees, then continue until you have done a complete rotation at least a dozen times. Next, move on to a higher-grit sandpaper.

You want to let the weight of the heatsink do the work for you, so don't apply any downward pressure on the heatsink. With pressure, you could end up creating an even more uneven surface because the sides will be sanded more than the center of the heatsink.

Start this process using 400-grit sandpaper, then move up to 600-, 800-, 1000-, 1500-, and 2000-grit sandpaper. When you're done, don't forget to wash the heatsink in soap and water and dry it completely. The whole process can take from 30 minutes to a few hours, but the result is better heat transfer and lower temperatures overall.

Air Cooling

Passive cooling is the simplest cooling method, but it can't deal with dissipating too much heat. Therefore, air cooling is far more commonly used. This simply involves using fans to blow cool air onto or pull hot air away from the hot components inside the computer to keep their temperatures down. In fact, fans are the cornerstone of air cooling. Most computers use several fans, on top of the CPU, in the power supply, on the graphics card, or even in front of the radiator in a water-cooled system (more on this later). The process of air cooling may seem simple, but there are many subtleties involved.

One thing to keep in mind is that all the factors that need to be considered when choosing a fan are interconnected. In the following sections, we'll go over the specific factors to consider when purchasing a fan—such as power usage, size, airflow, and noise. It's useful to look at these as separate elements, but they are usually connected. For example, a larger fan will typically have a larger airflow and larger power usage than a smaller fan. Reducing the voltage to that larger fan will make it spin more slowly, which will reduce the airflow and the noise generated (often making the larger fan's airflow equivalent to the smaller fan's, but with reduced noise). Of course, the quality of the various components come into play also—a higher-quality, smaller fan is often better than a lower-quality, larger fan in terms of noise production and reliability.

Fan Power Usage

Fans typically use 12-volt power, although that is not always the case. There are 5-volt fans as well, which are usually used in laptops or small-form-factor computers. It's also possible to undervolt a fan by providing less voltage to the fan than the fan is supposed to use, which will result in it spinning at a slower speed, but with a reduced noise level (again, more on this later).

Power is supplied to the fan through either a 3-pin fan connector or a 4-pin Molex connector (see Figure 2-4). But variations do occur. The 3-pin connector often only has 2 pins connected, and the 4-pin Molex connector usually has only 2 of 4 pins installed in the connector housing. Some fans even come without any connector, just bare wires connected to nothing.

Tip   The term Molex refers to the company of the same name, which produces various types of electrical connectors. However, in computer "slang" the term has become synonymous with the large 4-pin connectors commonly found on almost every home PC. These connectors are typically white, about 1-inch wide, and have four wires (one red, one yellow, and two black).

Figuring out how to attach the fan can take a bit of work. Assuming that the fan is a standard 12-volt fan (most are, except for fans designed for laptops), you will have two or three wires coming from the fan. If the fan has three wires, then those wires are for power, ground, and an rpm (revolutions per minute) sensor for the fan. If the fan only has two wires, the rpm sensor has been left off the fan (this is common, especially for cheaper fans). The darkest color wire

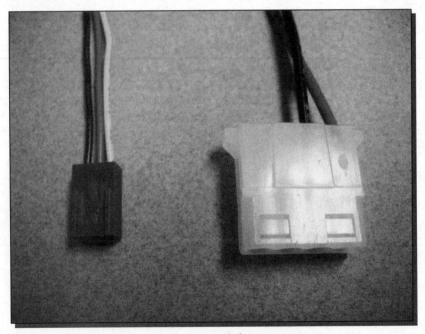

FIGURE 2-4: Both 3-pin and 4-pin (2 connected) fan connectors.

(usually black) is for the ground connection, but the colors from the fans are not always consistent. Sometimes fans include wires that are black/red/yellow, other times they are brown/green/yellow, or any number of other colors.

With two wire fans, the second wire is the power connector. Again, assuming that the fan is a 12-volt fan, this wire should be connected to the 12 volt power source. From the computer's power supply, the red wire is only the 5-volt positive lead. You should attach the red wire from the fan to the yellow wire from the power supply because the yellow wire is the 12-volt positive lead in the computer. If the fan is a three-wire fan, the process is more complicated.

If you are lucky, the fan will have come with a sheet of instructions that lists which color wire is for which function. If the fan came with a connector attached, almost certainly the fan is wired correctly, and you only need to plug the fan in. In the worse case, if the fan just has bare wires, and none of the wires matches the red/yellow/black color scheme, the darkest-colored wire is probably the ground wire and should be attached to one of the black power supply wires. Experiment by quickly touching one of the other wires to the red wire on the power supply to see if the fan spins. Then, touch the other wire (if there is one) to the red power supply wire and see if the fan spins. Repeat the process with the yellow power supply wire. Never touch the fan wires to the power supply wires for more than one second while trying to figure out the color mapping—the fan could be damaged if supplied with too much voltage.

In addition to all this, you also need to keep an eye on the power consumption of the fan. As well as the voltage required to run a fan, the fan will consume a certain amount of energy to run, just as the CPU, graphics card, hard drives, and other components do. If your power supply in the computer cannot handle the combined needs of all the components, including the fans, you will experience problems. Fans also range in power consumption, from 0.4 watt to 8 watt or higher.

For the record, fans use either DC (direct current) or AC (alternating current) for power. Fans used inside computers all use DC, because that is what the computer power supply puts out. AC is the type of power that comes directly from the wall socket and is used by fans that fit on a desk or in a window to keep you cool on a hot summer's day.

Fan Size

Fans range in sizes from tiny to insanely large. Fans for computer use are measured by the length of one side of the fan. Typical sizes are 60 mm, 70 mm, 80 mm, 92 mm, and 120 mm, although you can find some odd sizes as well. The depth of the fan is also important and is usually either 15 mm, 25 mm, or 38 mm. Both dimensions are important for simply fitting the fan in the case, but the length is the most important because there are only a few places where depth matters (for example, when putting a fan in the front bezel).

Most case fans are attached to the case by four mounting screws in the four corners of the fan casing. However, this does not necessarily apply to some of the specialty fans used for CPU cooling. The specialty fans attach with many different mounting mechanisms, which are specific to that fan and heatsink combo.

In addition to the sizes listed above, you can also purchase fan adapters that look like a cone with the top cut off. These allow a mounting hole for one-sized fan to accommodate a different-sized fan, although this will add considerably to the overall depth. Instead of just having to accommodate the depth of the fan, now the case has to be large enough to accommodate the depth of the fan plus the depth of the adapter.

Airflow

All fans are rated by how much air they can either push or pull. The rating unit for this is cubic feet per minute (CFM) and refers to how much air the fan can move over a unit of time. Of course, there are other factors that affect the CFM rating, including air density and humidity. But in general, a fan with a higher CFM rating is better at moving air, and therefore better at cooling, than a fan with a lower CFM rating.

Typical CFM ratings of fans designed for computer use vary in range quite a bit. They sometimes start as low as 0.5 CFM and go up to 125 CFM and beyond. In addition, there are tools that you can use, such as fan controllers (more on that later), to control the CFM by lowering it quite a bit. By lowering the speed (and hence the CFM), you reduce the cooling capability of the fan, but you also reduce the noise the fan generates.

Noise

Fans generate noise. There's no way around that. But different fans generate different amounts of noise based on the size of the fan, design, vibration, and so on. The amount of noise a fan puts out is measured in decibels (abbreviated as dB). Fans typically range from 20 to 35 dBs although fans both above and below this range are out there. Using a device such as a fan controller (more on that later), you can use to lower your fan's dB output. But as with everything else, there are trade-offs. While a lower-dB-output on a fan makes it easier to live with, it typically comes with lower CFM. Consequently, higher CFM means higher dB output.

Fan Types

For PC cooling applications, there are two basic types of fans and one much less common type. The most common fan type is the basic square fan that everyone is familiar with ($2 to $25). It has a motor in the center and spins the fan blades by using the motor to rotate the fan blades. Although they're common, these don't distribute even airflow across their surface. The center of the fan actually has lower airflow than the outside edge of the fan because the relatively large center spindle blocks some of the air.

The second type of fan is commonly known as a blower (approximately $8 to $30). It's often used as a PCI slot exhaust system or CPU cooler. It provides lower airflow than standard fans but does a good job at collecting air from one side and expelling it at a right angle. It also provides more even airflow across the surface it is pointed at because there is no fan hub to get in the way. However, most standard fans can outperform blowers even with this advantage.

The last type of fan is known as a magnetic tip fan (approximately $7 to $10). This type of fan has for motors in the four corners instead of a motor in the center of the fan. Magnets in the tips work with the motors in the corners to rotate the fan blades. Supposedly, this leads to greater airflow and lower noise, but only 70-mm fans are available with this configuration.

Getting Your Bearings

All fans use bearings of some sort. Bearings are what allow the fan blades to efficiently rotate and cool a computer.

The concept behind a bearing is very simple. Things roll better than they slide. When things slide, the friction between them tends to slow them down. But if the two surfaces can roll over each other, the friction is greatly reduced.

The most common type of bearing is the ball bearing. These have a life expectancy or around 50,000 hours but tend to generate a little more noise than other methods.

The next most common type is the sleeve bearing. The life expectancy is only about half that of ball bearings, but they make slightly less noise. Keep in mind though that the lesser noise output is only about 3 dBs, making this somewhat of a nonissue.

Finally, there are rifle bearings. These offer the life expectancy of ball bearings, while providing low-noise output similar to that of a sleeve bearing. Rifle bearings are patented, so they are only available from one manufacturer (Cooler Master).

In the end, does it matter what bearings your computer fans use? In general, no. Most computer components will be upgraded or otherwise disposed of long before a fan will fail. There are exceptions of course—server grade equipment should probably use ball bearing fans for their long life. For most other uses, most any bearing type is fine as long as the fan manufacturer is a reliable one.

Special Features

There are also a few other things to keep in mind when selecting a fan. Special features associated with fans increase their value tremendously. Modern fans include features such as different lighting effects, automatically adjusted speed, and unique grill designs.

Fan Lighting

Modern fans can be lit up in a number of ways. The original way that is still practiced by a small number of people is to add your own lighting by embedding LEDs (light emitting diodes) in the fan blades or the outer perimeter. This was a somewhat difficult mod in that you have to plan for the fan blades spinning and what will happen to the wires when the blades spun. Now many manufacturers sell fans with LEDs already attached. In addition to having multiple LEDs attached to the fan, the manufacturers also make the fan and fan blades themselves clear to help the light shine through.

This leads to another variation of fan lighting—the use of UV-reactive substances. As you probably already know, ultraviolet light is the blue/purple light seen in novelty stores used for lighting up glow-in-the-dark paint and other items. Many fans are now made from colored UV-reactive material, so when a UV light source hits it, the fan appears to glow brightly. The better UV-reactive fans also have UV LEDs embedded in them.

A few variations on LED lighting have recently appeared. A couple of companies have released fans that include not only the usual LED lighting around the perimeter, but also a set of sequencing lights in the center hub for extra visual appeal. Also, Aerocool has recently released its Chameleon Fan. This fan changes color when the temperature changes, so you have a visual indication of the temperature of your case.

Temperature Monitoring and/or Control

Many fans include a third wire, which is used for monitoring the speed of the fan, in rpm (rotations per minute). When plugged into an appropriate header on the motherboard, the motherboard and its utilities can read the rotation speed of the fan and present that information to you.

Some fans include a temperature probe as well. This probe measures the temperature at the probe and can increase or decrease the speed (rpm) of the fan automatically, depending on the readings. This functions similarly to a fan controller (more on that later) but in a simpler way.

Fan Accessories

Fan accessories have really taken off in the modding world during the last few years. These accessories are typically easy to install, look nice, and add significant value.

Fan Grills

Fan grills ($1 to $20) should be immediately recognizable to everyone. As far back as the 1980s, computer power supplies had chrome-plated fan grills. These are for functional purposes, to keep small items such as fingers or pets out of the path of spinning fan blades. To reduce costs, power supply manufacturers have been eliminating the separate fan grill altogether and simply cutting holes in the power supply's metal to make a cheap fan grill (see Figure 2-5). But now fan grills (or fan guards, as they are sometimes called) can be customized to look great as well.

Fan guards in the past have been of the chrome-plated wire variety or the makeshift holes punched in power supply boxes. Now, not only can you get those in various colors, but you have more material and design options as well. They come made from clear acrylic, resin, metal mesh, or any number of other materials. The designs on them range from simple geometric patterns to common logos such as the biohazard or radiation symbols. In addition, many people have even started fabricating their own fan guards using resin or other materials.

Caution

Although these new fan guards are often great looking, sometimes they fail in the original purpose—keeping things out. Some "new style" fan guards leave such large areas exposed, the fan itself could still be accessed and is therefore dangerous. This is good to keep in mind if you have small children or pets.

FIGURE 2-5: Fan guard cut into a power supply housing.

Tip

Some of these decorative fan guards also lead to poor airflow when compared with their simpler counterparts. When choosing a fan guard, try to temper your urge for good aesthetics with a desire for a fan guard that provides good airflow.

It should be mentioned that while the decorative fan guards can actually reduce airflow as compared to wire fan grills, they still generally function better for airflow than the cheap, punched-out holes that manufacturers often use as fan guards. Cutting out the manufacturer-supplied fan guard and installing your own fan guard is one way to increase cooling performance along with modding.

Fan Filters

One other potential addition to your fans are fan filters ($1 to $10). With the need for as much air flowing through modern computers as there is, a lot of contaminants can be drawn in as well. Dust, pet hair, dead skin, and smoke can all be drawn into the computer by the fans and clog up your heatsinks and other components. One solution to this is using fan filters.

Fan filters can be purchased at most computer stores. Basically, these are small pieces of mesh cloth, nylon, or metal cut to roughly fan size along with some sort of plastic or metal holder to attach the filter to the fans. The idea is that all contaminants will get caught by the filters, which you can take out and clean or replace regularly.

Tip For a cheap alternative to expensive fan filter material, you can use either panty-hose or anti-static dryer sheets cut to the right size. Keep in mind that you will still need something to hold the filter material in place. If possible, the homemade filter can be kept in place just by the tension between the fan and the surface it's attached to. Never use a permanent method such as glue—eventually the filter will need to be replaced.

The upside to using filters is that they keep a lot of dust and dirt out of your computer, which will help improve the performance by keeping temperatures down. On the other hand, adding a filter will significantly reduce the airflow into your case, which will raise temperatures.

You have two options:

- **Use a fan filter**—Your system will remain clean and functioning well for longer, but may require more fans. Also, the fan filters need to be taken out and cleaned or replaced every so often or your temperatures will increase.

- **Don't use a filter**—The system will get dirty relatively quickly, and the whole system will need to be cleaned with compressed air every so often. However, you will need fewer fans.

The choice, once again, is up to you. Some people wouldn't dream of running their computers without filters on the fans. Others simply clean the inside of their computer more often.

Additional Fan Lighting

For those who want more than just a few LEDs to light up their fans, you can also get a cold cathode fluorescent light (CCFL) to attach to your fans for between $8 and $20. These lights are similar to old neon lights you might see in the window at a bar or club, but typically use less power and generate much less heat. They use an additional small inverter that takes the 12-volt DC power input your computer power supply produces and changes that to the thousands of volts AC, which is needed to light up the gases contained within the glass tubing.

These lights now come in round patterns with mounting brackets for attachment to fans. You can get the usual assortment of bright colors or ultraviolet varieties, which work well for lighting up both your case and a UV-reactive fan itself. In addition to standard round shapes, they come in spiral patterns, although those other patterns can block some airflow.

Fan Controllers

Fan controllers allow you to adjust the amount of voltage going to a fan to slow down the fan's rotation. With slower speed, the fan does not cool as effectively, but it also makes less noise. Better fan controllers actually measure the temperature of your CPU and case and increase the fan's speed only when it's necessary. There are literally dozens of these devices on the market; they come in all shapes and sizes, and with different price tags, but typically cost between $4 and $50.

The simplest fan controller is called a bay bus (see Figure 2-6) and was done by modders in the early days of modding. You know that most fans are powered by 12-volt current. You also know that there is easy access to both 5-volt and 12-volt power inside the computer. As it turns out, this also enables access to 7 volts. The 12 volts or 5 volts you would use to power a fan is the difference between the ground wire (0 volts) and the hot wire (12 or 5 volts). By using the 5

FIGURE 2-6: Bay bus installed below a CD-ROM drive.

volt wire as the ground wire and using the 12 volt wire as the hot wire, it is possible to get 7 volts. That amount is enough to run a fan at a slow speed, while 5 volts isn't. A bay bus is simply a set of switches that selects between 12 volts and 7 volts for running fans.

A step up the ladder in complexity is using something called a rheostat to control your fan speed. A rheostat is just a device with variable resistance and a knob that you can turn to vary the voltage that passes through it. The way it's hooked up is even simpler, just put two of the leads from the rheostat in between the fan you want to control and the power source (usually the 12 volt wire), and you can vary the resistance and therefore the fan speed. The only thing you have to watch out for is using the right specifications for the rheostat (usually 3 watt and have a resistance of 20–50 ohms) or you could burn it out.

The last two methods of controlling fans are all-electronic methods: PWM or voltage regulators. Some controllers use *pulse width modulation*, or PWM. This involves chopping the supply of power to the fan to short bursts or pulses. This is very efficient, giving virtually 0–100 percent speed range. Unfortunately PWM has two side effects, the chopped supply renders the speed-sensing circuitry inside the fan inoperative, and it can produce growling noises as the fan speed is reduced.

The last method uses an alternative technique that depends on voltage regulators. These circuits use the voltage regulator to vary the voltage supplied to the fan and hence control its speed. It does have one drawback—it generates heat and therefore requires a heatsink. On the plus side, the voltage-sensing mechanism does work. What type of fan controller should you use? It depends on your needs. There are some very nice all-digital units that sense the current temperature and adjust the fan speed based on what you have programmed into the device. There are cheaper devices that have nicely glowing dials to alter fan voltage. Even the old-school-style, do-it-yourself rheostats and bay buses have their place. They can be modded easily into the exterior of the case and not cost you a drive bay that could be better used for a CD-ROM or hard drive.

Planning Ventilation

Now that you know everything you need to know about fans, you need to use those tools to plan intelligent airflow within the case you are building. Without proper airflow, it doesn't matter how many fans your system uses. With poor planning, you could simply be blowing hot air back across the components that need to be cooled and making the situation worse.

Most cases include fan mounts in several locations, usually near the front bottom and the rear just below the power supply. Some better cases also include fan mounts in the top center of the case or in the left panel (often within the window installed there). Take note of what size fans can fit into these locations, since the wrong size won't mount properly in the case.

The goal here is simple—remove as much heat as possible. Basically, you want to draw in cool air (usually from the front and sides) and expel hot air towards the back or top. You want to have even airflow. Bring in just as much air as you expel. There are some who believe in positive or negative airflow—when you bring in more air than you expel or expel more air than you bring in. Many will claim advantages for both, but this is largely untrue. With too much positive airflow, the fans will be straining to push more air into the case, and with negative airflow the fans will strain to try to remove enough air. Just having a roughly equal number is the best bet.

Bringing air into the case via the front fan mounts does a couple things. First, it starts the process of cooling the computer by bringing cool air into the computer. Second, it helps to cool the hard drives usually mounted directly behind the fans. Modern hard drives can generate a lot of heat, and actively cooling them will help greatly towards lengthening their lives.

When mounting any fans, pay attention to the direction in which the air will flow. Generally air will flow toward the label side of the fan, and it's important to mount fans in the right direction. Mounting a fan in the front of the case, which will blow outward, will do little to cool the computer, even though it may help warm your desk.

How much is enough airflow? It depends on the case, how many heat-generating cards you have, how many and what type of hard drives you have installed, and other factors. A rule of thumb is to include around 25–30 CFM of airflow if you have a single 7200-rpm hard drive up front. You should use have more airflow if you have multiple drives and/or faster drives.

As you already know, you want to remove all the heated air from the back or top of your computer. The power supply is probably already doing some of that for you, but often that simply isn't enough. The back of the case is a great location for a fan blowing out. That area is probably the warmest area in the computer due to the CPU, memory, and video card all being in that small space. As a matter of fact, some power supplies feature fans in the bottom of the power supply to help remove the heat directly from the area and get rid of it.

If adding a fan in this area, just make sure the fan blows out and not in. While taking cool air and running it directly over those components may sound like a good idea, the air in that area is rarely cool. The power supply is expelling hot air right above that space, and an intake fan right below would simply take already heated air and recycle back over the components that heated the air in the first place, starting a vicious cycle.

If your power supply already has a fan in this area, you may want to consider a blowhole. This is simply a hole in the top of the case, usually between the power supply and the optical drives, with an exhaust fan attached to it. A blowhole can also help to cool down the optical drives, since they get hotter than most people realize.

Finally, door- and window-mounted fans come into play. These can be very helpful when you're trying to cool the latest-and-greatest video card, especially if it has been overclocked. Placement of the mounts for these fans vary greatly, so some cases will work better with exhaust fans while others work better with intake fans. You may have to experiment to find the best type for your case.

| Cross-Reference | Be sure to check out Appendix A for a discussion on overclocking. |

Water Cooling

At its simplest level, water cooling is an effective means to cool computer components to levels unachievable with air cooling. At it's scariest, water cooling is a nightmare of water dripping over your new CPU, motherboard, and video card, turning them all into nothing but expensive modern art. However, the process of water cooling is not difficult, so don't be intimidated.

1. Inside your computer, a waterblock is attached to your CPU and sometimes graphics card or motherboard chips. A waterblock is a piece of metal, usually copper or aluminum, with channels cut into it for water to flow through. The waterblock also contains an inlet and an outlet to which plastic tubing to connected. One waterblock's outlet is connected to the next waterblock's inlet, and so on.

2. Eventually, the final waterblock is connected to a radiator much like the one in your car. It contains small channels or pipes for water flow that are designed to radiate heat. Usually, a slow moving fan is also attached to the radiator.

3. Finally, a pump is attached to the system and water is added. The cool water leaving the radiator first goes into the waterblock attached to the CPU and gains heat, then leaves the CPU and goes on to the next waterblock if present. At the next waterblock, the process continues and the water gains more heat, and so on until the water reaches the radiator. The radiator then cools the water and the process repeats.

This is a simplified view, of course. Most water-cooling systems also include a reservoir, which is a holding tank for additional water. The reservoir also gives air trapped in the system a place to go, since air in the water flow would cause serious problems.

Water Cooling with Less Danger

Everyone always thinks of water was electrically conductive. In other words, if someone threw a toaster (still plugged into the wall) into the bathtub while you were taking a bath, you would get a severe electrical shock and could possible die. But, while the bathtub example is a real danger, it turns out that chemistry says that water is *not* conductive. How can both be true?

Pure water, just hydrogen and oxygen molecules in the right proportion, do not conduct electricity. But virtually all the water people ever deal with (yes, even bottled water) is not pure. Those impurities make the water highly electrically, conductive. Even if you used truly pure water in your water-cooling setup, if it leaked the dust in your case would make the water impure and the risk of frying your components would be there again.

But water cooling is really misnamed. Liquid cooling would be a better term. There are lots of other liquids, and not all of them (even in an impure state) are electrically conductive. One such liquid is a new substance on the market called FluidXP from Integrity PC (`www.integrity-pc.com`). This liquid is nonconductive, environmentally friendly, and offers only slightly worse heat transfer abilities than water itself, although it's a little expensive (about $50 per 32 ounces).

There are other nonconductive fluids as well, such as various oils, but they usually suffer from serious drawbacks such as degrading the plastic used for the tubing to carry the liquid.

If you are concerned about possible leaks, using FluidXP can help provide a little more piece of mind.

External Kits

Since late 2002, several external water-cooling kits have become available. These are probably the easiest way for a novice to be introduced to the technology of water cooling. By moving all of components of the water-cooling system outside the host computer, kits offer relative safety and near-silent operation.

External kits generally come as a small box of some sort that sits beside, below, or on top of the host computer. Housed within that box are all the usual components of a water-cooling system—reservoir, pump, radiator, fan, and tubing. Coming out from the external box are a number of tubes (at least two, one for water flowing in each direction) and some sort of water-block to attach to the CPU inside the host computer.

These systems are nice because the number of components that contain water inside the host computer is minimized. In addition, should you ever decide to upgrade to a better computer system, the external system will easily move on to that system. The downside is that these kits almost always include proprietary parts. If something breaks, you must go to the original manufacturer and pay a premium.

External kits are available from a number of vendors including Koolance, Corsair, and Thermaltake. These kits will run you about $200 to $250.

Internal Kits

As when upgrading any component of your computer, measure twice and cut once, as they say. A properly planned water-cooling system will function well and be nearly silent, but a poorly planned one can lead to disaster. Buying a preassembled kit is one way to minimize the risk involved, but even then, knowing the details about the individual components can help you to avoid problems before they begin. Internal water-cooling kits are available from dozens of vendors, including Koolance, Evercool, Asetek, and Swiftech, among others. The price ranges are nearly as varied, with prices starting as low as $80 or as high as $350 or more, but typically around the $200 range.

The following sections give you the rundown on the basic components in a water-cooling system as well as some advice on why certain components have advantages over others.

Tubing and Clamps

One of the first decisions is what size tubing you will use. Tubing is measured one of two ways: the inner diameter (ID) or the outer diameter (OD). Inner diameter is the most common way to measure it, but double-check everything just to make sure that you are always using the same units.

Most components now use $3/8$-inch ID tube, but there are nearly as many $1/2$-inch and $1/4$-inch accessories as well. Basically, the bigger the tube the more water flow you can get but the trade-off is the inability to make tighter turns. Bigger tubes are harder to bend without causing a kink and impeding water flow.

Besides tube size, you must be concerned about the material the tube is made from. The best type is silicone- or latex-based surgical hose available from surgical supply stores. However, the most common tubing is vinyl (also known as PVC) tubing.

Plastic PVC tubing is available from $0.20 to $4 per foot. It's somewhat stiff and fairly resistant to kinking. The main drawbacks are that it ages poorly, and after a few months it will start to discolor and lose its transparency. After about a year it can become hard and brittle, making it prone to cracking and water leaks at fittings if mishandled. Overall, it's a cheap and effective tubing solution for most water coolers, and is the tubing type most commonly shipped with kit systems.

Silicon tubing usually has is white and is the near perfect tubing solution for water cooling. It ages well, stretches well, binds well onto fittings, and is fairly flexible. Its main drawback is its fairly high cost, often being 10 (or even more) times as expensive as PVC tubing.

Optional, but recommended are tube clamps. A tube clamp is responsible for binding the tubing tight to any fittings on the waterblocks or pump to prevent the chance of leakage. Some of the major types in use include:

- **Metal worm-drive ring** ($0.25 to $0.80 each)—Strong and effective. Many industrial strength tubing applications use this style of clamp. But there can be issues with corrosion as with all metal clamps

- **Metal spring type clamps** ($0.10 to $0.60)—These are squeezed apart with a pair of pliers then released over the area you wish to clamp. While they are cheap and effective unfortunately they are difficult to use. The corrosion problem exists here as well.

- **Metal wire screw clamps** ($0.25 to $1)—These are both effective and lightweight. They are strong enough for use in a water-cooling system, but the narrow wires may cut softer tubing types if tightened too much. Corrosion problems exist here too.

- **Plastic ratchet clamps** (about $1 each)—They are easy to use and remove. Since they are plastic, they won't corrode or react with any metals and are cheap. The plastic clamps generally provide enough pressure for use in a water-cooling system.

- **Cable ties** (under $1 for several)—These can make an effective and cheap hose clamp. In most water-cooling systems the water pressure is relatively low so the small amounts of pressure that cable ties provide is good enough.

Waterblock

Water blocks are the devices that remove heat from the hot components and transfer it to the water flowing through it. There are many different designs available, and each has some particular reason that its manufacturers claim it's the best design for you. Some adventurous individuals even make their own waterblocks by machining solid pieces of metal. Waterblocks vary in price quite a bit, but typically fall between $40 and $100.

There are two important considerations when choosing a waterblock. First, the waterblock must have mounting mechanisms for your processor. While some waterblocks can work on multiple types of processors, some are specific to an individual manufacturer (i.e., Pentium 4 vs. Athlon XP, ATI Radeon 9800 vs. Nvidia 5950, etc.). The second most important decision is the fitting size. If the tubing you are planning to use is too big or too small, the waterblock isn't going to work for you.

One common trend today is the use of a clear cap on top of the waterblock and a rubber O-ring seal to prevent leakage (see Figure 2-7). The advantage of these waterblocks is that the top can be removed should you need to fix the waterblock (for example, if something becomes stuck in the small channels). In addition to the ability to service the waterblock, the clear top allows you to see if you need to service the waterblock, which is hard to determine otherwise.

Caution

When a waterblock becomes clogged with something, the best case is just that water flow is restricted and the temperature of the processor will climb. In the worst case, not only will temperatures rise, but pressure will build in the system leading to leaks and possible pump failure. In either case, the situation is very dangerous and can easily lead to a damaged computer.

Water Pump

There are a couple of major types of water pumps, those that can be submerged in water (submersible) and those that cannot (inline). There are a few pumps that can operate either way. In addition, different pumps use different power sources. Some use DC power direct from the computer, and some use AC power directly from the power outlet in your wall.

Finally, you need to decide on the water pump capacity. All water pumps will have a flow-rate—how much water can be pumped over a given time (often listed as gallons per hour). How much actual water is pumped through the system depends on a few factors, such as the length and diameter of tubing in the system as well as the layout of the components. In other

FIGURE 2-7: CPU waterblock with acrylic cover permitting the insides to be seen.

words, pumping water uphill is a much more difficult task. The flow rate you need is simply whatever flow rate is enough to keep your processor cool when it's under load and computing something. Remember that it's better to have a high flow rate rather than a lower flow rate—extra cooling won't hurt, but too little certainly will.

Tip Some water pumps have adjustable flow rates, while some others can be adjusted by using a rheostat (i.e., certain types of fan controllers). Read the instructions to determine if the flow rate of a water pump is adjustable via one method or another.

The choice of a submersible or inline pump, as well as power source, depends on your own needs. A submersible pump may lead to a smaller water-cooling system because the pump can be contained within the reservoir. However, a system with an inline pump may be easier to service. As for power, DC is easier to hook up inside the computer but difficult to service because turning on the pump without turning on the computer (for example, when bleeding air out of the system) is more difficult. Using AC power makes the pump easier to work on but means an extra power cord to the computer.

Tip It should be possible to mod an AC-power-based pump to pull power directly from the power supply. This would involve modding both the pump and the power supply by cutting off the plug on the pump and soldering it inside the power supply where the AC plug is. It's dangerous, but potentially useful.

The main factor used in differentiating pumps is the gallon per hour or liter per hour rating of how much water it will pump. Many people think the most important factor, however, is the ability of the pump to lift water (the term used is "head"). If your pump is at the bottom of the case but the CPU is near the top, then the pump will need to have sufficient water flow (at least 20 gallons per hour) while pushing the water up hill.

Of course, there are also other factors such as noise and heat generated by the pump, but these details are often difficult to determine ahead of time. Water pumps for computer water-cooling setups typically go for between $35 and $100.

Radiator

The radiator is similar to the one installed in your car, only smaller. It is usually composed of aluminum or copper tubing surrounded by flat, corrugated aluminum fins. By forcing air over these fins via a fan, the water running through it is substantially cooled. There are two common types of radiators used in water-cooling systems today: tube style and fin style.

Tube style radiators are composed of a single long tube of metal that is curved back on itself several times. Many thin fins of metal are soldered onto the straight sections of the tube. Such radiators often suffer from poor flow-rate efficiency, meaning that the water pump will struggle to push water through the long sections of pipe. They also tend to be bulky but are cheaper to manufacture.

Fin style radiators consist of a number of thin flat tubes and an entry and exit tank. Between each tube an extra fin is soldered to the tubes at the fold point. These radiators often represent one of the most efficient water-air heat exchangers available for their size, but are more expensive. These radiators also don't impede on water flow rates as much as other types of radiators. Due to their compact size, they make good additions to most cases. Fin-style radiators with higher folds per inch (fpi) are more efficient coolers than ones with lower fpi, when the coolers themselves have equal dimensions. You can't judge efficiency by the dimensions of the radiator alone.

Radiators for designed for computer use typically run between $50 and $350. Radiators designed for automotive uses run several hundred dollars but can usually be had much cheaper from junkyards.

Reservoir

A reservoir is optional, but a very useful addition. Having a reservoir adds to the cooling capacity of the system by providing a larger capacity of material to absorb and dissipate heat. In addition, the reservoir helps to trap air bubbles that would otherwise be trapped in the system lowering cooling efficiency. The main drawback to using a reservoir is that in addition to the extra space it takes up, it is usually not totally sealed and could leak if the case were accidentally moved.

There are many styles and sizes of reservoirs. One popular option is a reservoir that fits entirely in a $5^1/_4$-inch drive bay. Such reservoirs are often somewhat easy to add or remove fluid to and from, and are easy to monitor fluid levels in. On the other hand, they also have limited capacity, so you may be better off with another solution if your case has space for it.

Simple reservoirs run between $30 and $80. Don't forget that with a little work, using acrylic, you could fabricate your own reservoir more cheaply, but the peace of mind that comes from using a professionally created one is usually worth it.

Additives

When the water-cooling system contains components made from different types of metal, there is the possibility of corrosion caused by the different metals reacting with one another. This can result in all sorts of problems, not the least of which is a blockage building up in some components, thereby reducing the effective cooling of the system or damaging components. In addition, there is also the chance that algae might start to form.

To solve this problem, a water additive is often introduced into the cooling fluid. Here are some of the common water additives used in water-cooling setups:

- **Automotive antifreeze** ($0.06 to $0.13 per oz.)—This substance typically contains boron suspended in an ethylene glycol mix. You can also use just pure antifreeze instead of the typical water/antifreeze mix. For systems that actively chill the liquid coolant to below freezing, some sort of antifreeze mix is a necessity.

- **Redline Water Wetter** ($0.59 to $1.20 per oz.)—This product, found in any auto-parts store, can be used to provide rust and corrosion protection. According to the manufacturer, it provides much better heat transfer properties than glycol-based antifreeze.

- **Laundry bleach** ($0.01 to $0.16 per oz.)—Laundry bleach is a cheap and good additive for killing off and preventing any fungal growth in the water system. Just a tablespoon of bleach is typically enough per liter of water to be effective for many months.

- **Dishwashing detergent** ($0.05 to $0.16 per oz.)—A few drops of dishwashing detergent (liquid variety) can also be useful when using water cooling. Water has a somewhat high surface tension, which means that air bubbles can be some sometimes get stuck in the system. Some detergent in the water reduces the surface tension of the water so that air bubbles trapped in the system are less likely to adhere to surfaces inside the system.

- **Coloring/UV dyes** ($7 to $10 per oz.)—Often, people like to add some sort of colored dye (especially the UV-reactive variety) to the fluid to give it a nice science-fiction-type effect. These are available at several online stores listed earlier in the water-cooling section.

Tip You can also cut the end off a highlighter pen and let the inner ink reservoir sit in tub of water for a cheap alternative to the expensive dyes from the online stores.

Tips for Installing a Water-Cooling System

Every water-cooling installation will be a little different, based on your case and your water-cooling kit. But there are some common tips that will help no matter what the specifics are in your situation.

- When installing the radiator, the best place is usually the front bottom of the case, with the fan between the outside and the radiator. The fan should pull air from outside the case and push it through the radiator.

- Even the best water pumps cause vibration, so keep that in mind when placing the pump. Most pumps have rubber suction-cup feet that help to dissipate noise, but you may want to use extra insulating material.

- Some waterblocks require access to both sides of the board they are attached to. While removing you video card to attach the waterblock is relatively easy, removing the motherboard may be a pain, so plan on this before you do too much mounting work inside the case.

- When mounting the tubing, remember to keep it away from anything sharp and be careful not to kink the tubing.

- Remember to use cable ties on all tubes where they attach to components. This step is optional, but isn't your hardware worth the extra precaution?

- Fill the reservoir and run the pump for a while with the computer off. This lets you "bleed" air out of the system before any damage is done, and it's a good check for leaks in the system. If anything leaks at this point, with careful work you can clean that component off and dry it for a few days, and it should still work. This is not the case if the computer was already started.

- Many computer BIOSs (basic input output/systems) allow you to set specific thermal shutdown limits. Thus, if your processor gets too hot, your computer will shut down before any permanent damage is done. Turning this on is, in general, a good idea, but even more so in the case of water cooling. Should a pump or fan fail, this will protect your investment in your processor and other components. The specific temperatures that the limits should be set to vary by processor, so consult the manufacturer's Web site for the standard operating temperatures for your specific chip.

- Many people like to assemble the water-cooling components (waterblocks, tubing, pumps, reservoir) completely outside the computer and run water through them for a few days first before reassembling them in their systems. This has the advantage of finding any leaks in the waterblocks themselves.

Build Your Own

With both internal and external water-cooling systems, you always have the option of building your own kit. All the parts you could ever need are all available from various retailers, and you can simply mix and match the components that meet your needs for performance and price. It's a lot more work to go with your own setup, but the knowledge you gain and the feeling of pride is often worth the cost. In addition, something you put together yourself has the potential to perform better that a one-size-fits-all type of kit.

There are quite a few people who have built their own water-cooling rigs, often including the creation of a custom reservoir from pieces of acrylic. Much less common are custom-built external water-cooling setups, but for no good reason. Wouldn't it be great to have one of the first custom built water-cooling setups in your area, while still maintaining the advantages of an external system?

Other Options

Air cooling and water cooling are not the only options for cooling a computer these days. Air and water cooling are the most popular and typically the least expensive, but for specific cases other options may be the best thing. Take a look at few competing technologies such as heatpipes, peltier cooling, and phase-change cooling. Those looking for a short-term cooling solution for benchmarks sometimes even go so far as using liquid nitrogen to cool their computers!

Heatpipes

Heatpipes are metal tubes that are vacuumed out (i.e., have no air is inside) with a bit of a special fluid inside. Heatpipes work on the principle of phase change, whereby a fluid changes state from liquid to gas at a specific temperature and pressure. Thus, they are effective means of moving heat from one place to another, but that heat needs to be removed via a heatsink/fan outlet.

A traditional heat pipe is a hollow cylinder filled with a liquid that vaporizes at a specific temperature. At the bottom of the cylinder, the heat boils the fluid inside until it changes to a vapor. That vapor then rises in the cylinder to the top, at which point the heat vapor is cooled (usually via an external heatsink or fan) and condenses back to a liquid. That liquid, due to gravity, flows back down the cylinder, and the whole process repeats itself.

Heatpipes are nice in that they, by themselves, require no power and have no moving parts. The downside is that with today's processors and graphics processing units, a heatpipe alone (at least one that would fit inside a case) is not efficient enough to remove the heat needed. Thus, it requires a fan and heatsink attached to it. Of course, this means added noise.

Heatpipes work well as part of a bigger solution. Many modern CPU fan/heatsink combos include some form of heatsink technology inside them. Of course, heatsinks that include heatpipes are usually a few dollars more expensive than heatsinks without them, but considering the vastly different designs of heatsinks, the addition of a heatpipe to the design doesn't always mean a more expensive heatsink.

Peltier Cooling

Peltier cooling (also known as thermoelectric cooling) is usually used in conjunction with other cooling methods such as water cooling. The idea is that when an electric current is applied to two dissimilar materials a temperature differential is the result. Thus, a peltier is a small device with a hot side and a cool side when power is supplied.

A typical peltier is composed of two ceramic wafers with some semiconductor material sandwiched in between the wafers. When current is applied, the positive side begins to lose electrons to the negative side, and they take heat with them as they go. The cold side is placed against the CPU (usually through a cold plate to better distribute the cooling effect) and the hot side is placed against a heatsink or water-block.

Using a peltier cooler has some serious drawbacks. If the peltier itself goes bad, not only will it stop cooling your CPU but it can actually heat the CPU causing damage. In addition, under normal circumstances a peltier can cool a CPU below the ambient room temperature, leading to condensation that must be insulated against. Also, the cooling does not happen for free. The peltier itself also adds heat to the equation, so you are trying to get rid of unwanted heat for both the processor itself (which is transferred through the peltier) *and* the heat the peltier itself creates.

Thus, while peltier cooling does have the advantage of being able to cool CPUs below ambient temperature, it has serious drawbacks should something fail. In addition, the cooling system working in conjunction with the peltier must be able to dissipate even more heat than the processor itself since the peltier adds to the heat generated. This is not a very efficient cooling method.

The cost for a peltier usually ranges between $20 and $40. Sometimes manufacturers embed a peltier into a water-block, which gives all the advantages of a separate peltier while only raising the cost of the waterblock by a few dollars.

Phase-Change Cooling

Phase-change cooling is also known as vapor-change cooling. Basically, this is the same as what happens in your refrigerator or freezer. The process consists of a refrigerant (commonly R134A, which is also used in automobile air-conditioning systems), compressor, condenser, expansion value, and evaporator.

The process starts when the compressor compresses the refrigerant to a high pressure and passes it through the condenser, which turns the refrigerant into a liquid. During that process, heat exchanging coils dissipate the heat created by the condensing process and exhaust it. The refrigerant then passes through the expansion valve, which reduces the pressure of the refrigerant. During that pressure reduction, the liquid evaporates and absorbs heat, making the temperature in the expansion valve cold. The cycle then repeats itself.

You can purchase complete phase-change cooling systems from companies like KryoTech and Asetek, and some companies even sell complete systems with all the computer components and phase-change cooling system already installed. However, these systems, whether just the cooling system or the complete computer system, are generally expensive. Some truly hard-core modders even build their own systems, although this is a dangerous and difficult task at best.

For the record, one of the main problems with phase-change cooling is how to avoid condensation on the CPU or nearby components. This is precisely why sticking your new, top of the line computer into the refrigerator is a bad idea.

Phase-change cooling systems are available for around $850.

Liquid Nitrogen

Nitrogen, for those who don't know, is the most common gas in the atmosphere. To change it to liquid form, it must be radically cooled. Because of this fact, the liquid form of nitrogen can actually be used to cool your computer—at least for short periods.

 It cannot be stated too many times how dangerous liquid nitrogen is. If you have ever accidentally spilled any liquid, try to imagine the damage it would have caused if the liquid would have caused instant freezing and brittleness.

Some daring people attach a sort of cup-shaped container directly to the component they want to cool (almost always the main CPU itself). The liquid nitrogen is poured into this container and immediately begins to boil off, taking the heat generated by the CPU with it. However, this cooling is short-lived and only lasts for as long as the liquid nitrogen takes to boil off. In addition, large amounts of condensation will appear on the container itself, causing a risk of complications because this condensation may drip onto the motherboard or other components.

This technique is great for producing quick benchmarks of what computing power is possible, but it is clearly impractical for any serious use. Bragging rights are the only long-term gain from this method, and serious injury can occur from using this substance. In all those science fiction movies where the villain is covered with liquid nitrogen and then gets smashed into a thousand pieces, they were not exaggerating.

Liquid nitrogen is available for approximately $2 per gallon, but you need special containers to transport it.

Wrapping Up

What cooling method you choose to use for your computer is based on compromise. A water-cooling method will cost more and require more maintenance than an air-cooling method, but will generally lead to cooler temperatures and increase your chance of overclocking. An air-cooled setup can be cheap and easy and will generally lead to acceptable results for most people but not serious overclockers. The other methods are generally used for the hard-core over-clocker with serious money to burn.

 See Appendix A for a brief discussion of overclocking and how to accomplish it.

At the same time, the extra cost and maintenance of a water-cooled system may be worth it if you really hate the sound of living in an air tunnel. But if you want a system that you can build and then forget about maintenance on, air cooling is your best bet. There are no clear winners (although liquid nitrogen is a shoo-in for a clear loser, considering the risks).

With modding, your cooling method is entirely up to you. If one of the available methods doesn't quite work in the case your computer sits in, mod it. Not enough fan mounts? Mod some more into the case. No room for a water-cooling system with reservoir? Buy a much smaller case for the water-cooling components and mod it to attach to your current one. It's all about seeing something in your head that hasn't been built yet.

Just remember, if you're not overclocking your system, there's no need to go overboard with cooling. All the various fans, fan controllers, heat pipes, and so on are unnecessary for most people. Let common sense prevail. There is no reason that a normal computer needs to sound like the flight deck of an aircraft carrier during combat maneuvers.

Cable Management

Ith the rise of case windows and lights, the rat's nest of wires found inside most computers simply won't cut it anymore. Aesthetics play a very important role in terms of computer mods, and nobody likes to see a case full of multicolored spaghetti (see Figure 3-1). In addition, all those poorly arranged cables actually impede airflow and lead to higher case temperatures, which are very bad for computer components. The solution, of course, is to manage that mess of wires and keep the interior of your computer clean. This is known as cable or wire management.

The methods for cable management are really very simple. Basically, there are only two things that must be remembered when trying to clean up the wires in your case. First, use the right cables for the job. Having the right length cables and the right type will do wonders for the general look and functionality of your system. Second, whenever possible, bundle the cables together in a logical and efficient manner. Anything less and you will likely end up with the mess seen in Figure 3-1.

Using the Right Cables

Buying the right cables for your case is important. But it's not just a question of making sure that you don't accidentally buy a USB cable when you need an IDE cable. The right cables need to be the right type, length, and possibly even color.

Creating or Hiding Cables

Sometimes the right cable doesn't exist because it's not made in the proper length for your needs. If the cable is something simple, like a serial cable or USB cable, you can make your own. This may be more expensive and time-consuming than buying a cable, but at this point you may have no other option. Buy a few male or female connectors and some wire and try your hand at soldering those connectors and cable to create exactly the cable length you need. Be extra careful to make sure that all your connections are soldered cleanly with no shorts between pins and that the entire cable is properly insulated with heat-shrink tubing and/or hot glue.

FIGURE 3-1: Example of poor cable management. Note the flat ribbon cables and excess of wiring from the power supply.

Be sure to check each and every pin to make sure that two pins have not accidentally been soldered together, potentially causing a short circuit in the computer. This can easily be accomplished by using a multimeter (set to the diode setting) and attaching one probe to a single pin while attaching the other probe to each pin one at a time on the other end of the wire.

Unfortunately, sometimes not only will you not be able to purchase the right cable because it's not made in the right length but also the cable will be beyond anything you can make at home. In those situations, try to hide the unused portion of the cables. Perhaps you can hide the extra length of cable behind the motherboard tray or behind the drive racks and hold them there using cable ties or some other mechanism. Above all else, try and make it look organized.

Round Cables

One example of using the right cable for your case would be IDE cables. Modern IDE cables are round instead of flat. The round cables impede airflow much less, which leads to lower case temperatures. In addition, these cables come in all types of colors that ribbon cables never came in, including varieties that use electroluminescent wire or tape to make them light up. Round cables are definitely the way to go to help manage the wires in your case. Even the older ribbon cable style can be brought into the modern age by making them round yourself.

Rounding cables is the process of taking an existing flat ribbon cable and separating some of the wires into smaller collections of wires so that they can be grouped together into a round "bundle" of cables rather than the original flat ribbon.

To accomplish this, you are going to need a sharp hobby knife (or razor blade), some method of combining the cables together (such as cable ties or tape), and some patience. This whole process should take less than 30 minutes to accomplish, and cost less than $15, including all the supplies (other than the cable itself). Depending of the cable type, luck may also be an important element!

1. Take a standard ribbon cable and decide how wide each individual strip should be. In this example, the cable is a 50-pin SCSI ribbon cable. For the rounded cable, you will separate the strips into collections of four wires each.

2. Make a small incision between every fourth and fifth wire with a hobby knife. The incision needs to go completely through the cable, but only needs to be a few millimeters long. Be careful to separate the existing wires without exposing any of the metal in the wires.

Caution

If you accidentally expose any of the metal inside the cable while making the incisions, you *might* be able to fix the cable by using a little electrical tape to cover the exposed area. If you cut completely through one of the small wires, most likely you have ruined the cable and will need to purchase another cable and start over.

3. Carefully rip apart the strips of cable by pulling them apart at the cuts you just made (see Figure 3-2). This should be easy because the cables are designed to separate at the meeting point between the wires. Remember to leave the connectors at the ends of the cable attached—don't rip them off the cable.

4. Bundle the strips of wire together (you can stack them or simply mash them together, whatever is easiest) about an inch or so down from the connector (see Figure 3-3). Use a cable tie to hold the wires together. Do this at both ends.

5. Finally, use cable ties to hold the collection of wires together. Use enough cable ties to make sure that the cable stays together and looks cleanly done. One cable tie every two inches is usually good.

Tip

Wire management devices other than cable ties can be used to hold the rounded cable together as well. These other wire management devices are discussed later in this chapter.

FIGURE 3-2: Ribbon cable in process of having the strips of wires separated from the main cable.

FIGURE 3-3: Ribbon cable with the strips of wires collected into a bundle.

Store Bought or Home-Made?

The question comes up frequently whether someone should make his or her own round cables or purchase them. Quite simply, store bought is always better.

Modern ultra-DMA100 or ultra-DMA133 cables involve such small gauge cables that the chance someone could round one themselves without actually cutting one of those cables is small. In addition, there might still be issues with signal crosstalk if done improperly.

If existing round cables don't offer the look you need, many of the wire management techniques (such as split loom or spiral wrap) can be used to improve the looks of the cables.

In addition, round cables are now dirt cheap. Sometimes, modern rounded cables are even cheaper than their ribbon cable counterparts.

Then why bother even learning how to make your own round cables?

Rounding cables is still a useful skill. Sometimes motherboards come with flat ribbon cables that are custom cables and could do with being round instead. For example, the DFI LANparty PRO875 revision A motherboard lacks a MIDI/gameport connector on the back panel. Instead, they provide a header on the motherboard for that port and a flat ribbon cable that leads to a DB15 port. This cable does not come as a rounded cable in any computer store, but can be rounded by hand following the techniques explained in this chapter.

Bundling Wires

You want to bundle your wires together in logical groups so that they are easy to use but also look good. Usually, the best way to accomplish this is to use some type of material to cover the wires and bind them together. For example, a standard power adapter for a hard drive or CD-ROM is composed of four separate wires that leave the power supply at one point and connect to the device at another point. Rather than have those four separate wires, wouldn't it make sense to have a single bundle of wires?

The best way to start the bundling process is to decide on what type of material you will use to cover your wires. All the commonly available methods have advantages and disadvantages, so let's go over them in detail. After the discussion, you should have a good idea of what materials are available and be able to pick a material that suits you.

Cable Ties

Cable ties are small plastic clips that you tighten around wires or cables to bind them together (see Figure 3-4). They are probably the most popular and effective method of cable management in current use. Cable ties can be purchased for between $0.02 and $0.30 each, but often come in bundles from 50 to 650.

The advantages of cable ties are numerous. They come in all different sizes and colors. They are simple to use and hold wires together very well. Multiple cable ties can be attached together to

FIGURE 3-4: Cable ties used to manage the wires from a floppy power adapter. Next to the adapter are a couple of different-sized cable ties.

make even longer cable ties if need be. They take up very little space and don't require removing the connectors from the cables.

Of course, there are downsides as well. Once applied they require cutting to remove them, but due to the tightness with which they are usually attached to the wires they bind together, you risk cutting the wires when cutting the cable ties. Also, they are not reusable.

Applying them is very simple. Place the cable tie around the wires to be held together. Bending the cable tie back on itself, place the flat side of the cable tie through the square piece attached to the other end of the cable tie so that the "teeth" on the cable tie are on the inside towards the wires. Then pull the flat piece through the square connector. You should hear a clicking sound as you pull the cable tie tighter and tighter. Once it's fully tight, use a pair of wire cutters to cut off the excess plastic sticking through the square connecter.

Few good case mods are done without using a lot of cable ties.

Electrical Tape

Electrical tape is truly the worst of the worst as far as cable management is concerned. In simple terms, you wind electrical tape around your wires to bind them together (see Figure 3-5). When this is done well, the effect is at best okay. Done poorly, this actually makes the case look worse. Electrical tape is available for between $0.80 and $5 for around 12 feet of tape.

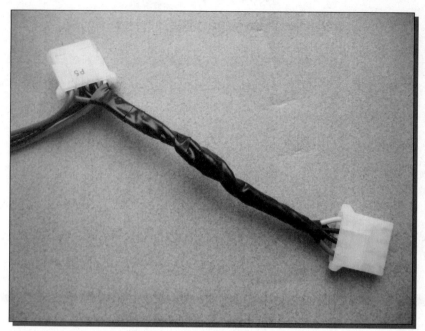

FIGURE 3-5: Electrical tape used as a method of wire management.

There are only a few upsides to using electrical tape. It's cheaply available all over the place (even at grocery stores). Electrical tape also comes in different colors (although anything other than black is harder to find) but so do most other methods. The tape can also insulate against electrical shorts. But the point of wire management is to bind several cables together, so any wires with exposed metal must be individually wrapped with electrical tape before using more tape to bundle them together if you need to prevent electrical shorts due to accidentally cutting into the wire.

The downsides are many. Electrical tape tends to come loose and start to unbind as time passes. This leaves a nasty, gooey residue on all the wires. In addition, the tape is difficult to undo if you ever need to work on the wires again (and of course leaves that same residue). The effects are even worse in a warm environment, such as the inside of your case.

To apply electrical tape, attach one end of the electrical tape (while still attached to the roll of tape) to one end of your wires. Now wind the tape over the wires in a spiral pattern till the wires are completely covered down their length. Finally, cut the piece of tape from the roll.

Heat-Shrink Tubing

Heat-shrink tubing is another possible material for wire management. Typically used for electrical work, this tubing is a nonconductive rubber-like material that when exposed to heat shrinks down to 50 percent of it's original size (see Figure 3-6). This creates a snug fit for the

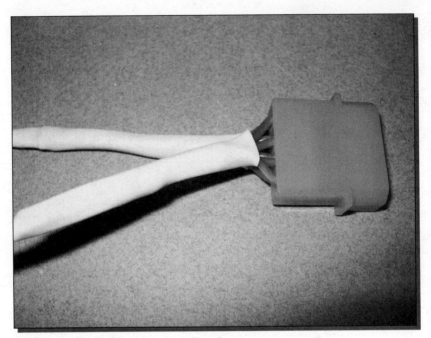

FIGURE 3-6: Heat-shrink tubing used alone for wire management.

wires beneath it and protects them from electrical short circuits. Heat-shrink tubing is available for between $1 to $5 for a few feet.

The advantage to heat-shrink tubing as a management material is that it is easily available from any electronics store and tightly binds together the wires beneath it. It's somewhat inexpensive and comes in a variety of colors.

On the downside, to remove the heat-shrink tubing you must cut it with a sharp knife and risk damage to the wires beneath. In addition, the heat-shrink tubing and wires beneath it tend to be quite stiff, which makes it difficult to move them. Finally, you may have to remove the connectors from the wires before you can place the heat-shrink tubing over the wires you want to bundle together.

To apply heat-shrink tubing, place the tubing over the wires you wish to bundle together. Remember to use a slightly longer piece of tubing than the wires you are covering, since the ends of the heat-shrink tubing can contract a little like the diameter does. Using a hot-air gun or hair drier, blow hot air over the heat-shrink tubing until it contracts and forms a tight seal over the wires.

Tip When blowing hot air over heat-shrink tubing, you may want to try to avoid blowing the hot air into your case because the other computer components might suffer from the additional heat. It would be best to remove the piece you are trying to attach to the heat-shrink tubing from the case first and place it back in the case later.

In general, heat-shrink tubing is best left as an addition to another wire management technique rather than a technique on its own.

Wire Loom

There are two types of wire loom—split loom and spiral wrap (see Figure 3-7).

Split loom is a flexible plastic tube that looks a bit like a radiator hose from a car. Down one side it has a slit that allows you to place it around a collection of wires. Spiral wrap is a spiral piece of plastic that looks a bit like a spring with flattened sides. It wraps around a collection of wires to bundle them together. Either type is available for under $10 for a few feet of material.

These methods share the same advantages. They are typically cheap and easy to apply. They do not require connectors to be removed when you apply them. They can be cut to any length desired. Unfortunately, the color choices for both are somewhat limited. Other colors besides the typical black and white are available, but only from specialty stores (not even most modding stores) and are much more expensive.

Sleeving

Flexible sleeving has become the preferred way to do an extensive wire management job, but it's also the most labor intensive. Flexible sleeving is a type of nylon mesh tubing that can

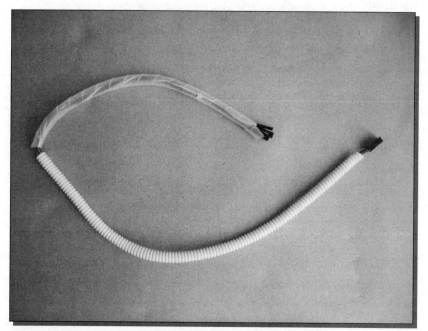

FIGURE 3-7: Spiral wrap and split loom used on the same wire bundle. Spiral wrap is on the top, and split loom is on the bottom.

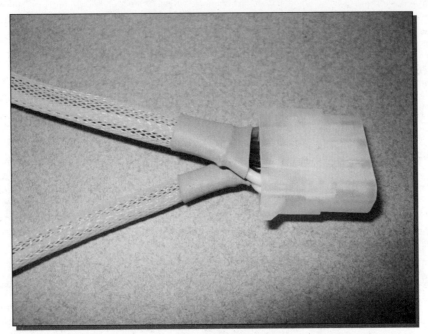

FIGURE 3-8: Flexible sleeving as wire management. Note that some heat-shrink tubing is also used around the connector itself to secure the sleeving in place.

expand or contract a good deal to accommodate whatever wire you need to fit it over (see Figure 3-8). Bare sleeving is available for between $0.60 and $1.50.

There are quite a few advantages to flexible sleeving. The sleeving itself comes in various sizes, and each of those sizes can fit a fair number of wires since the sleeving can contract or expand. In addition, it comes in a wide variety of colors, including UV reactive. There are kits on the market that include colored flexible sleeving, heat-shrink tubing (typically used to secure the ends of the sleeving), and cable ties for under $20. A properly (or even only somewhat properly) done sleeving setup looks very professional.

The main disadvantage of flexible sleeving is that in most situations the end of the cable you are sleeving needs to be removed before the sleeving can go on. This limits flexible sleeving use to those who are brave enough to actually take the risk of not getting things put back together properly.

The installation of the sleeving is a medium difficulty task:

1. Remove the connector from the wires you are trying to add the sleeving to. Remember to mark where each wire went.

2. Cut the appropriate length of sleeving (most sleeving requires you either to cut it with a hot knife or to quickly run the ends under a flame to seal them against fraying) and place it over the cables.

3. Cut a section of heat-shrink tubing about 1 inch long and place that over the sleeving.

4. Reattach the connector and use a heat gun or hair drier to shrink the heat-shrink tubing and secure it in place.

Few methods of wire management look as professional as a nice sleeving job. The time spent sleeving wires is always worth the result.

Chameleon Springs

Chameleon springs, from a company called Lizard Tree, is a new type of cable management. Basically, these are plastic "springs" that can be used to bundle your wires together (see Figure 3-9). Packages containing several 12-inch pieces in different diameters are available for around $12, while a package containing 36-inch pieces is around $22.

The company sells several different kits of various lengths and colors, including some UV-reactive colors. The springs themselves come in 13 mm, 8 mm, and 6 mm diameters (all in the same package) to accommodate the main motherboard wiring harness and the other collections of wires typically found in modern computer cases. There are over a dozen colors available, and most are UV reactive.

There are a number of advantages to this method of wire management. The installation is easy and doesn't require removing the cable end to install the springs. The colors are bright, and the

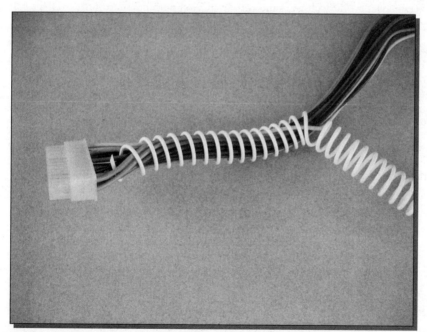

FIGURE 3-9: Chameleon springs being added to a motherboard power connector harness.

UV reactive ones, when combined with a UV light source, look like fancy EL-wire cables but require no separate heat-generating inverter. In addition, they are easy to remove and reuse, something that cannot be said of other wire management techniques.

But no wire management method is perfect. These springs suffer from a lack of availability. They can only be purchased from a couple of dealers (who only carry a small selection of the available colors) or from the manufacer. Shipping times from the manufacturer can be quite long, up to a month or so. The price is okay, less expensive than some flexible sleeving kits but more expensive than the other methods.

Installation of the chameleon springs is straightforward. Simply twist the springs onto the collection of wires you want to bundle together in a clockwise fashion. After a bit, the spring will work it's way over the wires you are trying to cover. You can then use a pair of scissors or wire cutters to cut the spring to the right length. If you find the length you have is too short or too long, you can expand or compress the spring by taking it back off the set of wires and pulling or pushing each coil individually. The spring will retain the new shape and can be put back on the set of wires you are working on.

Additional Techniques

With great case modding, you sometimes have to go over the top to really get noticed. There are some additional techniques for cleaning up your wires that can help you accomplish this. These techniques are difficult and time-consuming, but nothing can compare to the results you can get this way.

False Bottom

If you are truly interested in spending some quality time with your cables, there are some things you can do to clean them up even more. For starters, run as many cables as you can along the bottom of your case. Cut a piece of Plexiglas or metal the exact size of the bottom of the case and make a false bottom for the case, hiding the wires beneath it.

This technique can be applied to the drive bays as well. You can usually hide a good deal of wires behind the $3^1/_2$-inch drive bays between the motherboard side of the case and the drive bays themselves. The problem is that wires can be seen through the holes in the drive bay racks. By cutting a piece of Plexiglas or metal and attaching it to the drive bays, you can hide all those wires (see Figure 3-10).

For that final touch, you can use mirror-tinting trim (available in auto-parts stores) on the false bottom to create the impression that the case is bigger than it really is. If you have painted the inside of the case, you can then paint the false bottom or side the same color and from a short distance no one will be able to tell where the wires are.

Precision-Length Wires

As mentioned previously, the best type of cable management involves not only having the wires you do use covered in some type of material such as sleeving or spiral wrap, but having the wires the right length.

FIGURE 3-10: Behind the wires and pump is a false side that hides all these messy wires when viewed from the other side.

Some modders (and boutique dealers) have gotten very good at hiding the extra lengths of cable out of sight. Also, purchasing the right length cables, such as with round IDE cables, does a world of good in terms of making your case look good. But there is no standard length for power supply wires, so the chance that whatever power supply you purchase has exactly the right number of connectors and exactly the right the length of wires is extremely small.

The most extreme thing you can do is to cut and resolder every wire coming from your power supply to the right length. It's a lot of work and the chance of catostophic error is reasonably high, but nothing else can yield the same results. Of course, this requires knowing exactly where every device will be in your system so careful planning is required.

Cross-Reference Chapter 12, containing the "Scientist" mod, features this type of work. All the wires for the power supply were cut and soldered the exact length needed, and then covered with UV-reactive chameleon springs. It took just under two hours to cut and solder the wires themselves, not counting the time spent planning how the cables should be positioned, but the results speak for themselves.

Wrapping Up

With case modding, wire management describes the process of turning a mess into a showpiece. Starting with miles of unsightly wiring you relocate, conceal, and contort the wires until they are organized. It's a time-consuming process, but it's critical if you want a great looking case.

In this chapter we've looked at all the common methods for organizing the wires in a case—rounding, sleeving, wire loom, cable ties, false bottoms, and even cutting and soldering wires to the right length. But don't let any of these ideas constrain you from developing your own ideas. Just hide or bundle the wires in your case until they look good to you, and don't block the airflow in your case.

Lighting

When you finally bring your new, top-of-the-line computer home you probably want it to look cool just like all those computers in the science fiction shows you used to watch. One great way to do that is to have your case light up to showcase all the hard work you've done on it. With a lot of computer cases coming with windows preinstalled, what better way to show off that $500 video card you just bought?

Thankfully, there are many different ways to get your case to light up. Every color combination you can think of is attainable with just a little money. By combining these different methods, you will be able to achieve unique lighting schemes that will truly be your own.

The best way to decide what type of lighting your computer should use is to go over the differences between all the available types. After that's over, you should be able to get a good idea about what type of lighting best suits your case.

Types of Lighting

Before we discuss anything else, it's important to understand all the different options for lighting a computer. Different types of lighting will work well in different situations due to space concerns, amount of light produced, or the colors available. Neon tube, cold cathodes, EL-wire, and LEDs all have their place. The trick is knowing which one to use where.

Neon tubes

Neon tubes were the first items used to light up computer cases. Originally intended for lighting up store windows, advertising products, and car modifications, they are now often employed to make computers look great. Typically, the price ranges from $20 to $30 for a single neon tube but there are exceptions.

Neon lights are gas-filled tubes (available in all lengths and sizes) that change color as a result of metal electrodes on each end being charged with a high voltage. Different gases within the tube will give off different colors when they are charged. This offers an easy way to add a dash of vibrant color to the inside of a computer.

Neon tubes do not work with the DC current that is present inside computers (or cars, for that matter). All these tubes require an AC voltage of around 1,000 volts to operate. Because of this, small devices called inverters are usually supplied with neon tubes for computer or auto use to convert the 12-volt DC current readily available in the computer or car to the AC voltage the device needs.

Caution

Don't ever run an inverter without the neon tube attached. Doing so will damage the inverter and will at least reduce its life if not permanently destroy it.

Many computer retailers currently provide preassembled kits for computer cases, and auto stores often carry neon tubes for use in cars. The principle is the same for both, so many times you can find a better selection of neon tubes at auto stores. These auto-grade neon tubes can be easily modded for computer use.

The downside of neon tubes is heat. Sometimes they can generate a good deal of heat, so neon tubes are shunned by the overclockers. But heat is an issue for everyone, so it's best to avoid neon tubes, except in specific circumstances such as cases with especially good airflow.

However, there has been a recent advance that could shift the scales back in favor of neon tubes. Now on the market are a number of specialty neon tubes referred to as "liquid neon" or "plasma neon" that offer more than just a solid light (see Figure 4-1). These lights dance around in spiral patterns like lightning, making the lighting experience somewhat active rather than with just a static solid-colored light. Kits are available for both cars and computers in a number of colors, and it looks like the selection will only expand. In addition, these lights generate only small amounts of heat, thus rendering the main disadvantage of neon insignificant.

Adapting Auto Parts to Computers

Because the car modification scene has been around longer than computer modification, there are often a lot more varieties of lights and accessories in your local auto store than in your local computer store. But there are easy ways to adapt auto accessories for computer use, opening up a brand-new source of high-quality supplies.

Almost anything electrical in a car can be modified to run in a computer: neon lights, cigarette lighter, even the radio. Most auto accessories use 12-volt power by plugging an adapter into the cigarette lighter. Those that don't, use 12-volt power through some other sort of connector. Adapting the accessories will vary depending on how they access power:

1. If the part uses a cigarette lighter adapter (such as most neon lights), cut the wires that go to the adapter. Quickly plug one bare wire into your 12-volt source (the yellow wire on any Molex connector in your computer or test power supply) and the other wire into your ground

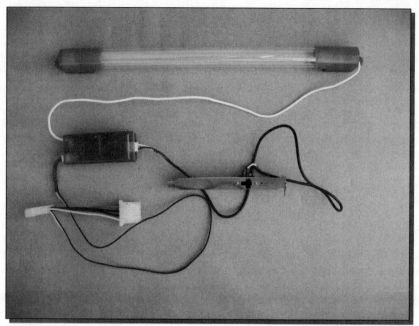

FIGURE 4-1: Liquid neon kit including neon tube, inverter, control switch, and Molex connector.

source (the black wire on the Molex connector). If nothing happens in 1 second or so, try reversing the connector.

Or

2. If the accessory uses some other connector, hopefully the wires are labeled. Usually, the red wire indicates the 12-volt power line and black represents the ground power line (but consult the documentation if you have it). Try attaching the bare wires to the Molex connector—red wire on the device to the yellow wire in the Molex, black wire to black wire.

If all went well, mark the cables as 12 volt and ground on the accessory, permanently solder a female Molex connector on the device, and you're done! If it still doesn't work check your wiring for a short or some similar type of problem.

Caution Be aware that some devices really hate being plugged in backwards (power where ground should be and vice versa) such as light emitting diodes (LEDs). These devices may burn out or spark if plugged in incorrectly. But by and large, most electronic devices can withstand the reverse voltage for a second or so.

Cold Cathode Fluorescent Lights

A newer and thinner variation on neon tubes has all but taken over the computer and auto modification market—the cold cathode fluorescent light, or CCFL. Unlike most fluorescent lamps, these do not contain a filament and therefore produce less heat. Hence the name "cold cathode," although these lights do generate some heat and are warm to the touch. CCFLs can be purchased for between $3 and $20.

Basically, these glass tubes have a combination of gases inside them as well as a phosphorous coating applied around the inside of the tube. When the electrode ends of the tube are charged, a great deal of ultraviolet energy is given off inside the tube. This UV energy reacts with the phosphorous coating and produces various vibrant colors depending on the exact makeup of the phosphorous coating inside the tube. Just like neon tubes, CCFLs need an AC voltage to operate and come with an inverter to handle the job.

Caution

CCFLs, like neon tubes, have an Achilles heel—the inverter. Do not ever run the inverter without a device (be it CCFL, neon tube, or another device) attached to it or you will damage the inverter and maybe even start a fire. Also, inverters can make a high-pitched whining sound. Some inverters are worse than others and make a louder noise.

CCFL tubes are quite small in diameter, about one fourth of an inch, so they tend to be very breakable. Most CCFL kits come with a protective acrylic tube around the tube itself to help prevent problems, although you can purchase bare bulbs from some dealers.

Because of the bright light and small size of CCFLs, they are used in many electronic devices. The liquid crystal display (LCD) screens used for laptops and desktop displays all use a CCFL behind the LCD panel itself, often referred to as a backlight. Also, most flatbed scanners or fax machines use a white CCFL to light up the document they are scanning.

CCFLs are simply the best way to light up a large area all at one time. Many different colors are available. Some even have three different colors in the same cathode with segmented color 1, color 2, and color 3 sections. Also, many dealers sell dual-inverters, capable of powering two CCFLs off one inverter.

Tip

Sometimes it may seem like a good idea to hide the inverter when placing the CCFL. Adding length to the wires may seem an obvious way to do this, but changing the length of the wires between the CCFL and the inverter will dramatically change the light output of the CCFL. However, the wires between the power source (usually a Molex connector) and the inverter can be changed without any problems.

EL Wire and Tape

One relatively new type of lighting available is electroluminescent wire, or EL, wire (see Figure 4-2). EL wire is a thin copper wire coated with a phosphorus material and wrapped with two tiny transmitter wires, then sealed in a clear or colored casing. Like neon tubes or CCFLs, EL wire must be powered by an inverter in order to glow. EL wire typically costs between $7 and $20.

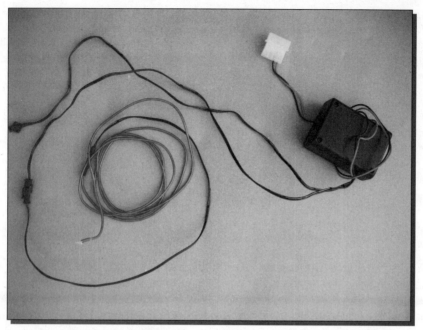

FIGURE 4-2: EL-wire setup including EL wire, inverter, and Molex connector. The various different colors for EL wire are obtained by covering the aqua EL wire core with different colored plastic tubes.

Note The inverters included with EL lights typically run at 120 volts AC, so the inverters for EL wire and CCFLs or neon tubes are all separate and cannot serve dual purposes.

When powered, the phosphorous coating on the copper wire glows a bright aqua blue. Other colors are made possible by covering the aqua wire with another color plastic tube. Thus, the aqua EL wire is the brightest.

Because EL wire can come in different lengths, it's important to get the right inverter for the length of wire you have. Different inverters can run different lengths of wire, and the length of wire used also affects its brightness. You also want to run an inverter with at least 3 feet of EL wire or the inverter may be damaged.

EL wire is a great tool for case lighting. It can be cut to the specific length you need (remember the 3-foot minimum), and can be bent to cover some pretty tight angles. However, it is not the perfect lighting system. The amount of light put out is small compared to a CCFL. Also, although EL wire never burns out, it will become dimmer over time. In general, EL wire will last between 1,600 and 5,700 hours at a reasonable brightness level.

EL wire and EL tape can be cut (as long as the power is off) with an ordinary pair of scissors. However, you should cover the end of the cut with some nonconductive material like hot glue or heat-shrink tubing. Otherwise, you could risk shorting out the connection and sending 120 volts AC through the outside of your case! Besides likely damaging your computer, you could easily burn yourself.

Electroluminescent tape works off the same principles as EL wire, except that you have a thin strip (generally with adhesive backing) that is about a centimeter in width and a millimeter or two in thickness instead of a round wire (see Figure 4-3). As such, it provides an even light source across its surface that would not be possible with EL wire alone. However, with EL tape the ability to bend the light source is limited to two dimensions, while EL wire can be bent in any direction. EL tape usually costs between $8 and $30.

Adding Length to EL Wire

Pieces of EL wire and regular wire can be soldered together to form longer wires, as well as to enhance the glowing effect by having glowing and nonglowing portions in the same string. Two pieces of EL wire can be soldered together as well, which is very effective when combining different color EL wires in the same string. The process requires a steady hand, but is not very hard.

Combining regular wire and EL wire, or two pieces of EL wire, together can be accomplished in only six steps. Assuming that you have all the materials available and a clean place to work, the whole process should take less than 20 minutes.

1. Collect the wires you want to connect. You will have either two pieces of EL wire or one piece of EL wire and two regular wires.

2. Strip about 1 inch of the insulation off each wire. For the EL wire, you should strip all the way down to the inner copper wire and two hair-thin transmitter wires.

3. With the EL wire, twist both transmitter wires into a single bundle. Also, strip away about a ½ inch of the phosphorous coating on the inner copper wire.

4. Carefully solder one regular wire and the bundle of two transmitter wires together. If you are combining two lengths of EL wire, solder the two bundles of transmitter wires together.

5. Slide a piece of small-diameter heat-shrink tubing on the copper wire and solder it to the other regular wire. Once again, if you are combining two EL wires, solder the two copper wires together but remember to still use some heat-shrink tubing. Heat the heat-shrink tubing until it makes a tight seal.

6. Finally, use a slightly larger diameter piece of heat-shrink tubing over the whole collection of wires, making sure to completely seal the connection. Heat this heat-shrink tubing until a tight seal is made. You may want to then use another piece of heat-shrink on top of that. The stiffer the connection is, the stronger and less likely to break the connection will be.

FIGURE 4-3: EL tape applied to the outside of a computer case.

Light Emitting Diodes

Light emitting diodes, or LEDs, have a long and distinguished history. Since the 1960s when they were invented, they have shown up in electronic devices all over the world as the leading form of power and indicator lights on electronic equipment. Advances in the materials used for LED construction in the last 15 years have enabled LEDs to be created that have thousands of times the light production of older models. In addition, those same advances have allowed LEDs to output light in all colors of the spectrum, from red and green to blue or even ultraviolet. Most LEDs are available for under $2, but there are specialty LEDs that can go for over $40.

Some of the most common mods in the world involve changing the LEDs in the power or hard drive light of the computer to be brighter or a better color (blue is very popular among modders). A slightly more advanced approach is replacing the LEDs in CD-ROM drives or other components.

LEDs are small electronic components (diodes, actually) that, due to being constructed of various elements, emit light when the right type of voltage is passed through them. These electronic components are generally housed in a clear or colored dome-shaped plastic package with two metal leads sticking out (see Figure 4-4).

Tip

There are many types of LEDs in common use today. Not all have just two metal leads, some use many more than that. Also, some come in unusual shapes and have rather unique properties, such as generating huge amounts of heat. However, the details expressed here are true for well over 99 percent of LEDs commonly available.

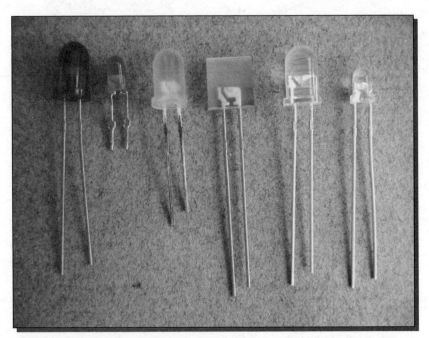

FIGURE 4-4: Various LEDs. Modern ultrabright LEDs typically look like the ones on the right, 5 mm and 3 mm water-clear LEDs.

There are many advantages to LEDs. They are small, they generate no measurable heat, and they come in very bright colors, from the usual red or green all the way to ultraviolet. The disadvantages are relatively few. They burn out quickly if fed the wrong type of power, and they have a small angle of light to project.

LED Size

LEDs come in many different shapes and sizes, but the most common are LEDs with 3-mm and 5-mm diameter dome-shaped packages. These two sizes are often referred to as T1 size (3 mm) and T1-3/4 (5 mm).

The package itself is made of plastic/epoxy that can be any color. In the past, the most common colors were red, yellow, or green. Today, modern ultrabright LEDs typically have a clear plastic package referred to as "water-clear." The older colored packages were diffused packages, which means that the light leaving the LED element itself was somewhat dissipated by the package and sent in all directions. Modern "water-clear" packages don't do this, so the light leaving the LED is relatively concentrated in a small area.

Tip Today's "water-clear" packages can be made to be diffused. Simply take some 400–600 grit sandpaper and sand *all* the sides of the LED slightly. This will create an excellent diffused effect.

LED Colors

Until 1995 or so, LED color selection was limited to red, yellow, green, or orange. But since a breakthrough in the technology that year, nearly every color of the rainbow is possible.

LEDs today can be purchased in the original colors and also blue (popular among case modders), white, ultraviolet, infrared (used in remote controls), pink (rare), and even true violet (more rare). Most of the modern LEDs come in what is called a *water-clear package*. This means that the LED itself looks like a clear piece of plastic, while the actual color in which the LED lights up depends on the chemical composition inside that plastic. Older LEDs were typically plastic pieces the same color as the light they produced.

Caution Ultraviolet LEDs are dangerous to look at, so you should never look directly at the LED when they are lit. These LEDs give off a lot of light, but only a small portion of that light is visible to the human eye so your eye doesn't dilate to protect itself. The invisible light beyond the range of human eyesight can actually cook the inside of your eye!

The brightness of the color is rated in millicandelas, or MCD. A higher MCD rating means a brighter LED. Common LEDs you would use on a computer range from a couple hundred MCD (very dim) to tens of thousands of MCD (literally painful to look at directly). Note that if you have two LEDs with the same MCD but different viewable angles, the LED with the wider viewable angle will appear darker, because the same amount of light is now spread over a wider distance.

LED Power

All LEDs have at least two metal leads that protrude from their plastic body. One lead is usually longer, which tells you that it's the anode (positive). The shorter lead is the cathode (negative). It usually won't damage anything, but the LED will only light up if it's hooked up to power in the right direction (unless you have one of the older and now uncommon dual-polarity LEDs).

If you find an LED that uses 5 volts (limited selection, but available), all you need to do is attach the anode to the 5-volt positive line on a Molex connector and the cathode to the ground line on the Molex, and the LED will light up. But usually, ultrabright LEDs require around 3.6 volts, and regular LEDs require 15 volts. To solve this, you need to use a resistor.

Resistors are simple devices that convert excess electrical energy to heat. They have specific ratings for both how much current can flow through them (wattage) and how much resistance they add (ohms). To attach a 3.6-volt LED to your system, you will have to calculate the resistance for the LED.

The easiest way to calculate resistance for LEDs is to use any of the widely available LED calculators on the net. These have the added bonus of deciphering the resistor color codes, so you will always know exactly what the resistors will look like in addition to what they should act like.

Tip   There are a number of these resistance calculators on the net. A couple of them include www.unitechelectronics.com/resistors2.htm and www.broadcast.net/resistor.html.

Calculating Resistance for LEDs

The basics of calculating resistance are easy. What resistor to add when using a specific LED can be computed using one of the most important laws of electronics, called Ohm's law. With this law, there are three variables—R is resistance in ohms, U is the unwanted voltage, and I is the current flow. Really, it's easier than it looks.

- When you know the voltage and current, you can calculate the resistance with the equation: $R = U / I$

The following example will make things clearer. Say you are using a modern ultrabright LED that uses 3.6 volts and has a current draw of 20 mA (milliamps, or 0.02 amps). You want to hook this up to your computer's 5-volt power line. Because you need to know the unwanted voltage (U), you take the 5-volt source and subtract the 3.6 volts to get 1.4 volts of unwanted power. Plugging the numbers in, you get:

- $R = 1.4 / 0.02$
- $R = 70$

This means that you need a 70-ohm resistor. Because 70 ohms isn't a standard resistor size, the next biggest available resistor (always go for a larger one, never a smaller one) is 75 ohms. Attach the 75-ohm resistor to either the positive or negative side of the LED and the remaining leads (one from the LED, one from the resistor) to the 5-volt power and ground from the computer. It should light up, but if not, simply reverse the positive and negative connections.

How and Why to Use Lights

How to use lights inside your case is simple enough. For most cold cathode lights, simply use some velcro or double-stick tape to attach the lights somewhere inside the case (usually around the bottom, top, front, or back of the case near the removable door). Attach power to the light via the included Molex connector and mount a switch to turn the light on and off (usually included), and you're all set.

Lighted fans are even easier, because they provide a lot of light but take up no additional space. Other lights like EL wire allow you to be more creative—outline your window with one or form it into a cool pattern on the front of the case. Superglue or hot glue is a great way to keep EL wire in place. But knowing how to attach and use lighting is only a small part of the work—the more important aspect is why you are using them.

Quite simply, adding lights to your computer is purely an aesthetic upgrade. True, individual lights that show hard drive activity or fan speed are very functional. But adding lights to the inside of a computer so that all the parts can be seen through a side window is a mod just for show. Your computer doesn't run faster when bathed in blue light, and your processor doesn't heat up more when surrounded by a red light. No, lighting effects are just to make your computer look "cool."

That being said, many modded computers have tons of lights in them but look horrible! If lighting is an aesthetic mod, why do modders sometimes have such horrible-looking computers? The problem is that computer builders often have a horrible sense of color coordination.

Some colors work well together, but others don't. Using fewer lights, but in the right colors, will simply look better that jamming every single lighted component you can find into a case. Try to keep a flow or a theme going with the lighting design for the mod. Using colors that go well together will make a mod much more impressive.

Wrapping Up

The type of lighting you use is entirely up to you. Each type has advantages and disadvantages, so there is no clear winner or loser. Of course, the lighting methods listed in this chapter are not all the types available but are the main types in use today in computer mods.

Also, there are endless variations on the types of lighting described here. There are EL-tape based light-up case badges, and LED-based case badges. There are round CCFL lights for attaching to fans. There are sound-activated neon tubes. But all these, and the doubtless many more varieties still to come, are based on the technologies discussed in this chapter.

Making Holes

By this point, you've probably realized that all modders eventually need to make additional holes in their cases. Whether you need to add a window to your case or another fan to your already cramped system, it's time to break out the power-tools and get to work.

Whenever attempting to make any serious modifications to a case, always remember to "measure twice, cut once." You can usually remove more of the case should your hole be too small or the wrong shape. But adding material back to the case if your initial cuts are too big or in the wrong location is difficult if not impossible.

Just remember the most important rule of working with power tools and you will come out fine. You're starting out with ten fingers, ten toes, and two eyes, and you should aim to keep them all working!

 Caution You can seriously hurt yourself and others using the tools described in this chapter. Remember to read all the directions that come with any tools you purchase and keep the tools in good working order. If you have any questions about how to use a tool, consult an expert before you start. This advice can save your life.

Common Case Materials

In theory, you can use any material to create a custom computer case. In practice, there are only a few different materials commonly used. These materials all have different characteristics, and it's important to understand the differences between them before you decide which techniques and tools to use. Knowing the properties of your materials and what tools to use will help prevent some costly mistakes.

 Tip The type of case material you're working with is also important for other reasons. For example, different materials require different types of paint. Taking this into account at the start of your project will save you time and money.

Steel

Steel is the original computer case material. Except for some very rare instances, all cases were made from steel up until about 2001. Most cases, and especially most cheap cases, are still made from steel. Steel is a very strong metal that provides excellent shielding against radio signals and other sources of interference, and it offers a strong surface to work on.

Cutting steel will always take more time than cutting through a softer metal like aluminum, regardless of the tools used. Jigsaws are a good choice for cutting steel as long as you use a blade designed for cutting metal. Rotary tools such as a Dremel are also a good choice, as long as you use reinforced cutting wheels and have a good deal of time. When cutting steel, heat generated during cutting can also be an issue because this heat can discolor the metal along the area you are cutting, although this is seldom a problem when cutting relatively thin steel like that cases are typically made of.

The main advantages of steel are its strength and low cost, while the main disadvantage is its weight. In general, steel cases will cost about half as much as aluminum cases, but feel stronger and resist dents better. Of course, they will also weigh three times as much.

Aluminum

Aluminum has become the most popular case material among modders. Aluminum is a relatively soft metal, much softer than steel. However, it's still a great material to work with partly due to its incredibly light weight. Because aluminum is so soft, most tools cut through it as if it were paper.

Unfortunately, aluminum also scratches and dents very easily, so the case must be handled carefully or you'll ruin the finish. Most aluminum cases are treated with a process called anodizing that hardens the outside of the case and protects it against scratches, but a small slip with anything sharp will leave a permanent mark.

Aluminum does not produce as much heat as steel when it's cut, and it's a lot lighter than steel, so aluminum cases are much easier to carry. The downside is that aluminum cases are likely to scratch if not properly handled.

Tip While aluminum does scratch more easily than steel, the difference in weight makes aluminum cases the best choice for LAN party cases. When the computer is full of components and a mouse and keyboard are strapped to the side, everything gets to be quite heavy. Every pound saved on the weight of the case will make it that much easier to lug around.

Plastic

Plastic is typically used for the front panel of many cases (especially steel cases), but some cases are now made entirely from plastic. Plastic is an easy material to work with because of its softness, but it's also fragile and can crack, bend, or warp with little or no warning. Heat is also an issue because if the plastic gets too hot it will melt. The heat generated by rotary tools is often enough to cause melting. Plastic scratches even more easily than aluminum so great care must be taken when working with it.

That being said, the sheet styrene plastic used for plastic model kits is becoming more and more popular among modders. It's cheap, easy to form and work with, and somewhat strong. Just remember how easily plastic can be scratched or cracked. Building a skeleton of metal and covering it with a shell of plastic is one effective way to make a completely custom case.

Sheets of styrene plastic can be bought at most hobby stores for under $5 each. While these sheets are not big enough for an entire case panel, they are a good source of material for building additions and details onto an existing case. Larger sheets of plastic can be special ordered as well.

Acrylic

Acrylic plastic, or its variations such as Plexiglass or Lexan, is another popular material for cases and case mods. As with aluminum and plastic, it's cheap and easy to cut with home tools but scratches easily. It also exhibits the same problems with melting as plastic when exposed to heat.

But acrylic is the only workable material that's clear, and that's a great advantage. Many nice looking cases for sale today are made entirely from acrylic, allowing all the components inside to be viewed easily. Almost all case windows are made using acrylic.

The cost of acrylic panels can vary depending on the exact type of material (see the sidebar "Acrylics . . . what's in a name?") and the dealer, but the cheapest acrylic panels can usually be purchased for around $3 per sheet.

Tip When purchasing acrylic sheets, try to purchase the sheets with a paper backing. Some acrylic sheets come with a plastic film, but it's impossible to mark that with any pens or pencils.

Acrylics . . . What's in a Name?

There are different types of acrylic plastics out there, and the properties they exhibit can confuse even experienced modders. To help clear up this confusion, it's important to understand some of the basic terminology.

Lexan is polycarbonate, while Plexiglas, Lucite, Acrylite, Perspex, and acrylic are polyacrylate. (The names Lexan, Plexiglas, Lucite, Acrylite, and Perspex are just brand names that refer to specific products.)

Polycarbonate is harder than polyacrylate and therefore more shatter resistant. However, poly-acrylate is more scratch resistant than polycarbonate.

Polyacrylate material comes in two types—extruded and cell cast. Extruded material is less expensive and more difficult to work with (it tends to melt along the edge being cut), while cell cast is more expensive and easier to work with (has less tendency to melt). Cell cast acrylic comes in different grades as well, so be sure to ask your dealer if they carry different grades of cell cast material (many only carry one grade) and which grade is right for your application. The price of polycarbonate is roughly the same as that of extruded polyacrylate, around $3 per sheet. Cell cast polyacrylate can be up to 10 times as expensive or more. But with both of these, the prices vary wildly from dealer to dealer based on what materials they normally stock and who their supplier is.

Both materials have their supporters. Some claim that polycarbonate can store a static electricity charge, which would be very bad for electronics. Others claim that Lexan can become cloudy if exposed to sunlight or UV rays, making polyacrylate the better choice.

In short, use what is locally available to you and within your price limit.

Wood

Although you might think wood was more appropriate for fine furniture, some great case mods have been made out of wood. There are dozens of varieties of wood available, each with its own look. In addition, every tool imaginable for woodworking is commonly available at any hardware store. As an added bonus, spouses are typically less resistant to case mods made from wood. You might even be allowed to put your mods on display in the living room.

There is one significant drawback to wood, however. Wood is an excellent insulator, so any heat generated by the computer will be kept inside the case, and this is very bad. If you're planning to create a wooden case, make sure that you have great airflow through the case to avoid overheating and damaging your expensive components.

See Chapter 2 for a discussion on proper cooling methods.

The cost of wood varies a lot depending on the type of wood you purchase. A lot of wood is very cheap, but there are exotic varieties that can cost over $30 per square foot or more. It all comes down to what type of hardness and finish you would want for your case.

Other Materials

Almost any material can be used for cases although the applications might be more limited than with traditional materials. Advanced modders have made cases from all sorts of interesting materials. Some of the more exotic materials are:

- **Cardboard**—This material has gotten a bad reputation over the years. Besides being relatively strong for it's size, cardboard can actually look really nice. Corrugated cardboard, the type that looks like waves inside, cut at the right angle can make for a case that's truly great eye-candy. Of course, common sense says that a water-cooling system makes little sense in a case made of cardboard.

- **Carbon fiber or fiberglass**—For modding purposes, these materials are equivalent. They start out as sheets of cloth. Added layers of resin cause the sheets of cloth to harden. They can be quite strong and allow the creation of totally free-form shapes for mods. Working with carbon fiber or fiberglass can be messy, however, and the dust is quite toxic. Still, these materials offer the ability to create abstract forms that are strong and thin.

 Be aware of health and safety precautions when working with fiberglass. You will need to follow the manufacturer's instructions and wear a face mask when dealing with this material.

- **Styrofoam**—This material is usually used on top of or below other case materials. For example, modders have built structures on top of normal cases from Styrofoam because of its wonderful abilities as a canvas for sculpting. It can then be covered in fiberglass to create a hard shell for a case.

- **Cloth**—Several people have made computer mods by putting working computers inside toy stuffed animals. You would still need a frame for the case from some other materials, but the case itself can be covered is cloth.

- **Food**—Yes, there have actually been mods made of food. For example, there have been case mods made of both gingerbread and pumpkins. While not a long-term solution for a case material, it does make for an interesting case mod. Cleanup when cutting holes is certainly easy enough—just eat the scraps.

Drilling

Drilling involves making a perfect hole in your work surface by using a round metal cylinder, the drill bit, with grooves cut along its surface. Drill bits come in different sizes, but common sizes range from $1/16$ inch to $1/2$ inch (see Figure 5-1). The actual pattern of the grooves along the side and at the tip of the drill bit can also vary. There are specialty drill bits specifically for plastic, but standard drill bits work well for both metal and wood.

Many drills come with a number of drill bits, but if your drill doesn't, make sure you pick up a set. Nothing is more frustrating than being unable to make that last hole just because it's suddenly midnight and you lack the right size drill bit. Even worse, using the wrong drill bit and ruining your piece because the hole you just made is too large can really dampen your mood.

As always, most of the important work is in the planning stages. Just attacking your case with a drill set is a dangerous thing to do. Time spent doing proper prep work is well worth it.

Prep Work

You should start preparing the surface that you are working on by completely covering it in masking tape. This offers some protection against making accidental scratches on the work sur-

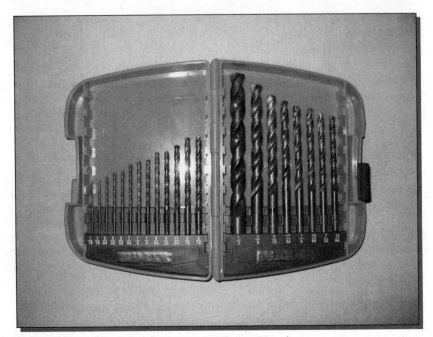

FIGURE 5-1: Drill bit set with sizes from 1/16 inch to 1/2 inch.

face and allows you to mark the work surface with a pencil to help guide your cuts. Using pencil is important, because pencil marks can be erased and redrawn if necessary.

In addition to the masking tape, placing a block of wood behind the surface you want to make a hole in will increase the cleanness of your cuts and help you control the tool better. When cutting a shape with a rotary tool, for example, you stand a good chance of making a clean cut because you have more control over the cutting tool due to the relatively small cutting surface and the angle at which you should be cutting. When drilling, you will almost always be perpendicular to the work surface, so you are certain to cut right through the work surface with no chance of stopping before you go beyond the intended material. Once the initial hole is made, the drill will have a tendency to slip because the force the tool exerted on the work surface has nowhere to go. A block of wood behind the work surface allows your drilling to continue through the work surface without the drill bit slipping.

Another important step when drilling a hole is to properly mark the surface. Of course, you should mark the center position with a dot using a pencil or marker, but that's not enough. Drill bits have a tendency to "walk" their way to the right of where they start because of the way the drill bit itself is tapered. You can get around this by using a tool called a center-punch.

Basically, a center-punch is nothing more than a somewhat sharp metal stick, similar to something a dentist might use. You should place the center punch at the location you want to mark and tap it lightly with a hammer, thus making a small depression in the surface that will help to guide the drill bit. In a pinch, your smallest drill bit can be used as a cheap center-punch. But since a center-punch usually costs less than $4, it's easier and safer to get a real center-punch.

It should go without saying that you should wear some sort of eye protection when working with power tools, but I'll say it anyway. Accidents do occur sometimes, and your eyes are very vulnerable to small particles of metal or plastic. Do yourself a favor and grab a pair of clear plastic safety glasses from any hardware store.

Hand Drills

There are two basic types of hand drills—corded and cordless. With a cordless drill (see Figure 5-2), you have freedom to move around and drill holes anywhere. The downside is that you need to keep the battery charged, and cordless drills typically have less torque (the strength at which they can turn something) than corded drills. Corded drills have the extra torque, but they need a power plug nearby, which limits their range somewhat.

The price of cordless and corded drills is roughly the same, but the range is pretty large. A cheap corded drill may go for as little as $23, while a nice cordless drill goes for close to $300, but there are many different drills of both types across the range.

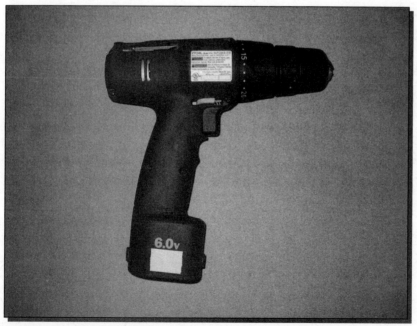

FIGURE 5-2: Cordless drill with nonremovable rechargeable battery.

Tip

For most at home modders, the mobility of a cordless drill far outweighs its disadvantages. In addition to modding, hand drills are helpful for mounting pictures to walls or other household chores.

Another consideration when selecting a hand drill is the drill chuck. The "chuck" is the part of the drill to which the drill bits are attached. This consists of a number of teeth that expand or contract to hold the drill bit itself. There are two types of chucks, keyless chucks and regular chucks. With a keyless chuck (see Figure 5-3), the chuck is tightened by hand while with a regular chuck the chuck is tightened by using a special tool (the "key"). The problem with a regular chuck is that the key is often misplaced, even when attached to the drill via a cord of some kind. For modding, a keyless chuck is the best way to go.

Make sure to read the instructions that come with your drill. Despite the fact that no instruction booklet will ever appear on the bestsellers list, they are important reading. Each drill is a little different and offers certain features such as the ability to reverse the direction of the drill bit or vary the amount of torque the drill applies before the drill bit will slip. All these features will be described in detail in the instructions.

Special care must be taken when drilling different materials. For example, standard drill bits won't drill plastic, and particularly acrylic, very well. When using standard drill bits on these materials, the drill bit will tend to rip large chunks out of the material rather than make a smooth, even cut. Instead, purchase drill bits specially designed for plastics from specialty plastic stores. These drill bits are cut differently and won't ruin good plastic like standard drill bits can.

FIGURE 5-3: Keyless chuck on a cordless drill.

Drill bits themselves range in price. Single drill bits can be purchased of course, but it's probably best to get a set of different-sized bits. A set of bits costs between $20 and $200, depending on the number of bits and the material they are made from.

Tip

If you really, really have to or are extremely cheap, standard drill bits can be used to drill acrylic or plastic. The trick is to exert very little force on the material itself and go slowly. Using a bit of soapy water as a lubricant also helps. Note that the smaller the drill bit, the better the chance of success. Larger drill bits greatly increase your chance of chipping and breaking.

Drill Presses

A drill press is really just a fancy mounting mechanism for a drill. It usually consists of a free-standing table of some sort with a drill mounted on an armature above it. The material to be drilled is placed under the drill and a handle attached to the drill is pulled down, bringing the drill bit down into contact with the work surface.

For such a simple concept, the advantages of a drill press cannot be overstated. One of the most difficult problems with a hand drill is being able to drill holes straight or at a consistent angle, rather than at whatever random angle you accidentally hold your hand at. A drill press solves this problem by aligning the work surface exactly 90 degrees from the drill.

Each drill press is a little different in how it's turned on, how the drill is lowered, and other aspects of the process. Just remember to follow the same rules as with hand drills, and the quality of work from a drill press will beat a free-hand drill every time.

A cheap drill press can be had for around $100, while larger models with more features cost several hundred more.

Hole Saws

Hole saws are round, circular pieces of metal with teeth around the circumference (see Figure 5-4). In the center of a hole saw is a regular drill bit that is longer that the circular metal for the rest of the hole saw. The drill bit extends upward and attaches to the drill like a normal drill bit. The big advantage of a hole saw is the ability to drill large holes, such as holes that are exactly the right size for a 80-mm or 92-mm fan.

Hole saws can be pricey, however. Sometimes a single-size hole saw can cost $25 or more. That being said, they are the right tools for cutting large holes, and you typically only need a few of them for case modding. For example, if you purchase an 80-mm hole saw, that will generally work for most of the cooling-related holes you will ever need to make.

To use the hole-saw, first find a drill bit that matches the size of the drill bit in the center of the hole saw. Using the drill bit and not the hole saw, drill a guide hole in the surface you want to cut. Some people do use the drill bit in the center of a hole saw to drill the initial hole. The problem with this technique is that after the initial hole is drilled, the hole saw will have a tendency to continue down until the circular teeth come in contact with the work surface. When using a hand drill, there is a good chance that this won't happen at exactly a 90 degree angle,

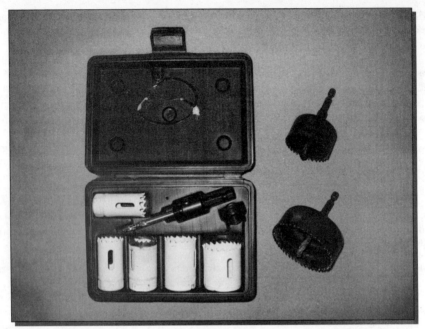

FIGURE 5-4: Various hole saws. The two on the right are complete, one-piece hole saws. The case on the left contains a modular hole saw set, with one center drill bit and several different-sized hole saws that mate to the drill bit.

and you will be left with large nicks in the work surface just to the side of where the real hole will ultimately be drilled. By using a separate drill bit, you will have more control and make cleaner holes.

After that hole is drilled, insert the hole saw drill bit into the guide hole until the circular blade for the hole saw is resting on the work surface. Then use the drill as you normally would to finish the hole. When you're using a hole saw, the drill will want to twist out of your hands much more than when you're using standard drill bits, so go slowly and make sure that you hold the drill firmly in your hands at all times.

Note that this cutting process will make a lot of noise, and that's normal. Some people use a little lubricating oil to help keep the noise down and prevent the metal from over-heating. In most cases, simply going slowly will help to alleviate these problems just as well as using oil and will also lead to nicer cuts.

After drilling the hole, the remaining piece may be lodged in the hole saw itself. Use extreme caution when trying to remove this, because the material (especially true for acrylic or plastic) may have heated and slightly melted during the cutting process.

Cutting

Cutting something sounds simple enough. But in reality, getting a nice smooth cut takes planning and a knowledge of what tools to use on a given type of material. Sure, a sharp knife can make a nice cut into a piece of cardboard, but it will take years to cut a piece of steel with that same tool.

Opinions vary on which tool is the best for cutting as it relates to case modding. Each tool has its own merits, but with a little information the best tool for your job should be apparent. Of course, cost is also a factor. Purchasing an expensive tool for a job you are going to do only once is a waste. Often it's better to buy a more general-purpose tool even if it takes longer to make the cut with that tool than with the perfect tool for the job.

Prep Work

Even more so than with drilling, prep work before cutting is very important and can mean the difference between a nice clean cut and a horribly mangled case. Fortunately, the prep work is simple and logical.

Start by completely covering the surface you need to cut with masking tape, available at any office supply or home improvement store. Cover more than just the area you are cutting, cover the entire panel. Should the cutting tool slip, the extra masking tape will provide at least some protection to keep the rest of the surface from getting damaged.

In addition to scratch prevention, the masking tape will allow you to draw the pattern you want to cut onto the working surface without marking up the surface itself. You should use a pencil for this purpose, because pencil lines can be erased if the drawing isn't right the first time, and you won't have to re-cover the panel with tape again.

Tip

When working with acrylic, leave the paper backing on the material when you cut it. The paper backing eliminates the need to cover the acrylic with masking tape, because you can draw right on the paper. If you use acrylic with a plastic covering, you may want to remove it and cover both sides with masking tape. The plastic covering tends to melt into the acrylic itself when the acrylic is cut.

Since you are drawing the pattern you want to cut, make sure that the pattern is correct. Keep your lines straight and your curves curved. Use drafting tools such as T-squares, rulers, and compasses to help draw the pattern 100 percent correctly, and rely on free-hand drawing only when absolutely necessary.

Remember to account for what is beneath the panel you are going to cut. For example, if you're preparing to cut a window in the side of your case, remember the teeth that connect the side panel to the case itself and make sure that you don't accidentally cut them off. If you're cutting a blowhole for hot air to be vented out (see Chapter 9) the top of the case, remember to leave space for the power supply in the back of the case and a CD-ROM up front.

Assuming that you have followed all the previous instructions, it's now time to decide on the proper tool for the job and start cutting.

Once again, don't forget the need for eye protection!

Rotary Tools

Rotary tools are the most loved and used tools in any modder's arsenal. The most common rotary tools are made by Dremel, but other manufacturers make similar tools. Rotary tools have literally hundreds of replaceable tips for every imaginable task (see Figure 5-5). Of course, all those attachments cost extra money, but they are usually worth it for the tasks they accomplish. Also, there are multiple variations on the tool itself such as variable speed models, cordless models, professional models with more torque, and so forth. Rotary tools range in price depending on what attachments come with the package, but in general they range from $40 to $60 for the basic set of equipment.

For modding work, stay away from cordless rotary tools. They have far less torque than the corded models, and the batteries tend to die quickly when presented with a large job. Something like cutting out a side window is a lot of work, and even with a soft metal like aluminum a cordless rotary tool will drain its batteries at least two or three times before making it through the job.

FIGURE 5-5: Dremel rotary tool and a very small selection of the available attachments.

Rotary tools can cut most materials, are capable of very fine detail work, and are great for engraving or etching. There is no perfect tool, however. When used for large tasks such as cutting out a case window, especially on a steel case, progress will be slow. Also, the cut-off disks used for such tasks quickly wear down or even shatter. This means a lot of time spent changing the disks, not to mention the cost involved.

Caution

When cutting disks shatter, the pieces fly off in different directions. Because of the small mass of the pieces, they don't really have the ability significantly hurt your hands or arms by cutting them. But the flying disk shards do have to ability to damage your eyes, so once again, please remember to wear eye protection.

As with anything, using a rotary tool takes a little practice. With time and patience, anyone can become good at using rotary tools to cut complex designs. Here are a few tips to help you on your way:

- Use reinforced cut-off discs (see Figure 5-6) for most materials. Only soft plastic is appropriate for the regular cut-off discs.

- Once the cut-off discs start to get small, take them off the rotary tool and replace them with fresh ones for large cuts. Save the smaller cut-off discs for detail work, like in the corners of intricate designs. Smaller cut-off discs are easier to manipulate in small spaces.

FIGURE 5-6: A regular cut-off disc and a reinforced cut-off disc. Note the grid pattern of the supporting fibers in the reinforced disc.

- Kickback is a common problem when using cut-off discs. Always use both hands to hold the tool, and make small incisions as if you were making a connect-the-dots type of image. Then go back over the design and finish the cuts.

- You will get better results by rotating the work surface after every incision rather than moving the tool around. This allows the incisions to be made from a consistent direction.

- Don't cover the air vents on the tool when holding it. Covering the vents will make the tool heat up and possibly fail, as well as heating your hands and making them uncomfortable.

Jigsaws

Jigsaws are good at cutting straight or curved lines in all kinds of materials including metal, wood, or acrylic provided you have the right blade for each. Blades for jigsaws are measured in teeth per inch (tpi), with higher tpi blades working well for thin materials. Jigsaws (with the right blade) also work well for cutting thick materials like wood where rotary tools often have difficulty. Jigsaws range in price from $30 to $200. Blades for the jigsaws cost between $5 and $15 each, but some sets of various blades can be had in the same price range.

Because of the need for separate blades for each type of material, the cost for the jigsaw can quickly rise. Another downside is that the vibrating action of the jigsaw tends to scratch the cutting surface unless you are careful. Also, very thin materials such as plastic or thin aluminum can be distorted by the cutting process.

Even with these limitations, many modders consider a jigsaw to be the best tool for powering through straight cuts or simple curves.

Tip   Use masking tape to cover the surface the jigsaw rests on. This will minimize any scratches caused by the vibrations from the jigsaw. Of course, as proper technique for any case cutting you should have covered the entire surface with masking tape anyway.

Band Saws

Band saws are great devices for making precise cuts in metal, plastic, or wood. The blade is a continuous band of metal with teeth that spins at a high rpm (revolutions per minute). When the material to be cut is pushed up against these teeth, the teeth grind away the material and leave a relatively clean cut. Different blades with different teeth per inch (tpi) are available for band saws much as with jigsaws, which enable band saws to properly cut different materials.

One significant problem in terms of case modding for band saws is the inability to start a cut in the center of a panel. Band saws need to cut from the edge of the panel only. While this is usually not an issue for an acrylic window panel, it is an issue for the metal that must be removed from a side panel to create the window. Thus, band saws are typically not purchased by modders.

Finally, price is also a factor. While cheap tabletop band saws are available for around $100, the more sturdy and reliable band saws easily cost around $300 to $400. Don't forget the cost of the blades at $6 to $10 each.

Nibblers

Nibblers are interesting tools, but only work for cutting metal. They work by cutting, or "nibbling," a small semicircular piece of metal off the work surface. There are several different types such as manual nibblers, electric nibblers, and pneumatic nibblers. Before starting to use a nibbler, you will have to drill an initial hole that the nibbler can start its work from.

On the plus side, nibblers can be very cheap—at least the manual ones. The electric and pneumatic ones easily cut through metals such as those used on computer cases. The manual nibblers can be bought for as little as $10, while the powered versions of the tools cost upwards of $200. As far as power tools go, they are relatively safe because the cutting edge is somewhat contained and not easily accessible to fingers and other small body parts.

On the downside, the electric and pneumatic nibblers are more expensive and less general purpose than rotary tools. The manual nibblers require a lot of grip strength to use and are very limited in the thickness of metal they can cut. Also, the small leftover pieces from cuts can be very sharp and cause injury. Often, it can be difficult to cut a straight line with a nibbler due to the circular shape of the cutting area.

Never use a nibbler on plastic or acrylic. As best, the plastic will become distorted and discolor along the cut. As worst, the whole plastic piece can shatter into a hopeless mess.

Scoring

When working with acrylic, there is another method of cutting that can be used called scoring. This entails using a sharp knife to cut a line across the material to be cut and snapping it off at that line. In general, the edges of the cut should be relatively smooth and clear, getting around one of the classic problems related to cutting acrylic.

Remember that hobby knives and scoring tools are extremely sharp. The sharpest steak knife in your kitchen is nothing but a dull butter knife when compared with these precise tools. Always make sure to cut or score by starting at the edge closest to you and pulling away on the blade. Also watch out for fingers, toes, paws, or other appendages that might get caught under the blade.

The best way to score a material is to use a straight edge, such as a ruler, and a sharp knife, such as a hobby knife (see Figure 5-7) or a specialty scoring tool, to mark and cut a line across the acrylic sheet. Remember to score all the way across the sheet of acrylic. If need be, you can score again along the same line to make the cut deeper. The exact depth of the cut is dependent on the exact type and thickness of the acrylic. Finally, place the acrylic sheet on a flat tabletop with one side of the score on the table and the other side hanging off. Finally, exert equal pressure on both sides of the scoring—one hand holding the acrylic against the table and the other hand pushing downward on the acrylic. If the score was deep enough, you should end up with a clean break.

FIGURE 5-7: Hobby knife with very sharp blade. Such a tool is very handy in modding and a necessity when attempting to use scoring to cut acrylic sheets.

Scoring can only be used on straight cuts and is a somewhat difficult skill to master. It's a great quick technique for "cutting" a piece of acrylic that you don't care too much about, but using this technique on a piece of acrylic you just spent 10 hours making a custom etch on seems a little foolish. At the very least, cut the acrylic first before starting an etch of any detailed work.

Hobby knives are available for under $5, and are immensely useful for modding. The special tools for scoring acrylic are a little easier and safer to use, at least for scoring acrylic, and are also available for under $5.

Laser or Water Cutting

One technique that can't be beat for cutting any design you want into your case is to use laser cutting or water cutting. Both require disassembling your case and taking it to a professional to perform the work, but nothing will achieve the same results that you can get with this method. Of course, this also means additional expense (sometimes a great deal of expense depending on how complicated your cuts are). Places that offer these services range often charge per minute of cutting time, and even a soft material like acrylic can take several seconds per inch to cut.

Laser cutting involves using a 5,000 watt laser to burn right through the case material and make a cut. Laser cutting can cut almost all materials except highly reflective materials up to 0.4 inch thickness. The cuts are very precise, down to 0.006 of an inch.

Tip There are small laser-cutting and engraving machines available that would be somewhat appropriate for home use. However, these smaller units are limited in what they can cut and as well as the thickness of the materials they can work on. If that doesn't turn you away from these machines, the $10,000 and up price tag may.

Water cutting involves using a high-pressure water jet at over 55,000 psi (pounds per square inch) to cut through the case material. Water cutting can cut right through even more materials than laser cutting, and at much greater depths (up to 6 inches thick). However, the cutting process is much less precise—the smallest cut is can usually be only 0.02 of an inch.

If your project demands high-quality, precise cuts, either of these methods is a way to go. The specific shop you have the work done at may request the design in a number of different file formats, but they will work with you to get your design into their computers that control the cutting machines. Often these shops charge by the number of cuts they need to make, so the complexity of your design is something to consider as well.

Cleaning Up Edges

Cuts made with power tools are seldom completely clean cuts and have somewhat jagged edges (except for laser and water cutting). Given this, it's a good idea aesthetically and safety-wise to clean up those edges and make the cut surface smooth. In addition, if you're attempting to glue acrylic pieces together you'll need a somewhat smooth surface to bond two pieces.

The technique you use is somewhat dependent on the type of material you use. For most materials, some form of sanding is the way to go. However, for acrylic and some plastics, the flame method might be the right choice.

Sanding

The process of sanding is tedious but is often the best way to get results. You start with the roughest grade of sandpaper you need to wipe out the deepest marks then use successively finer grades to polish out all the rough areas. This is a very time-consuming task, but cutting corners will quickly lead to poor results.

When using sandpaper, use a sanding block or some solid flat piece of material behind the sandpaper. This will help ensure that the sanded surface is flat rather than full of undesired hills and valleys. Of course, if you want more rounded features (for example, near rounded corners), use your fingers as the sanding block behind the sandpaper.

Sandpaper is actually quite cheap, so don't be afraid to get too much. Sandpaper can usually be purchased in single sheets for less than $1, or packs of several sheets for slightly more.

The first thing to understand about sanding is the grade of the sandpaper, otherwise known as the grit.

Grit

Sandpaper comes in a number of grades, from coarse to medium to extra-fine (see Figure 5-8). More specifically, these grades refer to a range of grits which are numerical and

FIGURE 5-8: A small selection of sanding paper grits. The paper on the top right is 320 grit, the top left is 100 grit, and the bottom is 600 grit. The 100-grit paper is standard sandpaper, while the other two are wet/dry sandpaper.

indicate exactly how fine the particles attached to the sanding surface are. Common grits go from 150 to 2000, with higher numbers indicating smaller particles and therefore smoother surfaces.

The smaller the particles are, the longer it will take to remove excess material and sand a surface smooth. Thus, you want to start out sanding by using a sanding surface with larger particles to remove the most excess material and move to a sanding surface with smaller and smaller particles to obtain a smooth surface with the least amount of work.

Wet or Dry

Commonly, you will see two different types of sandpaper—standard sandpaper and wet or dry sandpaper, often just called wet/dry sandpaper. The difference is that on wet/dry sandpaper the abrasive is attached with a waterproof resin, while standard sandpaper often uses water-soluble glue. The end result is that wet/dry sandpaper can be used when it's either wet or dry, while standard sandpaper can only be used dry.

The price difference between the two is negligible, so it is recommended that you use wet/dry sandpaper for all your case modding work. In addition, if you use water as a lubricant when sanding, the water helps prevent clogging of the paper and leads to a smoother finish. Just be aware that the process of wet sanding can be even more messy than dry sanding.

Files

Files are simply long metal sticks with a rough surface. As with sandpaper, you rub the file back and forth over the material to be smoothed and allow the file to work away all the rough edges. Files also come with different-sized abrasive surfaces on them, although much more limited than with sandpaper, so you can somewhat tailor the roughness of the file to the size of the imperfections you need to remove.

When trying to smooth a rough metal edge, sandpaper has a tendency to catch and rip. This makes the sanding process both slow and expensive. With a metal file, this will never happen. But by the same token, using a metal file on acrylic is asking for trouble because the metal teeth will tear chunks out of the acrylic. Always use sandpaper to smooth acrylic, never a metal file.

Flame Method

When working with acrylic, after the cutting process the edges are bound to be a little rough even if the acrylic was professionally cut. One method that can return the edges to crystal clear appearance is to use a flame to slightly melt the edges until they are smooth again. Professionals use machines to get some truly outstanding looking results via flame polishing, as it's sometimes called.

The idea is simple—the edges are not clear because they are not smooth. Tiny ridges and grooves that catch and distort the light are present, making the edges not entirely clear. Using a flame, you melt these tiny ridges and grooves together till they provide a smooth surface.

In practice, it takes a while to get the hang of this, so you will need to practice on scrap pieces first. Using a small butane torch (see Figure 5-9), hold the tip of the flame about an inch away from the edge you want to smooth. Now quickly draw the flame down the edge, holding it in one place for only a fraction of a second. If done properly, the edge will now be smooth. If not, simply go over the edge again. If the flame is held for too long in any one spot, bubbles will form that are nearly impossible to remove. Never flame polish any edge you are going to glue.

 Tip Small butane microtorches, such as the one in Figure 5-9, are commonly available in cigar shops and similar stores for under $10 each. There are also more expensive models available, but they offer no advantages over the cheaper ones (other than looking cool).

All this being said, flame polishing is somewhat difficult to do, or at least to do reliably without professional equipment. Better results can be had by other means, such as sanding.

Polishing

Once again, even with the best sanding, the edges of acrylic can be less than crystal clear. If flame polishing doesn't give you the results you are looking for, or simply sounds too error prone, you should fall back to old fashioned polishing techniques.

FIGURE 5-9: Small butane torches like this one are essential when attempting flame polishing. Using anything smaller, like a match, simply won't work.

Using a polishing agent specifically designed for acrylic, such as Novus #1 or Novus #2, apply the polishing agent with a soft rag and some pressure. Then switch to a dry soft rag and keep buffing the surface till the surface becomes smooth and slippery.

Depending on how smooth the surface was to begin with, you may have to spend more or less time/effort using the polishing compound(s). For an already smooth surface, a compound like Novus #1 is all that is needed. For a less smooth surface, start with Novus #3, then #2, and finally #1.

Each of the various Novus polishing agents can be purchased for around $3 for a small bottle.

See the sidebar "Acrylic, Sanding, and Novus" in Chapter 17 for a detailed discussion of polishing using Novus polishing agents.

Wrapping Up

There are a lot of ins and outs when using power tools to cut things. The most important thing to remember is to use the tool that you feel most comfortable with and can handle safely. Cost is also a concern, because buying the "right" tool for every job can quickly drain your wallet and is hard to justify if you will only be using the tool once.

No serious modder will ever give up his or her rotary tool, because they are just too useful and too general purpose to do without. Every modder needs one. The other tools you will need depend on the specific mods you want to perform.

Creating Exterior Finishes

Creating a great exterior finish for your case is one more way that it can be customized and made as unique as you want it to be. Standard beige boxes, while less common than they used to be, are unfortunately still fairly common. All those boxes deserve something a little more flashy, or at least a little less boring.

Finishing (whether by painting or another technique), on the surface (no pun intended), seems simple enough. But in reality a nice exterior finishing job takes some time and effort to pull off right. In addition, the sheer number of choices of colors, types, and techniques for finishing a case can be a little overwhelming at first. This chapter aims to give you a head start in creating a nice exterior finish job (using paint and other techniques) on any mod you come up with.

Preparation

As with most aspects of modding, proper preparation is more than half the battle. Without this, any exterior finish you give your case will not meet your expectations. While errors in a paint job can be undone, this generally means cleaning off whatever paint you have already applied and redoing the whole thing. Sometimes this can double or triple the work required if you just took your time the first time and did it right. Why waste all that effort? Don't cut corners. Stay the course and follow through.

The actual painting process is small compared to all the work necessary before you start pulling out the spray cans.

Protecting Your Health

This is perhaps the most important thing to mention. You should wear a mask (sometimes called a respirator) to prevent paint fumes and more importantly, paint overspray, from entering your lungs. You can get some simple white disposable masks that will cover both your mouth and nose from most hardware stores for a few dollars, and it's a good investment. You could also go all out and purchase a complete rubber mask with eye protection and replaceable air filters. These masks range from $8 to $200 dollars, depending on whether the mask is reusable or good for just a couple of paint jobs.

Tip

Not all masks are created equal. Some are designed to just block larger particles such as metal or wood and not smaller particles such as paint. Make sure to purchase a mask that can block paint particles.

Choosing a Respirator

What's the right type of face mask or respirator for you? It depends on how serious you are about case modding.

If you are working on single case, then purchasing a couple of cheap $8 masks would be the right choice economically. Just be careful reading the specs, not all masks can prevent paint fumes from getting through. Some masks are designed to handle the dust from sanding rather than paint fumes. It can sometimes be difficult to find cheap masks that protect against paint fumes. Check out your local home improvement warehouse, these usually carry a range of different cheap respirators. If you can't find exactly what you're looking for, ask for help—sometimes they can special order just what you need.

If you are working on several cases or are planning a career in case modding, the full-face masks with eye protection might be worth purchasing. They range in price from $20 to $200 and beyond. They have replaceable air filters as well, so remember that these add to the overall cost. Finding filters against paint fumes for these masks is much easier.

Another consideration is your own body chemistry. If you tend to have easily irritated skin and/or irritated eyes, the investment in a full-face respirator is worth it. You only have one set of lungs, and a good-looking computer isn't a good trade for them.

Besides, wearing a full-face respirator will make you look just a little bit like Darth Vader. And let's face it, that's pretty cool.

Readying Your Workspace

The place where you paint is very important. The ideal place would be similar to where they paint cars or motorcycles—a long room with lots of bright lighting, temperature control, and good ventilation with filters to prevent dust. But most people don't have access to such a room.

A good alternative is a garage. Try to limit the amount of dust in the area by limiting the movement of items or people in the room during the painting or drying process. Also, remember to cover any surrounding surfaces with newspaper or plastic. You will be surprised how far the overspray from spray paint can reach. In a pinch, you can always paint outside, but as soon as the paint starts to dry be sure to move the piece to somewhere more protected. Bugs and dust live outside, and many of them will want to check out your freshly painted case.

Caution

In weather below 60°F, or when the temperature changes radically between day and night, paint does not dry very fast or very well. Try to avoid painting in this environment, or at least limit the exposure of painted pieces by moving them to a warmer and more temperature-stable environment as soon as possible.

For something a little more elaborate than just a garage, some people construct makeshift painting booths. The idea is simple: Use large sheets of plastic to construct a small room by hanging the plastic from the ceiling. Use a small fan in one corner to exhaust the paint fumes. Finally, before beginning to paint, use a small spray bottle to dampen the floor and air slightly to help keep dust from being kicked up into the air. This technique, though effective, is usually overkill for most modders.

Readying the Parts

Cleaning any parts to be painted is very important. Always remove dust, dirt, and any adhesive or stickers on the part before painting. Stickers and adhesives can be tricky. Remove what you can by hand, then move on to the cleaning agents. One good product (available in many hardware stores for around $10) is product called "Goof-Off," but it can also melt some plastics, so you always need to test it in an inconspicuous place first. The same is true for most other cleaning products, so be careful.

For dust and dirt (after adhesive removal), it's best to clean the case using some warm water and soap. Always remember to let the pieces air dry for 24 hours after washing. If you are in a hurry (which is not recommended), you can use a lint-free cloth and some compressed air to speed up the drying process.

Tip

If your water is "hard" water (i.e., if your dishes sometimes have spots on them), using a lint-free cloth and compressed air to dry your piece would be a good idea so that you minimize the chance of water spots forming. Water spots can affect the look of paint or dye.

As a general rule, you always want to separate pieces before painting them. Just because both the front faceplate of a CD-ROM drive and the eject button are going to be the same color doesn't mean that you should paint them while they are still attached to each other. If you don't separate them, you will miss all the deep crevices where the parts are attached to each other, and the job will look unprofessional. Even worse, the paint may cause the pieces to become "glued" together.

Traditional Painting

When painting your case, you can use a number of different types of paints. Almost any spray paints you find in your local home improvement or auto-parts stores would be a good choice for painting a case, and some truly impressive results can be had by just using these spray cans. Typically, a can of spray paint costs around $6 per can, but to do a nice job on a complete case you could easily use two or three cans.

Tip   Paints designed and marketed for automotive use are typically thinner than other types of paints. This is both an advantage and disadvantage. These paints will go on more evenly than other paints because of the smaller particles of paint. On the other hand, you will need more coats of paint (and therefore more time), and the chance of the paint running is increased.

But painting a case involves more work than most nonmodders would imagine. Just buying a can of paint and spraying may be a great way to draw graffiti, but it's a poor way of painting a case. Lots of sanding, painting, waiting, and more sanding go into painting a case that you can be proud of.

Sanding and Applying Primer

The first step is to sand down the existing paint or anodized finish (mentioned later) to get a smooth surface to work on. Using 400-grit sandpaper wrapped around a sanding block, wet sand the surface of the case until it feels completely smooth. Note that the use of a sanding block is not optional. Without the sanding block you won't be applying even pressure. The case may feel smooth to the touch when you are done, but there will actually be hills and valleys where your fingers exerted uneven pressure. That uneven surface will show up when you are finishing up the paint job.

Tip   Buying a sanding block is not necessary. A simple piece of wood can also function as a poor man's sanding block, but is just a little less comfortable to hold. On the other hand, a nice sanding block only costs around $5 and holds the sandpaper in place with metal or plastic grips which helps make the job a little easier.

You don't have to completely remove the existing paint, just sand until the finish is even. The one exception to this is when working on an anodized aluminum case. The case will already feel smooth, but it's a good idea to sand through the anodized finish. Painting on top of the anodizing will yield inconsistent results. It works for some people and some paints, but not others.

When sanding, try to use even strokes moving in the same direction across the case, at least for the last stages of sanding. Also note that wet sanding is a messy business (see Figure 6-1), so be sure to wear clothes that you don't care much about because you will get paint particles all over your hand and clothes. You may find that it helps to place the part on a flat surface, therefore preventing (somewhat) the part from flexing due to the pressure of sanding.

Finally, when the case feels completely smooth, sand it some more. You can then use soap and water again to wash the case off, and dry it using a lint-free towel. Let the part air dry for at least 24 hours.

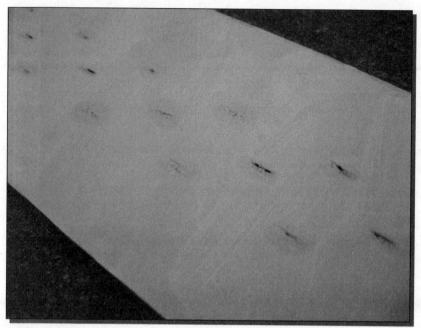

FIGURE 6-1: Original paint is being sanded off this panel. Note that all the extra paint that has been sanded off has collected in the recessed surfaces.

Tip

Sometimes after you clean the part, you will be able to see areas that were not sanded evenly by the reflection of light on the surface. Don't ignore them; go back and wet sand some more.

Next, take a can of sandable primer, and shake the can vigorously for at least a couple of minutes. Using even strokes, but being careful not to use so much as to cause runs of primer, apply the primer across the surface of the panel. You don't have to make a completely even coat the first time. Once the primer is dry (read the instructions on the primer for drying times), wet sand it using 600 grit sandpaper until the surface is smooth again. Finish it off by cleaning with soap and water again, drying it with a towel, and air drying overnight.

You may have to repeat this process a couple of times until the panel is evenly covered in primer as well as being smooth (see Figure 6-2).

Caution

Use primer from the same manufacturer as the paint you are going to use. This is not optional. Different paints have slightly different chemical makeups, each designed to work with primers from the same manufacturers. Primers from other manufacturers might have a chemical reaction to the paint and cause all manner of problems.

Figure 6-2: Primer on the case panel after sanding. Note that some areas are thinner than others. This is fine so long as some primer is still covering every section.

Applying Color

Time to decide what color you want your case to be. Really, the choice is up to you. You can get paint in hundreds of different colors, and if you are willing to pay a little more some paint stores or home improvement stores can even color-match paint to any color. The basic rule to keep in mind is that with darker colors it's easier to get a mirror-like finish, while lighter colors show fingerprints and dirt less. Also remember that you really want a paint from the same manufacturer as the primer if at all possible.

Once you've decided on a color and purchased some spray cans of it, it's time to apply the paint. Using even, thin layers of paint, cover the entire panel you are working on with paint. Don't worry about using too little. Using too much is a much larger problem. After the first layer of paint, let the paint dry 48 hours before continuing.

Tip

Nowadays, many spray paints have plastic covers that require you to use a screwdriver to remove them. You can spot these types by the small square hole near the bottom of their plastic tops. Be sure to remove the top by rotating the screwdriver clockwise or counterclockwise rather than pushing the screwdriver in/out/up/down. If you push the screwdriver, it's possible to knock the spray nozzle off the spray can and have a fountain of paint covering you.

After the panel is dry, sand the panel down with 600-grit sandpaper again trying not to use too much pressure. If you go through the surface layer of paint in a few spots, that's fine for this coat. After the panel feels smooth and you are confident you have sanded every portion of the surface, wash the panel again and towel dry it. Allow the panel to dry for 24 hours before continuing.

Tip

When drying a panel with a towel, be careful around any surfaces you cut such as windows or blowholes. Those cuts can sometimes be a little sharp and grab fibers from the towel. These fibers will show up in the paint job and will need to be removed, so it's best to try and avoid them in the first place.

After the panel is dry, paint it and sand it just as you did the last time. The difference here is to try hard to avoid sanding all the way down through the layer of paint you just added, so use less pressure to sand. You may find that giving up the sanding block and just sanding with your hand will help you avoid this problem. Once you're done sanding, wash the panel and let it dry overnight again.

Continue this process until you have no areas that seem thin in color. Then, move on to 1,000-grit sandpaper and repeat the same sanding, washing, and drying process.

You need to make a choice at this point as to whether you want a smooth semigloss appearance or a mirror-like finish (see Figure 6-3). If you are fine with just a smooth finish, you can proceed

FIGURE 6-3: Case panel with a smooth semigloss appearance (not completely mirror-like).

to the clear coat phase. If you want a true mirror-like finish, continue the sanding process with 1,500-grit and 2,000-grit sandpaper.

Note that a mirror-like finish is much easier to produce with dark colors. Light colors don't show a mirror finish as easily as darker ones. Another thing to ask yourself is whether or not you truly want a mirror finish. They look nice on cases used as display models and similar applications, but for everyday use (especially at LAN parties) these cases show fingerprints, dust, and dents like nothing else. A smooth consistent color paint job without a mirror finish may be more practical.

Tip If you're using metallic colors, don't sand the last coat prior to the clear coat. Just use some soap and water to clean the panel, let it dry, and skip the last sanding step.

Masking and Stenciling

A smooth, glasslike finish on your case is great. But these days, even that can be a little boring. By using masking and stenciling, you can add interesting patterns to the finish to really put it over the top.

Some tips for masking:

- Use the right type of tape. Masking tape or painter's tape is the right type to use. Other types of tape may work, but there are no guarantees. For example, certain types of artists' tape use an adhesive that reacts badly with vinyl dye and leaves a gooey, colored residue.

- Using a dull tool of some sort, such as a butter knife covered in a soft towel, go over the edges of the masking tape with a little force. This is referred to as burnishing, and it helps prevent paint from getting in the small air pockets that are sometimes present around the edge of the masked area.

- Don't use too much paint. The more paint you use in a single pass, the greater the chance that the paint will get under the masking tape and leave an uneven edge.

You always want to do any masking work before the final clear coat. The areas that you have masked and added another layer of paint to will be slightly raised above the rest of the surface. Adding enough clear coats and sanding them smooth is your only hope of a smooth finish on the case. However, never sand the newly added detailing. Because it's raised above the rest of the surface, the new paint will sand right off.

Clear Coat

Paint by itself looks nice, but for a truly glasslike finish you will need to apply a top clear coat for that extra shine. Also, the clear coat helps to seal in any masking and stenciling you've done.

The longer you can wait before applying the clear coat, the better. Some paints take up to 30 days to dry and harden fully. If you don't wait for the paint to fully harden before adding the clear coat, the paint may form an uneven surface and lose it's mirror-like finish (if that's what you are going for).

If your case has been sitting for a month or so, it's best to do another light sanding and cleaning with the highest grit sandpaper you previously used, such as 1,500 or 2,000. Wash the panel and let it dry for 24 hours before continuing.

Now apply the clear coat in a similar fashion to the paint, except lay it on a little thicker (but not so thick that you see runs in the clear coat). Let that dry for 48 hours, and wet sand it with either 600 or 1,000-grit sandpaper, depending on how bad the "orange peel" effect is on the surface (use the lower grit paper for worse cases of orange peel effect, of course). Wash that down, and let it dry for another 24 hours.

Tip

If you look closely at any freshly painted surface, you will see that it's not an even, smooth finish. Instead, the surface will look like it has tiny crater marks, like the surface of an orange. This is referred to as *orange peel effect.*

Finally, lay on the last clear coat. After that dries for 48 hours, wet sand it with 2,000 grit sand paper and go through the usual process of washing and overnight drying. You now have one last step left.

Using some fine-cut rubbing compound (available at any automotive store for $10) and some smooth rags, apply the rubbing compound to the case as per the instructions on the bottle. This should leave you with a perfectly smooth and glossy finish (see Figure 6-4).

Tip

If there is a slight haze left after you use the rubbing compound, you can go one step further by using swirl remover. This substance is also available at automotive stores (for approximately $10) and goes on similarly to rubbing compound but helps remove even smaller scratches.

Tip

You can also wax the case much as you would a car; just make sure that you wait at least 30 days for the clear coat to fully harden before attempting this. Wax will add yet another layer of protection for the paint and increase the shine even more.

Vinyl Dye

Vinyl dye is a type of coloring originally intended for the interior of cars, such as the dashboard or armrests, but it is also one of the best things ever to happen to case modding. Vinyl dye is not really a paint. It's a dye that seeps into the plastic and colors it. As such, it doesn't suffer the

FIGURE 6-4: Finished case panel.

problems that paint does. It won't flake or wear off as easily over time. Vinyl dye simply colors the plastic and makes it indistinguishable from plastic that was originally the color of the dye. It doesn't work well on other surfaces though. It's really only appropriate for all those plastic bits on a computer. Vinyl dye is simply the best way to color the front bezel of a floppy drive or CD-ROM/DVD-ROM drive.

Vinyl dye is available in most automotive stores for roughly the same cost as a can of regular automotive spray paint, around $5 per can. The color selection is somewhat limited when compared with paint though. So why use it rather than typical paint? The answer is that a dyed surface retains the original texture of the material and the dye doesn't fill in the small details as much as paint does (when the dye is used properly). Therefore, it's an easier coloring to use than paint, quicker because it requires less surface prep, and generally provides better results for beginners.

Tip   Lighter colors of vinyl dye let some surface details (such as logos or icons) show through , while darker colors usually cover them up. However, both lighter and darker colors are equally ineffective in masking the smoothness of a dyed surface. For example, most CD-ROM bezels have a slight texture to them except where the manufacturer's logo is painted on the surface. This surface is smoother and will remain smoother after the dye is applied. Be aware of this because it can have an impact on your results.

For the record, vinyl dye doesn't work on all types of plastic. Some types, such as the waxy types of plastic that many Barbie™ toys are made of, simply won't allow the dye to seep in. Just as with the cleaning agents, if you have any doubts, test it out. Put a little vinyl dye on an inconspicuous area of your case before you begin the major work.

In addition, with vinyl dye you won't need to do any surface preparation such as sanding or using primer. However, it's always a good idea to wash the part you intend to dye with warm water and a little soap before you begin. (Don't forget to let the part air dry for a day or so after the wash.)

Some people like to use a special cleaning agent called Plastic Prep for cleaning plastic parts. It has a chemical composition that more easily removes the oils associated with plastic production and also contains antistatic properties. Plastic Prep is available in better hobby stores for $8 for 16 oz.

There are some myths about vinyl dye that need to be dispelled. It's been said that vinyl dye won't fill in surface impressions like paint will. It won't—it will fill them in differently than paint! Vinyl dye acts slightly like a solvent, so when you dye a piece of plastic the plastic may actually become a little soft until the dye dries. In fact, the plastic may become so soft that some very small details may be destroyed in the process. But if you get that sort of effect it means that you are using too much dye. You need to slow down and use more coats of less dye to get the effect you want. For example, if you look at a CD-ROM bezel closely you will probably notice a texture to it. If you use too much dye in a single pass, that pattern will change. Worse, if you use too much dye on one corner of the bezel that corner will stand out because of the different texture.

This leads to the next myth—that it takes someone with an IQ below their own shoe size to ruin a dye job. Not true, it's actually easy to use too much dye if you are trying to rush. Take it slow, and you shouldn't have too many problems.

In simple terms, the best results when using vinyl dye result from using several light applications rather than one heavy coat.

Using Vinyl Dye

Start by making sure that the can is fully mixed by shaking it well for 30 to 60 seconds. Whenever you use any can of spray paint or dye you always want to hold the can mostly horizontal, at no more than a 45-degree angle down. More than that and the paint or dye won't flow evenly. Start on one side of the part (but not yet aiming at the part), holding the can about 8 to 10 inches away and press the button. Quickly but smoothly move your hand in a sideways motion until you have completely passed the part and are no longer aiming at it, then let go of the button.

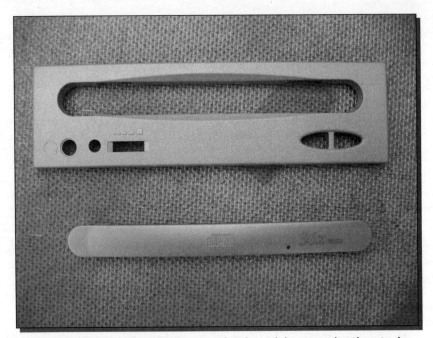

FIGURE 6-5: CD-ROM bezel partially covered with vinyl dye. Note that the raised details and the painted details are still visible.

The reason you start and stop the flow of paint or dye while not aiming at the part is simple—whenever you press or let go of the button the flow of paint or dye is uneven, often sputtering a little and sending out larger drops of dye. These drops of dye, if they land of the piece you are working on, will give the piece an uneven appearance. Continue this process until you consider the part to be 60 percent covered with dye (see Figure 6-5). Then, let the part dry for at least 30 minutes (longer in cold weather).

Continue the process for at least two more coats, and more if the part still needs them. Just remember not to use too much in one coat (you will use the most at one time during the first coat), and don't forget the drying time in between. After the final coat, wait at least 12 hours before assembling the parts or attaching them back to the computer.

Potential Issues

There are a couple of situations that you should try to avoid when working with vinyl dye—cracking and the dye rubbing off. Usually when the dye appears to have a cracked appearance, it's due to temperature changes. Try to keep the piece you are coloring at a consistent temperature while drying. If you do experience cracking, more coats of dye (after you have solved the temperature issue) will help, but the surface may always have a somewhat cracked texture due to the original problem. Once again, using less dye and more coats can somewhat help you avoid the problem in the first place.

As for the dye rubbing off, usually this is caused by certain types of plastic such as the waxy or slippery plastic found on toys for toddlers. If the plastic feels very slippery, you may want to rough up the surface using some sandpaper (around 320 or 400 grit) a little before dying the plastic. It a little difficult to know the types of plastic that may have problems, so some experimentation might be required. Suffice it to say that this won't be a problem with most bezels, but might be an issue with some keyboards (particularly the underside) or some mice.

One final thing to remember—since vinyl dye is a dye and not a paint, colors sometimes don't work as you might imagine. If you took black plastic and tried to dye it red, you would get black plastic with a red tinge. If you dyed white plastic red, you would have red plastic. So if you want to go from a darker color to a lighter color, you first need to use white vinyl dye to lighten the base color. In theory there is no limit to how many times you can dye a piece of plastic. In actuality there is a limit to how much dye a piece of plastic can take before it won't take anymore. If the small details and textures of the plastic are being distorted by the dye, you've already used too much. You may be able to correct the problem by sanding the entire piece down and starting over, but doing so successfully is difficult.

Special Features

There are a few aspects of vinyl dye that most modders don't know about or seem to ignore. These special features may be exactly what you need to make your mod into the creation that you envision.

One technique most modders rarely use is masking off certain sections with tape to make custom designs using vinyl dye. Using masking tape, place the tape over the section you don't want colored. Just make sure to watch the coats of dye and not use too much or there will be a very visible ridge when the tape is removed.

Many people also don't realize that cables can be dyed as well as plastic parts. You can use vinyl dye to dye cables another color, and, after drying, the cable can be bent and used without the coloring chipping off. For example, you could buy several USB cables and color-coordinate them for the function they are going to serve. Or you could use the masking technique mentioned above to create cables that looked like snakes or other designs (see Figure 6-6). Once again, the applications are endless.

Vinyl dye in spray cans is good, but in some instances you may want to add some detail work that just can't be done using spray cans. Some rare places sell bottles of vinyl dye as well as spray cans. But if you can't track down the bottles, you can spray dye into a disposable cup to capture the liquid and use cotton swabs or toothpicks to do detailed work. If you're trying this, you may want to use a plastic glove when capturing the liquid since overspray has a tendency to fly back at you and color your hand.

Vinyl dye, like paint, really likes to stick to skin. If you accidentally get some of it on you, you can try to wash it off but the majority of it will probably stay on you until it eventually rubs off a within a few days. You may want to wear latex groves when using dye.

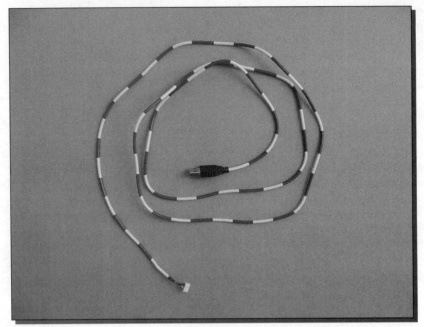

FIGURE 6-6: Custom vinyl dyed cable created by masking off portions prior to using vinyl dye.

Tip

If using a disposable cup to collect dye from a spray can, avoid Styrofoam cups. The solvent in the dye eats right through the Styrofoam, leaving a gooey mess. Use any other type of disposable cup, such as paper and wax based or plastic based.

Some auto-parts stores can color-match vinyl dye and mix a custom color for you. These same places can generally put the dye into spray cans or bottles for application by hand. The ability to color-match is very useful—it allows you to exactly match the paint used for the rest of the case while gaining the advantages of dye for the plastic parts rather than going through the error-prone method of painting the plastic parts.

Other Options

There are lots of other techniques for painting or coloring your case that go beyond the simple paint or dye work discussed in the previous sections. Many of these techniques are specific to certain situations, but they may be right for what you have in mind for your project(s).

Specialty Paint

There are a lot of specialty paints available that create special effects such as the appearance of rust or rock, among others. Walk through any home improvement store or arts and crafts store, and you will find a lot of these paints available. Since one of the points of modding is to make something unique, these specialty paints can go a long way toward making that come about.

One paint that is very good for a unique appearance is Plasti-Kote Fleck Stone paint (available at craft stores and home improvement stores for around $8). This paint is available in several colors and gives a textured appearance similar to stone (see Figure 6-7). This paint is very unusual, and the particles that come from the spray can are quite large and multicolored. Even the feel of the paint changes as it dries, becoming somewhat rubbery. It's also essential that you cover this paint in the associated clear coat for strength.

Tip When using Fleck Stone paint, make sure that the paint is dry before applying the clear coat. A full case panel can take as much as two weeks to dry completely. However, you can speed up the process by letting the panels sit in direct sunlight for as many hours as possible.

There are many other specialty paints available. Some paints simulate rust. Others simulate a cracked finish or turn a surface into a chalkboard. You can also simulate frosting, opening up

FIGURE 6-7: Fleck Stone paint. Note the textured surface.

new options for window etchings. There are even UV-reactive paints that can be used both inside and outside the computer.

Painting an acrylic panel is another case where some specialty paints can come into play. Some enamel automotive paints (the most common type) can have a bad reaction to the acrylic and cause tiny internal fractures in the panel. For painting acrylic panels, try to find spray cans of acrylic-based paints, because these won't exhibit the same problem.

Tip What is enamel paint as opposed to acrylic paint? The main difference is what substance the paint is based on. Enamel paints are oil-based products, while acrylic paints are water based. Enamel paints are generally considered to have a harder finish, but that is open to debate with modern acrylic paints performing just as well.

For example, one mod I was working on required a large tabletop that was painted black except for a see-through window in the center. I originally used color-fleck paint, a specialty paint that puts particles that reflect different colors of light on the painted surface. This went fine, but when I used a layer of black automotive paint behind this, the acrylic panel cracked in a spider-web pattern around every cut I had made in the panel. Starting over with a fresh panel, I was able to use the color-fleck paint and an acrylic spray paint with no problem.

Another specialty paint that may be useful is Krylon Fusion paint. This paint is specially designed to adhere to plastics, requiring no sanding or primer. Note that it doesn't work on all plastics, but it has a higher chance of working than most paints.

Hiring a Professional

One option that many modders overlook is the possibility of having their case professionally painted. Any auto painter (look in the phone book to find some in your area) should be able to paint your case for you, assuming that you do all the work of breaking it down into individual panels first. The paint shops may have never done anything like this before and might want to help out just for the fact that it's something different from what they normally do. The cost can range anywhere from $100 to $200 or higher, depending on the paint you want.

Only the very best of the best paint jobs done at home can match even an average professionally painted case, so don't be critical of yourself if your paint job doesn't match what the professionals can do. Professional painters, such as auto painters, have access to painting booths and specialized spray guns that make it much easier to get a high-quality job. As if those two things weren't enough of an advantage, the type of paint they use is thinner than the paint from spray cans and goes on much more smoothly. Be open to the idea of having someone else paint your case if it gets you the results you want.

Also, even if you do the basic painting yourself, you may want to have an expert artist airbrush a design or some picture on the side of the case before you put down the clear coat. You can find many talented airbrush artists willing to do the work for you in many locations, from specialty T-shirt stores in malls to the art departments of local colleges. Just be sure to see examples of their work first before handing over any money and/or your case panels.

Tip The cost of having someone airbrush a case for you can vary wildly, sometimes upwards of $300 or even more. Therefore, you may want to bring up the price early in the conversation with any artist you consider hiring.

Anodizing

One problem with aluminum, such as that used for computer cases, is that it is a relatively soft metal. It doesn't take much to dent or scratch the soft metal. In fact, aluminum is so soft that it can actually, with a little difficulty, be cut using nothing more than a hobby knife! So how come so many modded cases are made from aluminum, and what prevents them from quickly becoming ruined? The answer is *anodizing*.

Anodizing is an electrochemical process by which an aluminum oxide layer is grown on the surface of the aluminum. This is accomplished by placing the metal pieces in an electrolytic solution and passing current through the solution.

The main advantage of anodizing is a dramatic increase in the hardness of the surface of the metal. Hardness is typically measured by something called the Rockwell C scale. Aluminum as is typically used for computer cases rates around a 25 on the scale, while anodized aluminum is rated between 50 and 80. For comparison, diamond rates a 100 on this scale.

The secondary advantage of anodizing is the ability to give a deep, rich color to the metal by impregnating dye into the anodized surface. Expensive colored aluminum cases, such as those from Lian Li, are typically colored in this way.

The best way to anodize your case is to separate your parts (i.e., remove the rivets by drilling them out) and take them to a local shop that can do the anodizing for you. You can search the phone book under anodizing, plating, or electroplating, but make sure that the shop you choose does the work themselves. Many shops simply send your parts out to other shops to do the anodizing, and there is no need to pay for a middle man when you could send the parts yourself just as easily. Prices vary, but expect to pay well over $400 for the anodizing service.

Tip While anodizing is expensive, the results are top-notch and very professional looking. You can also take the anodized panel and laser-etch a design on the panels. If you're using laser-etching on a colored anodized panel, the color will be removed by the etching process and leave the original metal color or some shade in-between the anodized color and the metal color. This effect is very impressive.

It's interesting to note that some brave modders have taken on the task of anodizing parts themselves at home. This can certainly be accomplished, and for a relatively low cost, between $200 and $400 for the equipment and supplies to do a couple of complete cases. However, besides the fact that it takes some skill to work out how to accomplish this, there are serious safety concerns. If working with multiple types of acids were not scary enough, the process also involves the creation of flammable and poisonous gases. Honestly, it's better 99.999 percent of the time to just pay professionals to do the work.

Powder Coating

Another way to get a nice, automotive-grade paint job is through powder coating. This involves spraying powdered paint onto a metal surface, such as the panels for a case (of any type of metal). The powdered paint is charged with static electricity, which attracts the paint to the metal surface. Once the spraying is done, the part is heated to 400 degrees Fahrenheit for approximately 10 minutes. While in the oven, the powdered paint melts and flows into an even, durable, and beautiful finish.

The advantages are numerous. Besides the durability of the finish, runs and drips are nearly impossible. If too much paint is sprayed on a surface, it can simply be blown off with a little compressed air (prior to the heating, of course). The process is cheaper than anodizing, and there are more shops that perform the work. Again, prices vary considerably but expect to pay around $200 and up for powder-coating services.

Tip To find a place nearby that does powder coating, try calling some of the hot-rod shops and custom motorcycle places near you. While they usually don't do the service in-house, they will know where to get it done.

On the negative side, after the paint is heated mistakes are hard to remove and can only be removed by sand blasting or burning. Also, the process can only be used on metal, since the heating process would melt plastic.

Tip Most of the cost of powder coating is the setup fee—the cost to load the paint gun with the right color paint. Once you find a place that does powder coating, ask them to give you a call when someone else orders some work in the color that you want. Often the shop will waive the setup fee (or at least reduce it) and only charge you for the paint if they are already doing some work in the same color. Computer cases are small compared to the work that these shops usually do.

Once again, there are some people who do their own powder coating at home. While this is less scary and less expensive than anodizing, it is still a somewhat expensive procedure in small quantities considering the cost of the paint gun. In addition, the fumes given off during the heating of the paint can be flammable and toxic. Heating your case panels in mom's oven and then eating the dinner she cooked there would be a very bad idea.

Case Wrap

Case wraps have been rising in popularity in the modding and LAN party scene recently, and will probably continue to do so. The idea is simple—complex artwork is printed on adhesive-backed vinyl sheets that can then be applied to your case. This gives the impression of nice airbrushed art at only a fraction of the cost. In addition, the case wrap can be removed later with no damage or permanent alteration to the case if you get tired of it (although the case wrap cannot be reused).

On the negative side, even after spending the money (around $60 for a full case wrap), your front bezel will still look as boring as it ever did. In addition, if you are taking your computer to a LAN party, there is always the possibility that someone else may have the same case wrap as you.

Installation of case wrap is a simple. After cleaning the surface with soap and water, dry it completely. Next, lay the wrap over the case to make sure the wrap will completely cover the surface. Don't worry about excess material—that can be cut off later. Now start pulling back a small portion of the backing and slowly apply the wrap to the surface ensuring that it's lined up straight. Working slow is the key—going too fast will lead to excess bubbles and wrinkles. Repeat this process a little at a time until the case is completely covered.

Once the entire sheet is applied, go back and work out any bubbles that exist using your fingers or a small plastic card (such as a credit card) wrapped in a soft towel. Some of the case wraps actually come with a tool for this—just remember to wrap that tool in a soft towel as well or you may accidentally nick or scratch the case wrap. Using a hobby knife, cut a slit for ventilation holes and push the wrap through the holes until it conforms itself to the shape of the hole.

Tip Using a hairdryer to heat the wrap will allow it to expand slightly, which can help when forming the wrap around tight or irregular areas.

The Small Details

Painting the whole case is great, but sometimes your aim is a little smaller. Rather than painting the entire side panel, maybe you want to add an image of your favorite cartoon character. Maybe you have a custom logo for all your mods that you want to add to the front of the case. There are hundreds of instances where full-blown painting just isn't what you are looking for.

In such an instance, there are a few techniques that can help to remedy the situation. Things like using hobby paints for plastic models, airbrushing, or water-slide decals might be able to do just what you need.

Using Hobby Paint for Details

For all the small details on your case, especially for the plastic parts, the best paints to use are hobby paints like the ones used on plastic model kits. There are two basic types of paints, enamel paints such as those by Testors (although that company makes a small line of acrylic paints as well) and acrylic paints such as those by Tamiya.

Enamel paints are cheaper, come in hundreds of colors, and are far more commonly available—even many drug stores carry them. Acrylic paints are harder to find and more expensive, but go on thinner and have a more professional appearance. You also need special thinners to clean off brushes that were used with enamel paint, while acrylic paint can be cleaned off with ordinary water (before it dries, that is). A small bottle of enamel paint should cost around $3, while acrylic paints usually cost a dollar or two more.

Enamel paints dry more slowly than acrylic paints, but you can use this fact to your advantage. Although acrylic paints allow you to complete your work faster, enamel paints allow more blending of colors. It's much easier to blend colors when the new paint you are applying and the one you just applied are wet at the same time.

If you are working with a highly textured surface, such as imitation rock or some sort of skin, hobby paints are a great way to bring out those details using a method called dry brushing. You dip a small brush into a jar of hobby paint, then rub the brush against some scrap paper until there is only a hint of paint left in the brush. Lightly rub the brush against the textured surface and the paint will adhere to the raised surfaces only. This is a great way of bringing out details or creating an impression of greater depth.

Airbrushing

An airbrush is really just another version of a spray can, although it offers much finer control and many more color options. All airbrushes are built on the same concept—a small tank of paint (usually about the size of a bottle of nail polish), the airbrush itself (vaguely looks like a gun), and some sort of method of forcing air through the system (either cans of compressed air or an air compressor). Airbrushes, in talented hands, allow beautiful images to be painted because of the even flow of paint in relatively small spaces. Airbrushes range in price from around $40 to well over $400 and can be purchased from any decent hobby store.

It was previously mentioned that you can stencil a design on a case before adding the clear coat. This is true of airbrushing as well. You can paint an intricate image on a case and protect it from damage by covering it in clear coat.

That being said, an airbrush is a great tool for working on plastic model kits and gives a lot of flexibility colorwise for painting those kits. But developing the skills to airbrush a cool image (rather than just a solid color) can take some time.

Water Slide Decals

Sometimes you will need to label the function of some component, such as a rheostat or switch on the front of your case. How can you do that and still have it look professional? One quick answer is to use water slide decals. This is the same type of material as model builders use to add details far too small to paint, such as the markings or insignia on model planes and ships. The big difference is that you will need to make your own, as opposed to using some that came with a model kit.

Decal sheets come in two colors—white and clear. Both can have other colors printed on top of them, but white and clear are the two base colors. White allows you to have white elements on your decal (since white can't be printed using standard printers), while clear allows the details behind the decal to show through in areas.

Water-slide decals are extremely thin pieces of clear film with an adhesive backing. These decals come attached to sheets of somewhat thick paper. When placed in water for 10 to 15 seconds, the adhesive on the decal loosens, and the decal slides off the paper backing and onto the final surface (see Figure 6-8) usually a plastic model kit. Wipe away the excess water and wait for the decal to dry, and you have a permanent marking with more detail than would be possible to produce by hand.

Over the last five years or so, companies have started marketing special paper that enables hobbyists to make their own decals. This paper comes in two different types—paper designed for inkjet printers and paper designed for laser printers. Both types of paper are available from better hobby stores and also online (a good selection is available at www.kustomrides.com). Prices vary a bit, but generally decal paper costs between $1 and $2 per page.

The problem is that inkjet inks are water-soluble, so dipping paper with printing from an inkjet printer on it would never work. The solution is to spray a clear lacquer over the printed image on the page. Once dry, the decal can be used like any other decal. Laser printer decal paper is easier to use since laser printer ink isn't water soluble—just print on the laser decal paper and use it like a normal decal.

Tip

Although the inkjet decal paper makers would like you to believe their paper makes great decals, it really doesn't. The additional lacquer makes the decal thicker and heavier than ordinary decals, and they have less-than-great adhesive on them. Laser printer decal paper, on the other hand, works great.

FIGURE 6-8: Laser printer decals for replacing keyboard lettering. At the top is a piece of printed decal sheet, at the bottom left is a cutout decal, and the bottom right is a decal being removed from it's backing and applied to a piece of plastic.

Tip

If you don't have access to a laser printer, print out your image on normal paper and take the decal sheet to a local print shop. There, use their color photocopy machines to photocopy your inkjet image onto the laser decal paper.

The procedure for using decal paper is simple:

1. Using an art program on your computer, design your graphic image. Try to fit as much on one page as possible to avoid wasting the expensive paper. Use high-res graphics and text whenever possible.

2. Print out several test runs using normal paper first, to work out any spacing issues (don't skip this step, it will be an expensive mistake). Set your printer to the highest resolution output possible.

3a. If you have a laser printer (or a color laser printer), insert the decal paper into the printer so that the glossy side will be printed on. Print your image.

3b. If you own an inkjet printer, print out the image in the highest resolution possible and take it and the decal sheet to a local print shop. Have them photocopy the image onto your paper's glossy side.

4. Cut out the sections of the decal paper with printing on them. Cut as close to the edge as possible.

5. Place the cutout decal in a warm, shallow amount of water. Saucers make good holders for the water since you don't need much, and they're shallow enough that you can easy grab the decal should it sink.

6. Wait around 15 to 20 seconds, and remove the decal with its paper backing. Place the decal and backing next to the area where you want the decal. With your finger, gently slide the decal off the backing paper and onto the destination surface. Quickly discard the paper backing.

7. Again using your finger, position the decal in its final place and use some paper towel or absorbent cloth to remove excess water. Press down across the whole decal to remove any trapped air bubbles. Let the decal dry overnight.

8. (Optional) paint over the decal with some clear top coat to help permanently seal the decal in place.

Wrapping Up

Creating an exterior finish for a case is one way to clearly personalize a system to your tastes. When you combine the different types of paint you can use with the different colors and techniques, the possibilities are endless. It's all a question of what picture you have in your mind for your case. Conservative or wild? Textured or mirror-like? Paint or case wrap? You make the call.

Soldering Skills

For any "extreme" case mod, you need to know how to solder. Even just cleaning up the wires inside an existing case may require some level of soldering, and it's also a very handy skill for fixing things around the house. It's really not that hard so long as you take into account all the safety precautions. Soldering can be time-consuming and downright boring, but the skills required are fairly basic. You won't be an expert the first time out (it's really more of an art than a skill), and you'll need some practice. But there are plenty of tricks that can make the experience relatively painless.

The basic idea behind soldering is to attach one metal component to another by using a special metal that can easily be turned into a liquid. Take two wires, for example. To attach two wires you can uncover the metal wire beneath the plastic coating and twist the wires together, but those wires are easy to pull apart again. If you take some of the special metal (called solder), heat it until it becomes liquid, and then add it to those two twisted wires at the connection point, the liquid will seep into all the holes between those two wires. The liquid then cools so that it becomes solid, and you have two wires that cannot be pulled apart. Add some way for that connection to be shielded from the outside, and you now have one much longer wire.

When most people think about soldering, they tend to think of it as dripping molten solder onto a joint. This is incorrect. Instead, you want to heat the components involved to such a temperature that when solder is added it melts and flows into all the small holes and crevices. If you just drop a ball of solder onto something, the solder will immediately cool when it touches the component and not flow into all the crevices. This is called a "cold solder joint," which is a poor electrical conductor and not as physically strong (i.e., the connection is weak and may break).

Caution

Safety precautions are mentioned several times throughout this chapter, but it's important to mention up front that soldering can be a dangerous business. Besides the obvious risk of severe burns from both the soldering equipment and the molten metal (solder), the fumes from solder are considered dangerous and carcinogenic by the state of California. In common practice, if you are careful and follow all the precautions, you won't have any problems, but soldering is not something for people who tend to be a little clumsy.

Equipment

There are several tools you will need in soldering, but the most important is the soldering iron itself. These come in several types—wand type, gun type, butane wand type, and torch. Each has its own unique personality.

Tip The discussion here focuses on soldering irons for home users. There are professional-grade soldering stations for people who spend their whole day soldering, which are significantly more expensive, ranging from several hundred dollars to several thousand dollars when you include all the accessories such as air filters.

Types of Soldering Irons

Wand-style soldering irons (see Figure 7-1) are probably the most common and typically the cheapest currently available($5 to $20). They are great for getting into small places and don't weigh much. Replacement tips are readily available at most local electronics stores, as are the soldering irons themselves. But they lack the amount of power needed for large areas or for soldering large numbers of connections in a short period of time. They also take a while to heat up to the proper temperature before you can begin soldering and lack any sort of temperature sensing. They often heat up to temperatures that are a little too hot. That being said, they are really better tools than they would appear. They make great entry-level tools, and in general they are all you need for most case-modding jobs.

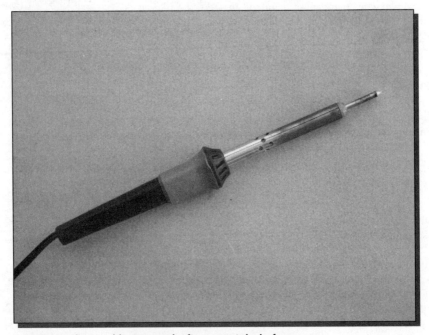

FIGURE 7-1: Cheap soldering wand, after a great deal of use.

Gun-type soldering irons are more professional tools, and therefore more expensive ($30 to $99). They have more power and can handle continuous use much better than wands and heat up much quicker as well. On the downside, they are heavy and difficult to get into tight areas. While useful for most types of soldering, they are often overkill for most case-modding projects.

Butane-powered wand-style soldering irons are also readily available and reasonably priced ($20 to $40). These are wand-style soldering irons that use flames to heat their soldering tips. While they do work, does using anything with a flame make sense indoors? Combine this with the relatively short working time (due to limited fuel) and the cost of buying additional fuel, and these factors limit the functionality of butane-powered soldering wands so much that they become a bad investment.

Some people also use small torches (usually butane based) for soldering. In general, these types of soldering irons (if they should even be called that) are good for one type of job only—they can heat a large area quickly. If you were trying to strip every component off a board for some reason and didn't care too much about potentially destroying the parts, you could use a torch. Simply hold the board upside down with the solder side up, light the torch, run it quickly over each component and watch them fall to the ground. But other than that rare task, this is not a good way to solder for any purpose. Torches typically cost $5 to $25.

Caution
Using a torch to remove a lot of components from dead circuit boards is quick and easy , but it also involves significant risks. When doing this, apart from the obvious risk of starting a fire, the board you are trying to remove components from will burn. These fumes are dangerous and unpleasant to smell. You also risk damaging the components you wanted to spare. But this method is also a real time saver when done right. Just be extremely cautious.

Other Tools

There are other tools you will want in addition to the soldering iron itself (see Figure 7-2). These include needle-nose pliers (less than $25 for a decent one), wire cutters (also less than $25), some component holding device (optional), and a wet sponge. Very often, you will need to solder a small piece that is too small to hold by hand, and that is what needle-nose pliers can help with. Also, by holding the soldered part with pliers you can avoid burning your hand should the component heat up too much. Wire cutters are really useful for cutting and strip-ping wires. While one can live without them, once you have a pair your success rate will sky-rocket, and you could never imagine living without them.

Many electronics stores also sell strange-looking devices with lots of clips and adjustable arms designed for holding pieces together while you solder. Such devices are not a necessity, but also really help you achieve the final result and are worth the investment. Last, a small wet sponge for cleaning the soldering iron during the soldering process will make your equipment last much longer and make your connections cleaner and stronger.

Tip
During the soldering process, a lot of dirt can get stuck to the soldering iron tip. Melted wire insulation, not to mention extra soldering flux, can contaminate the tip and make the process more difficult. A small, damp sponge that you can quickly wipe the tip against during soldering will clean the tip and improve the quality of the soldered connections. Make sure not to hold the sponge with your hand though—the hot soldering tip will burn your hand.

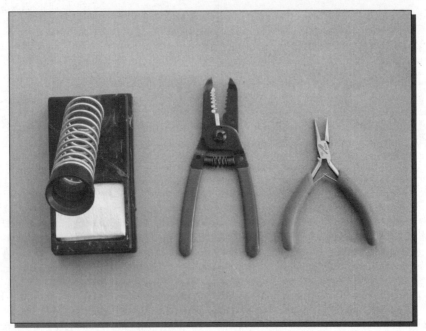

FIGURE 7-2: Tools of the trade. Left to right they are a soldering iron holder, wire cutters, and needle-nose pliers.

The last tool that should be mentioned is some sort of holder for the soldering iron. Since the soldering iron gets so hot as part of its normal job, you just can't put it down on a desk surface. Some soldering irons come with holders, but many cheap ones do not. If your soldering iron doesn't come with a holder, purchase one separately.

Associated Supplies

The solder itself comes in several different compositions and thicknesses. The standard composition is 60 percent lead and 40 percent tin with a resin core. For virtually everything you will want to do for case modding, this is fine. As for thickness, the thicker solder allows better control when applying it to a component, but any thickness should work.

One thing to remember is that the fumes from soldering are toxic, so try not to inhale them or get them in your eyes. One technique is to use a fan near your work area blowing away from you, and another technique is to simply hold your breath with each connection you make. You could also invest in a filtering mask, but you have to pay attention and make sure that the mask you get is appropriate for blocking soldering fumes, such as a respirator with a true HEPA filter. Different masks have different filtering capabilities, and HEPA filters for respirators are rarely available in home improvement stores. They are available, however, and an online search will yield several dealers that carry them.

Tip

The technique of using a small desk fan to keep soldering fumes away works well when done properly. The proper way is to aim the fan away from the soldering area, but have it close by so that the fumes are drawn into the fan and exhausted away. If the fan is directly facing you, even more fumes can get in your lungs and eyes. If the fan is placed beside the soldering area, the fumes might not get to you, but cool air would flow over your soldering iron, cooling it down and making your work all the more difficult.

Heat-shrink tubing is another important item for soldering. This is a round sheath or rubber-like material that insulates connections and prevents shorts. When heat is applied, it shrinks and forms around whatever is inside. It's available in many different sizes and colors.

This stuff is great for covering the connections you make between wires. Simply cut a piece of the right length, slide it on one side of the cable you intend to connect and slide it as far away from the connection point as possible. After soldering the wires together, slide the tubing over the exposed part and heat the tubing using a hair dryer or a small flame a few inches below the tubing. The tubing will shrink around the connection and protect it from conducting electricity where it shouldn't (see Figure 7-3).

Cross-Reference

Heat-shrink tubing's primary use is to connect wires and insulate them. However, heat-shrink tubing is also useful for grouping wires together such as when you're doing cable management, as shown in Chapter 3. The selection of colors and sizes for heat-shrink tubing also make the results of cable management attractive when you use it.

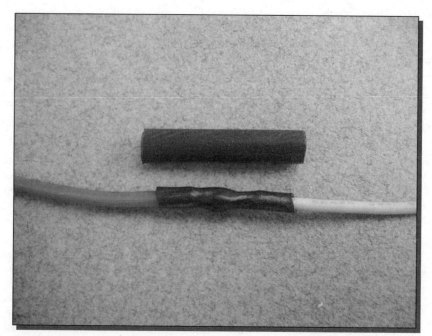

FIGURE 7-3: Heat-shrink tubing, both before and after the shrinking process.

Tip

In a pinch, you can also use the side of the soldering iron tip (away from the tip itself, about one inch up the soldering iron) to heat and shrink the tubing.

Of course, wire is also an important item to keep in supply. Wire comes in two varieties, stranded and solid core. Solid core is one fat wire, like a metal coat hanger (but on a smaller scale). Stranded wire is a bundle of smaller wires. Wires vary in thickness (called gauge), with the main difference being the amount of electrical load they can carry. But for most wires and voltages/amperages you will deal with in case modding, almost any gauge of wire will work. One rule of thumb is to use roughly the same gauge of wire that was already in use. Don't connect a small gauge wire to a large gauge wire—keep them the same gauge. You should use solid core wire for internal connections between switches and components and stranded wire when the wire has to travel somewhere (like the power connectors for the hard drives).

Heat Transfer Basics

The concept of heat transfer is simple—when the tip of a soldering iron touches some part, that part begins to heat up. However, heat will not flow through that part all at once. The piece closest to the soldering iron heats up first, then the part next to it, and so on.

Now, remember what the original goal was all along—to heat up the part enough so that the solder next to that part will melt and join the two pieces together. But what happens if the soldering iron wasn't hot enough to melt the solder in the first place? The part you are trying to solder will just heat up, the solder will never melt, and most likely you will ruin the part you are trying to solder because all the associated plastic around it will melt.

By touching the soldering iron to the piece you are trying to solder you are taking away heat from the soldering iron itself. Imagine that the soldering iron is just barely hot enough to melt solder. When you touch the soldering iron to a component, the soldering iron loses some of its heat as that heat is transferred to the component, and the soldering iron won't be hot enough to melt solder any more.

However, if the soldering iron is very hot, the area where you touch the iron will heat up rapidly and reach the point where solder melts very quickly. Since the solder will flow well, the actual time that the heat is applied is so short that the heat doesn't have time to flow through the rest of the part. This means that the solder connection is complete, and none of the plastic further away had time to be damaged. The trick to achieving this is called *tinning*.

Tinning the tip of your soldering iron allows better heat transfer between the tip and the components you are trying to join. To tin the end of your iron, let the iron heat up and then right before you are about to solder a joint, lightly brush the tip of the iron with the solder (see Figure 7-4). You can buy dedicated tinning compound, but for most jobs it's really not necessary. The tip of the iron should take on a shiny appearance, looking as if the tip were chromed. If you have a droplet of solder on the tip, you are being too liberal, and need to use less solder. Improper tinning won't hurt the soldering iron in any way, but will reduce the quality of your connections.

FIGURE 7-4: Soldering iron tip with a bit of solder to "tin" the tip.

By tinning the iron properly, you are creating a soft buffer area between the soldering iron and the component you are trying to solder. Think of it this way—if the surface you were trying to heat up were flat and the soldering iron tip were rounded, the iron would touch the surface at one small spot only. But with a properly tinned soldering iron, the iron would heat a larger area because the "tin" would help fill in some of the area where the iron wasn't. Thus, heat is more efficiently transferred to the part you are trying to heat and you can avoid overheating the component.

Soldering Techniques

The simplest soldering task (and probably the most common) is to attach two wires to make one longer wire. First, take two wires and strip them with a wire stripper. This is a simple procedure where you place the wire into the appropriate hole on the wire stripper, close the blades of the tool, and pull off the plastic surrounding sheath from a small section (about 1/2 to 1/4 of an inch) of wire. Do this to one end of both wires. Now cut a small piece of heat shrink tubing (about a 1/2 inch longer than the amount of wire you stripped).

Take one wire and put the heat-shrink tubing on it first, moving it as far away from the exposed section of wire as possible. Remember, you cannot add the heat-shrink tubing after connecting the wires. I guarantee that sometime or other you'll forget and will be kicking yourself about it, but it happens to everyone. Take the exposed part of each wire and form a U shape, hooking the wires together. Then, twist the wires together. The exposed wire should not be much larger in diameter than the regular wire with the plastic covering.

Next, heat up the soldering iron and tin the tip. If the tip was properly tinned, you should be able to hold the solder on one side of the exposed wire and the solder on the other side of the wire. Touch them both to the wire and the solder should melt and flow into all the little spaces between the two wires. If a good flow of solder doesn't happen quickly, just brush the tip of the solder against the iron itself for a fraction of a second and the process of solder flow should be accelerated. The whole process should take less than 5 seconds, preferably 2 to 3 seconds. You should still be able to see and feel the texture of the wires after the soldering, but the wires should be strong and inseparable (see Figure 7-5).

Give the connection a few seconds to cool (blowing on it will help). Finally, slide the heat-shrink tubing back over the exposed connection. Heat the tubing as discussed earlier, and it should form a close bond to the wire.

Another common type of soldering involves using something called perf-board. Perf-board is for connecting multiple components such as resistors, switches, and integrated circuits. Basically, perf-board is a piece of nonconductive material with many regular holes drilled in it and a small circle of metal (usually copper) around each hole. The idea is that you take some component such as a resistor, bend the leads off the resistor till they fit through some of the

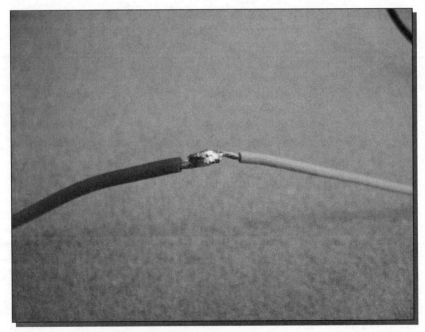

FIGURE 7-5: Wires properly soldered together.

holes in the perf-board, and solder it into position. It's then a simple matter to connect two adjacent holes with solder to create a circuit.

The procedure for soldering to a perf-board is even easier. Simply take a component and place its leads through the perf-board with the copper side of board (and the leads from the component) facing you. You can bend the leads slightly so they stay in place by friction. Then, touch the properly tinned soldering iron to both the component lead and the copper hole and touch the solder to the other side of the component lead (in effect sandwiching the component between the soldering iron and the solder). The solder should flow evenly into the hole attaching the component. Take the soldering iron away and let the connection cool. Use wire cutters to clip off the extra length leads from the component.

Desoldering Technique

It's inevitable that some time you'll need to undo a connection that you already made or remove some component someone else put together. For a wire connection, it's simple. Just cut the wire in two and connect the two parts again using standard soldering techniques. But if instead you have some component attached to a piece of perf-board, you will need to desolder it.

The first way to do this is also the most error prone. Holding the component with a pair of needle-nose pliers, apply the soldering iron to the connection point. Once the solder has melted, you should be able to pull the part away. But often this technique doesn't work because you may have several connections from the same piece, such as a resistor or switch. You can still try to use this technique by heating each connection one at a time and moving the component a little at each solder point until it's fully disconnected. It's workable, but you run a significant chance of overheating the component and ruining it.

There are devices sold called desoldering pumps ($5 to $10). These are typically long plastic syringes with a spring in them. Push the plunger in until it snaps, then heat the solder point with the soldering iron. Holding the tip of the pump close to the solder point, press the button on the pump. This will cause the plunger to spring back and create a small vacuum that pulls solder away from the solder point, and you will then be able to remove the component by persuading it with a pair of needle-nose pliers.

There is another variation on a soldering iron that can help in these circumstances. Usually these are similar to a wand-type soldering iron but have a rubber bulb on the end of a long metal tube running parallel to the soldering iron itself (see Figure 7-6). They also have a different-style tip, usually a round tapered tube of some sort. The idea is that (somewhere safe, away from the component) you press and hold the bulb until the hot air and solder are expelled. Next you move the desoldering iron over to the component, heat it using the tip, and let go of the bulb. The vacuum created will draw away the solder. These are available for $15 to $45.

Finally you can also use a soldering iron and something called a "solder wick" to remove the solder (less than $1). Basically, you hold the solder wick on the item you want to desolder along with the soldering iron, and the solder will be drawn up into the wick. You then remove that piece of wick and start again with a clean piece of wick.

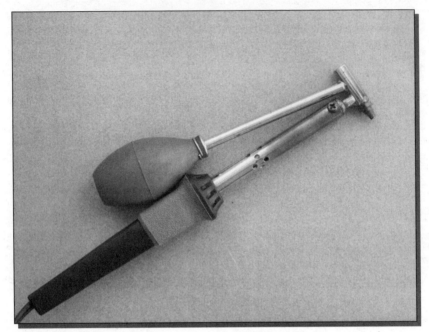

FIGURE 7-6: Well-worn desoldering iron with attached rubber bulb.

Common Problems

There are some common problems that people encounter when soldering, most with easy solutions. While certainly there are a hundred variations on the problems you might encounter, most of them will be due to improper technique of some sort. Here are a few of the more common problems when learning to solder:

- **When holding the soldering iron to the component and holding the solder to the other side of the component, nothing happens for a long time**—Several things could be wrong. You might not have tinned the iron's tip properly, so not a large enough area on the component is heating up. Also, the piece you are trying to heat might be too large and you need a higher wattage soldering iron.

- **When holding the soldering iron to a component or wire, the area around the part goes soft and the plastic melts**—Most likely the soldering iron was too cold before you touched the iron to the component. Also, it could be a matter of poor heat transfer due to an improperly tinned or dirty tip.

- **You have to solder very small components, and the solder keeps bridging two connections**—There are a couple of solutions. First, try getting a smaller, more pointed tip for the soldering iron. Second, purchase some solder flux paste and coat just the lead you want to solder with a small amount of the flux before soldering it. The flux will help the solder flow more easily over that piece. Note that solder flux is usually unnecessary for most modding jobs, but it can be useful for really small connections such as those to single leads on chips attached to motherboards.

Wrapping Up

Any project requiring some electrical changes is a project that needs some soldering. Soldering is a dangerous process that requires paying attention to detail and has serious repercussions if you don't (burnt skin and small fires are not out of the question). However, with the basic skills outlined in this chapter and some time to learn the "art" of soldering, those projects are within your grasp. Just remember that having the proper tools and paying attention to detail are your keys to success.

That being said, don't be intimidated by the process. Every day, thousands of people (if not tens of thousands) all over the world are soldering, and I've never heard of anyone seriously injured. If you want to solder, you have to start sometime, and there is no reason to put it off. As long as you pay attention to detail and have a nice clean work area, you'll do fine.

Electronics

A lot of case modding can be done without ever touching a soldering iron or knowing much about the underlying electronics, but these will just be "assembled" case mods. In other words, they are just one step up from premods. For a truly unique case, you will need not just to use a soldering iron but to use it to assemble electronic circuits that perform some action apart from the typical functions of the computer inside the case. To accomplish this you will need to understand basic electronics.

Electronics can take years of study to understand in detail. Thankfully, for all but the most extreme case mods you won't have to go that far. Designing a circuit to flash some LEDs is actually somewhat complex, but there are lots of people who do that stuff for a living and make the diagrams freely available on the Internet. For most case mods you won't need to completely understand what goes on in the circuits, but you must be able to build a simple circuit based on the circuit diagrams available. With a little information, this should be within your grasp.

But before you go that far, you should know some basic electronic theory. Without this understanding, assembling circuits (even from existing diagrams) will be difficult.

Simple Circuits

A circuit is exactly what the name implies. It's a complete circle that electrons (i.e., electricity) can flow around. The idea is that while traveling along that path, the electrons can perform some work such as lighting something up, turning a motor, and so on. The path the electrons flow around goes from the power source's negative terminal, through the various components, and on to the positive terminal.

A simple circuit comprises a power source (a battery, a computer power supply, etc.), a load (something that uses electricity to perform some action, such as a light bulb), and a path from the power source to the load and back again (some type of wire or other conductor). There are two basic types of circuits: a series circuit and a parallel circuit, although any moderately complex circuit will contain elements of both.

A series circuit is one with all loads in a row, like links in a chain. There is only one path for the electricity to flow. If this circuit were a string of light bulbs, and one blew out, the remaining bulbs would turn off.

A parallel circuit is one with two or more paths for the electricity to flow around. In other words, the loads are parallel to each other. If the loads in this circuit were light bulbs and one blew out, there would still be current flowing to the others because they would still be in a direct path from the negative to positive terminals of the battery, and they would continue to light up.

When there is an error in a circuit and the electricity finds a shorter loop back to the power source than expected, this is referred too as a "short circuit". A short circuit can lead to some real problems such as damaged components and fire.

Circuits are typically shown as a series of diagrams with simple icons representing the various electronic components and the connections between them. There are literally hundreds of different symbols to describe all the various electronic components, but some are more common in case modding than others (see Figure 8-1).

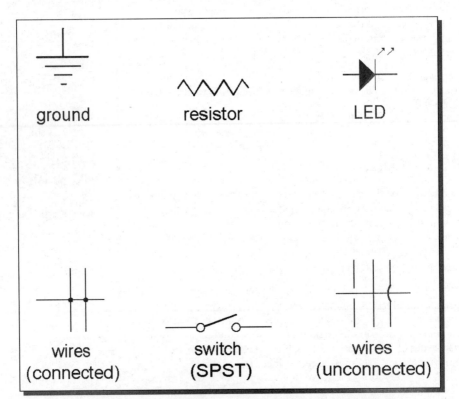

FIGURE 8-1: A few of the common electronic component symbols and their names. There are hundreds more, but these are the basics used for many case mods.

Multimeters

With all the different things that can go wrong with electronics, testing parts as you go along can be very useful. Using a tool called a multimeter (see Figure 8-2), you can test all the different aspects of electronic circuits before problems arise.

Multimeters have the capability to test resistance, AC or DC voltage, capacitance, current, and much more. There are multimeters in every price range from $15 to $500, but even the cheapest one can help greatly when you're assembling circuits or trying to debug someone else's circuits.

That being said, digital multimeters (those with a digital display) are generally more useful and accurate than those with an analog display. Digital multimeters can be purchased at any electronics store.

Powering Electronics

There are two basic forms of electricity, known as alternating current (AC) and direct current (DC). In addition to AC and DC electricity, you should also be concerned with the voltage and the current of the electricity. If electricity were water flowing through a pipe, the voltage would

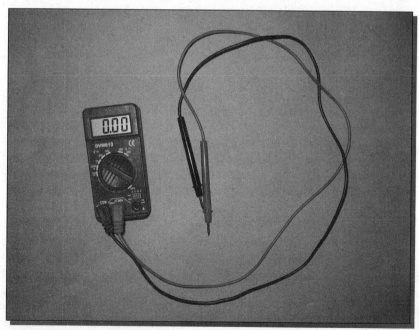

FIGURE 8-2: Cheap digital multimeter with included test probes.

be the water pressure, while the current would be the amount of water that passed through the pipe over a given time.

For almost everything built during a case mod, DC electricity is used. The problem is that the electricity available in wall sockets is AC electricity. However, your computer's power supply converts AC electricity to the DC electricity that the computer needs to run. The power supply creates several different voltages of DC electricity, and the current varies depending on how many devices attached to the power supply need power.

Note   Batteries also supply DC electricity.

In general, the power supply will have at least three different types of connectors (but possibly more). The most common connectors are the IDE hard drive power connectors (commonly called Molex connectors), the floppy drive power connectors, and a large connector with many wires that plugs into the motherboard itself. Some power supplies also have an additional 4-pin cable that also plugs into the motherboard in a separate location and/or power connectors for SATA hard drives, but not all power supplies have these.

Ignoring the motherboard power connector, the IDE hard drive and floppy drive power connectors have exactly the same function but different physical plugs. Both connectors have 4 wires—one red, one yellow, and two black. The red wire supplies positive 5 volts DC, the yellow wire supplies positive 12 volts DC, and the black wires supply a ground connection (both black wires typically go to the same place).

Other devices or circuits plugged into the computer are powered off these connectors. If the device being plugged in needs any voltage other than the 5 volts or 12 volts provided by the connector, the circuitry in the device must derive those voltages itself using the 5 and 12 volt lines as a basis.

There are other factors you encounter when trying to understand wiring for electronics that can be quite complex. The thickness (gauge) and length of wire used can create all sort of issues—the wire itself actually causes resistance to the electrical flow and a corresponding voltage drop. Using too small a gauge of wire can cause the wire to heat up and melt, causing a short circuit. Thankfully, when dealing with low-voltage components, such as LEDs and simple circuits, these issues rarely come up.

Building a Test Power Supply

One thing comes up frequently when working with electronics—the need to test them. If there is an error in either the design or the assembly of a circuit, too much electricity can flow through the wrong areas and burn out components. Should this happen while testing a circuit in your computer, the power supply itself can be damaged and burn out itself or other components in the system. For this reason, it's best to test anything you build someplace other than your working system before you know it's safe to install. To accomplish this, it's best to build yourself a power supply that is dedicated only to testing purposes.

First, you'll need a few supplies:

- **Power supply**—Because this power supply is dedicated to testing devices and circuits (but not motherboards or complete systems), a cheap and small-wattage power supply will be fine. For example, the power supply used for this discussion is a 350-watt unit that came as a package with a case for $29.99 with $10.00 rebate.

- **LEDs and resistors**—You want a visible sign that the power supply is on and another that the power supply is plugged in. Depending on the type of LED you use, you may need some resistors as well. Here, I've used two ultrabrite LEDs (red and green) and the corresponding resistors (150 ohm and 100 ohm). Chapter 4 provides instructions on calculating the right resistance. You should be able to pick up a couple of ultrabrite LEDs with the appropriate resistors for under $8.

- **Toggle switch**—This switch controls whether the power supply itself is on, but doesn't need to be large. A small two-position toggle switch is all that is needed. These usually go for $3 to $7 dollars new, but are available for much less through second-hand electronics stores.

- **Miscellaneous supplies**—Heat-shrink tubing, electrical tape, 400-grit sandpaper, and LED holders are also required for the power supply mod. All these should be available for under $10 combined.

The construction of a test power supply is easy, but caution is necessary. Allowing a short circuit across the wrong set of wires could lead to serious burns or fire, not to mention electric shock. Make sure that the power supply is unplugged from the wall socket before starting this work. Also, these instructions are only valid on standard ATX power supplies. Custom power supplies such as those from Dell or Compaq may or may not work.

1. Start by opening the power supply and separating the wires for the strings of Molex connectors and the motherboard connector.

2. On the motherboard connector, cut every wire about 1.5 inches from the circuit board inside the power supply except the green wire, the purple wire, one red wire, and three black wires.

3. For every wire cut, cut a piece of electrical tape about 1 inch long and wrap it around each cut wire to prevent any accidental shorts.

4. Next, loosely place the cover of the power supply back on the power supply itself taking note of at least three areas where holes could be drilled into the cover with no obstructions for at least 1.5 inches below the holes.

5. Take the power supply cover back off, and drill the three holes—one big enough for the toggle switch and two just a little larger than the LEDs' diameters (i.e., the holes should be just large enough to place an LED holder into the hole). When done, mount the LED holders and the toggle switch into the holes (see Figure 8-3).

6. Place the power supply cover upside down next to the power supply itself. Cut the six wires remaining on the motherboard connector so that the wires can reach the holes you just drilled in the power supply cover while still having a little room to move around.

7. Solder one black wire and the green wire to the switch in adjacent terminals on the switch.

8. Ultrabrite LEDs have a very narrow field of light projection (i.e., a narrow band in which they shine light), but you can modify that area a little to spread light more evenly. Using the 400-grit sandpaper, carefully sand the entire face of the LED all around until the clear plastic of the LED becomes a little rough and somewhat white. Use a little water to clean the LED and dry it.

9. Next, solder the appropriate resistors to the short legs on the LEDs.

10. Finally, solder the purple wire and one black wire to one LED and solder the red wire and the remaining black wire to the other LED. The black wire will go to the leg of the LEDs with the resistors. Don't forget to use heat-shrink tubing on all the wires before you solder on the LEDs.

11. Push the LEDs into the LED holders and reassemble the power supply (see Figure 8-4).

Plug the power supply into the wall socket and test it. If all went well, one LED will light up as soon as the power supply is plugged into the wall, and the other LED will light up when the toggle switch is turned to the on position (which will also turn on the power to the Molex connectors).

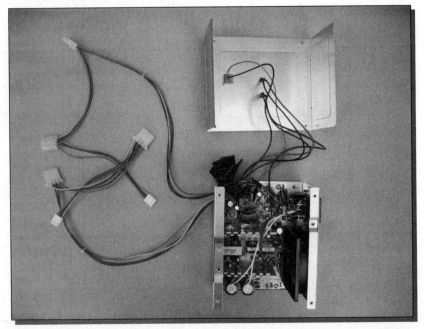

FIGURE 8-3: Power supply with cover removed and motherboard connector wires cut.

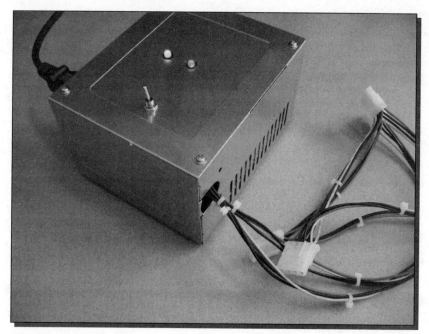

FIGURE 8-4: Completed "test" power supply with LED indicators and on/off switch.

Common Components

As there are hundreds of different electronic components, it would take a lot of space to describe them in detail. However, there are some components so common in case mods that they really deserve some special attention. In this section you'll learn about a few of the most important components necessary for the electronics used in case mods.

Understanding Switches

The switch is probably the most important electronic device to understand, and thankfully it is actually very simple. Basically, a switch is nothing more than a collection of metal and plastic that when activated connects two of the terminals of the switch together allowing electricity to flow. There are a number of things that differentiate switches from one another—momentary versus constant, number of poles and throws, specs, and physical construction.

Momentary switches are switches that connect their terminals only while the button is pressed, such as the power and reset buttons on a computer. Constant switches are ones that maintain the connection between their terminals even after you stop pressing the button, such as a light switch in your house.

The number of poles and throws that a switch has may seem confusing at first. The number of poles a switch has is the number of separate, individual switches contained in the switch itself.

A dual-pole switch is really just like having two switches right next to one another that are activated simultaneously. The number of throws a switch has is the number of possible states a switch can have. Most switches, such as toggle switches, have two positions (up and down) and are therefore known as single-throw switches. But some toggle switches have multiple positions (up, center, and down), and are known as dual-throw switches.

The number of poles and throws that a switch has are lumped together in the description of the switch in an abbreviated form. Thus, a single-pole single-throw switch is called a SPST switch, and a triple-pole double-throw switch is called a TPDT switch.

The specs, or specifications, of the switch relate to how much electricity the switch can handle. If too much electricity is drawn across the switch, the switch will heat up and literally melt (causing all sorts of problems). The specs are usually written on the side of the switch itself, or on the packaging for the switch if it's too small to write on. For most case mods, almost any switches will work, and you don't need to concern yourself too much with the specs.

Since most case mods use DC electricity, almost every switch out there can handle the loads that the DC electricity inside a computer could place on them. So which switch to use is up to you. Which switches physically fit in the space you need them to? Which switches are the right type (pushbutton or toggle)? Which switches are the right color?

Tip

How much electricity a switch can carry is rated in amps, and it varies greatly between AC and DC voltage. When reading the specs, keep in mind that most case mods will need to use the switch with DC electricity not AC.

The physical construction of the switch refers to how the switches are put together. There are toggle switches, pushbutton switches, slide switches, and lots of other specialized types. Switches truly come in all shapes and sizes (see Figure 8-5).

Finally, much less important but still notable, are switches with internal lighting. These switches have additional terminals to supply power to internal lighting systems in the switch itself.

Using Resistors

Resistors are probably the second most common electronic component in modding use. They come in all shapes, sizes, and colors, but they all do the same thing—limit current. For example, you might have an LED that needs no more than 3.2 volts but you have a 5 volt power source. Using a resistor, you could limit the voltage such that the LED would only see the voltage it needed. Resistors are measured in "ohms."

Each resistor is marked with a color code that describes its resistance (see Figure 8-6). Typical resistors have four bands of colors around their diameter, which detail exactly what the resistance is. Starting from left to right, the two leftmost bands detail the base number for the resistance, while the next band is the number the first two numbers are multiplied by. The last band of color shows the tolerance, or how accurate the preceding description is.

The colors black, brown, red, orange, yellow, green, blue, violet, gray, and white represent the numbers 0, 1, 2, 3, 4, 5, 6, 7, 8, and 9, in that order. The first and second bands represent the tens and the ones columns of the final number, while the third band represents 10 to the power

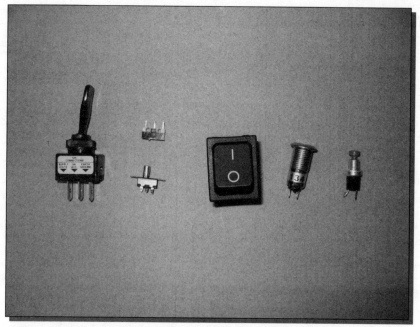

FIGURE 8-5: A small selection of different types of switches.

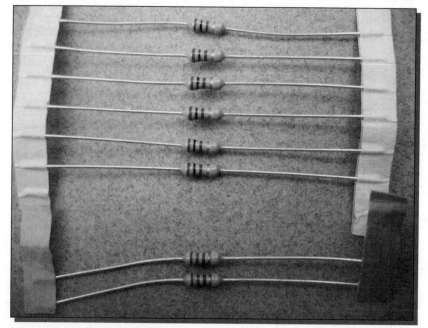

FIGURE 8-6: A collection of resistors.

Table 8-1: Resistor color codes

Color	Band 1 (tens)	Band 2 (ones)	Band 3 (multiplier)
Black	0	0	1
Brown	1	1	10
Red	2	2	100
Orange	3	3	1,000
Yellow	4	4	10,000
Green	5	5	100,000
Blue	6	6	1,000,000
Violet	7	7	10,000,000
Gray	8	8	100,000,000
White	9	9	(none)

of the color code (see Table 8-1). The colors gold or silver as the fourth band of color indicates a 5 percent or 10 percent tolerance, while the lack of a fourth band indicates a 20 percent tolerance. The best way to see this is with examples.

If a resistor has color bands in brown, black, brown, and gold, that equals "1," "0," "1," and "5 percent," the first two bands show the base number, 10, and the third band shows 10 (10 to the power of 1). This means that this resistor has a rating of 100 ohms with a 5 percent tolerance, meaning that the actual resistance is somewhere between 95 and 105 ohms.

If a resistor has color bands in yellow, violet, orange, and gold, this equals "4," "7," "3," and "5 percent." The base number is therefore 47, and the multiplier is 1,000 (10 to the third power), which means 47,000 ohms. Because of the 5 percent tolerance, the actual resistance is between 44,650 and 49,350. Resistors that are this high are typically just referred to using the abbreviation "K" for 1,000, making the resistor in this example a 47 Kohm resistor.

Tip For those not so good in math, there are several online resistance calculators available. These calculators, such as `http://www.electrician.com/resist_calc/resist_calc.htm`, allow you an easy way to see exactly what the resistance of a given resistor is.

Example Simple Circuit

Using the basic components discussed here, you can now build a simple circuit. This circuit will attach to a Molex connect and light up an LED when a switch is turned on. Using the circuit component symbols, the circuit diagram is quite simple (see Figure 8-7).

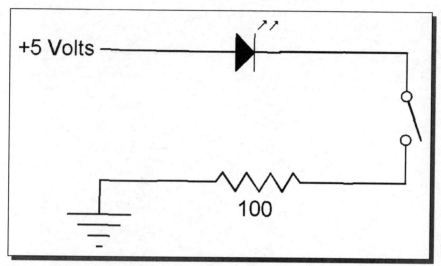

FIGURE 8-7: Simple circuit diagram. This circuit turns on an LED when a switch is pressed.

The circuit, when actually assembled, is still just as simple in appearance (see Figure 8-8). Note that this circuit has been quickly assembled to show the basic concepts of the circuit assembly. If you are actually using a circuit similar to this in your computer, all connections and exposed metal should be covered in heat-shrink tubing to prevent accidental short circuits. Heat-shrink was left off this circuit to show the components more clearly.

Caution

It's very important to make sure that all connections are properly insulated (for example, with heat-shrink tubing). Even a small, simple circuit like this one can cause a short circuit should any of the exposed connections accidentally touch a metal surface such as the exterior of the case. Yes, even something as simple as this circuit can cause your power supply to burn out if done without the right precautions.

You can obviously expand this idea a great deal. Add more LEDs, either in parallel or in serial (adjusting the resistor as needed), and mount the LEDs and switch in a blank drive bay. Or use a switch like the one in this circuit to control power to a fan. The possibilities are limitless.

LCD and VFD Panels

One electronic component that has been gaining popularity, especially among overclockers, are LCD or VFD panels. Functionally, they both do the same job—display some sort of information about the computer aside from what the monitor shows. For example, they can be used to show the temperature reported by the CPU or motherboard—information that otherwise wouldn't be seen while playing a full-screen game.

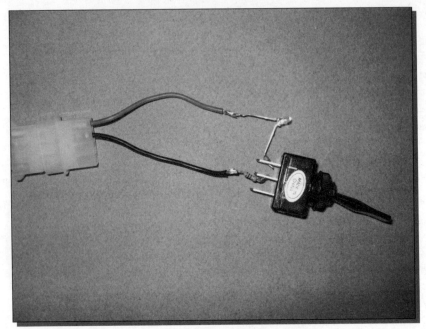

FIGURE 8-8: Assembled circuit. Note the lack of heat-shrink tubing on the connections—never allow such a circuit inside your computer.

Cross-Reference

Appendix A covers the topic of overclocking. See that section for a discussion of what it is and why anyone would want to do it.

Both types of panels come in two varieties, character based and graphic based. Character displays simply show a fixed number of characters using a certain number of rows and columns, although the characters themselves are composed of individual pixels. Graphic displays can display any arbitrary picture.

LCD displays come in various background and foreground color combinations, everything from gray and black to blue and white. In addition to the one-color LCD displays, complete multicolor LCD panels such as those used in car headrests and portable DVD players can also be interfaced with your computer. VFD displays are generally limited to one color—aqua, but this can be changed somewhat by using colored filters in front of the VFD display.

Traditional LCD panels are cheap but have a limited viewing angle and unless they are backlit can be hard to see from a distance. VFDs are more expensive but are extremely bright and have no viewing angle problems. Full-color LCD panels are relatively expensive and may or may not suffer the same limited viewing angle problems as cheap LCD panels.

Nice units can be purchased from companies such as Matrix Orbital, Crystalfontz, and Virtual Lab Systems. These units range in price from $40 to $100 and are generally high quality. For

FIGURE 8-9: VFD display bought as a separate component, attached to an empty drive bay and interfaced through the parallel port.

those who are more the do-it-yourself type, bare LCD panels and VFD panels (see Figure 8-9) can be purchased for as little as $15 at some times. Those units require a lot of additional setup and wiring, however, and not all of those LCD and VFD panels can be interfaced to existing software.

These panels connect to the computer in several different ways, namely through the parallel port, the serial port, or the USB port. The exception to this is the advanced full-color LCD panels, which attach through an RCA or VGA port.

Parallel port hookups are sometimes the best way to go—the cheapest LCD and VFD panels are based on the Hitachi HD44780 controller chip. The mapping between the HD44780 pins and the parallel port pins is easy enough (see Table 8-2), but connecting them requires soldering a lot of wires.

Serial port hooks are nice because they require a smaller number of wires to be soldered, but a serial interface must be provided on the LCD or VFD display, which raises the cost and makes them harder to find.

USB interfaced panels are even more complex and are generally just serial panels connected through USB to serial converters (and are therefore the most expensive). The big advantage of USB panels is that they can often be connected completely internally to the computer without requiring a cable to run outside the computer to the back of the motherboard.

Table 8-2: Parallel port to HD44780 pinout mapping

LCD pin	Connect to
Ground	Ground (black wire on Molex connector)
Power	+5 Volt power (red wire on Molex connector)
LCD contrast	Ground (black wire on Molex connector)—this could be replaced with a 10K pot for adjustable contrast, grounding sets maximum contrast
Register select	Parallel port pin 16
Read / Write	Ground (black wire on Molex connector)—since there is no reading from the LCD, set it permanently in write mode by grounding
Strobe	Parallel port pin 1
Data bit 0	Parallel port pin 2
Data bit 1	Parallel port pin 3
Data bit 2	Parallel port pin 4
Data bit 3	Parallel port pin 5
Data bit 4	Parallel port pin 6
Data bit 5	Parallel port pin 7
Data bit 6	Parallel port pin 8
Data bit 7	Parallel port pin 9

Caution   While hooking up an LCD panel to the parallel port, always attach the LCD to both the parallel port and the power connectors at the same time. Hooking up one without the other and turning on the computer will burn out the parallel port on the computer, the LCD panel, or both.

Definitions

The following table of definitions will help you keep things clear as to what component does what. By no means is this list complete, but this will be a good start for components and concepts you might hear in case mod discussions:

- **Circuit**—A path for electricity to flow around. Along the way, the electricity can perform some useful work such as powering lights. The path runs in a complete circle from the negative terminal, through the various components, and on to the positive terminal.

- **Voltage**—The electrical force that causes the current to flow in a circuit. It is measured in volts.

- **Current**—The movement of electrical charge, that is, the flow of electrons through the circuit. Current is measured in amperes (amps).

- **Conductor**—A material (usually a metal) that allows electrical current to pass easily through it.

- **Insulator**—A material that prevents electrical current flow, otherwise known as a non-conductor. Note that with enough current and/or voltage, electricity can go through any nonconductor.

- **Resistance/impedance**—Anything that causes electricity to not want to flow through a circuit. For example, the plastic covering over a wire (an insulator) has very high resistance, while the wire itself (a conductor) has low resistance. Remember that everything in the circuit causes resistance, even wire itself. Resistance is measured in ohms.

- **Resistor**—One of the most common components in electronics. It is typically used to control current and/or voltage within the circuit. You can identify a simple resistor by its cylindrical shape with a wire lead coming out of each end. It uses a system of color-coded bands to identify the value of the component. There are other types of resistors, but simple resistors are the most common.

- **Potentiometer (pots)**—A variable resistor. This lets you vary the resistance with a dial in order to alter current or voltage on the fly.

- **Capacitor (cap)**—This varies in size and shape, from a small surface-mounted rectangle up to a huge electric motor cap the size and shape of a paint can. The purpose of both is the same—they store electrical energy in the form of electrostatic charge. The size of a capacitor generally determines how much charge it can store. A small surface-mount cap will only hold a very small charge, while a large cylindrical cap can store a much larger charge, even enough to kill a person.

- **Diode**—A one-way valve for electrical current. It lets electricity flow in one direction (from positive to negative) but not in the other direction. Most diodes are similar in appearance to resistors and will have a painted line on one end showing the direction of flow.

- **Light emitting diode (LED)**—A diode that emits light of one form or another. They are used all over most electronic devices and can be one of the most effective tools a modder has at his or her disposal. They come in many shapes, sizes, and colors.

- **Transistor**—This serves two purposes. First, it acts as a switch, turning current on and off. Second, it can act as an amplifier making an output signal that is a magnified version of the input signal. They come in all sizes, including microscopic.

- **Integrated circuit (IC)**—A complex circuit encased in plastic housings. Usually, they come in some rectangular or square form with many metal "pins" coming out of them. The number of applications is immense—everything from memory to specialized micro-processors.

- **Microprocessor**—A very-large-scale IC. At the core of these are thousands to millions of transistors that provide the logic for everything from computers to TVs to just about everything electronic.

Wrapping Up

Understanding electronics at even a superficial level can take years of study. The details given here barely scratch the surface of what can be accomplished, the benefits, and the dangers or doing certain things with electronic circuits.

What this chapter has hopefully given you is enough knowledge to whet your appetite and make you want to experiment and try things. Using the simple ideas in this chapter, expanded with a little creativity, can lead to much more exciting and customized case mods.

Common Mods

By this point, you've gone over many of the issues and techniques related to case modding. You've even touched on a few mods here and there in passing, but nothing serious. It's now time to take the knowledge from the previous chapters and create a few mods.

The instructions presented in this chapter are by no means the only way to perform these mods—there are infinite ways to do them. But these instructions will get you started down the right path and allow you to branch out from there. Be creative, and if you think of a way to perform some mod that seems better for you than the technique presented here, go for it!

Creating a Case Window

By far the most common case mod these days is the classic case window. Many people think windows are too common now, with so many premod cases that come with windows preinstalled in them. The truth is the very same reason that case windows were popular years ago is still true today— there is simply no better way to show off all the money and hard work you've spent putting together your system than with a case window. The trick is to find ways to make the window special, one step above or beyond what comes in the premod cases.

Tip If you still need extra justification for a case window, remember that windows allow you to see the amount of dust build-up in your system. This lets you know when to clean it out before heat build-up leads to damaged components.

Using unique designs and just the right combination of other accessories such as window etchings can make a window that stands apart from the rest. But before focusing on all the details, you have to be familiar with the steps and common techniques for case windows. The place to start is with the general window design.

Window Design

When designing a window cutout, there are a few things to consider. The first and most important thing to keep in mind, especially if you want something unique, is what your general case design is going to be. Maybe you have a theme, such as a brick wall, that you can use to make the basic design. Even if you don't have a full theme in mind for the case, try to come up with a feel for your own sense of aesthetics for the case. Maybe you like clean, straight lines so a rectangular window would suit you best. Or maybe you like more rounded shapes and something a little more organic for the window.

Another important consideration is letting the case help you. Look at the case you will be working with. Are there obvious designs that would work well for the window? Are there already recessed areas that would make for a good window shape (see Figure 9-1)? While almost any design can be cut into a case, working against the natural flow of the case will complicate your work 1,000 percent.

Think about the inside of the side panel that the window will be cut into. The side panel will be mounted on the side of the case in some manner, probably using some metal teeth on the top and bottom and some screws in the rear, although some cases use plastic handles or other means to attach to the case. Keep in mind that the acrylic panel for the window will probably need to extend a little way past the cutout. Make sure that this will not interfere with the panel-mounting mechanism.

After measuring twice, cut once. In other words, after thinking about where the window should go in the case, make the cutout for the window. The options for how to cut the case window vary based on a number of factors, but remember that you are not restricted to just a single method. If the window design you chose is somewhat complex, for example, you may want to

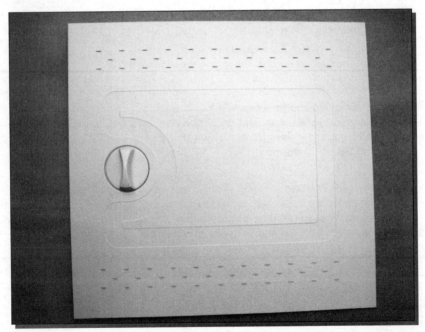

FIGURE 9-1: The recessed area of this case panel are an obvious place for cutting out a window.

make the major cuts with a jigsaw but add details using a rotary tool with some cutting discs. After the major cuts are done, don't forget to smooth the cuts with either a set of metal files or a sanding drum on a rotary tool.

Cross-Reference Chapter 5 contains information about the various tools you can use to cut your case, and some of their pros and cons.

Tip If you want to paint your case or side panel, remember not to start painting until after the window is cut. Painting before cutting a window makes little sense. The risk of damaging the paint during the cutting process is high, and the cutting process can deform the edges of the cut so that they are no longer smooth (thus destroying certain paint effects).

Attaching the Window

There are a number of different methods for attaching an acrylic window to the case panel itself. All these methods have some advantages and disadvantages, so it's really up to you how to get the look and feel you want.

Tip The type of acrylic panel you use really doesn't matter—they all work equally well for this application. Some people even use real glass for their windows, but that both significantly increases the weight and limits what type of work you can do with the panel because professional-grade tools are generally needed to cut and etch glass.

Window Molding

The oldest way to attach a window, popular in the early days of case windows (around 2000 and 2001), is window molding. The molding is an H-shaped piece of rubber that fits the window in one channel and the case panel in the other channel. It sometimes has an additional channel for another strip of rubber that helps to lock the window and case panel into the molding (see Figure 9-2).

Molding usually comes in black, but sometimes clear, chrome, or gold molding is available as well. The advantage of molding is that it helps hide a poor job of cutting the case window because the edges of the cut are obscured by the molding itself. However, the molding can be difficult to work with, and it requires a smaller window because part of the cutout is taken up by the molding itself. Prices vary, but molding typically costs $2 to $4 dollars a foot.

Silicone Glue

Another good option for attaching case windows is to use silicone glue. Any hardware store will have several types of silicone glue available in the plumbing section. If you use silicone glue under the obscured portions of clear plastic and the edges (see Figure 9-3), the window will be attached relatively securely. The advantages are that attaching a window this

FIGURE 9-2: Window attached with molding. The window is on the left, the locking strip is in the middle (not fully set in place), and the panel is on the right.

way is very easy and requires no means of attachment that is from the outside that could ruin the theme or effect you're going for. But on the downside, a good hit or too much pressure on the window itself can cause the glue to let go. A tube of silicone glue usually costs around $3.

Other Options

Some people use strips of Velcro to attach their windows as an even simpler alternative to glue. You place strips of Velcro on obscured areas of the window and the surrounding panel, and the window is attached. The main advantage is that this technique is easy enough for anyone to do. Another advantage is the ability to have different windows that you can quickly swap in and out (perhaps with different color acrylic or different window etchings). The downside is that the window isn't as strong as it could be, and it won't be flush with the surface of the case (letting dust and perhaps worse into the case). A couple of dollars will buy enough Velcro to attach a single window.

One more common method for attaching windows is to use either rivets or nuts and bolts to attach the window to the case. Such a connection is very strong and still removable in the case of nuts and bolts. However, these methods require making several holes around the edge of the window on the case panel, which can ruin a theme. A set of nuts and bolts will cost less than $5, but to use rivets you would need to purchase both a set of rivets and a cheap rivet gun. Together, the rivets and rivet gun should cost less than $25.

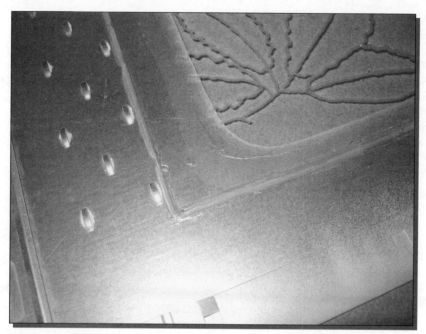

FIGURE 9-3: Window attached with silicone glue. With all the edges covered in silicone glue, not only does the window adhere to the panel but it also protects your hand from sharp edges.

What is the right method is entirely up to you. If you were going for a Frankenstein's monster type of look, using nuts and bolts or rivets would work fine with the theme. If you wanted something more organic, using glue so no visible blemishes show on the surface is probably the way to go. If you are making a case for a child, you might want to use Velcro so you can replace the case window with a new one (with a new window etching) every few months.

After you decide what method to use, cut out a piece of acrylic of the appropriate size. Remember, if you're using window molding to attach the window, the acrylic window will need to be a little smaller than the cutout you made. For all other methods, the acrylic window should be a little larger than the window cutout. Remember to double-check and make sure that the acrylic panel won't interfere with attaching the case panel to the case itself.

Before installing the window with one of these techniques, you should think about any additional enhancements or finishing touches that you may want to do to the window. In general, these are easier to do before the window is installed.

Finishing Touches

There are a number of things that can be done to spice up a window design. Not that a plain window is necessarily boring—it may be exactly what the theme of your case calls for. But there are additional steps that can enhance almost any window such as etchings, appliqués, and tinting.

Etchings

The most common addition to a window is a window etching. When you scratch the surface of the clear acrylic, the scratch will catch light better than the smooth portions of the acrylic and will seem to glow. The most common way to accomplish this is by using the etching attachment of a rotary tool to etch a design into the acrylic panel. In addition, some shops (such as www.koolpcmods.com) offer the ability to use a laser to etch designs in acrylic panels that have varying depths and look photorealistic. But you can do simple etchings yourself using a rotary tool.

To create your own etching, just follow these steps:

1. Come up with a design you want to etch. Remember to make it from simple lines, the fewer the better. Since the actual etching needs to be on the inside of the window, you will need to create a mirror image across the horizontal plane.

2a. The easiest method is to print use an image-editing program on the computer to flip the image horizontally and print it out.

2b. If using the computer isn't an option, you can create the mirror image by hand. Attach a regular piece of thin white paper over the original image. Using a black marker, trace over the original image. Don't be too light on the lines—you actually want the marker to soak all the way through the paper. When done, flip the paper over. Where the marker soaked all the way through the paper, you'll have a mirror image of the original.

Caution The original may be ruined by the marker soaking into it as well, so you might want to use a photocopy of the original.

3. Attach the mirror image to the piece of acrylic panel face down on the surface that will become the outside with masking tape.

4. Flip the acrylic panel over so that the opposite surface is facing you. You should be able to see the image through the acrylic panel. Using the etching attachment on a rotary tool, turn the tool on its lowest setting and gently trace over the lines (see Figure 9-4).

5. When you're done, brush away the extra bits of acrylic and remove the paper. Your etching is complete!

Tip If you move the rotary tool in the same direction as the rotation of the tool's shaft (toward yourself), the lines will be a little cleaner because the rotation of the tool helps clean up the edges of the etching.

FIGURE 9-4: Simple window etching. Note that the protective paper on the acrylic has only been removed from as small a section as possible.

Appliqués

If you want to go for something a little simpler, you can purchase appliqués for the window. These are nothing more than clear stickers with some frosted sections. These frosted sections also pick up the light similarly to a window etching. The prices vary, but they generally go for between $6 and $10.

A variation on case appliqués are EL appliqués. These use electroluminescent tape to create a multicolored lighted case appliqué. On the positive side, they are bright and attention grabbing and often incorporate sections that flash on and off. On the downside, they are expensive (around $25), and there are only a few different designs currently available. These EL appliqués, sometimes misnamed case badges, are available from many of the online modding stores (such as www.frozencpu.com or www.svc.com).

Tinting

Finally, there is a technique that is only occasionally used but can have dramatic effects in the right case. By using window-tinting material that is ordinarily used to tint windows in cars, you can create some great window designs. For example, using mirror-like window tinting on the inside of your case window makes the case look solid from the outside, but when you turn on an internal light (such as a cold cathode light), all the components inside the case suddenly become visible. Window tinting is available from most auto-parts stores for between $7 and $30 for enough material to do a few windows.

A Sample Case Window

The main thing to remember is not to limit yourself. You can use one of these techniques, a combination of these techniques, or some other ideas to enhance your window design. All in all, some interesting techniques not normally associated with case windows can be used to good effect with just a bit of thought.

In the following example of a case window (see Figure 9-5), I have employed some of the techniques discussed in this chapter. This is a standard window cutout with clear acrylic window. In addition to that, I have added a window etching of some leaves, but those alone were not enough to make it stand out from the crowd. I also glued some teardrop-shaped pieces of wood painted green around part of the cutout as fake leaves. To complete the image, I added a do-it-yourself sun-catcher with glow-in-the-dark elements. If I added a couple dual-green and UV cold cathode lights in the case with some UV green wire sleeving, this window might really come to life.

Expanding the Concept

Having seen how a standard case window is created, including the bells and whistles that can be added, what else is left? A lot. While a standard case window is placed on the removable case panel on the left side of a case, there is no reason to limit yourself to that location.

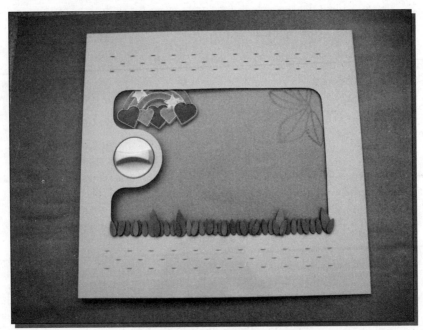

FIGURE 9-5: Sample case window combining some typical techniques with a few uncommon techniques.

Case windows of one sort or another can be placed in several locations. In addition, windows are not limited to just cases but can be applied to peripherals as well.

Windows in Other Components

Some of the peripherals in your system can be modded with windows, including hard drives, optical drives, and power supplies. As you might expect, the difficulty of these mods is a little greater because of the tight spaces and delicate nature of the components, but the effect can be truly great.

The easiest component to add a window to is probably the power supply. All that is required to add a window to a power supply is to open the power supply up, cut an appropriate hole in the top cover, lay an acrylic panel over the hole, and close it back up.

 Caution Remember that power supplies, even when disconnected from the wall, can still carry voltages powerful enough to kill. Don't touch any of the components (especially capacitors) when opening the power supply.

 Tip When adding a window to a power supply, use silicone glue to attach the window. Velcro has the potential to catch fire, and bolts or rivets could add some additional height to the power supply case making it difficult to put the power supply back in the computer.

Optical drives are slightly more difficult to add a window to. The basic idea is the same—remove the top cover, cut a hole, cover it with acrylic, and close the drive back up. But there are extra concerns when working with optical drives. Each optical drive is a little different, but many actually use the top cover as part of the mounting mechanism for the media, so be sure that no internal components will be rendered inoperable by the window cutout. Also, the thickness of the acrylic panel can sometimes cause a problem so be sure to get the thinnest acrylic possible and make sure that the addition of the acrylic won't cause a problem.

Finally, one of the more difficult mods is adding a window to a hard drive. When successful, hard drive window installations offer exciting visuals as the hard drive read/write heads move wildly all over the disk surface. This mod is also very dangerous and prone to error, since too much dust or fingerprints inside the drive can render it inoperable.

The procedure for modding a hard drive with a window is simple:

1. Open the hard drive in a dust-free environment.

 Tip For a dust-free environment, some people run the shower on hot in a closed bathroom for a few minutes. The humidity in the air actually causes the dust particles in the air to settle to the ground. Just don't make the room too humid—hard drives don't like water either.

2. Place everything except the top cover for the hard drive in some airtight container such as a Tupperware container. You could also use a large plastic zip-lock bag, but the bag itself might touch the platters or the head, which should be avoided.

3. Cut out a section of the top cover, and smooth out the cuts.

4. Cut a matching piece of thin acrylic panel and glue it in place with a good amount of silicone-based glued.

5. Go back to the dust-free environment and reattach the top piece to the drive itself. Make sure that the acrylic isn't touching the platter or the read/write head. If it does, find a thinner material for the window. The hard drive won't work if anything touches the platters or the read/write head.

6. Test the drive in your computer. Make sure to format the drive, and run several passes of reading and writing data throughout the entire drive to find any problems.

7. Done!

This process can be somewhat error prone. In general, only drives that run below 7,200 rpm have ever been successfully modded with a window. Some drives also don't have the space inside for even a thin sheet of acrylic. A few drives also use the center of the top cover as an additional stability point for the spinning platters, and removing that metal can disrupt the functioing of the drives. But modding is about being adventurous, and small 1-GB drives can be found cheaply at many places, so give it a shot! Just don't try this on a drive that contains critical data.

Alternate Case Window Locations

On a standard tower case, the left side panel is where windows typically go. The front is usually completely full with all your optical drives, buttons, and sometimes an air inlet for a fan. The back has all the ports for the motherboard and PCI cards. But the top and the right side are just flat pieces of metal. These may seem like strange locations for a window, and the applications are more limited, but they certainly can be used for windows as well. Also note that a window in the top of the case is an excellent way of showing off the windows you put into your power supply or optical drive.

While creating a window on the top of the case is somewhat straightforward, putting a window on the right side of the case presents some interesting problems. In most cases, the space between the panel the motherboard is attached to and the right side of the case is only about 1 cm. How can a window here show anything interesting? It's easy with a little imagination.

A regular window wouldn't be interesting here because all you would see through a window here in most cases would be a bare piece of metal that has the motherboard attached to the other side. Don't use a full-sized window on the right side of the case, but instead use a smaller window intended to highlight something. Put a picture of some sort on the inside of the window. Take some old circuit boards and attach them underneath small windows exposing the fake electronics. Even put an oil painting there.

Because right-side windows are rarely used in case mods, this is one more area in which you can customize your case and make it a little more extraordinary.

Making Blowholes

Heat build-up is a common problem in all computers, hence the need for fans and heatsinks. One problem rarely addressed in stock cases is the heat build-up from the optical drives and the top right-hand corner of the motherboard (often the location of the system memory). One way to combat this problem is with a top-mounted blowhole.

A *blowhole* is nothing more than a hole in the top of the case with a fan mounted on it to help expel the hot air out of the case. While it would seem that the majority of the heat in the case would be exhausted out the rear of the case, anyone who has a blowhole on their system can attest to the fact that the air coming out of the system at the top is quite warm. Without a blowhole, that heated air would be trapped in the system.

1. The first order of business when creating a blowhole is to measure, measure, and measure again. Remove all the components from the case except for the power supply and the topmost optical drive. Test fit your fan on the inside and visually inspect the area to make sure that there is space between the optical drive and the power supply, especially with all the cables attached to both.

2. If it looks like there will be space, cover the top center of the case with masking tape.

3. Measure the proper distance from both the back of the case and the front of the case to account for the power supply and optical drive. Find the exact center of the remaining space front to back and the exact center side to side of this area and mark it with a pen or marker.

4. Remove all the components from the case.

5. Find a hole saw with approximately the same diameter as the fan you are using (probably an 80-mm fan is best, but there may be space for something larger). Cut the hole using a hole saw, remembering that drilling a pilot hole first will make the job easier.

 Cross-Reference Chapter 5 discusses the use of hole saws, plus other methods of making holes in your case.

6. Once the hole is cut, take a fan guard and lay it across the hole in the direction that you want it to go. Mark the four holes for mounting the fan guard with a pen or marker.

7. Remove the fan guard and drill those four holes using a $3/16$ drill bit (approximately).

8a. Now clean up the large hole. Using either a sanding drum on a rotary tool or a round file, smooth the edges of the hole till it feels somewhat smooth.

8b. (Optional) if the hole itself just doesn't look professional enough, consider picking up some auto-trim molding. The molding itself is shaped like a C or an L and comes in a variety of colors, such as black, gold, and chrome. Using the adhesive backing you can get it to conform to the edges of the blowhole and it makes the cut look much cleaner.

FIGURE 9-6: Blowhole with chrome molding.

9. Finally, attach the fan from underneath the hole. Using some long screws with matching nuts, attach the fan from the inside of the case and a fan guard on top of the case (see Figure 9-6). Put everything back in the case and hook up power to the fan.

Tip If you use window molding, you may find that fan guards don't fit over the molding so well. You can use extra nuts to raise the height of the fan guard so that it goes over the molding.

Stealthing Optical Drives

One common complaint among modders is that the front of their optical drives don't match the general look of the front of their cases. Because modern operating systems can instruct the optical drives to open and close on their own, many modders hide or "stealth" their optical drives by replacing the front faceplate of the drive with the empty drive bay inserts that come with their cases. The downside is the lack of an eject button or activity light, but that really isn't a problem because modern operating systems provide other eject options.

Caution

This guide only refers to tray-loading optical drives. While drive stealthing is still possible with slot-loading drives, the mod is far more complex and involves fabricating some sort of hinged panel that can rotate out of the way.

It turns out this mod is a pretty simple one. All that is required is an empty drive bay insert, the optical drive itself, some hot glue, and perhaps some spare pieces of plastic or wood. This mod really does help to clean up the look of your drives, and can be a great fall-back plan if your painting experiment on the front of your optical drive went very, very wrong.

The process of stealthing your drives is simple:

1. First, you need to prepare the pieces for the mod itself. Take an empty drive insert and cut off all the little tabs that hold the insert in place in your case (see Figure 9-7).

2. Remove the optical drive from your computer and hook it up to your test power supply. Turn on the power and eject the drive tray, then remove the drive from the power connector.

3. Remove the front piece on the drive tray and remove the front panel of the drive itself. Both front pieces are removed a little differently on each drive. Generally the front of

FIGURE 9-7: Drive bay insert with one tab cut off and one tab still in place.

the drive tray is held in place by a couple of plastic tabs underneath the tray and the front of the drive is held in place by several tabs around the perimeter of the drive itself.

4a. With most drives, the front piece of the drive tray is a flat surface—but not on all drives. If the piece is flat, reattach it to the drive tray.

4b. If the front piece is not flat, you will have to fabricate an additional piece to help the drive bay insert stick out from the drive the right amount. You can use almost any type of material for this, such as styrene plastic or wood, and attach it to the drive tray with hot glue (see Figure 9-8).

5. Now, reapply power to the drive and close the drive tray. Place the drive back into the drive bay (not attached to the computer) but back further than normal.

6. Using hot glue, cover the edge of the drive tray (either the front tray faceplate or the fabricated panel) with hot glue. Quickly attach the drive bay panel to the surface with the hot glue. Allow the hot glue to cool for five minutes or so.

Tip   You may want or need to remove both the audio jacks and the power/activity LED from the front of the optical drive. Test fit the drive bay panel against the front of the drive before applying glue to see it the audio jacks or the various LEDs cause any problems.

FIGURE 9-8: Extra plastic attached to the front of the drive tray.

FIGURE 9-9: Stealthed drive with the drive tray open.

7. Now you can test the drive by screwing the mounting brackets in place so the front of the drive sits flush with the front of the case. Attach all the cables to the drive, such as power and IDE cables, and boot up the system. Using the operating system, eject the drive and try closing it several times to check the alignment of the drive (see Figure 9-9).

8. Tighten the mounting screws for the drive to secure it in place.

Changing Mouse LEDs

Optical mice are nice components, much better than mechanical mice from years ago. They function by using a very bright red LED and an optical sensor that works like a small digital camera. The mouse uses the LED's light to take pictures of the surface the mouse is sitting on, and by comparing those pictures to one another the mouse can tell if it's moving and what direction it was moved in. The one problem with these mice is the color of the LED—red. If your entire computer was put together with a color scheme with anything other than red, the mouse sticks out like a sore thumb. But that can all be changed.

The first step in changing the mouse LED color is finding the right type of LED to use. As you might recall, LED brightness is measured in something called MCD. You want to find an LED in the color you want with the highest MCD you can find (at least in the several thousand range). Mice generally can deal with a wide range of LED voltages, so it's not too important to pay attention to the voltage needs of the LED as long as it's a typical 5-mm ultrabrite LED. These usually cost around $2 per LED, but some cheap sources for LEDs do exist (for example, www.lsdiodes.com).

Tip — Ultrabrite LEDs are available in many colors such as red, green, blue, amber, yellow, white, and UV. Other colors are also available but are much harder to find.

Once you have secured the right LED, to replace your mouse LED:

1. Open up your mouse. Each mouse is a little different, but generally they are held together with a few screws and some sort of plastic tabs. After the mouse is open, remove the scroll wheel (if present).

2. Remove the circuit board from the bottom plastic piece. Removing the circuit board from the plastic bottom is a little different on each mouse—some use screws and some just use plastic tabs. Also note that after removing the circuit board you will find a clear plastic lens that was sitting underneath the board. It's important not to get scratches on the lens.

3. Now that the circuit board is free, you will notice that there is a plastic shroud covering the LED itself and the top of the sensor chip (see Figure 9-10). This plastic piece is

FIGURE 9-10: Optical mouse circuit board with LED shroud still attached.

usually black, but in some cases it's clear. Remove this piece by gently lifting up on the plastic piece that sits over the chip and pushing on the two plastic mounting pins near the back underside of the circuit board. Once the plastic piece is at about a 45-degree angle, you can remove it by pulling forward and unlatching a tab on this cover that holds onto the LED itself (some mice have this latch, some do not). This should expose the LED.

4. Heat up your desoldering iron and remove the LED on the circuit board.

Cross-Reference Chapter 7 contains all the procedures and tips you need to successfully solder and desolder.

5. Take your new LED and place the leads through the holes the old LED was in. Now take this bare circuit board over to your computer (which should already be on). Lay the circuit board down on something nonconductive (wood, plastic, etc.) and plug the USB or PS2 cable into your computer while putting some slight pressure sideways on the LED with your finger so that the leads from the LED touch the side of the holes they are mounted in. If the LED lights up (don't look directly into the LED itself), simply mark the right lead of the LED with a marker pen. If the LED doesn't light up, unplug the mouse and reverse the LED. Then, try the same procedure again. Eventually, you should be able to figure out which lead from the LED is the one on the right. Unplug the mouse from the computer.

6. Heat up your soldering iron. Before soldering you new LED in place, measure the length of the leads on the new LED and cut them to the same length as those of the old LED. Now solder the LED in place, remembering to solder it in using the same lead orientation that you tested previously.

Tip When soldering the new LED in place, make sure that you don't accidentally connect two other leads on the circuit board. Also, make sure that you use the same orientation for the LED that you identified earlier.

7. Now, reassemble the mouse the way you took it apart. Put the plastic shroud back on the LED and bend it back into position. Put the circuit board back into the mouse shell (remember to put the clear lens underneath the circuit board first, of course). Replace the scroll wheel. Close it all up with whatever screws were holding the mouse together.

8. Test your mouse out by plugging it back into your computer. If all went well, you now have a mouse with whatever color light you wanted. If it doesn't work, unplug it from the computer immediately and start over from the beginning to find the problem and correct it.

Creating a Bay Bus

Years ago, if you wanted to help silence your computer there were few options. One option that did exist, however, was to run the fans in the system at half-speed by supplying 7 volts to them instead of the 12 volts they typically ran on. Some adventurous people wired up their fans to switches so that they could either turn the fans completely off, run them at half-speed (7 volts), or full speed (12 volts). Since these switches were typically mounted in an empty drive bay, the term "bay bus" came to be used to describe these devices (or sometimes "fan bus").

These days, more elaborate devices called fan controllers are available with more features. But that does not mean that the bay bus is dead. Simple bay bus devices can be used to control general-purpose components such as fans, lights, or other cool accessories on the system. Creating such a bay bus is actually one of the more simple wiring jobs for a mod.

Chapter 2 contains information about fan controllers of all sorts.

For this example, you will create a general-purpose bay bus that can switch the power on or off to devices that require a regular Molex connector. You will need all the following components for this mod:

- **Switches**—You will need a few nonmomentary dual-pole dual-throw (DPDT) switches, although you could also use triple-pole and/or triple-throw switches. You will need as many switches as devices you want to control, but for a typical drive bay five switches work out nicely. These vary widely in price from $0.99 to $3.99 each (or even more).

- **Male and female Molex connectors**—You will need one female Molex connector (with associated wires) and as many male connectors as you have switches.

- **LEDs, LED holders, and resistors**—This is not a necessity, but indicator lights for on/off status are nice. Therefore, you will need as many of each of these as you have switches. Get the right resistor for the LED you purchase, planning on a 5-volt power source for the LED.

Chapter 4 contains instructions for calculating the right resistor values for an LED.

- **Liquid electrical tape**—This is a liquid latex rubber compound that you brush on bare metal connections. When it dries, it forms a thick coating that insulates the metal connection and prevents short circuits. It comes in several colors and any can be used for this project, but avoid the clear color because it's difficult to see any spots you missed when working with the clear liquid. Liquid electrical tape can be somewhat hard to find, but some auto-parts stores carry it. It should cost less than $10 a can.

■ **Empty drive bay panel**—You did save all the extra ones that came with your case, right?

To create a bay bus, follow these steps:

1. Start the process by preparing the empty drive bay panel. Drill five evenly spaced holes across the center of the panel the same diameter as the switches. Above that, drill holes for the LEDs, remembering that to use an LED holder the hole drilled must be a little bigger than the LED itself.

2. Mount all the switches, LED holders, and LEDs in the holes (see Figure 9-11).

3. Take the female Molex connector and cut all four wires so that they are approximately 8 inches long. Remove one of the pins connected to one of the blade wires on the connector and discard it. Take the male Molex connectors and cut all wires in all the connectors to equal lengths, at least $1^1/_2$ inches long.

Tip If you trace all the black wires on the Molex connectors back into the power supply, you will find that they are all connected to the same location. This means that you can use any of the black wires interchangeably. The only limitation is the gauge of the wires, which limits the number of amps the wire can carry.

FIGURE 9-11: Front of a simple bay bus with five switches and five indicator lights.

4. Starting 3 inches down from the female Molex connector, strip a small section about $1/4$ inch long on the black wire. Place the exposed section of wire next to the bottom terminals of the first switch and measure the distance to the terminals of the next switch. Strip a small section of wire at that point, and continue this process till the final switch, and cut off any excess wire. If you are using triple-throw switches, you may need to strip a $1/2$-inch section of wire so that the exposed wire touches all the terminals.

5. Perform this same type of striping operation with both the yellow and red wires as well, except strip a section approximately $1/8$ inch long for both wires no matter what type of switch you use.

6. Take the black wire from the female Molex connector, and solder the wire at all the exposed sections to all the bottom terminals on the switches.

Cross-Reference   See Chapter 7 for information on soldering.

7. Take the short leg of each LED and wrap it around or through one of the top terminals on each switch. Solder that connection in place, and cut off any excess.

8. Cut one lead from each resistor to about $1/4$ inch, and cut the remaining lead of the LED the same distance. Solder the leg of newly shortened LED lead to the shortened lead on each resistor. Cover the resistor and the LED connection with heat-shrink tubing.

9. Now you can start attaching the male Molex connectors. If you're using double-throw switches, solder both black wires from the male Molex connectors to the remaining top terminal on the switches. If you're using triple throw switches, solder one black wire from the male Molex connectors to one terminal on the switches, and solder the other black wire to the other terminal.

10. Now, solder the red wire from each Molex connector to the exposed area of the red wire on the female Molex connector.

11. Cut the long lead from each resistor so that you can wrap it around the exposed areas of the red wire from the female Molex connector, and solder it in place.

12. At this point, you may want to check the functionality of the device with your multimeter and test power supply. Make sure that the unattached wires (the yellow ones) are kept out of the way or cover them with electrical tape temporarily. Plug the device into your test power supply and throw the switches—the LEDs should light up, and your multimeter should show 5 volts when attached to the red and black wires in the male Molex connectors.

13. Now, you have to insulate the connections to avoid a short circuit. Remove the device from the test power supply and use the liquid electrical tape to cover the exposed connections on the red wire(s). Brush it on the exposed areas in thick layers, and wait for it

to dry overnight. If any areas look thin or are not completely covered, go over them again with another layer of liquid electrical tape.

Caution

The fumes from liquid electrical tape can be pretty strong. Make sure to have adequate ventilation, and try not to breathe the fumes for too long at one sitting.

14. Finally, finish up by soldering the yellow wire from each male Molex connector to the exposed areas on the yellow wire from the female Molex connector.

15. Again, you may want to test the device at this point to make sure that you have 12 volts between the yellow wire and the black wire on each male Molex connector.

16. Cover the connections on the yellow wire with liquid electrical tape as well.

17. To finish off the device, you may want to use a number of cable ties to clean up the wiring (see Figure 9-12). Also, hold the completed panel up to a light bulb. If you can see light around the LED holders, you may want to cover the back of the LEDs and LED holders with a thin layer of the liquid electrical tape.

That's the basic technique to create a simple bay bus. But don't limit yourself to using this technique to create a bay bus in an empty drive bay. Instead of using of an entire drive bay in

FIGURE 9-12: The rear of the completed bay bus, showing cable ties and using TPTT switches.

your computer, try creating the bay bus into the front bezel of the case itself. Depending on the theme of your case, you might be able to cleverly integrate a bay bus into the theme and overall flow of the case without using up a drive bay.

Multiple Hard Drive Activity Lights

One common mod is to replace the LED for hard drive (HD) activity with a different-colored LED. But what if you want to use several LEDs to show activity, or need to control something else based on hard drive activity? The problem is that the activity header on the motherboard doesn't carry enough voltage or current to control anything other than a single LED. The solution is to use an optoisolator such as the 4N27 (available at most electronics dealers for under a dollar).

An optoisolator consists of a matched LED and phototransistor integrated into a plastic package. When the LED is turned on, the light shines on the phototransistor. The phototransistor then becomes conductive, allowing current to pass through.

In the sample circuit (see Figure 9-13), power from the HD header enters the optoisolator activating the integrated LED. When the LED is lighted, the phototransistor picks up the signal and allows current to pass from the 5-volt power supply to the next pin. On that pin, say that there is a resistor and then a couple of LEDs in parallel, which are then connected to ground. However, this is just an example. Any circuit that you want can be hooked up to the pin below the 5-volt power supply pin.

If there is any doubt about whether the HD activity header puts out enough power for your application, or if there is the chance of too much power being drawn from the HD header, use one of these circuits.

Tip Many different optoisolators are available, and all function somewhat the same. Read through the specs and example circuit diagrams of an optoisolator, and you are sure to find several that will work for most case-mod applications.

Wrapping Up

This chapter covered some of the most common mods done to computer cases. Windows, blowholes, stealthed drives, and more are all well-known mods in the modding community.

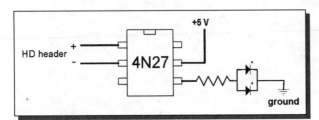

FIGURE 9-13: Circuit diagram showing sample use of an optoisolator.

But don't let that discourage you from trying them yourself. You have to start somewhere, and any of these are good places to start. As long as you take your time and perform these mods with precision and an eye for detail, no one can criticize you.

If you have accomplished even half of these mods (with a little creativity of your own), your system should be pretty unique by now. But don't stop here. Come up with some of your own ideas for mods you would like to see and take a stab at creating them.

Advanced Skills

Presented here are a few more topics that can help you in creating an awe-inspiring case mod. These are by no means every technique, because there are an infinite number of methods that you can use for making a great case mod. Instead, these are a few more well-known methods for improving your case mod.

Using some of these techniques is an additional way to make your case mod into a case you can be proud to show off.

Noise Reduction Techniques

Everyone loves the gentle soothing hum emitted by modern computers, right? Of course not. The sound from the fans that most high-end computers use can be very loud and annoying. Reducing these sounds can be a tricky process though, so some tips will help.

The most important first step is to identify where the sounds are coming from so that you can work on reducing them one by one. Once you have exhausted all those possibilities, if the computer is still louder than you want, you can move on to more elaborate techniques.

By simply putting you ear next to the computer with the panels removed and listening, you should be able to identify which components are making the most noise. The following sections look at the noisy culprits in detail.

Don't Forget the Basics

With all the emphasis on specialty components, cutting larger holes for increased airflow, and reducing power to make fan operate more quietly, sometimes it's easy to overlook the simple reasons why a computer may be loud.

Back in the early years of computers, even before Microsoft even existed, computer memory was expensive compared to hard drive space (this is still true, but less so). Some smart computer scientists came up with a way to use space on the hard drive as a (much) slower but cheaper form of memory. This is referred to as swap space, a swap file, or a page file.

When physical memory gets all used up, less used bits of data in memory are moved to the disk to make room for new data. This action is called swapping or paging.

When doing swapping or paging, the computer has to wait for the (relatively) slow hard drive to write all the data from memory or read it back into memory if it's needed again. During this time the computer will seem sluggish, and if your hard drive is even somewhat noisy (and 99.9 percent are), the computer will seem loud as the heads on the hard drive move back and forth to read or write the data.

Something like this cannot be solved adequately by adding more fans, or even by getting a less noisy hard drive (although that helps somewhat). The real answer is to buy more actual memory to reduce the amount of time the computer spends swapping or paging.

Modding is a great tool to solve many problems, but modding alone cannot solve every problem.

Low-Noise Components

First and foremost, when trying to lower the noise of a computer you need to pick the right components. There are a lot of different hard drives, power supplies, and graphics cards out there, and one of the key differences among the various models is the noise they produce.

Overall, water cooling is the way to go if you want a silent computer. If you're using water cooling, you make a trade-off between the sound of several fans cooling the case and the sound of the pump and possibly a fan cooling the radiator. Because water is such an efficient cooling mechanism, the trade-off almost always comes out in favor of water cooling.

Tip

There are other options for silent computers, such as some of the mini-ITX boards from VIA that operate completely fanlessly. However, for anything but Web surfing or playing a few MP3s, these fanless computers are inadequate due to the slower processor speed required for fanless operation.

Power Supplies

One area of concern, whether or not you use water cooling, is the power supply. While the usual concerns for power supplies are how many watts the device supplies and how many connectors it has, the sound it makes is just as important. A modem power supply always has at least one fan and often two. Those fans come in several different sizes and, consequently, many different sound levels. Some manufacturers, such as Vantec, Zalman, Antec, and others, specifically make low-noise power supplies. These low-noise power supplies utilize a number of techniques such as external heatsinks and autoadjusting temperature-sensing fans to lower their noise to the bare minimum. If you are concerned with noise, a low-noise power supply will cost more but is worth the investment.

Pricewise, low-noise power supplies range from around $100 to $200. This is nearly double what a similar non-low-noise power supply costs.

It is possible to water cool a power supply, but this is a rarely done mod and requires extensive modification to the power supply itself, including fabricating custom water blocks for the power regulators in the power supply. Pumping water directly next to components that carry AC voltage at high current is more than a little dangerous.

Hard Drives and Optical Drives

Another area that can't be avoided is the hard drive. Water-cooling kits exist for hard drives, but they only help with the heat that hard drives generate, not with the noise. To help lower the noise that a hard drive generates, first you have to understand the nature of the noise. Hard drives generate noise from three different sources: noise from head movement, noise from the center spindle, and noise from vibration against the case.

The noise from the movement of the drive read/write head might be fixable. Depending on the exact make and model of the drive, some manufacturers offer utilities that can modify the function of the firmware in the drive itself to lower and raise the noise output. This is called acoustic management. In the acoustic management software/firmware (if your drive has such a feature), you can tune the drive for slightly faster performance and slightly more noise or for slightly degraded performance but less noise output. This will help with the scratching noise you hear when a hard drive is seeking for data.

The sound from the center spindle as it rotates the internal platters in the drive cannot be adjusted. The best advice is to read online reviews of drives and preferably listen to the drive operate, if that is an option, before purchase. Some drives simply make more noise than others, and the general pitch of the noise can be more or less irritating, depending on your personal preference.

Finally, vibration from the hard drive can sometimes be transmitted to the case causing noise. This is an easy fix. Place rubber grommets (available at any hardware store) between the hard drive and the case where the hard drive attaches to case. This will help minimize the vibration transferred to the case itself and lower the noise.

As for optical drives, the best option once again is to read reviews and listen to the drives themselves, if that is an option. When listening for noise, remember that different activities such as reading or writing can generate different amounts of noise. Also note that different media can change the noise output. For example, DVD reading might be quiet, while CD reading might be noisy.

Heatsinks and Fans

Assuming that you are staying with air cooling for your computer, when selecting a heatsink and fan for the CPU pay attention to the noise rating of the fan. Something like the Zalman CNPS7000 series offers a large surface area and a large, slower-moving fan to help things keep cool. While the best performance comes from faster-moving fans, larger and slower fans will generate less noise.

Related to the CPU heatsink and fan problems are problems with the video card. Most modern video cards use some sort of fan and heatsink combo to cool themselves, because the heat they generate has gone beyond what most passive heatsinks can deal with. But card manufacturers are interested in the bottom line and how much money they can make from each card, so

FIGURE 10-1: Fan-fitting rubber gasket. This gasket covers the entire outer frame of the fan rather than just the screw holes.

cooling systems are designed around the bare minimum for both performance and cost. Any good online modding store will carry several different types of high-performance cooling solutions for video cards, from large monster heatsinks to improved fan and heatsink designs. Just be careful with your purchase, because these cooling solutions are often designed for a small range of cards or have other restrictions such as requiring additional empty PCI slots around the video card. These coolers for video cards range from $5 for a few small heatsinks to $50 for massive pieces of metal that completely surround the video card.

The advice about using a larger, slower-moving fan on the CPU heatsink applies to all the fans in the case. For noise purposes, it's better to have more fans at a lower noise level than a single fan at a higher noise level. In addition, the fans themselves can generate the same type of vibration noise that a hard drive can generate. The solution is also the same—just use some rubber grommets at the screw holes to minimize the vibration transfer (see Figure 10-1).

Fan controllers, especially automatic ones, also help minimize the noise from fans. The type of fan itself, as discussed in Chapter 2, contributes greatly to the amount of noise generated. Purchasing cheap fans for your case is never a good idea. You always pay the price in the shorter lifespan of the fans and the increased noise they make.

Sound Absorption Materials

If you exhaust all the options for trying to get the right components for your case, and your computer still sounds a little too much like the flight deck of an aircraft carrier, there are a few more things you can do to try and deaden the noise. The most useful technique is using special material designed to absorb sound.

The idea behind all these materials, more or less, is the same. In a normal room (or case) sound waves are emitted from a source and travel outward, bouncing off walls cleanly, and ultimately ending up at your ears. If you have ever seen pictures of a recording studio, you have probably have noticed that the walls are covered in a strange spiky foam material. The idea behind this material is that when the sound waves hit the surface, they don't bounce back but instead are absorbed and dissipated by the material.

Tip The problem of sound waves bouncing around until they reach your ears is even worse with computers than you might think. With all the sound waves bouncing around inside the computer, the side panels of the computer case vibrate and actually act like speakers, sending out noise in every direction. So, not only do the original sound waves cause noise, but the sides of your case actually act as amplifiers.

In a nutshell, materials that are solid actually conduct sound through themselves. Materials that have open space inside them, such as foam rubber, do not conduct sound well. So use foamlike materials as barriers between solid surfaces whenever possible.

Several manufacturers such as Dynamat and Akasa sell material designed for quieting computers. Applying these materials takes little more than peeling back a self-adhesive strip and attaching the material to as many of the inside surfaces of the case as you can. But be mindful or causing any electrical shorts (especially with Dynamat since the material contains an aluminum strip). These specialty materials usually range in price from $20 to $50 for enough material to fit an average case.

A cheaper alternative to using specialty materials is to get some foam striping from an automotive store. Listen to your case and try to identify the source of the noise. Assuming that you have used rubber grommets to attach the hard drives and optical drives first, try applying the foam striping around the sides of the optical drives near the front faceplate to eliminate any rattling from there. Use more of the foam on the inside between the side panel and the case itself.

Plugging Unwanted Holes

Sometimes a case may have a number of holes that you don't want anymore, such as extra vent holes or the locations of LEDs that you have relocated to another place. The best way to fill these holes is by using a substance called Bondo, available in several different forms from any auto-parts store. A small can of Bondo usually costs around $7, which includes both the filler and the hardener (these two substances must be mixed together).

Bondo, in all its forms, is nothing more than a gooey substance that hardens once its two parts have been mixed. It's commonly used to repair dents and holes in cars, so it's definitely able to bond to metal and most plastics. It can take some amount of flex, but too much and it will crack. It's not a miracle substance—it's best when used to fill small holes, just about the size of a pencil eraser. For larger holes, first cover the hole with some other material such as metal mesh so that the Bondo has something to cling to.

The procedure for using Bondo is actually quite simple:

1. Start the work by preparing the surface. This means any large open areas should be covered with metal mesh, permanently attached. Also, sand the surface with rough sandpaper, something like 100 grit, to give the Bondo something to cling to.

2. There are several different types of Bondo, but it's best to start with standard body filler. Following the instructions on the can, mix the right proportions of the hardener and the filler material. You can also mix based on color—many cans of Bondo (those that include both the filler and the hardener) contain a plastic spatula molded in the same salmon color as the properly mixed Bondo.

Tip   A coffee-can plastic lid makes an excellent surface for mixing Bondo. The Bondo will peel off the surface easily when dry.

3. Next apply the Bondo across the surface of the area with the holes you are trying to fill. Use multiple layers and smooth the Bondo across the surface somewhat (see Figure 10-2).

FIGURE 10-2: Bondo applied across vent holes in a case panel. The holes are only about half a centimeter wide, easily small enough for Bondo to cover. Note the uncovered holes on the left.

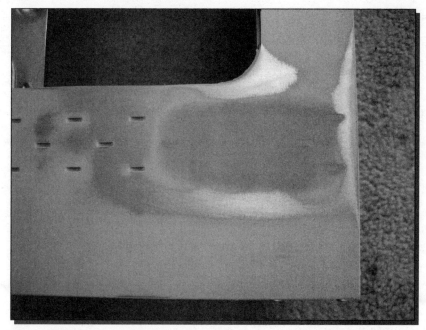

FIGURE **10-3: The sanded case panel. Remember to use a sanding block (similar to when sanding as part of the painting process) to keep the sanded surface flat.**

After the Bondo dries (see the instructions for approximate drying times), you can move on to sanding. Be aware that in most cases, you only have three or four minutes to mix the Bondo and apply it before it starts to harden.

4. Now, sand the surface with various grits of sandpaper. Start with something very abrasive, such as 100 grit and move on to 200- and 300-grit paper. Rinse the surface off once it feels smooth, and look for any holes or rough areas.

5. If you find a few, you can use Bondo spot putty (available in the same places as the Bondo, usually for under $5) to go over the small areas. The spot putty comes as a tube of premixed material and has a bit smoother texture to it. Once the spot putty dries, sand the surface and check for rough spots again (see Figure 10-3).

Sanding Bondo generates a lot of nasty dust. Using a respirator or filter of some sort is highly recommended.

6. Once everything looks and feels good, use some primer to go over the area (see Figure 10-4). If you find some areas that still don't look even (primer sometimes allows

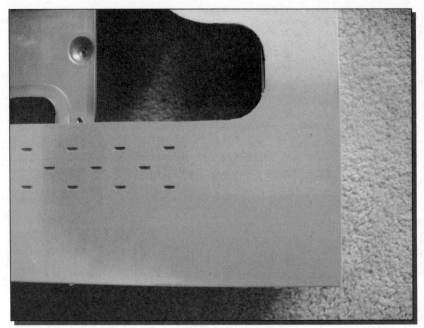

FIGURE **10-4: The case panel after a bit of primer. Hard to tell the holes were there!**

you to see things you didn't catch before), sand the area and start again with the Bondo spot putty.

7. Once everything looks and feels smooth with the primer, you can apply paint over the Bondo and primer.

Working with Acrylic Plastics

Acrylic is such a useful material for case modding that it deserves a little more discussion on some of the finer points of working with it. As you already know, it's cheap and easily available (and clear), but that is just the beginning of its capabilities.

Chapter 5 contains a discussion of common case materials, including acrylic.

Like metal, acrylic can be formed to arbitrary shapes with a bit of work. Unlike metal, acrylic pieces can be joined using only glue. Let's look at these properties, and the ability to remove scratches, in detail.

Removing Scratches

You already learned about smoothing the edges of acrylic pieces in Chapter 5, but the same technique can also be used to remove scratches in acrylic pieces. In most instances, the best result is had from just cutting a new piece of acrylic and starting over. But if you have just spent 10 hours etching an intricate design into the acrylic, starting over certainly doesn't sound like a good option.

Tip If the initial scratch is over 1 mm deep, you really have no choice other than starting over. Even if you did sand and polish enough to remove the scratches, the surface of the acrylic would be noticeably uneven.

The process is simple, if time-consuming:

1. Start the process by dry sanding the area with 1,000-grit sandpaper in circular motions to remove the acrylic around the scratch itself and make the surface somewhat smooth to the touch.

2. Repeat the process using 1,500- or 2,000-grit sandpaper, but use water this time. Make sure to cover every area that the 1,000-grit sandpaper touched.

3. Finally, use a polishing agent such as Novus #2 and a clean terrycloth towel to remove all the fine scratches left by the sandpaper.

4. (Optional) if this process isn't enough to remove all the sandpaper scratches, use Novus #3 and then Novus #2 after that.

The acrylic piece should be clear once again and without the scratch.

Joining Pieces

There are a couple of ways to join acrylic panels together. The first, and most obvious, way is to use nuts and bolts through holes to hold everything together. This is the method most often employed in clear acrylic cases. The second method is to use special acrylic glue that "melts" the pieces together into one larger piece.

Using nuts and bolts is the easiest way to secure two pieces of acrylic together, but obviously this won't work with pieces that are extremely small. One technique used to assemble some of the acrylic cases for sale is to use acrylic cubes as junction points for the acrylic panels. For example, say you wanted to join two flat sheets of acrylic at right angles to each other. Using a drill bit designed for plastic, drill all the way through the center of an acrylic cube, then flip the cube over 90 degrees and drill all the way through the cube, but slightly offset so that the two holes do not intersect. Drill a hole in the corner of one acrylic panel and use some nuts and bolts to attach the cube to that side. Now drill a hole through the other acrylic panel so that you can use some nuts and bolts to secure the panel to the other side of the acrylic cubes (see Figure 10-5). Repeat the process in the other corner where the two acrylic panels meet, and you have a secure right-angle connection between two sheets of acrylic.

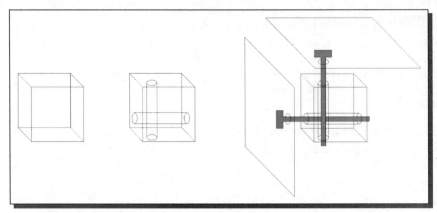

FIGURE 10-5: On the left is a plain acrylic cube. In the center is the same acrylic cube with a couple of nonintersecting holes drilled through it. On the right is the same cube with a couple of sheets of acrylic held together using bolts through the panels and the cube.

Tip

For that extra bit of detail, some plastic stores sell premade acrylic nuts and bolts (less than $1 for a matched pair of nut and bolt). Using these will give a more consistent look to the case, rather than breaking it up with visible metal bolts.

But for more general usage gluing acrylic pieces to each other is the best technique. When you walk into a plastic store, there seem to be dozens of different adhesives and other chemicals that might be of some help. But when it comes down to it, only basic acrylic glue will do what you want.

All the different types of acrylic glue on the market are basically the same and come down to two different types—prethickened ($3 per small tube) and unthickened ($4 for a small can). Prethickened acrylic glue is similar in texture to most other glues. In reality, prethickened acrylic glue is just unthickened acrylic glue with bits of acrylic already dissolved into the mixture. As such, it's easier to use because the glue doesn't run like unthickened glue, but the bond it forms between acrylic pieces isn't as strong.

Unthickened glue, on the other hand, makes very tight connections between acrylic panels. But the main drawback is that the glue is the same consistency as water, and has a tendency to spread and leak even more than water. Unthickened acrylic glue is usually applied by holding the two acrylic pieces tightly together with a clamp of some sort and then using a bottle with a needle-like applicator tip to apply the glue (see Figure 10-6). By dropping just a couple of drops into the small gap between the two panels, the glue will be drawn into the microscopic gaps between the panels.

Tip

The way that the liquid glue is drawn into the gaps is because of a force called capillary attraction, also known as capillary action. Capillary attraction refers to the greater adhesion of a liquid to a solid surface than internal cohesion of the liquid itself. This causes the glue to be drawn against the sides of the acrylic rather than stay as a single large drop of glue.

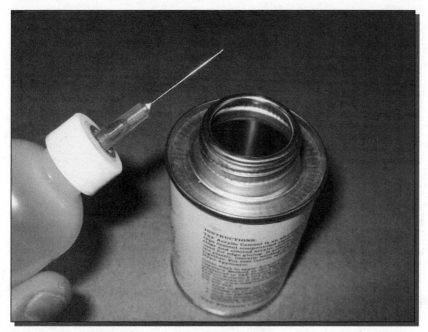

FIGURE 10-6: Unthickened acrylic glue and needle applicator.

Both types of acrylic glue work by melting the acrylic until the two pieces become one. Because of this, any excess glue that drips or leaks on the acrylic can ruin the smooth surface. The two types do vary, however, in drying time. Unthickened glue usually takes between one and eight hours to fully harden, while thickened glue can take up to 24 hours.

Tip — Edges that are to be glued should not be polished. You can sand them down so they are somewhat smooth, but polishing the edges will make the edges less able to melt together under the influence of the glue.

How to Use Unthickened Acrylic Glue

Using a glue as thin as unthickened acrylic glue is a different experience than using any other type of glue. With a normal glue, you add the glue to one surface and press the second surface against the first, but acrylic glue won't work that way. In addition, acrylic glue is even thinner than water, so keeping the glue from running and creating unsightly blemishes on your nice panel can be a bit of a chore.

Thankfully, a few instructions will go a long way towards helping your project look its best. To use this type of glue, just follow these steps:

1. Squeeze the syringe bottle to push out some air and hold it that way to prevent the air from reentering. Turn the syringe upside down and insert the needle into the can of glue until the tip of the needle is below the surface. Slowly release your grip on the bottle and let the vacuum draw the glue inside.

> **Tip** Syringe bottles do not come with the cans of glue, but can be purchased in the same places that sell acrylic glue for under $4 each. Do not try to use unthickened acrylic glue without a syringe—all you will end up with is a mess.

2. When you have a teaspoon or two of glue in the bottle, withdraw it from the can and replace the lid. The solvent will evaporate from inside the syringe, so only put as much in as you will use in a single session. Replace the cap on the syringe.

3. To apply the glue, first make sure that your parts are tight with no gaps. Use tape, clamps, or a friend to hold the acrylic parts together.

4. Remove the cap on the syringe and have a paper napkin handy. With the syringe held upright, gently squeeze it to expel some air. Hold the syringe tightly once again and quickly turn it upside down over the napkin. As soon as the solvent starts to come out of the needle, release your grip. The solvent will now stay inside the bottle until you are ready to glue the parts.

5. Now place the needle along the seam between the parts (see Figure 10-7).

6. Gently squeeze the bottle to let the solvent flow. Capillary action will draw it into the joint producing a strong, clean weld. Leave the joint clamped for at least several minutes. The glue sets up very quickly. The joint should be very strong in a matter of hours.

Bending

One of the aspects that makes acrylic so nice to work with is the ability to bend and shape it to the basic shape you need, assuming that you cannot find a premade shape to begin with (which is always the best bet). Unfortunately, bending acrylic is much more of an art than a science. But acrylic is cheap, so buying some extra pieces to practice your technique on is always an option.

> **Tip** Many stores that sell acrylic panels will cut your panel to the right basic shape for you, often for free. Whenever your store offers this service, go ahead and use it because their tools will yield better results than you can usually do yourself. In addition, some plastic specialty stores already offer some basic shapes precut (like circles of various diameters) for just cents more than a square panel of the same size.

The basic technique is to use either a heat gun (the best option) or your oven to heat the material till it starts to soften. Using a premade form, you take the soft acrylic and lay it over the form till it starts to cool and harden. At this point, you clean the material of any debris or dirt

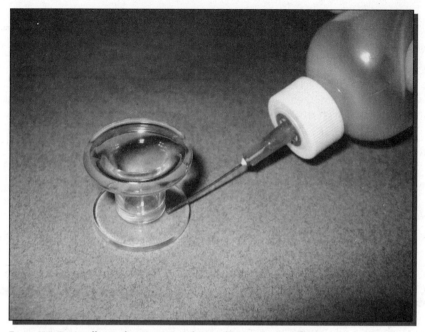

FIGURE 10-7: Needle applicator tip applying glue to acrylic pieces.

that may have become attached to the acrylic, and you are ready to go. In practice, there are a lot of variables that can complicate the process.

The steps, in detail, are:

1. Create some sort of a form that you will be placing the acrylic against to change its shape. The form should be made of some material such as wood or metal that can take a bit of heat without burning. Also, the form should be covered in felt to prevent the acrylic from sticking to the form. The form can be a simple 90-degree angle or a complex smooth curve; it's up to you. Usually the forms are nothing more than a couple of boards nailed together to make a solid "L" shape.

2. Heat the acrylic panel till it starts to soften. For heating the acrylic, the best option for a simple bend is to purchase a heat gun from a hardware store for $30 to $70. For something other than a single bend, such as curving the entire panel, it's best to use an oven to heat the acrylic. Never use a torch to heat the acrylic, because the acrylic is flammable and will catch fire. If you're using a heat gun, move the heat gun back and forth over the line you want to bend the acrylic along, using a moderate speed. If you're using an oven, set the oven at 275 degrees Fahrenheit, and put the acrylic panel on a very clean cookie sheet in the oven. The length of time required to heat the acrylic varies with the size and thickness of the acrylic, but in general you want to heat it just enough that the acrylic is soft when you lift a corner of it.

Using a hair dryer may seem like a good way to heat the acrylic, but hair dryers simply don't have the power to put out enough heat to raise the temperature of the acrylic enough. Heat guns are basically hair dryers on steroids, and they are the right tool for the job.

3. Now, quickly remove the acrylic from the oven or from underneath the heat gun and press it against the premade form to mold the acrylic. You should use additional pieces of felt between the acrylic and your hands to help form the acrylic to the desired shape. You have less than a minute of working time before the acrylic loses the ability to take the shape, so work quickly.

Caution Use clean BBQ tongs to lift heated acrylic. Never use your hands, or you will get severe burns. Remember not to press too hard with the tongs or you will deform the acrylic. Also, when holding the acrylic against the form, you should use a pair of oven mitts (as well as the extra layer of felt) to protect yourself from burning your hands on the acrylic.

4. After the acrylic has cooled, you may find a slight texture to the acrylic. You may need to lightly sand the surface with a fine grit sandpaper and use polishing agents such as Novus to regain the smooth, clear appearance of the acrylic.

Tip Earlier in this section, the process for removing scratches from acrylic was discussed. This same process can be used to remove the slight texture left over after bending the acrylic.

Molding and Casting

It should be clear throughout the modding process that attention to detail is one of the most important things. A nice idea, executed with little attention to detail, won't generate much interest. But paying attention to every little detail pays off in how professional a case mod is.

One thing that grabs people's attention is when you fabricate one-of-a-kind pieces, such as fan grills or drive faceplates. The problem with doing this is that most of the materials that are easy to work with are not exactly durable. The solution is to create whatever you want, such as a fan grill, with an easy-to-work-with material and create a mold from that. Then, using a more durable material, create a copy of the original part using the recently created mold.

The process involves a number of steps and requires a bit of practice to get right, but the results can be truly great. The process, broken down to steps, is:

1. The first order of business is to create the original model that you can duplicate. You can use almost any material you can think of—wood, plastic, or metal—it really doesn't matter. One material that is very useful for this is called Super Sculpy, a type of polymer clay (available in arts and crafts stores for a few dollars for a small portion). You can use

FIGURE 10-8: A original model for a fan custom fan grill. This model started as a star-shaped piece of styrene plastic, an outer ring from another fan grill, some skull-shaped tire stem caps, and some modeling clay.

Super Sculpy to make a shape just as you would clay, but then you bake it in the oven, and it becomes hard. Regular synthetic modeling clay can also be used (see Figure 10-8).

2. Next, prepare a mold for the piece. Take some solid backing such as foam board and build up some walls enclosing an area big enough to hold the model you just made. You can use any material for the walls, such as more foam board. The only thing to remember is that this area must be free of any areas where the liquid rubber could leak out. You can use a fair amount of hot glue to secure the connection between the backing and the walls, or use some modeling clay for this purpose. Remember that the walls must leave at least a half an inch around the edges of the original (see Figure 10-9).

3. Once this area is built up, it's time to pour the rubber for the mold (see Figure 10-10). Use some white glue or other weak glue, and glue the model in place. Several different molding materials are available, but one of the best is quick-set RTV silicone rubber from Allumilute (available at better hobby stores). Mix the rubber per the instructions (silicone rubber almost always comes as a two-part liquid that you have to mix). Once fully mixed, slowly pour the liquid over the part until it's fully covered. You want to use enough of the rubber to make sure that everything is completely covered and nothing beneath the surface of the rubber is visible. On the other hand, since RTV rubber is expensive at nearly $35 per pound, don't use excessive amounts.

FIGURE 10-9: Building walls around the original from foam board.

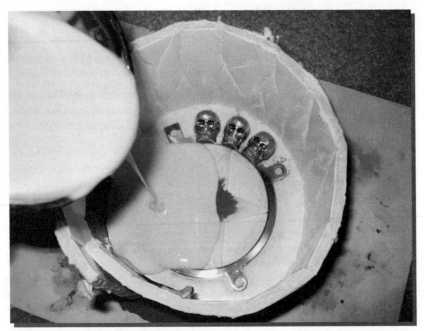

FIGURE 10-10: Pouring the liquid rubber over the original.

Caution

Pouring too fast can lead to trapped air bubbles in the mold. Try to pour slowly over the model itself, but more quickly on the areas not directly touching the model.

4. Now wait for the rubber to set per the instructions. Depending on the type of silicone, the time for the mold to set will be from a few minutes to a day. Once the mold is solid, it can be removed from the part easily due to the flexibility of the rubber. To help in removing the mold, you can remove the walls around the mold first.

5. Now you mix the casting agent, such as Allumilite casting plastic (available at better hobby stores for $40 for two 28-oz bottles). Measure equal amounts of the two-part casting plastic for exactly 20 seconds and pour it into the silicone mold. Let the plastic set for at least 5 minutes, at which time the piece will still be a little soft but can be removed from the mold (see Figure 10-11). Wait a few hours for the piece to fully harden. Timing is crucial—if you don't mix long enough, the piece won't ever fully harden. Since the casting agent goes from liquid to solid in around 3 minutes, wait too long and the liquid won't flow into all the details and the piece will be incomplete.

Tip

Allumilite also sells various dyes and metallic powders that can be added to the casting plastic during the mixing process. The result is a plastic with the color molded right into the piece itself.

FIGURE 10-11: The custom fan grill removed from the mold. Note that the color pattern is due to slightly too little mixing of the plastic—ideally this should not happen.

FIGURE 10-12: The final result, after some sanding and painting.

6. The piece is now complete and can be sanded, painted, glued, or anything else you need to do to make it work for you (see Figure 10-12).

That's it. The mold can be reused a number of times, making this a great way to duplicate hard-to-find or expensive pieces. Think about it. How many items can you think of adding to your case now that you know how to make your own custom plastic pieces?

Wrapping Up

By now, we've covered all the major areas used in case modding. But there are always new things to learn. Try and come up with some of your own ideas. There are still plenty of areas that can use more investigation as potential case mod techniques.

With all these techniques, what can be created? A lot. Keep reading to see what some modders have come up with using the methods from this book and a lot more.

Case Mod Projects

part

II

Matrimony Mod

Mike Johnson

chapter 11

Throughout the years we've been together, my fiancée has been very supportive of my modding habit. Whenever I came up with another idea, her attitude was always "do whatever you want." There were no limitations placed on me (well, I couldn't make a 24-carat-gold-plated case or something outrageously expensive) and on the weekends I have pretty much free reign in the garage. Keeping that in mind, I decided that this was one of the many reasons why I wanted to be with my fiancée forever. I decided to propose to her, and my first plan having been thwarted (she started to get suspicious—something tipped her off), I set out to find a new way to propose.

I had purchased her a ring and had been keeping it at my parents' house until I figured out how I was going to propose. At about the same time, the modding bug began to rear its ugly head again, and I was itching to mod another case. Also at this time (very coincidentally, I might add) my fiancée needed a new PC for her office. Her old Pentium 1 was not cutting it anymore, so being that I always have parts laying around, I told her I'd put something together for her that would easily blow her old PC away. I began to consider the crazy idea of modding the case to incorporate the wedding proposal.

I'd been trying really hard to find some original way to propose that no guy had ever done before. This seemed like the perfect way. It would allow me to bust out the Dremel and mod again, at the same time giving her a new, upgraded PC. What was even better about it was that if she was having a hard day at work, she could look over at the PC (see Figure 11-1) and think of the proposal and our relationship. Hopefully, that would make her day a bit better.

Timeframe and Costs

It took me roughly three weeks at a frenzied pace to complete this mod. Many of these days were only for an hour or so though, and there was a snow day in which I was unable to complete any work on the mod. To compensate, I took a couple of days off and worked all the way through. However, this time estimate is really rough because if you work longer days, you'll be done more quickly. It all comes down to how often and for how long your schedule permits you to mod.

FIGURE 11-1: Completed Matrimony mod.

Estimating the cost for this mod is also a little confusing because I had most of the parts already on hand. Hardware costs are up to you because you could use an AMD chip that is cheaper than an Intel, a 40-GB drive as opposed to a 60-GB one, and so on. The PC will still work. For my case, I didn't use all the craft materials I bought (lace, etc.) so you wouldn't have to budget for that. An educated guess for my PC would be roughly $700 to $750.

Required Parts and Tools

To perform this project, you will need a number of tools and supplies. Each section will also detail the specific tools and supplies you need for that section. In general, the typical modding tools are all required for this project:

- Screwdrivers
- Dremel with cutting discs and etching tool
- Jigsaw with fine toothed blade
- Drill with various bits
- Hole saws
- Utility knife

- Heat gun
- Scissors
- Measuring tape
- Masking tape
- Electrical tape
- Fine-grit sandpaper
- Can of compressed air
- Hot glue gun and gluesticks
- White craft glue

The Plan

Convinced that this was how I would propose, I began to gather some spare parts. I had a self-imposed time limit, because it was early December and I wanted to propose before Christmas (since both New Year's and Christmas are overused as times to propose). I knew it would be a difficult feat to pull off (seeing as how we live together and she couldn't catch me modding), but I knew that I could make it happen. I even went so far as to take two days off from work to go to my parents' garage to mod. My fiancée was none the wiser and thought I went to work as usual. My dastardly plan was beginning to take shape.

One good thing to keep the costs down was that I had most of the parts for the PC lying around as spares from other projects in the past. Scrounging around in my parts bin in the closet, I located the following:

- AMD Athlon XP 1700 + CPU
- Asus A7S333 motherboard
- 256-MB DDR-2700 RAM
- 40-GB Western Digital 7200-rpm hard drive
- Apollo GeForce 4 MX420 video card
- Lite-On 52x CD-RW
- Generic 350W power supply
- 3Com network card
- Eight silver anodized thumbscrews
- 80-mm fan
- 80-mm silver aluminum mesh fan grill
- Old Codegen case

I decided that the case would also need some mod supplies (because the above is a pure vanilla case setup). I began to formulate in my head how I wanted the case to look. Seeing as how it was to represent our engagement/marriage, it had to be white. This would mean I would have to paint everything white (case, power supply, drives, etc). The case had to have at least one window, and I wanted to incorporate a wedding cake topper of a bride and groom, and/or a tiered wedding cake.

I decided to put the cake topper on the floor of the case. To see it better, I wanted to cut a front window in the case and a fairly large side window. Since I had never etched a window before, I wanted to try my hand at it by putting a phrase on the window that would be visible with the lights on. I had toyed with the idea of inserting the ring into the CD drive (which would then pop out at the touch of a button) but decided against it, as I had roughly a three-week timeframe to get the PC finished. I wanted to wrap each wire from the power supply with white cable sleeving and heat-shrink and then accent the wires with lace or something "matrimonial" looking. With most of the case planned in my head, I set out to purchase supplies.

I looked online at my favorite Web mod shop and an online auto store I had dealt with in the past. I placed an order with these two companies, as well as with a wedding items Web site (for the cake topper). This is what I decided on:

- One 10" rounded single-device white floppy cable
- Two 18" rounded single-device ATA-133 white cables
- Two tailed white LEDs with white cable sleeves and white heat-shrink
- One 12" × 12" clear acrylic window Kit
- Four white PCI/AGP card quick screws
- Twelve feet of white $1/4$" nylon cable sleeve
- Two feet of white $1/2$" nylon cable sleeve
- One foot of 1" white heat-shrink
- Two feet of $1/2$" white heat-shrink
- Three feet of rubber window molding"
- Two 12" white cold cathode fluorescent lights
- Two cans of gloss white Rustoleum spray paint
- One can gloss white vinyl dye
- One cake topper

The mod supplies only ended up being about $250, which wasn't too bad. I began by writing out a list of tasks to be achieved and attempted to put dates on them to establish some kind of working schedule. I've found that this is very helpful when trying to mod a case. It helps you stick to a specific plan without skipping anything that may turn out to be a surprise for you later on. This is the rough outline that I made:

1. Cut side panel for the window

2. Take apart power supply for painting

3. Remove drive faces

4. Paint case and panels, drive faces, fan, and power supply

5. Remove power supply Molex connectors and sleeve wires

6. Cut front window

7. Vinyl dye front case panel

8. Etch side panel window

9. Attach side and front windows

10. Relocate power button

11. Assemble power supply and PC

12. Add accents to case internals/externals, including case topper

13. Install operating system and software

14. Make custom wallpaper and icons

15. Construct tiered wedding cake and attach to top of case

With a bit of humor, I saved the document in a password-protected folder named "Belltower" (after all, what does a belltower do? RING!). My plan now laid out, I began to work taking every lunch break I had from work and going to my parents' house to mod in their garage (and returning late most times as well).

Cutting and Painting

Before I could make anything look pristine and white, I needed to get some of the "dirty work" out of the way. This would begin with cutting of the windows—front and side.

Cutting the Side Window

I decided to start with the side window. This seemed to be the logical first step because it would more than likely be one of the easier steps of the project. Items needed:

- Jigsaw with fine toothed blade
- File set
- Pencil
- Window kit
- Drill

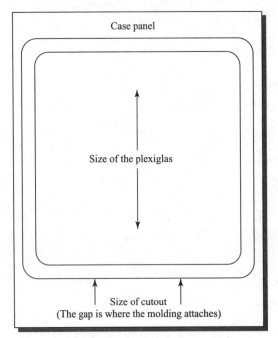

Case panel

Size of the plexiglas

Size of cutout
(The gap is where the molding attaches)

FIGURE 11-2: Diagram of cutout for case window.

I removed the side panel and unpacked the window kit I had purchased online. Placing the 12" × 12" Plexiglas against the side panel, I inserted my pencil into the included washer and traced around the window. The added width I traced onto the panel due to the washer's diameter would ensure that enough room would be left for the molding to securely hold the window in place (see Figure 11-2).

Once the outline was drawn, I drilled a $1/2$" hole into the middle of the panel to allow my jigsaw to pass through. Once the hole was drilled, I inserted a very fine-toothed saw blade (greater than 20 teeth per inch is recommended) and began to cut along the traced line. The more teeth per inch, the less the saw will buck and the smoother the cut. When the cutting was complete, I lightly filed the edge with my handy file set. I wasn't too concerned about getting it completely straight and smooth because the window molding would cover any ugliness from the jigsaw. This task complete, I moved on to the power supply.

Cross-Reference   See Chapter 5 for a discussion about the best tools to use for cutting holes in your case.

Preparing the Power Supply

Now with the panels cut and ready for painting, I needed to get the power supply ready. I wanted to paint everything that needed to become white in one shot to prevent having to set up my paint booth more than once because time was of the essence.

Items needed:

- Philip's-head screwdriver
- Masking tape
- Razor blade

I had a 350-watt power supply that was more than sufficient to do the job, but let's face it, power supplies are kind of dull with their matte gray color and mass of tangled wires. Since the theme of the case demanded that everything be white, I was going to have to make sure that the power supply followed suit. In order to properly achieve this, I needed to completely disassemble the power supply. This may seem a bit scary, but as long as you are careful not to scrape any leads from the power supply's PCB on the metal, you will be fine.

I unscrewed the four retaining screws (goodbye warranty!) and got to the guts of the power supply. Again, after removing all screws inside, I pulled the actual power supply board out and set it aside (for the time being). Because I could not fully remove the point on the power supply where the power cord comes in (the black plug area), I loosened it up the best I could and and covered the area with some masking tape, cutting it with a razor to ensure a tight fit. At this point, I was ready to paint the power supply.

When setting aside the power supply, be aware that it's a delicate piece of electronics that has high-voltage electricity running through it. Even when unplugged, the power supply's capacitors can store electricity that if touched will be happy to shock you. Be sure to set the internals down on something nonconductive to protect the power supply and yourself. Also, at its core is an exposed PCB that is fragile and can be easily broken if it falls or is stepped on.

Removing Drive Faces

Have you ever seen a red Ferrari with a brown rusted door on it? Yes, what's under the hood will knock your socks off, and yes, the rest of the car looks great. But the door is such an eyesore that it will detract from anything that is good about the rest of the car. The same concept applies here. One of the worst things that a modder can do is to have drives in a different color than his or her case. If you look on any forum online, everyone will tell you emphatically to match the drives and the case. So keeping that in mind, I needed to make my drives white. Luckily the way the case is designed, the floppy drive is hidden so I didn't have to worry about its color. My Lite-On CD-RW was beige, so I needed to rectify that. Inserting a small flathead screwdriver into the tabs on the sides, top, and bottom of the CD drive will allow you to pop the face plate off. Once this occurs, you're ready to color.

Painting

With all my pieces spread out in my little paint booth, I was ready to inhale some paint fumes! Just kidding, in all honesty, you should definitely consider investing in a face mask if you already don't have one. It will save your lungs and prevent the inside of your nostrils from being painted the same color as your case.

Items needed:

- Two cans Gloss White Rustoleum spray paint
- One can Gloss White SEM vinyl dye
- Masking tape
- One large and one small cardboard box
- Small flathead screwdriver
- Face mask

Usually when you have to change the color of something in your mod, you need to consider its material before painting. If what you have to color is made of metal, spray paint will do nicely as long as you use thin, multiple coats with plenty of time in between to allow for proper drying. If what you are coloring is made of plastic or acrylic, vinyl dye works much better than paint for several reasons. The first and most attractive reason to use vinyl dye is that it will not get thick and gunky after multiple coats like spray paint does. This is especially nice when coloring CD drive faces because it will not clog up the logos that are molded into the plastic. This will allow your dyed drive to look like it came that color straight from the factory. The second best thing about vinyl dye is that it dries very quickly, in approximately 5 to 10 minutes. This means that you can get your drive colored within an hour or two, tops. With spray paint you'd have to wait up to an hour or two between each coat.

Cross-Reference   See Chapter 6 for a discussion on painting techniques for different types of materials.

Before I began painting and vinyl dyeing, I located a fairly large cardboard box and a smaller cardboard box and laid them on their sides, with the openings facing me. The large box was to be used to spray paint the metal of the case and power supply. The small box was to be used to vinyl dye the CD-RW, the fan, window molding, and later the front panel of the case (the front panel is plastic while the rest of the case is steel). I flipped the plate for the CD-RW over and located where the activity LED flashes. There is a small plastic translucent cover over the location where the LED sits in the drive, and unless you want to block the light by painting over it, you're going to need to remove it. I simply wedged my small screwdriver in between the plastic and the drive face and popped it off.

Now I was ready to color. I vinyl dyed the CD-RW face plate, and while the first misting was drying, I taped around the volume knob on the actual drive and vinyl dyed that too (yeah, I know, no one uses it anymore, but if you don't dye it, it'll still be beige!). In all, I sprayed about six to eight coats of vinyl dye, waiting about 10 minutes in between coats. The drive face came out beautifully. I purposely held out on vinyl dyeing the front case panel because I knew I was going to have to perform some heavy modification on it. I wanted the window molding to match the case too, and the only color it comes in is black. I vinyl dyed the rubber molding and the 800-mm fan, and all looked good.

Next, I painted the case and power supply with my traditional 4 to 5 coats of paint, checking every hour or so. This is where I ran into a problem on the power supply. I was in a bit of a rush because the day was flying by, so I sprayed a little too much on one of the coats of paint. The result: one big gunky mess. I had to grab a bottle of Goof Off (it's great stuff—takes off just about anything you want) and remove all the paint from the power supply, which set me back a few hours. I was not happy about having to repaint that power supply, let me tell you. The actual case came out great though. I painted the top, sides (inside and out), back, basically anywhere that you could see beige or bare metal. After being forced to repaint the power supply, I was done making everything (with the exception of the case front) white that needed to be.

Modding the Power Supply

With the exterior of the power supply drying, I set about tidying the power supply's wires using cable sleeving.

Items needed:

- Universal Molex pin remover
- Twelve feet of white $1/4$" nylon cable sleeve
- Two feet of white $1/2$" nylon cable sleeve
- One foot of 1" white heat-shrink
- Two feet of $1/2$" white heat-shrink
- Heat gun
- Scissors
- Sewing needle
- Roll of electrical tape

The power supply cable sleeving is often a bit time-consuming. For whatever reason, many power supply manufacturers run wires between each other. For example, the four wire Molex connectors often intersect, making sleeving that much more difficult because you need to separate the wires before you can wrap them. I grabbed my universal Molex pin remover (it works for both female and male Molex pins and has been a lifesaver) and got to work. You can see in Figure 11-3 how messy wires can be. Generally, this is how most power supplies look inside.

One thing to consider when sleeving your cables is to make sure that after you remove the Molex connectors you reattach them in the right order. Otherwise, some very bad things could happen. If the wires are not attached in the proper order, the voltage coming off the power supply will be all mixed up, and you could end up frying one of your components (i.e., if you plug the yellow +12-volt connector into a slot where a black "ground" should go). When removing Molex connectors on your power supply, look closely at the connector, and you will see that yellow always goes into slot 1. Make a mental note of this. The reason I grab electrical tape when I sleeve cables is that it is very easy to mistake the two black wires for each other. I

FIGURE 11-3: Power supply opened, showing a mess of wires.

always cut a small square of tape and wrap it around the black wire directly next to the yellow wire, at the connector, and repeat this for each Molex plug. Once the Molex connectors are off, you're free to move each wire around to untangle the whole mess to make sleeving possible.

Once all the cables were as neatly separated as they could be, I sized them up by eye and cut a length of $^1/_4$-inch cable sleeve. I made sure to run the sleeve down far enough so that the full cable would be sleeved and that the heat-shrink would be inside the power supply when I put the cover back on. You might think that 12 feet of sleeving was a bit much, but I was planning on wrapping every single wire in the case (fan connectors and cold cathodes wires included). I figured that I would probably use most, if not all of it, before the mod was finished. In retrospect, I'm glad I bought that amount.

Note When sleeving, everyone always says to use a hot knife, rather than scissors, to sear the ends of the sleeve so it doesn't unravel. I don't do this for three reasons: one, I'm lazy and don't want to take the time to get a hot knife; two, searing the ends won't allow the sleeve to expand as fully as it could if it were unseared; three, even if the sleeve does unravel a little bit, the heat-shrink makes sure that it stays in place.

I cut about an inch's worth of $^1/_2$-inch heat-shrink for each side of the connector (two pieces of heat-shrink for each Molex plug) and slid it on over the cable sleeve. Once I had done this for all the Molex plugs, I reached for my heat gun and applied steady heat to each plug. The heat-shrink, as the name so cleverly implies, will shrink in the presence of heat to fit snugly around the wires. This gives a nice, clean appearance and covers the cut, slightly frayed ends of the cable sleeve (not to mention that it will increase airflow in your case by eliminating a rat's nest of cables all over the place).

The hardest connectors to sleeve in the case are the auxiliary and main ATX connectors. The auxiliary plug is a little more of a challenge because you need to temporarily flatten a tiny clip to slip the wires out. This is where my sewing needle came in handy. I stuck it in each of the four holes and depressed the clips, releasing the wires. Once the wires were free, I repeated the process of sleeving. After prying the clips up again with the sewing needle, the connector clicked back into place.

The ATX connector is almost always a bit of a problem for me and many others, from what I've seen online. The ATX connector poses a bit of a problem in that I don't want to remove and label 20 wires, and I just can't justify spending $25 for an ATX pin remover. The easiest way around this is to take the ATX connector and fold it down parallel to the wire stem, as flat as possible. Usually you can slip the $1/2$-inch cable sleeve over the wires fairly easily, and then slip $1^1/2$ inch or so of 1-inch heat-shrink over it and apply your heat gun.

With that, I was done sleeving the power supply.

Window Work

I now was at the point where I needed to make a cutout in the front of the case for the window.

Making a Cutout for the Front Window

I figured that I would want as big of a window as possible in the front of the case, to show off the cake topper I planned on attaching to the floor, so it was time get started on that project.

Items needed:

- Dremel with several reinforced cutting wheels
- Measuring tape
- Straight edge
- Marking pen
- Fine-grit sandpaper
- Bondo automotive filler
- Wood putty

I removed the front panel and mapped out just how big the window could possibly be. This was slightly difficult for two reasons. First, the case front was concave (whereas the rest of the case was flat). Second, by making the window as big as the case front would allow, I would need to relocate the power and reset buttons which sat directly in the center of the proposed window. Not a problem, really, just another detail to work out. That's what modders do!

After I measured out the size of the cutout and marked it on the case front, I brought out the modders' best friend—the Dremel. The Dremel made short work of the plastic case front, and after the window was cut out, I took some fine-grit sandpaper and smoothed out some rough areas.

With the window cutout finished, I now was free to make a few cosmetic changes to the front panel. There was a small hole in the panel to accommodate what looked like a USB port. Since I have plenty of USB ports on the motherboard, the front one was unnecessary and kind of ugly. I placed a piece of duct tape on the inside (for support) and filled the hole in with Bondo. This is also where I ran into a small snag. The best conditions for Bondo to dry in are sunny, fairly warm days. Well, this was December in New York. It was gray, cold, and not very inviting. Sunny days were far away. I tried to make the best of it, but the Bondo just would not dry. I left it for a few days, and it was still gummy. Since I had a big deadline (fast approaching at this time) I elected to remove the Bondo and use something that would dry quickly and easily. I chose wood putty, and after using the same procedure as for the Bondo, I set the panel aside to dry again. This time—success! I sanded it smooth, and the front panel was now ready to join the rest of the PC by being vinyl dyed white.

After the customary 6 to 8 coats of vinyl dye, the front panel matched the rest of the case. The mod was starting to come together, and was becoming easier to visualize.

Etching the Side Window

Items needed:

- Dremel with etching bit
- Piece of Plexiglas
- Transparency film
- PC with PhotoShop and printer
- Painters' tape
- Can of compressed air

As I said previously, I'd never etched before this project. I'd seen a bunch of people online do some pretty nice work, and I wanted to try it this time around. I chose to etch a phrase on the window, related to the proposal. "Will you marry me?" seemed a little cheesy, so I decided on "Will you do me the honor?" which sounded a bit classier. My handwriting is atrocious, so I knew there was no way I could ever do the etching free hand. I went into Adobe PhotoShop and found a nice-looking flowery cursive font, and typed out the phrase. I loaded a piece of transparency film into the printer, and I was ready to try it out.

I taped the transparency to the front of the Plexiglas with painters' tape. I laid a towel on the workbench, and placed the Plexiglas face down. At this point, I knew it would take a while to etch, because I wanted to make sure that it came out just right. I was willing to stop every so often if necessary.

Tip When modding, it's a good idea to use painter's tape because it's not permanent and won't leave a sticky film after it's removed.

FIGURE **11-4:** Close-up of etching on side window.

I found that the easiest way to etch the window was to first outline the letter you're working on, and then fill in the rest with broad strokes. It seemed to look the best this way. As a result of being so precise and holding the Dremel as steady as possible, my hand would begin to cramp after 10 minutes or so. I stopped every 10 or 15 minutes, moved my hand around to get the blood flowing again, and sprayed the window with a can of compressed air to get the flecks of Plexiglas out of my work area. This process took a couple of hours, but once the etching was finished I knew the time had been well spent. It came out exactly as I intended. I was very happy. My first time etching turned out better than expected (see Figure 11-4). In retrospect, it would have looked really cool if I had etched a picture of my fiancée and me onto the window, but hey, you've got to learn to crawl before you can walk!

Chapter 9 contains information on etching your own design into a piece of acrylic or Plexiglas.

Attaching the Windows

With the cutouts complete, I was ready to attach the windows into the case.

Items needed:

- Single 12 × 12" piece of Plexiglas
- Window molding
- Small (roughly 5" × 6") piece of Lexan or Plexiglas
- Utility knife
- Straight edge
- Bottle of Goof Off and paper towels
- Heat gun

This was a section of the project that I had not anticipated that I would spend as much time on as I did. The etched side window was easy enough except for one small issue. To attach the side window, I took the precut window molding from my kit and put the edge with the smaller lip over the cut edge of the metal and ran it around the circumference of the cutout. This is where the small snag occurred. To get the window into the molding, you have to ease one corner in, and then work the rest in by flexing the rubber of the window molding. Well, if you remember from before, I had vinyl dyed the rubber white to match the side of the case. Working and flexing the rubber made the vinyl dye crack and split, so instead of looking classic and clean, it looked antique, and very ugly and messed up. I had to remove the molding and apply Goof-Off to it, rubbing the vinyl dye off with paper towels. It didn't really take much time, but it was an annoyance because now I had black molding against a white case panel. It no longer matched my color scheme, but I decided to keep working past it and deal with it at the end.

Well, I must have been jinxed due to the window molding incident, because I ran into what was probably the most difficult and time-consuming aspect of the entire mod—the front window. If you recall, the front of the case is concave, so I quickly learned that I would need to bend the Plexiglas to get it to fit in the molding.

Another problem I soon discovered was that since this was a window of my own design it didn't have rounded edges like the side panel window kit I bought. My window was square, and the hole I cut in the case front was also square. This was a problem because the molding usually lines the window in a smooth, curved, semi-circular line. By cutting everything square, there was nothing curved or smooth anymore, which made the molding difficult to use.

I solved this dilemma by printing out eight perfect 45 degree angles on paper, using PhotoShop once more. I figured if I could cut each edge of the molding at a 45 degree angle, the two sides that joined at each corner would fit snugly together and look pretty nice. I taped the 45 degree cutouts onto the edges of the window molding and cut them with a utility knife. Some of the cuts were not exactly 45 degrees, but I planned on decorating them anyway so I wasn't too worried how it looked at the moment as long as it held the window in place.

To get the window to fit the curve of the case, I gently bent it by hand and heated the point of the bend with the heat gun. This allowed it to curve slightly and not cloud the Plexiglas with a severe bend. After a couple of tries, I got the Plexiglas to adhere to the curve I needed. This is where the difficult part came into play—actually getting the window in. Imagine trying to get a curved window into a curved hole with straight molding inside it. What was I thinking?

Just as with the side window, I tried to get an edge of the Plexiglas in and then work the window into the molding. Since it was curved, the other edges would nudge the molding, sometimes getting jammed, sometimes pull the molding completely out of the window cutout. I ran the heat gun over the molding to try to make it more pliable, and this seemed to help. Through *a lot* of trial and error (1 to 2 hours' worth) I finally got the window in place. I felt like Tom Hanks in *Castaway* when he finally started a fire. My elation was soon cut short when I looked a little more closely and realized that in my struggles I had scratched the Plexiglas right down the center. I ripped the window out, threw it against the wall and walked out of the garage.

After I calmed down a little, I went back to the window and cut a new piece of Plexiglas from the scraps I had in the garage and went through all the trials and tribulations of getting to fit into the molding. An hour or so later (I guess practice makes perfect—it took less time the second try) I got the window snug and called it a day.

I took a day off from work the following Tuesday. Again, my fiancée never knew I took the day off. When I left in the morning, I was dressed in my normal work clothes, and when I got to my parents' house, I borrowed a pair of my dad's jeans and a flannel shirt so as not to come home with paint and plastic bits all over my shirt and tie. I had the whole day to mod, so I vowed to make some serious progress because Christmas was fast approaching.

Relocating Power and Activity LEDs

Because the window was now occupying the location where the power and reset buttons had been, I had to find them a new home. It was now time to relocate them.

Items needed:

- 1" hole saw
- 2" square piece of Plexiglas
- White paint and paintbrush
- 5-mm drill bit
- Hot glue gun and gluestick
- Package of 20-mm rhinestones
- Measuring tape
- Scraps of lace
- Dremel and its smallest drill bit

I decided to ditch the reset button (I can't remember the last time I've used one) so that made it a little simpler. Looking at the case front, I decided the best place where the power button would not interfere with anything would be below the front window, in the center. I measured to the center of the front panel and marked it. Using a 1-inch hole saw, I cut through the front panel. I found a package of 20-mm rhinestones my mother had and decided that the clear one looked kind of like a diamond, which would be fitting for this project. Since 1 inch is roughly equal to 25 mm, I had about 5 mm of space between the rhinestone and the actual hole. I decided that the rhinestone could sit flush with the case front if it had something anchoring it on the back of the hole. I grabbed my hole saw again and cut another 1-inch hole, this time in a scrap of spare Plexiglas.

Because I was using the piece that was cut out by the hole saw (rather than using the hole itself) the Plexiglas fit in the case's hole nicely. As an added bonus, the Plexiglas already had a hole in it (from the hole saw's drill bit) for the switch and wires to sit in. I hot glued the Plexiglas circle in place in the 1-inch hole. Using the existing power button and wires, I placed the switch in the hole in the Plexiglas (from the hole saw's drill bit) and hot glued it in place. I also took the time to sleeve the wires with the spare sleeving and heat-shrink from before. Since the Plexiglas circle was visible, I took some white paint and covered it to make it appear part of the case front. It was a little streaky and looked unfinished, so once again, I raided my mom's craft cabinet and grabbed a scrap of lace. I cut a small round piece and glued it down, giving the backing a little more of an interesting look. With everything in place, I flipped the rhinestone over and used the Dremel with its smallest drill bit to cut a little hole for the power switch to sit in. When it was finished, I hot-glued it in place. The button was finished.

I looked at the case front and came to the conclusion that something looked weird. I finally put my finger on it. The power button on the bottom looked naked sitting there alone, with the activity LEDs sitting to the upper right of the CD drive bays. I decided to move the activity LEDs down to the same area the power button was in. I drilled a 5-mm hole to the left and right of the power button and hot glued into place the two presleeved and -tailed LEDs I had purchased (see Figure 11-5). Very quick and very easy. I had two holes above the CD drive bays now, but I was getting an idea of what I wanted to do with them.

Assembling the PC

After getting the external pieces ready, it was time to work on the internal pieces. At this point I was ready to put the actual PC together inside of the case.

Items needed:

- Philips-head screwdriver
- Four white PCI/AGP card quick screws
- Various parts you are installing

I installed the CPU and attached its heatsink, inserted RAM, and then screwed the motherboard inside the case. I used four white PCI/AGP card quick screws to hold the CD-RW and floppy drive in place in their respective bays. I inserted the network card, video card, and USB bracket in the PCI slots of the motherboard and bolted them in place. I attached two white 12-inch cold cathodes, one horizontally on the ceiling outside of the drive cage, and the other on the floor of the case. I ran the cables (already white—phew!) in the most unobstructive way that I could, and ended them inside the 5.25-inch drive bays where I had an extra space or two. In here I Velcroed down the cold cathode power inverters with the Velcro that came with the kit. From the outside of the case, you couldn't even see them in there. I connected the white IDE and floppy cables. The only thing I didn't install at this time was the power supply, because I felt it needed further decoration.

FIGURE 11-5: Relocated power and activity LEDs.

Internal/External Design Accents

Despite being white, the power supply looked like it needed something else. I decided to decorate each of the cables in something that would look "matrimonial."

Items needed:

- Two yards of satin ruffle
- Two yards of pearl rope
- Two yards of flat lace
- Two packages of faux minipearls
- One yard of white lace with silver accents
- Hot glue gun and glue stick
- Scissors
- One 6¹/₂" round doily
- One ceramic bride/groom cake topper
- Forty pink and white mini roses

- White paint and paintbrush
- Eight silver anodized thumbscrews
- Two 1" strips of Velcro

I kind of liked the look that the lace gave the power button, so I decided to go out to the local craft store and pick up some supplies to make the PC look "like a wedding," that is, lace, pearls, and so on. I ended up getting too much, but then again, I could have decorated more things to use the spare materials. Oh well, better to buy a little too much than to be short.

I began with the power supply. I decided that the plain white sleeving looked a little too plain, so I wrapped each one with a string of mini-faux-pearls. When I came to the end of each, I hot glued each string to the side of the heat-shrink that was facing away from the window. I figured that because the side of the power supply would be visible through the window, I should add something to that as well. I cut a small piece of lace with silver accents and ran it along the bottom of the power supply to liven it up a little. With that completed, the power supply could now be inserted in the case and all the Molex plugs connected (see Figure 11-6). Instead of normal screws, I used four silver anodized thumbscrews.

In the front window I wanted to attach the cake topper, so the bride and groom would sit in the white light and be very visible. I hot glued a 6½-inch doily to the floor of the case, right in front of the window. Rather than glue the cake topper down, I used two 1-inch strips of Velcro, in case it needed to be removed for any reason.

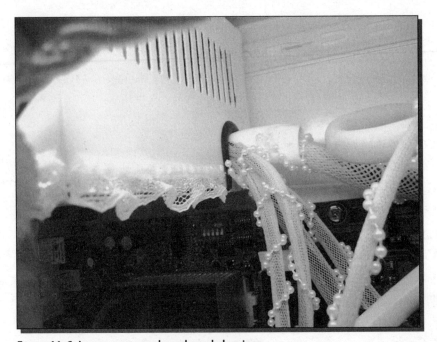

FIGURE 11-6: Lace power supply and pearl sleeving.

After the topper was secured, I attached the side panel in place with two more silver anodized thumbscrews. I did the same for the other side panel without the window. I thought the silver would go nicely because it looked classy and was the same color as the platinum in my fiancée's engagement ring.

The front of the case was decorated next. The window molding was still black, so I painted it white by hand and hot glued some lace over it. You couldn't even tell it had been black. To further improve its appearance, I hot glued three pink roses, one white rose, and one white leaf in each corner. In between the corners, I hot glued two white roses and one pink rose.

To further accent the case front, I ran pearl rope from the top of the case to the bottom, accenting it with pink and white mini-craft-roses (see Figure 11-7).

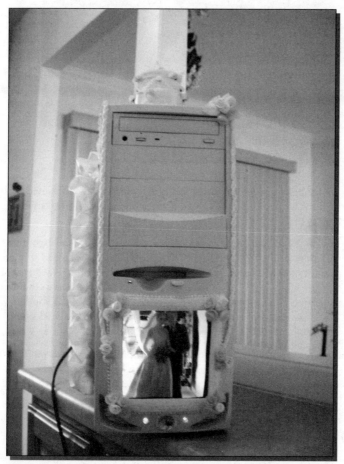

FIGURE 11-7: Front of the case with custom painted molding and accents.

FIGURE 11-8: Side panel molding with satin ruffle.

I still had two holes on the top-right side of the case where the old activity LEDs had been so I filled them with hot glue and inserted three pink roses, three white roses, and three white leaves. It doesn't even look as if there were LEDs there once.

If you recall, the side panel still had black molding as well. To remedy this, I ran satin ruffle I had purchased at the craft store around the perimeter of the window and hot glued it in place, completely covering any trace of black. It still needed something else, so I hot-glued two pink roses, one white rose, and one white leaf in each corner as well as two pink roses in the middle of each side. As a finishing touch, I ran more pearl rope around the inside of the window molding (see Figure 11-8). Again, there's really no set amount of decoration to use, I used the amount I did because it felt right to me. It depends on personal preference.

At this point, I booted the PC up for the first time and began installing Windows (the operating system this time). I ran it as an unattended installation so I could take a well-deserved break. I planned to create a custom wallpaper after a bite to eat and then I would stop for the day.

Making Custom Wallpaper and Icons

Items needed:

- PC with PhotoShop

FIGURE 11-9: The virtual desktop completed.

- Icon-making program
- Imagination

To begin, I first made an all white 1024 × 768 resolution image in PhotoShop. I went online and searched for a retailer that had pictures of engagement rings. I looked for the one closest to the ring I had purchased for my fiancée. I found it relatively quickly and pasted it into the white background. I used the same font I had for the window etching, and succinctly typed "Marry Me," which I then dragged underneath the picture of the ring.

I wanted to give her some custom icons as well, so I went to a shareware site online and searched for an icon-editing program. I found one called Icon Editor. I wanted to make three icons to replace "My Computer," "My Documents," and "My Network Places." For "My Computer" icon I used the top view picture of the similar engagement ring from the online retailer, and for "My Documents" I used the side view picture of the same ring. For "My Network Places" I used PhotoShop to take a circular sample of the diamond. I pasted the diamond as the network places icon. I saved all my work and applied the necessary changes in addition to whitening the desktop view as much as possible (see Figure 11-9). With the exception of the pièce de resistance, the three-tiered wedding cake on top of the case, I was finished.

Making the Cake

Items needed:

- Forty-two pink ribbon roses ($^1/_2$ inch or 1 cm)
- Sixty-five white ribbon roses ($^1/_2$ inch or 1 cm)
- Four white flowers with pearls and tulle

- Two packages of faux mini pearls
- One-quarter yard of white satin fabric
- Two feet of $1/8$-inch double face white ribbon
- Three wood circular boxes (3, $3^1/2$, $4^1/2$ inches)
- One 1" diameter Styrofoam ball
- One small decorative "wedding" ring
- One 3" diameter circle of Styrofoam (for inside top layer of cake)
- Approximately 3" × 3" scrap of black velvet
- White craft acrylic paint/paintbrush
- One $6^1/2$-inch paper doily
- Two feet of gathered lace trim
- Fray Check
- Piece of heavy cardboard
- Scissors
- White craft glue
- Hot glue/gun
- Straight pins
- Pencil

The cake was perhaps the most important part of the case, because it would be the delivery mechanism for my proposal. I planned to have the top layer of the cake hold the ring, and then once my fiancée saw me, I could pop the top layer off and put the ring on her finger.

The first thing I did was to remove the tops from the circular wood boxes. The bottom of the large and medium boxes would be flipped upside down to become the cake layers. The smallest box would be a little different than the other two layers, in that both the top and bottom would be used.

The first step was to cover the outside of the boxes in white satin. I took the largest box bottom and placed it bottom down on the wrong side of the satin (the unfinished side). Next, I traced around the bottom of the box and repeated the steps for the bottom of the middle box and the top of the smallest box.

To cover the sides of the boxes I had to measure the height of the "sides" of each circle and the circumference of each box (area around each box). For example, the height of the largest box from top to bottom is 1 inch. I added $1/4$ inch to this, allowing me to turn the fabric over to make a hem. This equaled $1^1/4$ inches high by 14 inches long (which is the circumference of the largest box). I then used an iron to crease the fabric, giving a clean edge to the sides. For the smallest box, I measured from the bottom edge of the box to the bottom of the top edge. In order for the small box to close, the fabric could only run as far as the top edge of the box.

I cut out fabric larger than the traced circle, leaving a small amount of material around the marked area. I then spread a thin layer of white tacky craft glue on the bottom of the large box and center over the wrong side of the cut circle, and pressed down. It was necessary to smooth out the satin to remove any creases or wrinkles. I had to be careful not to use too much glue because it will come through the fabric and stain if too much is used.

I then followed suit with the medium box and the top of the smallest box. When the glue was dry, I cut the circles close to the box edge and put Fray Check on the edges. This prevented the fabric from unraveling and/or fraying. I then repeated this for the medium box's bottom and the small box's top.

The next step was to work on the box sides. I lined the turned edges up with the box sides and glued as I did with the box bottoms, again being careful to use as little glue as possible. I had to overlap the fabric in what would be the "back" of the cake. A dab of hot glue held this in place. I was careful to not cover the "sides" of the top of smallest box (the lid). Instead, I painted the top sides with white acrylic paint, using three coats. When it was dry, I took some $1/8$-inch ribbon and glued it around the edges of the top of the small box twice to completely cover it. Once I completed this, I was ready to decorate the boxes.

The first thing to do was to measure the faux minipearls around the circumference of the large cake layer. When I came to the edge, I cut the string and hot glued them in place. It wasn't necessary to glue every pearl. A few drops of hot glue can go a long way. I repeated the process for the medium bottom and small top. Once they were complete, I ran a second line of pearls around the top of the smallest box. I then draped the pearls in a U shape around the sides, running from top to bottom of the layer. When I got it to look how I wanted, I cut off excess pearls and hot glued the strings into place. An easy way I found to keep the strings of pearls equidistant was to divide the pearl strand in half and glue on opposite sides.

I did the same for the remaining sides, and tried to line up the U of the large box with that of the medium box (see Figure 11-10).

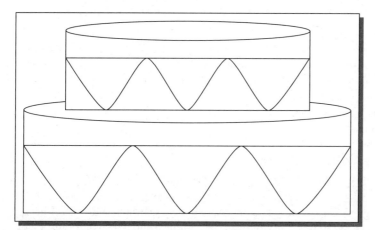

FIGURE 11-10: Example of lining up bottom and middle layer pearl strings.

I had to handle the small top layer cake bottom differently, as I wanted to be able to use both the top and bottom of this box. Using the same U technique, I strung the pearls from the bottom edge of the box to the bottom edge of the top of the box. This allowed the box to be opened and closed. Again I tried to align the U with the other two boxes. With my hot glue gun, I attached the medium box on top of the large box to form a tiered cake.

Now, I had to accent everything with flowers. I cut the flowers off the "stems" of the ribbon roses, trying to cut as close to the beginning of the stem as possible. For the medium box only, I alternated roses (two white and one pink) and hot glued at the bottom of each U. For both the medium and large boxes, I glued one pink rose surrounded by three white roses at the top of each U.

I then glued the small box on top of the medium box. For the smallest box, I glued one white rose at the top of each U (right below the lower edge of the top of box). I had to be careful not to glue over the edge as the top would not open if I had. On the top edges of the small box, I glued two white and one pink rose below the pearls, centering to the lowest part of the U.

To complete the outside of the small box top, I cut the Styrofoam ball in half, and cut four white silk roses with pearls/tulle off their stems. I pushed each rose into the Styrofoam in the shape of the four directions on a compass. The roses mostly covered the Styrofoam but I left room in the center for the decorative ring. I made a small slit in the Styrofoam and inserted the decorative ring. I held the ring in place with a small dab of white glue (I couldn't use hot glue on the Styrofoam as it would have melted). Next, I cut four pink roses and put a dab of glue on the stems and pushed them into the Styrofoam around the ring. Finally, I cut eight pink and four white roses and hot glued them to the top of the box alternating colors and centering between the roses on the top edges.

I was almost done with the cake at this point. All that remained was the inside of the top layer. I placed the Styrofoam circle on the edge and sliced it in half lengthwise. I then covered it with black velvet I found in my mom's sewing closet and secured it on the sides with four straight pins. I made a small indentation in the center of the velvet with a quarter. This indentation is what would hold the real engagement ring I had bought earlier in the month.

I wanted to make something to mount the cake on before I attached it to the top of the case. I ended up cutting out a circle $6^3/4$ inches in diameter from cardboard and painted it white with acrylic craft paint, edges included. After it dried, I tacked lace with the glue gun around the circumference of the cardboard overlapping in the "back." Then, I glued down another doily on the cardboard using a little more white craft glue.

I centered the cake on the doily and hot glued it in place. Next, I glued more strings of pearls around the bottom of the box. I cut 12 more pink and 12 more white ribbon roses, gluing them at the bottom of the U and in between each U. The in-between roses were lined up with those glued at the top of the Us on the large box.

Finally, I cut four 1-inch pieces of Velcro and attached them to the bottom of the cardboard. After attaching the cake to the top of the case, I took a step back and stared at my newly finished mod (see Figure 11-11). I was really happy with the way it came out—a perfect representation of my vision. I was so psyched about getting it finished and how well it came out, I threw caution to the wind and decided to get home as soon as possible so I could propose that night.

FIGURE 11-11: Completed cake with hidden compartment for engagement ring.

The Proposal

Items needed:

- One nervous guy
- His unsuspecting wife-to-be
- A monitor to display the custom wallpaper

Well, with the case fully finished, I didn't want to wait any longer. I decided to grab the case and bring it home right away and have it ready when she came home (which was about four hours away). I set my flat panel up on a small table and put the case on the floor at an angle that showed both the side and front windows. I turned the lights off so the only light was from the PC and monitor, displaying the custom wallpaper. It turns out that my fiancée was late from work that night, so I sat around in extended agony, nervous as anything though I knew beyond a shadow of a doubt she would say yes. Why then was I so nervous? I drank a bottle of water really quickly to calm my nerves, and took my post next to the window so I could see when she came home. Suddenly I saw her pull in, and the nerves were multiplied by ten. In the next few minutes we'd be engaged!

I kneeled down and waited for her to follow the light from the PC. She came into the room and her eyes nearly bugged out of her head! She was stammering and then her eyes moved to the PC. She was fixated on it, and I don't think she heard a word of my little engagement speech I had prepared for her. I "popped the question" and she said . . . "Yes." The way she said it was almost like "Of course—what took you so long?"

In her fixation on the PC, my fiancée had completely forgotten that she was getting a ring. She looked dumbfounded when I took the top layer of the cake off to reveal the ring inside, as if she thought I was breaking it. I slipped the ring on her finger and sealed the deal with a kiss.

The Happy Ending

People have asked me if building this mod was worth it. All the time spent, frustration endured, lunch hours, weekends, and days off from work spent in my parents' garage. Each time I have answered with an emphatic "yes." Sure, it was time-consuming and stressful, but the project allowed me to express my love through something that is near and dear to me, which is modding. Also, how many other women get to look at their wedding proposal every day? This was a totally unique wedding proposal, and in this day and age that is a very difficult thing to pull off.

As for the day that the PC gets outdated and obsolete? Well, I'll just have to get my tools out again and make her another one—maybe this time for our anniversary!

The Mad Scientist

Russ "JediKnight0" Caslis

I decided it was time for a new mod. Rather, I found an excuse to create one. One of my other mods was entered into a contest where the top prize was a pretty nice motherboard. I convinced myself that I would win that motherboard, and of course it deserved a new case around it (and new hard drive, and processor, and memory, and . . .).

I spent the next few weeks dreaming up features for the new computer and exactly what components should be installed in the computer. The overall decisions for the computer components were somewhat easy to make, because it was just a matter of compromise between the best components the motherboard could handle and the price. But the overall design of the case itself took quite a bit of sketching and daydreaming.

After getting the basic design down on paper and a bit of a discussion with my wife, I purchased a case and started modifying it for the new computer. I purchased pieces slowly, on an as-needed basis. This slowed the process down a little, but ensured that I paid the lowest prices because computer equipment continuously drops in price over time.

Tip For the first time in modding, I realized that chocolate is an essential part of modding. How? Whenever I needed to make an expensive purchase, I found the topic went over much better with my wife if I was holding a small box of chocolates for her!

In the end, I had a case mod that I was truly proud of (see Figure 12-1). Besides being a computer I can feel proud to display, it's been a wonderful machine to play Far Cry on. My old computer would never have the power to run such a game, but this one cuts through it without a single hitch.

Timeframe and Cost

This mod took approximately six months to create. The number is a little misleading, however. During this period, I spent many late nights at my "real" job, and I was limited in the time I could spend on modding. Also, I worked on another mod (the Chapter 19 Aircraft Carrier PC) during the same period, so my time was split between them. If I knew then what I

FIGURE 12-1: The completed mod.

know now, this mod would probably have taken only a month and a half. Even that number is misleading, because a significant portion of that time would simply have been spent waiting for paint to dry.

The cost of this mod runs over a thousand dollars, since most of the computer is new equipment. The case and the mods themselves would only cost $200 to $300, but add a new processor, memory, hard drives, and so on, and the cost skyrockets.

Required Parts and Tools

This was a computer built to be a "daily driver"—a computer I could use every day for every purpose. It had to excel at game playing, Web surfing, and video editing. In other words, all the things I use my computer for. As such, the parts are too numerous to list but include all the usual components you would think of—CPU, motherboard, hard drives, and so on. Some of the parts that are not so obvious are:

- Various paints, including Fleckstone textured paint (about $30 worth)
- Chameleon Springs for wire management ($25)
- Dual UV cold cathode lights ($15)
- White LEDs ($3)

- Three battery testers ($10 each)

- Old, unused circuit boards (free—old junk I'd saved)

- Various fans—standard 80-mm fan, green LED fan, blower exhaust fan ($30 combined)

- Various buttons, switches, and a rheostat (about $15)

- VFD display compatible with Hitachi 44780 display ($15)

- Various acrylic pieces including tubes, discs, flat sheets ($25)

The tools involved with this case are all the usual case modding favorites. Nothing too special here:

- Soldering iron with solder

- Dremel with cutting disks

- Hand drill

- Epoxy ($5)

- Masking tape ($5)

- Wire strippers

Design

As with many of my mods, I started out with a vague sense of the theme for the mod and a certain set of requirements. This mod was going to be different from the mods I typically did. This system would become my everyday computer and not just some dedicated-purpose system. I wanted something that was significantly more complex and more powerful than the mods I had done before, but one that would still be somewhat easy to upgrade or work on. Sketching out my list of requirements, they came out to be:

- The mod must be functional rather than just pretty. This meant that I had to have space for a full-sized motherboard and all the accessories.

- It had to be aluminum. It's just much lighter and easier to work with. It also looks much better (in my opinion). But my final design wasn't done yet, so I was open to the idea of painting the aluminum if it worked out better for the theme.

- It had to be easy to work with, which meant that the layout and wire-management must be better than anything I had done in the past.

- It should have a theme and be visually interesting to me and others.

It was also important to realize that time had passed since my first desktop system mod. In those days, ordering a window kit and installing it was something that made "normal" people (even people involved in computer support every day) stand up and take notice. I needed to find something that could wake them up again. So I decided on every computer user's worst nightmare—water.

Water cooling is not nearly as scary as it sounds, as detailed in Chapter 2. The car you drive to work every day is also liquid cooled and has to function in far worse environments than your computer, and it rarely has problems. However, most nonenthusiasts are still scared by the prospect of water spilling into or on their computers.

Some people use water (and an elaborate scheme of pipes, tubes, metal fittings, and other fun stuff) to water cool their PC. I agonized about whether I should water cool this new computer. In the end, I decided against it. I had a hard time finding a case that I liked the appearance of and was large enough to fit the computer components and all the water-cooling components that I liked into it, but mostly what killed the idea was my inability to water-cool everything. If I wasn't able to water-cool everything, I didn't want to even start.

Don't be afraid to change your modding plans if the techniques involved are beyond you. I found lots of info on how to cool everything that needed it, except the power supply. I did find info on one person who had done it, but it looked like the technique was beyond my ability and I knew it. I shifted gears and was still able to get a great result. You can too.

I had also seen several cases that used light tubes on the front bezel. These were tube-shaped clear plastic with bubbles in them that reflected the light from some LEDs at the bottom and top. I thought to myself, "why not do the same thing but with real water?"

So . . . what has cool bubbling water and interesting lights? Why something created by or for a mad scientist. I started sketching some designs (see Figure 12-2) during those moments at work where my brain was too fried to think about "real" work. After several iterations, I decided on a case where the back half looked like brick and the front was metal with big bolts sticking out the sides. It would have several bricks missing in the side that would allow me to put a window in, so the motherboard inside could be seen. I would use UV lights to light everything up with an eerie glow. The front would use analog gauges meters instead of lights for power and hard drive activity. Not to mention the vial of bubbling liquid up front.

The Shell

According to my designs, I wanted the sides and top to look like metal up front and like brick in the back. In fact, the left side needed to have a number of missing bricks in which I could install a window to show the inner computer components.

Brick Design

The first thing I needed to do was finalize the design of that piece of the case. I measured some bricks in my fireplace to get the general dimensions of a brick. The problem was, if I used that size directly, the whole case would be made from about a dozen bricks. Since

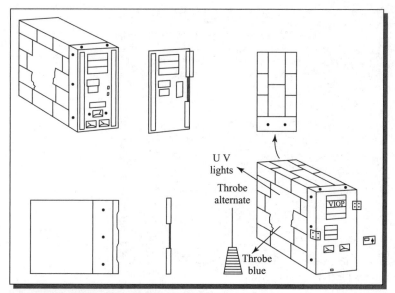

FIGURE 12-2: Initial sketches of the design.

I wanted a pattern for the side window like several bricks had fallen out, I needed smaller bricks. I scaled the numbers for the dimensions down quite a bit until I settled on bricks that were 10 cm × 5 cm × 5 cm. I then took a side panel and completely covered it in masking tape. Using a T ruler, I drew the brick pattern on the side panel, making sure that I left some room at the front that would remain the original aluminum.

Once I had the brick pattern copied on the side panel, I figured out exactly which bricks should be missing so that the appropriate amount of the interior could be seen. It was also important to remember that the side panel had to attach to the case via metal teeth along the bottom and top, so I had to make sure that I didn't remove any of these teeth with the window I was planning to cut. Once I had the design down, I lightly colored it in using pencil (see Figure 12-3). Time to cut . . . sort of.

I used the engraving bit on my Dremel to trace all the lines I had made with pencil on the tape, cutting through the tape in the process. I used a fair amount of pressure, but not enough to go through the metal or compromise its strength. The idea was that this would become the cement between the bricks. As such, it was important to make things somewhat irregular. I varied the speed at which I moved the Dremel across the surface and the amount of pressure I used so that I had a roughly straight line, but I also made it look a little unprofessional on purpose (see Figure 12-4). After this, I removed the tape that represented the bricks but left the tape that represented the front metal portion on the panel.

Cutting Through

The next day I fired up my Dremel and using a cutting disk I carefully cut out the window. I remembered to not go to fast and let the tool do the work, rather than just pushing the tool

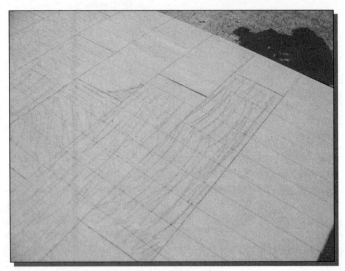

FIGURE **12-3: Pattern for etching and cutting.**

into the metal as quick as I could make it go. Control over the Dremel was key. It could easily grab someplace and either shatter the cutting disk sending sharp edges flying or drag itself across a side panel where I didn't want any nicks. I tried to get the window design so it looked somewhat realistic and not just a simple pattern. I also made sure to nick one of the bricks so that it would look like it fell apart on its own or due to some outside force, but not as though it was put together that way.

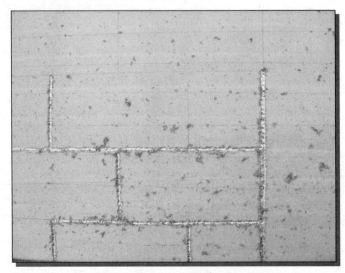

FIGURE **12-4: Etching directly through the masking tape.**

Once I had the window cut out, I used some 400-grit sandpaper to clean up the edges and make them somewhat smooth. The advantage of leaving the edges a little uneven is that brick itself is never perfectly straight, so some amount of imperfection is perfectly fine. It also leaves some room for error, which is always good.

All this work left a fair amount of gooey metallic sludge on the side of the panel. I brushed off what I could, then took the panel inside to the bathtub. Using warm water, soap, and a cheap toothbrush, I cleaned all the goo from the panel. I tried to keep the portion still covered by tape somewhat dry. After the panel was clean, I dried it using a towel and left it to air dry for a day.

Painting

Time to start painting. I used gray primer as the first coat on the panel. I made sure to spray everything thoroughly, especially all the little areas I had engraved out. I used two coats and let it dry for a few hours. I then used some graphic art tape to cover all the lines that I had previously engraved. I used tape that was $1/16$ inch wide and simply cut it to the right lengths and pushed it into all the grooves left by the engraving process.

Chapter 6 has a good discussion of painting methods, tools, and technique.

Now for the fun part. There is a special type of textured paint you can buy that instead of simply covering in a solid color, actually uses small particles of different colors to cover the panel and leaves a surface that actually has a bumpy texture. The brand and color I used was Plastikote Fleckstone Fiesta, which gives a nice slightly washed-out red color that simulates brick pretty well. I shook up the can and started spraying the side panel. The paint goes on very heavy, and the overspray is pretty intense, so I had to watch that I didn't get the overspray on other items in the area. I tried to get a somewhat even coat but not too much. Ultimately I used about four coats, with about two hours of drying time in between.

The overspray from this paint is nasty and likes to cling to everything. My screen door is still slightly brick colored and textured just from the overspray.

Painting with Fleckstone paint goes quicker in direct sunlight. If you paint in direct sunlight and let it dry there, you only need two hours between coats. Anywhere else and you would have to wait longer.

The drying time on this stuff took forever. I let it dry for two days, then I was able to continue work on it. I still felt a little tacky and wet, but at least I could start handling it. I carefully removed the graphic tape (leaving the masking tape on). This showed the beauty of the brick

FIGURE 12-5: With the graphic tape removed, the texture of the paint can be seen in relation to the gray primer underneath.

and cement pattern (see Figure 12-5). I then let it dry a whole week before touching it again, much of that time in direct sunlight.

After the paint was finally dry, I applied a clear coat on top of the paint. I let that dry another 24 hours, then applied another layer of clear coat. I let that dry for about a week, then removed the tape covering the front of the panel revealing the bare metal underneath.

A Window on the World

The panel still needed a window to prevent things such as dust, fingers, or my cat from getting into the computer and causing problems. This was a simple thing to create.

I purchased a sheet of $1/8$-inch acrylic panel from my local hardware store and cut it to the size of my side panel using my Dremel and a cutting disc. The only thing I had to remember was to cut a special rounded section in one side to accommodate the indentation for the handle.

Once that piece was cut and cleaned with a little glass cleaner, it was time to attach it. I made a line of silicone glue all around the window, about $1/4$ to $1/2$ an inch away from the edges and laid the acrylic panel on top of the panel. I built up a small stack of books on the panel to maintain an even pressure and left the panel alone for 30 minutes to let the glue set a little. When I returned, I used a thicker bead of silicone glue around all the edges to help hold the acrylic even more strongly. I let that dry for a full 24 hours before removing the books.

Cross-Reference Chapter 9 suggests several ways that windows can be attached to side panels, including this method.

Frankenstein's Mod

The design called for the front of computer remaining metal and looking like an old 1950s-style computer. Equipment from that day and age always had huge screws and bolts holding everything together, so I went to my local hardware store and bought some bolt covers about ¹/₂ an inch in diameter (quite heavy, actually).

I started by measuring three spots evenly spaced on the side panel in the section not covered by paint, and drilled three holes just smaller than the diameter of the nuts. I then attached the bolts over the holes using masking tape and applied a generous amount of epoxy through the hole and onto both the side panel and the inside of the nut.

After the epoxy was dry, I removed the masking tape from all the nuts.

Let Your Light Shine Through

The panel was almost complete now. One remaining problem was the lighting for the mod. The design called for the inside to be UV lit, but every location in which I tried to put the cold cathode lights was a poor fit. Either the lights simply didn't fit in the space provided or the lights themselves were easily seen from the outside (somewhat blemishing the appearance I was going for) or the light distribution was too uneven.

Then a thought occurred to me. Most cold cathode lights are shipped in an acrylic tube to prevent them from being damaged because they are very fragile. Some of the acrylic tubes, such as the tubes on the dual cold cathode light I had purchased, have square ends the make mounting them easier. Hmmm . . . acrylic panel . . . acrylic tubes. . . .

Using some acrylic glue, I simply glued the tubes to the panel in an L shape. Since inverters for cold cathode lights can be damaged by running them without the cold cathodes attached, I glued the inverter to the side panel using some silicone glue (see Figure 12-6). If I decided to

FIGURE 12-6: The completed side panel with UV lights.

remove the panel I would be cutting off power to the lights at the 12-volt DC power source rather than the high voltage AC source. Thus, no damage would occur to any component.

To facilitate the disconnecting, I attached a smaller connector to the DC side of the inverter rather than the standard Molex connector. I remembered to attach the male side of the connector to the side panel to prevent the loose connector inside the case from shorting out.

One Down, Two to Go

The cool part was that I now had a great looking side panel to inspire me to finish the rest of the mod. The downside was that after all this work, I wasn't even half done. There was still another side panel and the top of the case to finish up in the same fashion. All in all, the other panels came together pretty well using the same techniques.

The top panel was the simplest. I covered the panel in masking tape and used a pencil to trace in the brick pattern, continuing the pattern and shape from the already completed panel. The only difficult problem on this piece was that, due to laziness on my part, I chose not to remove the panel from the rest of the case. I simply masked off the other areas with tape and newspaper before doing any of the painting.

The other side panel was similar, in that I continued with the same pattern and techniques. On this side, however, I didn't cut just one window. I cut two small windows about half a brick in length each. The idea was to put some fake circuit boards beneath these to add a little life to an often underused and bland area of most cases.

Cooling

I decided that I'd include the common cooling design that a lot of modders use on their systems—one front intake fan and one exhaust blowhole up top. Even so, I still had a number of issues to contend with.

The front of the case I chose to use as a canvas for this mod had a horrible black square pattern painted on it. I carefully cut out this entire section, leaving a large hole in the front (see Figure 12-7). Looking at how much space there was to work with inside the front panel, I decided to move the front intake fan from inside the case itself to inside the front panel. I carefully cut out the extra metal between the case front and the inside of the case and drilled a few holes for the fan to mount onto.

For the top fan, I cut a jagged hole in the brick design , which I had carefully measured to make sure that everything would fit even after the power supply and optical drives were added. One problem I faced was how to attach the fan without having four bolts sticking up through the brick paint job. The solution was to make my own mounting brackets on the inside.

Tip   I really should have cut out the blowhole before painting, but I hadn't designed the cooling system at that that point.

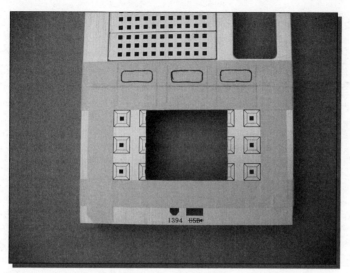

FIGURE 12-7: The font of the case with the fan area beginning to be cut out. Also visible are the markings for the analog gauge cutouts.

I took four long screws with matching nuts and cut the screws so that when the screws were placed through the fan mounting holes, they were just long enough to attach the nuts on top. I covered the nuts in epoxy and placed the fan and screws in position. I first had to rough up the edges of the nuts and the inside of the case with a combination of sandpaper and cutting discs to give the epoxy have something to grab onto. After the epoxy dried, I was able to unscrew the fan and remove it.

Next, it was time to clean everything up. I used some metal mesh that I sanded down and painted with copper paint to cover the fan areas as a fan guard. Because the label side was exposed on the top fan, I printed out a radiation symbol and glued it over the manufacturer's label (see Figure 12-8). On the front, there were open areas to the sides of the fans that allowed the internal wiring to be seen. I covered that with some spare plastic, painted black and cut to the right shape, and glued it in place.

Now, just the issue of noise control was left. I had decided on a three-stage cooling setup. While the two fans I purchased were both low-noise-producing fans, I wanted something even quieter. Using a couple of switches mounted in the front panel, I set up the fans so that when the first switch was in the lowest position, the intake fan ran at half speed, and the top fan was off. When the first switch was in the upper position, the intake fan operated at full speed and the top fan became active. The second switch controlled the low speed/full speed operation of the second fan, if it was active.

Of course, both switches had to be labeled with their functions. I used a bit of clear transparency paper and printed out several pieces that could act as labels and covers. I carefully cut out the labels and glued them on the front panel over the switches. I also used this technique through the rest of the mod, making sure that every display, switch, or dial had a label.

FIGURE 12-8: Top fan mounted in position.

Even with the power modifications made to the fans, I wanted this system to be as quiet as possible and to minimize any vibration noise produced by the fans. I purchased a number of gaskets designed to deaden the vibration sounds from the fans and installed them between the fans and the case. Now, the cooling aspects of the mod were taken care of.

Front Panel

The majority of this mod was spent working on the front panel. The front panel of any computer is where the majority of a person's interaction with the computer takes place (other than the keyboard and mouse), so this is only logical. Almost all elements of the design depended on changes to the front faceplate.

This mod, of course, was going to have the front faceplate of all the DVD-ROM drives vinyl dyed to match the case colors. But so many more mods were necessary that this piece consumed nearly all the time on this mod.

Power and Lighting

The computer needed power and reset buttons, as well as a switch to turn on the UV lights installed on the side panel. The exiting power and reset buttons on the case were cheap pieces of plastic with even cheaper switches underneath, so I removed those as well as the plastic mounting pieces for them. This left a hole in the right side of the front panel, but luckily the hole had nicely round edges that didn't look too bad.

For the power and reset buttons, I purchased some heavy-duty momentary automotive switches. I took a small piece of acrylic panel and drilled two large holes in the center for the two switches, and drilled four smaller mounting holes in the panel around the edges. I also drilled matching holes for mounting this piece against the front of the case. Then, I painted the acrylic with copper paint and mounted the switches.

The switch for the UV lighting was even easier. I just drilled a hole for a toggle switch further down the side of the front of the case and attached it to a Molex connector and the wire for the UV lights on the side panel.

All the switches were then labeled using the same technique as the other switches.

Analog Gauges

Another important design element from the beginning was including analog gauges to display hard drive activity. A single gauge wasn't very interesting, so in my design I added a couple more gauges to display the 5-volt and 12-volt power source status. There are a number of nice analog gauge mods on the Web, so my design would not be earth-shattering. But typically these mods suffer from two problems—the gauges were almost always round and somewhat large, and they were expensive. Both these things were issues I wanted to avoid.

 Tip   Analog gauges are not something new to modding—various people have modded gauges from cars into their computers. Also, companies such as CoolerMaster (`www.coolermaster.com`) have started selling their own analog gauge devices such as the Musketeer.

Problems and Solutions

The first problem was finding the right gauges. Without requiring far more electronics knowledge than I had, I would need to find a gauge that showed voltage (not any of a hundred other elements that could be measured—temperature, wattage, pressure, and so on. The exact range of voltage would be changeable with the right resistor, but I had to find one that measured voltage (and relatively low amounts). Also, I didn't have much space at all to work in the case, so the gauge had to be small.

Also, let's face it—I'm not rich. Convincing my wife to let me buy the computer stuff was hard enough, but trying to convince her to let me purchase a $70 to $100 gauge (three of them) that I might accidentally destroy during the modding process would be near impossible. But then I read about a solution to those problems.

Radio Shack sells a number of cheap battery testers for under $10 that use a small analog gauge to show the health of the batteries. I picked up a few and tore them apart to get at the gauge inside. These gauges, with a few modifications, solved both of my problems.

Adapting the Gauges

The gauges as they were used in the battery testers allowed the testing of batteries from 1.5-volt button batteries to 9-volt square batteries. Thus, adapting them was, in theory, easy—just use the right resistors to drop the voltages I had to work with (5 volt and 12 volt) down to 1.5 volt or so. I busted open the plastic housing and found a complex web of resistors attached to each gauge (see Figure 12-9).

FIGURE 12-9: Inside the battery tester.

I decided to clean the wiring up. I disconnected all the resistors from the gauges and slowly found the right amount of resistance to use with each gauge by trial and error. I hooked a gauge up to the 5-volt power source and put a 10-ohm resistor there—oops, too little. I replaced the 10-ohm resistor with a 10-Kohm resistor—oops too much. I replaced the 10-Kohm resistor with 5-Kohm resistor—still too much. I repeated this process for each power source, the 5 volt, the 12 volt, and the hard drive activity light (similar to 5 volt).

The second problem was how to mount the gauges. I carefully cut out three holes the right size for the gauge displays in the right spot on the front faceplate. The problem was that the gauges themselves needed to sit back a little from the front to allow the needle to move. I used a bit of the plastic from the battery tester—the clear piece—and attached it with tape to each gauge. I then used bits of spare styrene plastic to build the depth up a little more so that the needle would have the room it needed to move. This piece was painted black.

The last problem was how to light up the gauge itself. First, I replaced the background sticker inside the gauge with a piece of paper with some evenly spaced lines on it that I printed with my inkjet printer. Then, near the bottom of each gauge, I drilled a hole for a 3-mm white LED and resistor. This LED would shine through the gauge and reflect off the plastic piece I had previously built and illuminate the whole gauge (see Figure 12-10).

Mounting the Gauges

The gauges were all wired together so that the bundle of three gauges had only two connectors—a Molex connector and the hard drive activity header for the motherboard. I attached this bundle of gauges to the inside of the front panel with hot glue.

Finally, I just needed to label the gauges. While the gauge marks were already printed in appropriate colors (red for 5-volt power, yellow for 12-volt power, and gray for activity), that

FIGURE 12-10: The completed set of gauges.

just didn't seem clear enough. I used the printed transparency paper technique to create labels for all the gauges and attached them with glue.

I tested the gauges in place an everything seemed to work okay. Not too bad—for less than $35 in parts I had three small gauges that fit my theme. Just buying a single automotive gauge would have cost more than that.

VFD Display

LCD displays that can display vital computer stats such as temperature, CPU load, and other information are becoming common in computer mods these days. Slightly less common but just as useful are VFD displays. These display the same information as an LCD and can be controlled the same way, but have a bright display that can be seen well no matter what angle you look at them from (unlike LCD displays which suffer from a small field of view). Several LCD and VFD displays are available as kits for modders, but it's more fun to do it yourself—so that's what I did. I found a nice VFD display that was compatible with the common parallel port configuration for LCD displays and purchased it.

The first problem was mounting the display. While the circuit board did have four mounting holes, these holes were not exactly centered over the display but were offset to one side. In addition, I didn't want four huge screws sticking through the front of the case. I came up with the idea of making a mounting bracket of sorts on the inside of the bay insert.

I started by measuring the size of the displayable area for the display and cut out the same-sized hole in the center of a 5^1/$_4$-inch bay insert. I then took four screws with matching nuts and cut the screws until they were the same height as the display itself when mounted through the mounting holes. In other words, the nuts were screwed on the screws themselves just

FIGURE **12-11: The VFD display attached to the bay insert.**

enough so the nuts were level with the glass front of the display. I covered the edges of the nuts in epoxy glue and placed the display placed into the bay insert (see Figure 12-11). After the glue finished drying, I unscrewed the screws and was able to remove the display but the nuts stayed in place. Thus, I could reattach the display anytime just by screwing it in place.

The next problem was how to access the parallel port. There are no ways to easily access the parallel port from inside the computer, so I built a cable that went from the VFD display itself to the back of the case. Using one of the little-used extra punchouts in the back of the case, I mounted the edge of the cable there. I then built a jumper cable that went on the outside of the case from the VFD cable to the parallel port.

 The jumper cable is nothing more than a small cable that maps pin 1 in one connector to pin 1 of the other connector, and so on for the rest of the pins. The interesting work is in the cable from the VFD display to the jumper cable. A simple VFD mod like this one is described, along with the appropriate pinout, in Chapter 8.

I finished off the display by first printing and attaching a label to the front of the VFD bay insert like I did with the analog gauges. I also covered the jumper cable in the back of the case with orange UV material that was leftover from an unused IDE cable.

USB and FireWire Ports

Another problem with the front panel was the front-mounted USB and FireWire ports. While my motherboard did have headers for USB ports, it did not have a FireWire port. The computer needed a FireWire port, so I added that via a PCI card, but that card didn't have and headers either just a standard cable connector inside the case.

FIGURE 12-12: Front-mounted ports with cables directly attached.

I took a standard FireWire cable and cut off one end. Carefully, I mapped out which wires should go to each pin on the FireWire header and soldered a proper connector onto the FireWire cable. Plugging that cable into the PCI card, I now had a functioning FireWire port up front.

But that was too easy. With the small circuit board mounted up front, there wasn't enough room for the USB and FireWire cables to attach to the headers on that board with the front intake fan mounted. Determined to have front mounted ports, I removed the header from the circuit board with the connectors up front and directly soldered the cables to it (see Figure 12-12). This allowed just enough room that the cables could bend and go underneath the front intake fan.

Wire Management

Hiding and controlling the wires inside a computer case is essential for making it look clean and improving airflow (and therefore cooling). The downside to doing a really great job of wire management is that changing the layout of the case (i.e., where the wires need to go) is quite a chore. So I had an idea—what if I made messy wires a feature?

Any of the computer stuff in the old science fiction movies always looks a little like a rat's nest of cables. I didn't want a real mess, because that would cause heating problems. But because

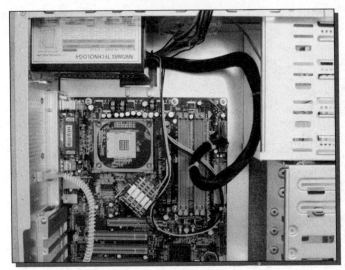

FIGURE 12-13: Some cables are clearly too long.

this computer would require quite a few cables, why not avoid hiding them? I would still manage the individual wires in bundles, but I would leave the bundles in clear view.

I started out by arranging all the components that needed power in the case, including hard drives, the motherboard, optical drives, the video card, and so on. It was obvious that the power supply I had purchased had some cables that were way too long and others that were too short (see Figure 12-13). I measured every cable and came up with a cable layout that I thought would work. I then cut every single wire and resoldered them to the proper lengths, including opening the power supply and changing the length of the motherboard power connector.

Since I was going to leave the bundles visible, I needed to make them more interesting. I decided to use some of the Chameleon Springs wire management material I had read about to bundle the wires together. This material comes in several different shades, and I purchased a small kit of blue UV reactive material and started cleaning up the wires. I then came to realize I didn't purchase enough of the material.

Chapter 3 includes info about wire management, including Chameleon Springs.

The IDE cables I was going to use were orange UV-reactive cables (they came with the motherboard). Since I needed more of the Chameleon Springs, I decided to purchase them in orange UV reactive as well. Thus, I came up with the loose concept that power-carrying wires would be blue, while data-carrying wires would be orange.

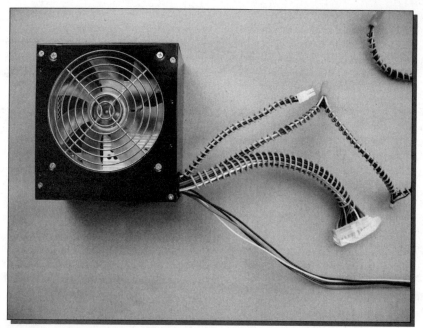

FIGURE 12-14: Power supply cables shortened, wrapped in Chameleon Springs, and with UV reactive Molex connectors.

Not content yet, I purchased some UV-reactive blue Molex connectors and replaced all connectors that I could with these UV-reactive connectors. In the end, I replaced about a half-dozen power connectors, a floppy power connector, and the motherboard power connector with these UV-reactive connectors (see Figure 12-14).

Another technique I used to manage the wires was a false back. What this means is that behind the location where the hard drives are mounted in the case, I used a piece of plastic to hide the mess of cables behind the drives.

Tip   Because it's often impractical to cover every single wire up and make them look good, the use of a false back or false bottom helps to hide a lot of the clutter inside the case.

Water Effects

One of the most interesting features I planned for this mod was a classic water tube with air bubbling up from the bottom. In addition, the tube would be lit with green light from below so the air bubbles would catch the light and give everything an eerie green glow. The concept was simple, just a clear tube and an air pump. But in reality, adding the tube was a lot of work.

The basic tube was easy to create. I simply purchased the right diameter acrylic tube and a matching diameter acrylic disc and glued them together. I drilled holes in the bottom of the tube and the disc as well. In the side of the tube, I glued an acrylic fish-tank air-hose connector in place with acrylic glue. In the bottom hole in the disc, I epoxied a water-clear ultrabrite green LED. I allowed all three glued areas to dry for a few days and then tested the tube for leaks.

The first problem was how to mount the tube to the case and still have it look somewhat professional. The tube needed to be removable for maintenance work or to empty the water. The first design I used was to attach small sections of acrylic rod at 90-degree angles to the water tube. On the ends of the acrylic rods, I epoxied some rare-earth magnets. At the appropriate height in the case front, I epoxied matching magnets. When the tube was placed on the front of the case, the connection wasn't too strong, but it was good enough to hold the water-filled tube in place. I then set this piece aside, securing it to the side of a piece of metal to keep it out of the way as I worked on other pieces of the mod.

When I came back to work on this piece a month or so later, the tube had cracked and spider-webbed all over. I never reached a firm conclusion as to why this happened, but I suspect this was somehow related to the stress placed on the tube. But for all I know, the magnets could have caused some reaction from the impurities in the acrylic or case-modding elves could have used it for a pogo-stick. In any case, I needed another method to mount the tube.

I ended up purchasing some small acrylic boxes just big enough to hold the tube inside them. I cut out round seconds at the top of one box and the bottom of the other box, painted them silver, and drilled holes in the back for mounting them to the case. The acrylic tube can be placed inside and the covers placed on it, which covers the ends of the acrylic tube. The front of the case was nearly complete now (see Figure 12-15).

The next problem was how to arrange the electronics to accomplish the bubbling air. I started by purchasing a battery-powered air pump from a pet store and adapting it to use power from a Molex connector rather than batteries. I experimented a while with different resistors to give me exactly the right flow rate for the air bubbles in the tube. I then fabricated a mounting bracket on the inside of the case for the air pump from half of a large acrylic box (see Figure 12-16) and painted it.

One problem that could occur was water backup up into the air pump itself. To prevent this problem, I used an air-check valve a couple of inches from the location where the tube attached to the front of the case. This handy device made it possible for air to flow only one way through the valve, preventing the water from flowing backward.

Finally, I added a switch to control the front panel (along with a label) to turn the water effect on and off. I also wired into the same switch a control for the LED embedded in the water tube.

Putting It All Together

At this point, I was ready to begin the basic assembly of the case. Along the way, I still needed to fabricate a few more parts and install them correctly, but the bulk of the work was already done. Time to see if everything would fit together as I planned.

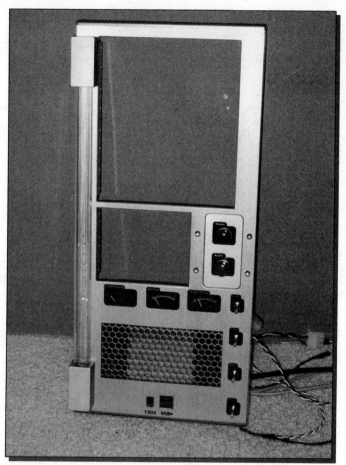

FIGURE **12-15:** The front of the case with water tube in place.

Hard Drive Brackets

Earlier, I had moved the front intake fan from the inside of the case to inside the front panel. This left an extra 1 inch of space in front of the hard drives. I decided that it would be great if I could move the hard drives forward 1 inch. That would give the IDE cables a little extra room to move around, since they still don't make 3-inch IDE cables, and motherboard manufacturers still insist on putting the IDE connectors along the right side of the motherboard. But if I moved the hard drives forward, the screw holes wouldn't line up and the hard drives couldn't be secured in place.

I solved this problem by taking some scrap pieces of metal (brass, actually) and making $1^{1}/_{2}$-inch extensions. I attached one end of these extensions to a hard drive bay (see Figure 12-17) and the other end to a hard drive in the bay below. This allowed the hard drives to be held in

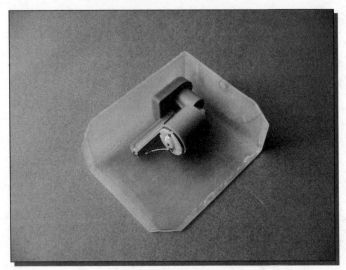

FIGURE 12-16: The air pump attached to the box mounting bracket.

place in a sort of cradle, and moved them forward the distance I needed. I used some rubber gaskets between the hard drives and these brackets to help silence any vibrations.

Tip

Fans, by their nature, are constantly vibrating as the blades spin around at high RPM. When the side of a fan is pressed against a case panel, the panel starts to vibrate as well, which turns the whole side into a speaker. This, of course, adds a lot of noise. But this noise can largely be eliminated or at least reduced by using rubber or silicon gaskets between the fan and the side panel. Several case mod manufacturers sell kits that include several gaskets, or you can save some money by buying small rubber gaskets at a local hardware store.

Exposed Circuits

I had previously installed two small windows in the right side panel of the case. The idea was to allow computer bits to be seen through these windows, as if the bricks had broken away and you could see the computer inside. Since all that was really visible under those windows was the back side of the motherboard mounting tray, I needed to do something else.

I, like any true computer geek, have collected many old pieces of computers over the years (many of which don't work well or don't work at all). I took a couple of these, an old SCSI card and an old network hub, and cut them open to expose their bare circuit boards. I modified the boards a little by sanding the back side smooth and removing any tall components. One chip had a company logo on it, so I covered it up with another radiation symbol I printed out. Then, I used hot glue to glue these to the back side of the motherboard tray directly underneath the windows.

FIGURE 12-17: Hard drive brackets in place.

Finally, I wired some ultrabrite green LEDs to the sides of both of these boards and attached a Molex connector (see Figure 12-18). The plan was to attach these to the same switch that controlled the UV cold cathode lights. Thus, turning on the lights would turn on lights on both sides of the case.

Finishing Up

The rest of the computer came together as one might expect. No major problems, just standard computer assembly. The motherboard goes there, the RAM goes here, the hard drives go over there. Pretty standard stuff.

The fun part was watching it all take shape. I knew everything should work, but there is always that feeling of dread the first time I turn a new computer on. Will it work, or will I have to pull everything apart looking for the proverbial needle in a haystack? When I first poured water into the acrylic tube for the first time with the computer running, I was worried that it would leak. So many pieces to assemble and so many chances for mistakes.

In the end, everything came together and worked just fine. A lot of worrying for nothing. But all in all, I'd rather worry over nothing than be justified in my worrying.

Oops! I'll Do It Again!

After all this hard, the mod was seemingly done. By dumb luck, that very week the game Far Cry was released. What better way to test the system that by play testing the system with a state-of-the-art game? I had a blast, literally, blowing up mutants and humans alike in this great game. It also showed me several design problems with the mod that needed to be corrected.

FIGURE 12-18: Fake circuit boards mounted against the motherboard tray.

Too Hot for You

The first problem I had was a few random lockups of the system. Not always during gameplay either, sometimes the lockups occurred just playing a few MP3s and light Web surfing. I went nuts trying to figure out the problem. I tried playing around with hanging extra fans off the side of the case while leaving the side panel off to see if it was a heat-related problem. For a while, I decided that the problem was too much heat around the area of the system memory and/or the edge of the video card. How would I solve that without placing a big fan in the middle of the side window, thus ruining the effect?

You may have seen the PCI card coolers that are for sale. Basically, these are nothing more than blower-type fans that attach to the PCI card slot mounting holes on the back of the case and take hot air out of the case. I had the thought that If I could just reverse the airflow, I might be able to bring extra cold air into the case, while avoiding cutting my window. In reality, this proved to be difficult.

Because I know nothing about taking fans apart and reversing airflow, I thought I could just mount the fan on the outside of the case by removing the mounting bracket and reversing it. I was able to get the mounting bracket off and reversed, but the fan was too thick. All the blower fans for PCI cards are thin enough to attach to the cage opening just for a few millimeters, then they grow in size. When I mounted this fan externally in a PCI card slot, the extra width made getting at the back of the other PCI cards impossible.

FIGURE 12-19: Exhaust blower fan turned into an air intake fan and mounted on the rear of the case.

Once again, I turned to one of the extra punchouts in the back of the case. I was able to remove that extra punchout and attach the fan through the hole there instead. I rewired the fan power wire to pass through the fan housing itself and replaced the typical red and black wires with UV-reactive blue wire. I also replaced the manufacturer's logo and fan specs with my own label (see Figure 12-19).

In the end, this mod didn't help or hurt the situation. My problem with flaky behavior turned out to be bad memory modules. No matter what the cooling was like, the memory I purchased (rated at 400 MHz) was unstable at speeds greater than 333 MHz.

Bubble, Bubble (or Lack of)

I was never happy with the water tube the way it was. It looked cool and was one of a kind, but it didn't work very well. If the tube was completely filled with water, the weight of the water was so great that the air bubbles simply couldn't make it up to the top. Perhaps worse, when the case (and water) heated up from the case simply being on, the flow rate of the air bubbles would change slightly.

I had tested the water effects by hooking the water tube up to the air pump with clear tubing before I ever placed the pump inside the case. I had attached the air pump to my test power supply, filled the tube with water, and watched the bubbles rise. Everything worked great

FIGURE **12-20**: Rheostat for adjusting air pressure mounted in the front of the case.

during the testing, but it turns out I made a few miscalculations. First, I never tested the air pump system with a full tube of water (to reduce the chance of spilling). Of course, the amount of water in the tube greatly affects the weight of the water and the strength required for the bubbles to flow. Second, I never tested it with exactly the same length of tubing I was using in the final mod. This also affects the air pressure. The solution was simple, if a lot of work. I took the entire front of the case off (no simple feat with so many wires and controls involved). I reworked the air pump to use a rheostat and a resistor instead of just a couple of resistors to adjust the air pressure, and thus the strength of the bubbles. Lastly, I mounted the rheostat in the front panel of the case (see Figure 12-20).

Gauge Problems

There was one last problem I had to overcome. The analog gauges simply didn't look very good. The gauges were lit unevenly, and two of the gauges had more of a blue look to the backlight than white. In addition, the white light tended to bleed up in the case, illuminating the bottom of the floppy drive in ways it wasn't supposed to. I bought three more battery testers, and started over from scratch.

The problem with the blue tint to the light in a couple of the gauges was easy to solve. I simply purchased LEDs from a different source, rather than just use whatever I had left around the house. That's why they were different colors—the LEDs came from different manufacturers originally.

FIGURE 12-21: A close-up of the finished interior.

FIGURE 12-22: The front and right side of the computer.

The problem with uneven light distribution was caused by the placement of the LED in the gauges—it wasn't centered. The problem with bleedthrough occurred because the plastic housing I used, left over from the original battery tester, wasn't completely enclosed on all sides. Instead of reusing that part, I built three custom enclosures from styrene plastic with the LED mounted in the center shining downward.

These changes solved all the problems with the gauges. They now looked much more professional, and the mod was finally complete and working as designed.

Conclusion

A lot of work went into this case. This was also the first case that I had to open back up a few weeks later to continue the modding process. This computer is also the most technologically advanced mod I've ever worked on. I'm happy to say that everything from the UV interior (see Figure 12-21) to the right side windows (see Figure 12-22) worked out just as planned.

This computer, this mod, has performed exactly as I wanted it to and looked good while doing it. It's played games, edited home videos, and even had chapters of a book written on it! What more could I ask for? Maybe a few more games. Time to present my wife with some more chocolate, I think. . . .

Picture Frame PC

Russ "JediKnight0" Caslis

These days at any good electronics retailer you can buy a digital picture frame that includes an LCD screen and plays pictures from memory cards (or in some cases via a phone line and a nightly call to a subscription service). These picture frames are usually several hundred dollars for a small 4 inch × 7 inch screen and are quite limited in what they can do.

To further this idea, some people have taken apart their laptop computers and tried to graft them into picture frames for the enhanced functionality that a real computer can offer. The problem is that very often the motherboard is bigger than the screen itself so they have to build some Frankenstein's monster of a case to house this motherboard and screen contraption. Even worse, they sometimes leave bare electronics sticking out the edges of the frame for anyone to touch and possibly damage the computer. Plus, these mismatched machines typically provide no way to actually use the computer itself without plugging in a keyboard and mouse or using some bulky wireless adapter. And don't forget that laptops are not exactly cheap.

One day I came across what I feel is a better and cheaper solution, when I was browsing the "cool cases" message board at one of my favorite sites, www.hardforums.com. Someone posted a message about a sale going on at one of the auction sites for an old Internet appliance called the Webplayer. Back during the dot-com days, several companies decided to make cheap computers that included a mouse/keyboard/screen setup for computer novices to use. They actually made their money from people paying a subscription fee, not the hardware itself. The Webplayer from Virgin was one of these computers.

Several of these Internet appliances, including the Webplayer, can be modded into cheap computers. Don't expect much in the way of processing power, but the form-factor presents many possibilities. The Webplayer is a 200-Mhz Pentium-compatible machine with built-in screen, modem, 44-MB disk-on-chip, and wireless keyboard/mouse combo. This system was the basis for my picture frame PC (see Figure 13-1).

Tip There were several varieties of Virgin Webplayers sold. Apart from the OS already on the appliance (different companies bought inventory of old Webplayers and applied their own OS without changing the hardware), there were two different confirmed types. The most common type came with a modem, but

FIGURE 13-1: Picture frame PC in operation.

some came with an integrated network interface card (NIC). There were also very rare versions that were supposed to have touchscreens, but these do not appear to have been fully functional.

Timeframe and Cost

The basic parts for this mod should run between $170 and $255, but that varies depending on what supplies you already have and what types of deals you can find. Sometimes none are available on any of the auction sites, but usually a new batch shows up in a week or two. They seem to go up for sale a few at a time, almost in waves.

- Webplayer: $35 to $75
- Wireless Ethernet mini-PCI card: $80
- Laptop hard drive and cable: $20 to $50
- Shadow-box picture frame and mat: $15 to $30
- Other miscellaneous supplies: $20

Once I had all the supplies, this mod was easily done in a couple of afternoons. Overall, I probably only invested 10 to 15 hours into the creation of this mod, but most of that time was spent just figuring out the placement and location of components. Knowing what I know now, this mod would only take four or five hours.

Required Parts and Tools

Despite appearances, this is actually quite a simple mod—particularly if you have a completely custom enclosure. Because of this, the tools and components didn't cost a lot this time around.

Parts

The only problems with the components used for this mod are that some are a little difficult to find.

- **Webplayer**—I used the modem variety, but the NIC variety should work as well. eBay is probably the best bet to find these now ($50 to $100).

- **Laptop hard drive**—Any size over 1 GB or so, but at least 2 GB is better ($70 for a 20GB drive).

- **Laptop hard drive IDE cable, at least 10"** — These can be rare. One place to purchase these is www.cablesonline.com ($8).

- **Linksys 802.11b wireless Ethernet card WMP11 revision 1**—Other cards may work as well, but it's difficult to say. The Ethernet card *must* include a mini-PCI type 3 card inside ($45).

- **Shadow-box picture frame**—Inner dimensions $9^1/2" \times 7^3/4" \times 1^1/2"$. ($20)

- **Thin sheet of tin**—Available at any hardware or hobby store ($5).

- **Foam board**—Cut to the shape of the back of the picture frame ($3).

- **Electrical tape**—($3).

Tools

The tools for this mod are the usual suspects for any case mod:

- Soldering iron with solder

- Desoldering iron

- Rotary tool with cutting discs

- Power drill with various drill bits

- Scissors

- Laptop to desktop hard drive adapter (This is not for permanent installation in the mod, only for temporary setup, so the adapter is more a tool that a component.)

Preparing the Webplayer

To prepare the Webplayer for its transformation into a picture frame PC, I needed to install Windows 98 on the Webplayer and verify that it worked properly. Since my Webplayer was fairly old and didn't come with a warranty, it was logical to verify its functionality and test it before I got too far into the mod. To do this, I needed the help of another computer.

Copying Necessary Files

I took the laptop hard drive and laptop drive adapter, and added the laptop drive as a secondary drive on another computer. (Of course, I made sure that the computer was off first and followed normal procedures for adding a hard drive.). Booting up the other PC and formatting the laptop hard drive, I made sure to do a full rather than a quick format because this was the initial install (it's always a good idea to exercise the drive before the first OS install). I made some directories on the laptop drive such as images, `images\win98`, and `images\drivers`. I then copied the complete Windows 98 CD to the `images\win98` directory.

Tip When copying the Windows CD, copy the actual files from the CD. Don't do an OS install on it. The actual OS install has to happen on the Webplayer itself. Also, remember to copy any hidden or system files. Leave nothing uncopied.

Next, I copied all the appropriate drivers to the `images\drivers` directory on the laptop hard drive. These drivers can be obtained from a number of places on the Web, such as:

- `www.webplayer.0catch.com/index.html`—Excellent general source of information about the Webplayers

- `www.larwe.com/technical/webplayer_main.html`—Main source of drivers and also a great description of the Webplayer hacking process

- `www.techdose.com/projects/Webplayer`—Another good source for Webplayer hacking including drivers

- `www.geocities.com/nojx2`—The rare but important power button (actually, sleep button) software hack

Tip Should you not be able to track down the drivers at the Web sites I suggest, there will probably be another source for them somewhere else. Just use a search engine to look for them or post a message on the I-Appliance BBS at `www.linux-hacker.net/cgi-bin/UltraBoard/UltraBoard.pl`.

In addition to these drivers, I copied over the drivers for the wireless Ethernet card I was using and also some utility programs like WinZip.

Caution

Windows 98 is not the only operating system option for the Webplayer, but it is the best one. Some people have gotten Windows 2000 to work, but usually with some problem such as non-functional sound. Keep in mind that Windows 2000 has additional overhead that will slow the system down even more than Windows 98. Some people have also gotten Linux to work, but finding drivers for the mini-PCI card may be difficult.

I then powered down the PC and removed the hard drive and laptop adapter.

Partial Disassembly of the Webplayer

Now, I started to take the Webplayer apart. I just needed to remove enough to get the hard drive installed so I could begin the Windows installation process.

I started by removing the side pieces on the main base, and they popped off with a little force. Next, I removed the two screws from the bottom of the base. The top of the base has two black rubber feet the LCD panel can rest on when it's folded down, and they can be removed simply by pulling them straight up. I removed the feet and then the two screws directly underneath them. Next, I laid the LCD down flat against the base and pulled the top front panel off, being careful because there were wires still attached to the red translucent panel up front. I removed the top-front piece completely and disconnected the small plastic holding plate for the LEDs attached to the red plastic. I then lifted the LCD panel up again and was able to remove the top cover.

Since this mod has no need for a modem, I removed the modem daughtercard by unscrewing it. The modem is the raised card toward the right side (see Figure 13-2) when looking at the Webplayer from behind. Once it was unscrewed, I simply lifted it off its posts. I also unscrewed and removed the phone jack connection daughtercard from the rear of the Webplayer. Next, I

FIGURE 13-2: Webplayer with top cover removed to expose the motherboard.

attached the IDE cable I purchased to both the hard drive and the Webplayer, and laid the hard drive flat outside the case. The IDE connection on the Webplayer is the long header on the left front of the device. Remember that pin 1 on both the motherboard and the hard drive need to be lined up with each other (pin 1 to pin 1) whenever attaching a hard drive to a computer (cables usually have a red stripe on pin 1).

I got the keyboard ready (installed fresh batteries) and plugged the Webplayer in. I needed to tweak the BIOS so that I could start the Windows installation. I entered the BIOS by hitting F2 (the notebook icon on the keyboard) and entered the BIOS password. The BIOS password is "schwasck" and cannot be permanently changed. I changed a couple of BIOS options such as Local Bus IDE Adapter: Primary and Large Disk Access Mode: DOS, and updated the date. I also changed the boot-up order to boot from the hard drive first, saved the options, and rebooted. This left me at the C:\ prompt.

Tip

The BIOS password on the Webplayer is a little strange. You *seem* to be able to set the BIOS password to anything you want when you are working in the BIOS. But as soon as the machine reboots, the BIOS password is set right back to the original password. It cannot be permanently changed.

I could now start the Windows install by doing a cd images\win98 and running setup.exe to start a standard Windows 98 installation. The only significant differences I found was when setting the time and date near the end of the installation. When setting those, the Webplayer crashed down to a blue screen but when the system rebooted everything continued normally.

After the system came up for the first time, I proceeded with installing all the other drivers for video, sound (although this mod didn't include sound, I thought it was best to include the driver so the system wouldn't prompt to install the drivers with every reboot), DMA drivers, and others. Basically, I installed everything from the main driver set. As a prerequisite for those drivers, I also needed to install WinZip.

At the point, I had a fully functional Win98 PC. I then shut down the system and unplugged it to get ready for the next step.

Networking the Webplayer

As should be obvious by now, the Webplayer has several expansion ports—some work and some don't. One of the ports that does work is a mini-PCI expansion slot for type 3 mini-PCI cards. If I wanted to network the Webplayer, I needed to find a mini-PCI wireless Ethernet card.

Under the Covers

It turns out one of the Linksys wireless Ethernet PCI cards (the WMP11) actually has a type 3 mini-PCI card hidden inside a metal shield on the card. Some people say that only the revision

1 WMP11 cards contain the mini-PCI card though. In any case, quite a few wireless PCI cards seem to have suspicious rectangular shielding about 1 cm high on them that probably house mini-PCI cards. Of course, to find this out for certain requires modding the card, which could turn into a costly set of experiments. Lucky for me, I found one of the WMP11 cards with the integrated mini-PCI cards.

The first problem I had to tackle was to remove the metal shield from the WMP11 card by unsoldering the connection points between the shield and the PCI card. The next issue was the antenna.

The antenna itself was connected to the PCI card by screwing itself onto a special connector on the PCI card. Once that was unscrewed, I looked at the metal traces on the PCI card. It was easy to follow those lines all the way back to a section just above the mini-PCI card. At that point, wires were soldered directly to both the PCI card and the mini-PCI card (thus, the circuit to the antenna was complete). I carefully unsoldered the wires attached to the mini-PCI card. After that, I unlatched the two side connectors for the card and pulled it out. I then plugged the mini-PCI card into the mini-PCI slot on the Webplayer and powered it back on (see Figure 13-3).

When Windows started, it detected the new wireless card. Using the drivers I had already copied over to the `images\drivers` directory, I installed the drivers for the device and the associated software. After one more reboot, I was able to configure the wireless card for my home wireless network.

FIGURE 13-3: Mini-PCI wireless Ethernet card. Note that some epoxy glue has been used around the wires attaching the antenna to provide strain relief, and a small heatsink has been attached to the metal RF shield on the card.

At this point, the wireless card was running without any antenna installed. I built an antenna later when I prepared the new case, but for now the range was very short. In addition, I experienced a minor headache when running the card without an antenna and have known others who have the same problem. I'm not sure what this really means, or if the effect is real, but I try to avoid running cards without an antenna because of this.

I took this opportunity to install all the Windows updates from the Internet. I made sure to get everything, especially since I would be relying on some of the Internet Explorer 6 features later on in the mod. These updates took quite some time to install, and several reboots as well.

Making an Antenna

The antenna was a difficult problem. I could have tried to remove the special connector for the antenna from the PCI card and reattached it to the mini-PCI card somehow, but that solution would mean having to use a large external antenna. A better solution was to use a concept known as a patch antenna. Basically, it's an antenna that's a couple of squares of metal separated by a small distance. With this picture frame, I was able to place one side of the antenna inside the frame attached to the back panel and the other side of the antenna on the other side of the back panel. Thus, I had an antenna that required no increase in size and no visible holes in the case.

Using directions and patterns from www.rc-cam.com/gp_patch.htm, I built a simple patch antenna. This was actually a simpler procedure than I had expected. Due to space concerns, I had to scale down the size of the antenna from that given in the description on that site, but for my purposes, performance wasn't the critical thing. The size and form factor were the real winners here.

I took the existing patterns from the site and scaled them down in a paint program so that the largest of the patches fit inside the picture frame. I then printed the pattern on a sheet of paper. I cut two square pieces of tin (available in most hobby stores or home improvement stores) to the right size and drilled holes in the center of both pieces. I mounted the larger piece on the inside of the foam board that serves as the back of the picture frame using hot glue, mounting it towards the upper left side. Then, I hot glued the remaining piece on the back outside of the foam board. I made a hole in the foam board with a sharp hobby knife where the holes in the tin plates were. I fed one wire through the hole and soldered that wire to the top piece. Then, I soldered another wire to the inside piece of tin. I twisted the wires together, making sure the wires were reasonably long. Finally, I soldered those wires to the mini-PCI Ethernet card where the original antenna was attached (see Figure 13-4).

Any amateur radio people out there will surely hate this design. It blatantly ignores the careful measurements that went into the design of the patch antenna and also ignores using the right type of antenna wire (one that has been properly shielded and measured for length). On the other hand, this design meets the size requirements, is cheap to make, and works well in all the environments it has been tested in.

As a final touch, it would be wise to cover the inside piece of the antenna with something non-conductive, such as a full-page adhesive label. This is a safety precaution—I didn't want the

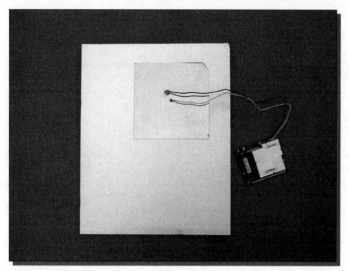

FIGURE **13-4: Wireless Ethernet card attached to the completed patch antenna.**

metal antenna touching any pieces inside the case and causing a short circuit. Because paper is generally nonconductive, this worked fine. If I were working with higher voltages and/or amperage, something like electrical tape would have been a better solution.

Preparing the Frame

I continued with the disassembly of the Webplayer at this point. This meant detaching the hard drive and cable, unscrewing the motherboard from the case, opening up the LCD portion and extracting the LCD screen and inverter, and in general just separating the components so I could see what I had to work with. The system separates into the following major pieces:

- Keyboard/mouse
- LCD screen
- Speakers
- LCD backlight inverter
- Motherboard assembly
- Hard drive and cable
- LED front panel with sleep button
- Modem and modem ports

- Power supply

- Case plastic and metal shield

It was time to do away with a few things. I set the case plastic aside, because I wouldn't be needing it anymore. I also put the speakers, the modem ports, the modem, and the LED front panel aside. Finally, I flipped the motherboard over and removed the disk-on-chip (the big chip socketed on the bottom).

Tip Removing the disk-on-chip (DOC) is a matter of some debate among Webplayer modders. It is possible to put a small Windows image on the DOC and have a Webplayer with no moving parts, but the image really is stripped down and lean. I needed to be able to install a full Direct-X installation so I could get access to some cool effects, so the DOC wouldn't work for me. Also, the DOC can be very slow—sometimes even slower than a hard drive. By removing it, there was also one less component generating heat.

The most important part of this mod was finding the right frame. Several frames would work for this project, but they need to have pretty specific dimensions. The frame I used was the minimum size needed for the project, but I could have used a bigger frame. Actually, the frame I selected for this project is not a frame so much as it is what they call a "shadow box" used to store knick-knacks such as sea shells. While it would be possible to use a metal frame, that would introduce the added complication of making sure that nothing shorted out against the sides of the frame. In addition, I thought the contrast of wood and electronics would make for a more interesting mod. But this decision left one significant problem.

The wood on this frame is very thick, around $1/2$ inch on all sides. I needed to mount the power connector and a couple of small switches on the side, but the wood was too thick. For this picture frame, I needed three external items—a reset switch, a sleep switch, and a power connector. I purchased two small switches and a female power jack that would fit the existing power supply, all of which used nuts to secure themselves in place. Since I wanted to mount them in the bottom-right side of the frame, I drilled holes for the switches and connectors. I used my Dremel with a sanding wheel attachment to hollow out the surrounding area inside the frame where the switches would go. I made sure that the frame was thin enough for the switches to fit through the hole with enough space for a nut to hold the switches in place. But I also made sure to leave the frame thick enough that it wasn't going to break (see Figure 13-5).

Modding the Electronics

There were a few mods that needed to be performed to the electronics to get them to work in the picture frame. Nothing really difficult, but critical changes nonetheless. Several of these connections required soldering to the motherboard itself, so using proper soldering technique was key. Too long with the soldering iron in one spot and the motherboard would have been destroyed.

FIGURE 13-5: The frame with the holes for switches and power, drilled and sanded down to size.

Motherboard Mods

First, I took both switches and soldered a long pair of wires to them. I soldered one switch to the previously unused reset header on the motherboard near the front audio connectors. The other switch was the sleep switch. I soldered those wires to the underside of the front header near the volume knob. The two rearmost pins on that connector were for the sleep function.

For the power connector, I first removed the existing power connector. It was a difficult desolder because of how tightly the connector fit the holes, but by using proper desoldering techniques I was eventually able to get it. I then soldered some wires (of a thicker gauge than the switches) to the three empty spots and connected those wires to the power connector I had already purchased.

Adding a CPU Fan

Since I was using a wooden picture frame, I knew it would store heat very well—wood is an excellent insulator. Also, the wireless Ethernet card and hard drive would add extra heat that the motherboard was never designed to handle. I wanted to actively cool the CPU with a fan instead of just the passive heatsink that was already installed. I thought it would be a relatively easy task—just attach a fan/heatsink combo to the chip and attach it to power. In reality it was a little more complicated than that.

First, the existing heatsink needed to be removed. I removed the two plastic mounting screws, but I found that the heatsink was still stuck on the CPU. To solve this problem, I attached power to the motherboard (without hard drive attached so it wouldn't boot up) for about 20 minutes to heat up the heatsink. I was then able to slide the heatsink off the CPU. I removed the power and waited for the CPU to cool, then used rubbing alcohol to clean off the leftover thermal paste.

Second, I needed to find an appropriate fan. I needed a fan/heatsink combo that was small enough to fit on the CPU without touching any surrounding components and that ran off 5 volts (the Webplayer doesn't put out the 12 volts that most fans run on). The fan also needed to attach to the CPU using thermal tape, since the chance of finding one that used the existing mounting holes was virtually zero. One solution was the I-Opener cooler from www.tennmax.com, but I got lucky and found something equivalent but cheaper at a local used electronics-parts store.

Different methods can be used to attach heatsinks to processors or other chips. See Chapter 2 for the various methods that can be used.

Finding a power source for the fan was easy, because there were multiple places to get the 5-volt power from inside the Webplayer. But there was another problem—the fan made a small amount of noise that was very distracting when the room was quiet. During normal hours this wasn't a problem, but in a silent room (when trying to sleep, for example) this was annoying. The solution was to put the fan to "sleep" when the frame itself was in sleep mode. This was accomplished through the use of a 5-volt reed relay attached to both the fan and the power LED header.

When computers, such as laptops, are put into "sleep" mode they are not really off. Instead, they go into a special mode where no more processing is done but the processor remembers exactly where it was before going to sleep. The advantage for laptops is that in such a mode they use very little power. The advantage for this mod is that reduced power means reduced heat.

In a perfect world, I could just attach the fan to the same place as the power LED. In that case, when the power LED was on (which means the computer was not in sleep mode) the fan would have power. However, the LED header only puts out around 3 volts of electricity, not enough to run a fan. Using a relay gets around this problem.

Basically, a relay is a switching mechanism. This particular relay has four contacts. The two contacts furthest apart are normally not connected, but when a current is available on the other two contacts (the "coil") the two contacts furthest apart are connected.

I soldered a wire between the two "coil" contacts, running to where the power LED was located on the motherboard (the power LED is the two frontmost pins on the header near the volume knob). The 5-volt power on the serial port (the inside pin on the rearmost set of pins where the modem was connected) was connected to one of the remaining relay pins. The final relay pin was connected to the positive power wire for the fan. The remaining wire from the fan needed to be connected to the ground lead on the serial port (the pin next to the power pin). I then used some hot glue to glue the relay in place on the motherboard near the hard drive header (see Figure 13-6).

FIGURE 13-6: CPU fan/heatsink combo attached to reed relay.

Now, the fan was only active when the Webplayer was on and not in sleep mode.

Cross-Reference This is only one way to accomplish the goal of a having fan that can sleep. Another, perhaps better, method would be to use an optoisolator in the same way you would hook up multiple hard drive activity lights. Chapter 9 discusses that method.

Odds and Ends

A few more tasks, and I was ready to start assembling the PC. At this point, it looked more like a small computer had exploded over my dining room table than as if I were assembling something. But just a few more steps and everything started coming together.

Attaching the Mat

First, I had a local frame shop cut a nice mat for me (and charge me way too much for the honor). On the bright side, the mat fit inside the frame perfectly and had exactly a 1-inch border on all sides. That 1-inch border was big enough to hide the ugly metal on the side of the LCD panel but small enough to show the LCD itself.

I took the LCD panel, placed it in the exact center of the mat, and hot glued it in place. I made sure to place glue around all the edges but not underneath the LCD panel's metal frame. If I put glue underneath the LCD between the panel and the mat, the glue would have held the LCD in place but would have created an unattractive gap. Also, when centering the LCD,

I remembered to center it over the viewable LCD itself and not over the metal border of the screen, which wasn't even on both sides.

Preventing Electrical Short Circuits

Next, I turned my attention to the possibility of electrical shorts. Again I used full-page adhesive labels on both the back of the motherboard and the back of the LCD panel to make sure there would not be any shorts. I used one sheet on the back of the LCD panel because it was basically flat and used three sheets on the motherboard because it had many sharp edges where the components were soldered to the motherboard. I made sure the adhesive stuck, but I didn't push too hard because this could have caused the solder spikes to puncture the adhesive paper. Finally, I did the same thing to the hard drive, but made sure to leave a hole at the breather valve on top of the drive (the little area that says "do not cover").

Electrical short circuits happen when electricity flows between two points using a path that it was not intended to follow (and in the process usually damages components). The solution to the problem is to place something nonconductive between the two potential points where a "short circuit" could happen. In this case, the back of the LCD panel was metal, and the underside of the motherboard had many bare metal spikes. The adhesive paper (when enough sheets are used) is nonconductive enough to prevent short circuits in this mod.

Creating an Air Intake/Exhaust

At this point, I was able to test fit the motherboard into the picture frame. I placed the mat/LCD combo down into the frame and positioned the motherboard on top of it. The motherboard needed to be as close to the left-top side of the frame as possible (when looking from the front of the frame). But I still needed to leave space for the mini-PCI Ethernet card, since that would overhang the left side of the motherboard a bit.

Next, I created a hole for the CPU to allow some fresh air in so that the hot air inside the case didn't just get recycled. I placed the foam board in place on the frame and marked the approximate location of the CPU fan. Using a sharp knife, I cut a large hole in the foam board backing over the location of the CPU.

Chapter 2 contains a detailed discussion of cooling methods, including information on different types of fans and how to power them.

Relocating the Keyboard

The one remaining problem was how to control the computer. The Webplayer IR detector is notorious for picking up signals from other remote controls, which causes the Webplayer to wake up from its sleep mode. Since the motherboard and IR detector were hidden inside the frame, it wouldn't see those signals and awaken, but how could I then control it using the keyboard? The answer was a removable reverse light pipe.

With most computers and electronics, the power light you see up front isn't actually the LED itself. Instead, it's a small piece of clear plastic that twists and bends the light from someplace deeper in the case and transmits the light to the front. It's the same idea that fiber optics use to transmit large amounts of data. I built something similar for the Webplayer to transmit the IR light from outside the case back into the case.

I started by measuring where the keyboard IR detector would be inside the frame with the motherboard installed, just as when measuring for the fan hole. I cut a piece of acrylic rod about 1^1/$_2$ inches in length. Then I drilled a hole above where the IR detector would be in the frame, the same diameter hole as the piece of acrylic. Using some 150-grit sandpaper, I sanded all sides of the rod to make it a whitish color instead of clear and cleaned it with water.

When the frame is together, I can temporarily put the rod into the hole so that it rests on the IR detector inside the frame while still sticking an inch out of the frame (see Figure 13-7). The IR signals from the keyboard hit the side of the rod and are transmitted down into the frame. When I'm done using the keyboard, I pull the rod out and store it somewhere. The hole is too small for any other IR signals to get inside unless the keyboard or remote is aimed directly into the hole.

The whole IR system is a little finicky about what height or angle I hold the keyboard at, but it beats having to open the case each time I need to install an OS update or something like that. Since this system primarily runs without any user intervention, this way of using the keyboard is acceptable.

FIGURE 13-7: The light pipe installed in the case. Also visible is the contrast control dial.

Final Assembly

At last it was time to assemble everything. First, I thoroughly cleaned every bit of dust, dirt, and wood shavings from inside the frame. Once it was closed, it would be a real pain getting back in so this step was important. I found it useful to lay the mat and LCD combo down in the frame, then stand the frame on its side while holding one edge of the mat and LCD combo in place until one side opened up as if it were on hinges. I could then use a can of compressed air to push out any last specs of dirt or dust away from the glass.

Tip   Cleaning your mods during final assembly is always a great idea. It's at this point in the assembly of the mod where each part is a separate entity and can be thoroughly cleaned easily. Sure, when the mod is complete parts can be taken off and cleaned again, but who really goes through all that effort? Save time by cleaning everything the first time.

Placing the Components

I placed the mat and LCD combo down into the frame. It fit like a glove.

Next, I laid a couple pieces of foam double-stick tape about 4 inches long onto the back of the LCD panel above where the motherboard would go. I put the motherboard on the foam tape, remembering to leave room for the mini-PCI card that still needed to be attached. The motherboard was placed as far to the left side (when looking from the front) as possible. I attached the two wires for the LCD to the motherboard now, making sure that the main data cable for the LCD didn't bend too sharply in the path it needed to take (the wires are hair-thin on that cable). I used a piece of clear tape to hold the data cable in place.

The connections for power and the external switches were threaded through the holes in the frame next. Because they were already connected to the motherboard, I just had to place them through the holes and tighten the nuts down. Then, I added the hard drive cable to the motherboard. I was able to bend the cable back and forth on top of itself in such a way that when the hard drive was attached, it sat on top of the cable. The hard drive was just a few fractions of an inch above where the foam back would sit on the frame. When the foam was added, it placed just enough pressure on the drive to keep it firmly in place (see Figure 13-8).

Next, I cut a small round hole in the back of the foam board directly above the contrast control on the motherboard. I carefully measured another piece of acrylic rod and cut it so that when it was placed on top of the contrast control, the rod stuck out of the case only a couple of millimeters. I then glued the rod in place with 5-minute epoxy and let the glue dry. Even though the glue was dry enough to continue my work after 5 minutes, the glue doesn't reach full strength until 24 hours later.

Finally, I attached the mini-PCI Ethernet card in the mini-PCI slot on the motherboard. I closed the frame by placing the foam board on top, securing it with the clips the frame came with (see Figure 13-9).

FIGURE 13-8: All components placed inside the picture frame.

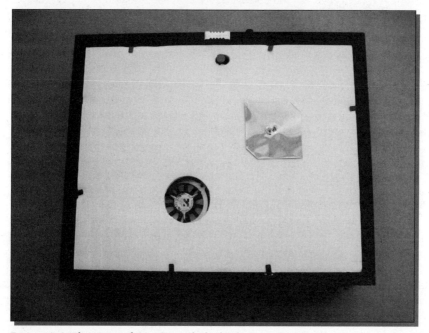

FIGURE 13-9: The picture frame PC with the back secured in place.

Software Details

One option for software to control the picture frame would have been to transfer a bunch of pictures to the frame itself and use some of the freely available screen saver programs that can load custom images to cycle through all my images. But the solution I chose was a little more complex.

Since I have my own Web server available on the Internet, I wrote a combination HTML and JavaScript Web page that would read in a list of picture files and display them in a browser. Sixty seconds later, it will randomly pick another picture from the list and randomly pick a Direct-X transition (such as fade, expanding circle wipe, or others) and display the new picture using the new transition. I even found a way to blank the cursor, but only using Internet Explorer 6. I then modified Internet Explorer's home page to point to that Web page, and set up Internet Explorer in the Startup program group so that it runs as soon as the system is booted. Whenever I power on the picture frame, it boots directly to my slideshow.

Tip You can get a copy of the code I use at www.xkill.net/outermods/SlideShow.zip.

One small finishing touch I used was replacing the windows startup and shutdown screens with my own. I created 256 color .bmp image(s) at 320 × 400 resolution and put them in the right places to replace the standard Windows 98 startup and shutdown images. For the startup image, I saved my image as C:\logo.sys and for the shutdown image the filename was C:\WINDOWS\logow.sys. I used a happy face and sad face as startup and shutdown images, respectively (see Figure 13-10).

Conclusion

This mod only took a couple of afternoons to complete and left me with a custom mod that truly has a real purpose in my house. It would even make a nice gift for a significant other or family member, even for less techie relatives. Of course, I could never bear to part with it so there is little chance of that happening.

That being said, there are a number of trade-offs with this mod over a traditional electronic picture frame from an electronics store. Should you want to complete a similar mod, keep these positives in mind:

- You will create it yourself and can take pride in your work.

- It's as unique as you want it to be. You can customize the frame with knick-knacks such as seashells or anything else you can think of. If you do this to a purchased electronic frame you will void the warranty.

- The screen is larger than any reasonably priced purchased electronic frame.

FIGURE 13-10: Picture frame PC during startup mode.

■ It has more functionality than a purchased electronic frame. You can pull pictures off the Internet or store them locally. You can store far more pictures locally that any available electronic frame on the market. You could even surf the Web from your wall.

But there are also some downsides:

■ The power cord hanging down isn't really attractive. That being said, all the other electronic frames on the market have the same disadvantage.

■ The brightness control needs careful adjustment, and the screen is not up to modern TFT screen standards. Replacing the screen in the Webplayers has been a longstanding dream of many people, but it seems it has never been accomplished.

One final note—all the techniques described in this chapter could easily be applied to more modern hardware such as the mini-ITX or yet unreleased (as of this writing) nano-ITX form factor boards. The main problem with those is the height of the boards, but if you're using a much larger frame and LCD panel, the relative dimensions of width to height to depth would not be that bad. Perhaps you can build the first nano-ITX picture frame!

Framed 8.0 Custom PC

William "ZeusEnergy" Shaw

In 1999, I needed to add a dedicated Web server and router to the growing family of machines that filled my office to the breaking point. I decided to mount a piece of plywood to the wall and add the machine plus all my networking equipment to it. This worked wonders since I didn't need to take up any of my dwindling desktop space. At the time, this machine was the talk of my tech friends. Everyone who saw it was quickly impressed by the idea, and equally disgusted with its appearance. The server itself was nothing more than a case with no panels, just a skeleton of aluminum and silicon. I wasn't going to win any awards with the looks of that machine.

Fast forward four years. Due to rearranging the apartment a bit, it was time to begin another wall-mounted PC. Over those four years I had given some thought to making another wall-mounted machine. The new design included six $5^1/_4$-inch drive bays, a motherboard tray from an Inwin Q500, and a top-mounted power supply. I needed room for four removable hard drive frames plus CD-RW and DVD drives. I also wanted lights and water tubes with bubbles between the drives and motherboard on both sides. The idea was to construct a wooden enclosure and then cover the front of it with a window panel, hinged for easy access. All the components would be attached with wood screws directly to the main wood panel. The drives would be exposed with their topsides viewable from the window. After literally hours of design changes, I was ready to build. Off to the hardware store I went, with dimensions and a list of parts in hand.

When I returned home that day I began work on the back mounting panel. As I was cutting the panel outside, some of the neighborhood kids showed up asking what I was building. None of them could remotely guess what it was. The Antec case I had been using for a computer housing had to be dismantled for the donor parts to be fitted onto the new mounting board, so I went inside and got it. Those kids couldn't believe what I was doing: taking apart a perfectly good computer only to mount its parts to a plain old piece of plywood. Obviously, they didn't have the same vision that I had. I tried explaining the project to them, but they scoffed at me and left moments later to get into some sort of trouble, I suppose.

FIGURE 14-1: Framed 8.0 custom PC completed.

A month later, Framed 8.0 was complete (see Figure 14-1). This mod was named after its picture frame appearance and this version number reflects the changes in design over the years since my first wall-mounted machine. I invited those same kids who were laughing about my ideas over to see the finished product. Mouths hung open, and drool soaked my carpet. It looked like I had completed my mission to astound and amaze with simple ideas that nearly anyone could follow. So, how did I build this contraption? Was it as easy as I say it was? What problems did I face while building this monstrosity? Read on!

Timeframe and Cost

With any project, your time is the most precious investment you will make. Framed 8.0 took at least 100 hours to build, probably more. Following the tips in this chapter, your version may take less time though. Of course, if you are inexperienced, the time may be doubled. Don't expect to breeze through your build. It's better to be thorough than to wake up from your carelessness just to see 10 hours of build time go up in smoke (or worse).

The cash spent on this mod was only around $200 to $250. Why so cheap? I used my current computer's internal parts to build it. Remember, this machine was a solution to my office space issue. If you need to buy any electronic components for your computer, the cost will go up considerably. Beauty came as a welcome side effect and is totally optional. The biggest purchase I made was the front panel of acrylic, at almost $30. The rest of the major purchases included the heatsink for the CPU (on sale), the LED fan, cold cathodes, and the tower vases. The nickel and dime items such as screws, hardware, and cables will increase your cost quickly. Just the hardware and cheap parts totaled over $100. Add another $100 if you plan on enclosing the sides of your wall machine. More acrylic and fans equal more cash.

Required Parts and Tools

Be prepared to hunt down some supplies and tools before starting work on your project. The following list represents the major components you'll need to finish a project based on my design. Feel free to add or replace any of the items with the parts that you want. After all, customizing a design to fit your style is what makes a modder mod. Be sure you don't mind voiding some warranties if you plan on cutting into PC hardware. Check your components for proper operation before modding them. They can't be returned after holes and windows are installed.

Parts

- High-quality plywood base panel, $^3/4$" thick (suggest a 2' × 4' section) ($15)
- Motherboard mounting tray, aluminum or steel from old case (free)
- A few feet of aluminum flat stock, $^1/{16}$" and $^1/8$" × $^3/4$" wide ($20)
- Screws, bolts, nuts, and other hardware ($50)
- Wire loom, a couple different diameters about 6' long any color you like ($5)
- Brackets—you might need to purchase or make these ($20)
- Wire and connectors—an extra power supply and leftover case front headers will work ($10)
- Wire clamps and cable ties, heat-shrink tubing ($10)
- Clear acrylic sections: $^3/{16}$" thick, 30" × 36"; $^1/8$" thick, 24" × 24" ($40)
- Optional: Water tubes, air pump, air lines, air rocks, and one way valves ($20)

PC-Related Components

- Motherboard of your choice with CPU and memory
- Hard drives and optical drives (older ones if you plan on adding windows)
- Lights and fans
- Removable hard drive frames (4) with locking feature
- Optional: NewQ equalizer or DSP
- Rounded IDE cables and/or SATA cables
- Power supply (some newer power supplies even come with clear windows and lights!)

Tools

- Soldering iron
- Hand-held jigsaw

- Rotary multitool with various bits and cut-off wheels

- Drill and bits

- Digital multimeter

- Various screwdrivers, pliers, and other hand tools

- Utility knife

- T-square and metal straightedge

- C-clamps and extra wood pieces for holding items in place

- Stud finder

- Masking tape, printable masks, scalpel, and fine marker

- Paint and paint pens

Starting Out

Your plan is the most important part of your mod. Without detailed ideas and specific measurements for what you are trying to accomplish, nothing will fit properly. I had a couple of problems (you'll find out about them in this chapter) because of new ideas that came up along the way. Start with the basics and go from there, especially when building a fully custom job from scratch.

In my case, I needed to find out the total dimensions for my project to build the mounting board. Some of the considerations for this design included:

- Number of drives per side

- Dimensions of the drives

- Dimensions of the motherboard mounting tray

- Overhang for the side panels (later utilized for the front cover aluminum subframe)

These figures were needed to decide how large the mounting board should be for everything to fit. I chose a center-mounted motherboard at the bottom of the mounting board with its connectors facing down. I wanted all six drive bays to eject or be removable from the sides of the machine. This allowed the connectors of each drive to be facing the motherboard and gave me room to mount the power supply, all the cabling, the NewQ equalizer, and the temperature gauge above the motherboard tray.

Mounting Motherboard Tray and Drives

The mounting board was made from 3/4-inch high-quality finished plywood. I cut out a section 34 inch wide × 24 inch tall with a jigsaw. The height of the mounting board was a function of all three drives stacked with 1-inch clearance between them for mounting brackets, plus

2 inches on each end for additional items such as cold cathode inverters and an overhang for the abandoned side panels. The width was based on my hard drive removable frames (the deepest drive bays I had) and the width of the motherboard tray. I left a little room between the drives and the motherboard (mobo) tray for cabling. I wanted an easy measurement of width so I rounded up the next couple inches for the added connector space. The drive bays met up with the outer edge of the mounting board once installed. With the mounting board cut, it was time to mount the motherboard tray. I found the center of the mounting board and the center of the motherboard tray, and placed the metal tray on the wood board, lining up the marks. I drilled holes in both materials and used $3/4$-inch sheet-rock screws to attach them together.

Tip

When attaching any parts to the motherboard tray be sure that all the metal screws and stand-offs do not contact the motherboard itself once it is installed. Any extra standoffs that don't line up with your mobo holes should be removed.

The drives were laid in place to find the best mounting locations. Later, I measured and marked the wood board in increments to locate the drives permanently. You need to divide the height of the mounting board in half and measure out 3 inches on either side of that point to get the middle drive centered since $5^1/4$-inch drive bays are actually 6 inches wide. Then, measure 1 inch from there for drive bracket gaps, and then 6 inches more for the top and bottom drives. In the end, the leftover space was 2 inches on either end of the mounting board as planned. Measuring properly is crucial to getting the drives to look right, rather than sloppy. All the lines I marked were drawn at 90-degree angles to each side of the mounting board with a square, so I could get each drive perfectly level with the rest of the machine. It's crucial to make all your parts line up properly or else you will have some trouble with them. The next step was to find some mounting brackets for the drives.

Tip

Most drives can be mounted in any configuration you choose, as long as optical drive trays have small tabs for holding your disk when the drive ejects it. Hard drives can be operated on any angle and some people prefer to show off the PCB below the drive rather than the front cover. Make sure that your drives will operate the way you want to mod them before cutting or mounting anything.

None of the L-brackets I found worked out of the box, and I was getting sick of searching for a perfect match so I decided on a custom design. Using flat aluminum strips about 1 inch wide, I cut smaller strips out of those to make each bracket "blank". The blanks were flat pieces with the final dimensions of the brackets before drilling and bending. I drilled holes using a wooden template as a guide after bending each piece to form custom aluminum L-brackets.

Using Wooden Templates

To make a wooden template, all you need is a piece of wood and a drill. Make one bracket with both holes first, then place the bracket on top of the wood and bend it in the right spot so that the hole for the drive lines up with the height from the bent portion. This leaves a small tab that can be screwed to the wooden mounting board. Now, you can mark the wood template so that all the brackets have holes and bends in the same exact spots, using the original bracket as a guide. The mounting board screw holes don't need to be perfect, but your drive holes do. These parts are hidden in my application, which is why I never gave them a nice finish. Strong, simple brackets with the right dimensions were all I needed.

Parts can be mass produced easily by using templates. I learned the technique doing factory work on assembly lines. Most of your time is spent making the template and the original piece, of course. But the time you save by following this step will save you hours of frustration trying to build 24 brackets as I had to in Framed 8.0. Use some imagination when designing parts and try to keep the template in mind during the design phase of your mod. The easier it is to make the template, the more time you will save. You will also get better, higher-quality results with simple templates.

You can finish these brackets any way you please, but if the drives will be exposed in your project, you might consider taking the time to make your brackets look good. After cutting, drilling, and bending 24 of these metal brackets, I attached them to the drives with the regular screws and used some small wood screws to drive the brackets into the wood (see Figure 14-2).

Power Supply Issues

I stood back and enjoyed the fruits of my labor for a moment until I realized that the power supply was missing. Originally, the power supply was supposed to be lined up with the upper

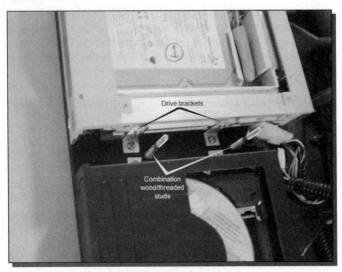

FIGURE 14-2: Drive brackets and drive mounting bays installed.

edge of the mounting board. But once the power supply was in place, it was obvious that the ATX power connections would never reach the motherboard.

I could have solved this problem by using an ATX extension, or better yet cutting the wires and soldering on extensions. But after moving the power supply closer to the center of the mounting board, almost directly against the edge of the motherboard itself, I could see how the cables passed over everything. Once the ATX wires were covered in some wire loom they would form a single, large cable almost in the middle of the motherboard. The visual interest it added to the finished project is one of those things a modder chooses to do rather than hiding the cables out of sight.

I decided to lay out all the cables emanating from this single area: power, ATX connectors, and the IDE cables all came from the same location and fanned out like a spider's legs. This is one of the reasons the power supply was offset to the left, so the power outputs were directly above the IDE cables. Offsetting the power supply also gave me room to route the IDE cables from the RAID controller in a more elegant way, passing under the temperature monitor.

Now that the cabling design dilemma was over, I still needed a way to mount the power supply to the mounting board. Upon examining the Antec 300 W unit I had, I found two small threaded fittings that were perfect for the task. I took out the motherboard tray and dismounted the motherboard from it again. I drilled two holes in the mobo tray almost at its top edge. I found screws with the matching threads in the parts bin and mounted the power supply to the large area of the Inwin motherboard tray furthest away from the connector backplane.

Another benefit of mounting the power supply to the mobo tray is grounding. This is an important subject that should not be taken lightly because you can damage expensive components without proper grounding. I would have used a ground strap between the mobo tray and power supply if they were not already attached to each other. They're attached to provide proper electrical flow between the power supply housing and the motherboard screw locations. It's possible to burn out a motherboard without this feature, because all of the ground wiring for the whole board would need to pass through much thinner circuit traces to reach a ground if the screws do not connect electrically with the power supply.

Electrical Grounding Considerations

If you don't know much about simple circuits and grounds, here's a primer. A circuit is a loop between a ground or negative path, and the positive power connection. With a battery and a light bulb, power is fed from the positive connection to the bulb filament and straight back to the ground (the negative terminal on battery in this case). To make a circuit easier to wire and manufacture, the ground is almost always attached to the case or housing and any other large conductive surface. This way only the positive lead needs to be run for power to be applied to a circuit, since the ground connection can be attached to any nearby metal surface. Built-up electrical charges released as electrostatic discharge can also be dissipated by the ground plane. Finally, the ground plane can shield an electronic device from RF interference.

With a large load such as high-powered processors, fast video cards, and multiple fans driven from the motherboard at the same time, more flow takes place. More flow means that larger connections to the power source are needed—bigger wires. But not just the positive connections need upgrading; the grounds are equally important and should have the same characteristics as the positive does.

Motherboard manufacturers add small connections under each of the motherboard mounting screw locations, expecting the board to be installed into a metal casing along with the power supply. Since motherboards are getting so complex, smaller connection traces are used on these boards to save space, and some of the ground connections are marginal where they meet up with regular ATX connectors. Most cases are metal, so this rarely presents a problem. Fully acrylic cases are becoming common now, and so far I have seen no grounding straps included with any of them. Just one screw and a wire with loop connectors is all it would take to reduce the problem, relieving some of the load on the smaller circuit traces on the board.

To make a grounding strap, use some stranded 14-gauge wire and attach a loop connector to one end. Attach this end to the power supply at any of the screw locations, then attach the other end to a motherboard screw with another loop connector (see Figure 14-3). Make sure that the loop connector does not contact anything else on the motherboard, or you will short it out. You can add more wires to this setup for multiple-screw grounding at the motherboard.

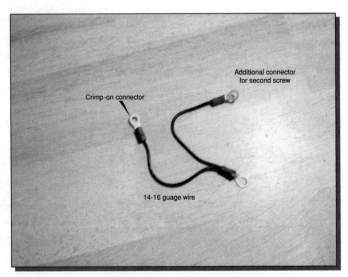

FIGURE 14-3: A grounding strap can be used to supply an extra ground source for the motherboard.

I imagine that there are a few people out there who have had a motherboard failure with custom or acrylic cases because of the lack of grounding straps. Even your drive casings should be grounded. I never did this to my drives in this mod, but it's much less of an issue because there is less current being drawn from these devices, and each one has two ground connections as it is. But electrostatic discharge (ESD) could damage a drive without a decent physical ground. ESD forces static through the drive's ground circuit rather than through the casing, directly to the power supply ground. I always make sure that I shut down my machine before handling plugged-in drives, and I also ground myself on the mobo tray to lose any built-up static charge. Make sure that any design you may have at least incorporates some grounding between the motherboard and power supply to prevent expensive damage or possibly even a fire from overheated motherboard traces.

Modifying Cables

With any power supply, the connectors are designed to be configurable for a range of applications within a certain distance from the power source. In this mod I needed to extend the connectors as well as adding more connectors. I purchased regular four-wire power splitters and extensions and set them up temporarily to find the perfect length for each cable and its path. Some were cut off, others were soldered back on and extended, and then all the power cables were covered with wire loom. The IDE cables were a bit easier. I knew I needed rounded cables that were much longer than standard. I installed the dual-connector black cables to the top drives although I don't like the extra connectors terminating above the power supply. Someday I might replace them with single-connector cables. The two lower-left drives were the opticals—CD-RW and DVD. They were on the secondary IDE channel and shared a dual-drive-cable. Similarly, the lower two right-side hard drives were on the primary IDE channel, sharing the last cable.

Cross-Reference Chapter 3 contains information on proper wire management.

Both of the regular IDE channel cables needed the same basic layout to look symmetrical. The computer store had a few types of rounded cables to choose from, including lighted ones. I decided to use plain black to take the eye away from the cables, since I didn't want to have too many colors, and the idea was to hide as much cable as I could. After installing the cables, I found the primary channel cable to be defective. When I went to exchange it, most of the store's merchandise was at a computer show, and the only remaining cable that was long enough was red.

The new red cable grew on me after installing and testing it. The primary and secondary cables look almost like large power cables coming from an automotive amplifier, which matched the automotive-grade wire loom I was using. Almost all the other wires and harnesses were hand made and took many hours to complete. Each fan wire was extended or shortened and covered with heat-shrink to get the best balance of appearance and functionality. I screwed wire clips to the mounting board in some spots to keep everything in place with help from the added zip ties.

If you want to extend cables and don't have soldering skills, you can use crimp-on connectors for this task. However, I don't recommend doing this for ATX power connections, because there are so many wires and the power requirements are tight enough with the regular connector. If one wire is poorly connected, you could experience a lot of trouble and assume hardware failures to be the culprit when it's just one badly crimped wire. The cabling turned out neat and organized, but still had a pattern to it, especially when viewed with the front cover installed.

Mounting the Plywood Backing

To mount this beast of a machine, I needed to find studs in the wall for attaching it. I bought a stud finder at the local DIY store along with four high-quality 3-inch wood screws. I found the studs and marked them at about the height of the machine. Read the instructions that come with your stud finder for proper operation. It's very easy to use, but without perfect calibration you might not get the holes lined up right. Almost all homes and buildings use 16 inches between stud centers. Verify this with your stud finder before drilling any holes in the mounting board. I offset the 16-inch difference to the left on the mounting board to line up the machine with the center of the wall, and drilled the top holes. Wait until the machine is on the wall before drilling the bottom holes.

Sometimes the studs in the wall are out of alignment. Even though the holes are not even with the center of my machine, the stud mounts are far stronger than they need to be. You might want to do the same with your project, so that the machine doesn't look odd where you decide to mount it. Say you want to mount your project directly above your desk. You might want to line up the machine perfectly with the desk location. You could just move the desk, but why go through all that trouble when the holes can be drilled closer to one side of the mounting board? You will know how far to offset the holes once you get your studs marked. Make sure that the mounting screw holes are at least 1 inch from the edges of the mounting board for strength.

Another thing you might want to think about is being able to remove the entire machine without disassembling it first. You will need to put the screws close to the edge of the mounting board, and accessory locations might have to be changed, such as the inverters on each side. Marking the wall is easy. Just use the stud finder to get marks up high and down low enough so that the mounting board will sit between them.

With help from my wife, we struggled to lift this heavy section of wood and computer up against the marks on the wall and I started the first screw. Use some washers on the mounting screws to make sure that the machine does not break free from them. The second screw was much easier. Pivoting the whole machine on the first screw allows for leveling. Don't tighten the screws fully; wait until all the screws are in place first. Be very careful, and have at least one other person on hand for this step.

Tip   Wall anchors could be used for this type of mounting, but they will need to be high-quality parts, and the wall must be made from high-quality drywall or paneling. Horsehair and plaster walls are common in New England and along the East Coast, and these walls will not support a heavy load without tying the load into the wall studs. Again, use washers on any type of anchor you might use to prevent the wood mounting board from separating from the fastener. You can paint the washers to match the color of the mounting board.

Once the top screws were set in the wall studs, the marks on the wall below the machine were used as a reference for drilling the lower holes in the mounting board. I stopped drilling as soon as the drill bit contacted the wall to give the screws more to grab onto. You don't need to predrill the wall itself; only the mounting board needs this attention to prevent the screws from splitting the mounting board. Each of the holes is slightly bigger than the screws to accomplish this. Tighten each screw slowly with a regular screwdriver so that the screw holes in the studs do not strip out. If your wall is a bit lumpy or has irregularities, the mounting board might flex. Make sure that you don't tighten the screws too much so that your mounting board stays flat. After mounting the machine, I attached everything temporarily to get the computer up and running.

NewQ Graphic Equalizer

With the machine wall mounted and bootable, I could concentrate on some of the other details I had planned. A few years ago I had a NewQ 5$^1/_4$-inch drive bay equalizer given to me along with a PC that I used for a mobile computer in my old Audi. That Audi and the computer are long gone, but the NewQ has always found a home in one of my machines. One of the coolest features provided by the equalizer is right and left channel VU meters, composed of red LEDs. Whenever sound is played back on Framed 8.0, the LED bars light up and dance to the music, even if I'm not using headphones. This adds to the "living" qualities of the windowed drives and water tubes. I planned on using an audio splitter on the front channels to give the NewQ its input.

The NewQ is primarily for tuning headphones because of the fairly poor-quality sound that it provides on only two channels. I've been using it this way since my first four-channel card. Headphones can be problematic because they never seem to have the right qualities. Most have very little bass and terrible midrange. With the equalizer, sound can be tailored to near perfection for games and music when used with headphones.

The NewQ in its original state was around 6 inch deep, making the top of the device nearly square. I wanted to mount it under the front panel because the settings are modified only when a new pair of headphones is used. I dismantled the casing and examined it for further modification.

I looked inside the open casing to find a single face plate module with all the wiring leading to a single PCB mounted to the bottom casing panel. After removing the components, I played with the layout of the internal parts. After deciding that the top cover should remain off, it was easy to modify the lower casing into an L-bracket. The exposed green PCB could be seen under the front cover and continued the bare component look well.

I cut pieces out of the lower cover to form notches so that the cover could be bent. The front faceplate module faced out and still mounted solidly to the original screw locations on the newly modified mounting bracket. Once the cutting and bending was done, I took the device apart once again for painting and then reassembled it. I used another small PCB (intended to be mounted to a PCI slot) for connecting the NewQ to audio jacks. The tiny board came off its bracket easily, and I mounted it next to the modified NewQ for a bit more PCB exposure (see Figure 14-4). I ran two extensions along the mobo tray to meet up with the audio splitter and a jack for remote headphone connection at my desk.

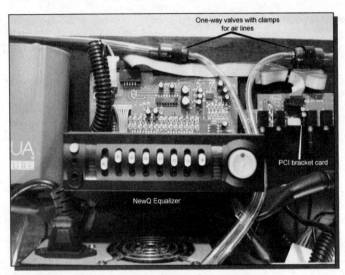

FIGURE 14-4: NewQ equalizer modified and mounted.

Attaching Components

The mod really started to come together when I finished up all the computer-related components. After attaching all the components, the computer would be fully functional and would need only cosmetic additions.

At this point the whole machine needed to be taken apart again for mounting the side panels and painting the mounting board. The acrylic side panels were designed with fan openings and cutouts for the drive bays. I had the materials and the design, so it was time to begin constructing the panels. I remembered how loud the machine had been with its CPU fan, Northbridge cooler, and video card cooler. Adding another four 80-mm fans would increase the noise quite a bit, and with the power supply in its centrally located position, I needed to create an exhaust duct if I was to install side panels to box the project in.

Another issue was ventilation for the water tubes I planned on installing. They would need to be mounted within the casing somehow, and the top of these needed to be outside the case to prevent excessive humidity from forming. All of these problems forced me to reconsider the idea of enclosing the sides. The solution was to use standoffs to support the front panel, leaving the sides open and allowing the light created by the machine's accessories to spill out onto the walls around it. The new design required a lot of thought because all my ideas of mounting the front panel had to be scrapped. I decided to worry about the design later and began concentrating on some of the other features I had planned from the start.

Making Drives and Bays Visible

The most important aspect of the design for Framed 8.0 was the flat mounting of the drives. This was done to show off each device through windowed openings. Both optical drives were removed, and the top covers were taken off.

Tip

When you add a window to an optical drive, the disc can be viewed when it is spinning or ejecting, and there is never a question of which disc has been inserted in the drive. This is one of the coolest, most "elite" mods, and it's quite easy to accomplish. A cut-off wheel, masking tape, and a marker are just about all that is needed.

Two different manufacturers made the optical drives in my machine. An optical disc needed to be "clamped" by the drive mechanism once it was inserted to keep the disc straight on the drive spindle. My CD-RW had a separate bracket attached to the drive subframe instead of the outer top cover. This made it easy to cut a rectangular hole wherever I needed it, but the DVD drive presented a new problem. The upper bearing that clamps the disc was built into the DVD drive's top cover. I had to cut around this section in a half-moon shape to keep the bearing in place. Always mask these bearings with tape before cutting, since small particles of metal can fall into the bearing while you cut.

For future design possibilities, I decided to leave the drives open instead of adding an acrylic window to them. Each drive cover was then cleaned and painted black to match the mounting board, effectively blending the drive casings into the background. You might want to cover the area above the laser's range of travel; mine can aim right at the eye when you are standing in front of the machine. Indirectly, the lasers give a nice red shine when in use. But be aware you can burn someone's eyes out if you're not careful. I also removed the covers from each of the four removable hard drive frames to expose the hard drives themselves. The covers slide off the trays that insert into the hard drive frames.

Caution

Laser radiation isn't dangerous until it meets the eyes. My drives are at the same height as a standing adult's eyes, so they need to be used carefully when other people are around. Drive manufacturers cover the laser emitter for good reason. When you window a drive that operates on laser principles such as a CD or DVD drive, this may expose the laser enough so that it can be seen and therefore become dangerous to people in the vicinity of your computer. The best solution is to cover or mask off a small portion of the window directly above the laser's path, or leave some of the metal cover in place over the laser's eye when you cut the window. Otherwise, you might have vision problems from viewing the laser light. Even with a DVD in my drive, I can see the laser through the disc itself when it's in use. I'm not sure if this is as dangerous as viewing the laser directly, but when you mask the window you won't have this problem.

I installed a 4.3-GB IBM hard drive in the bottom-right drive frame. This drive was intended to be sacrificial. In other words, I didn't care if the modding process destroyed it. For this particular application I decided to give the IBM a bit of a test and see how long a hard drive could last with no cover at all. I was also interested in seeing an operational hard drive and didn't want to spend a lot of time to see my results.

Cross-Reference

For information on how to add a window to a hard drive, see Chapter 9.

My sacrificial hard drive was so small and old that a window would be wasted on it. The covers on hard drives generally have Torx fasteners, and mine was no exception. Some of these screws are underneath the label on top of the HDD; you need to feel the label for low spots and then cut through the paper to get to the screws. Once all the screws are removed, the cover can be pried off. If a good drive is being used, and a window is planned for it, once the drive is open it needs to be placed into a new plastic bag and sealed up immediately after removing the cover. I won't get into details of windowing hard drives, but you need to know that these devices are probably the most sensitive to dust of all computer components. The tiny read/write heads at the tips of the armature are so small it takes a powerful microscope to see them. Even the smallest speck of dust can land on the drive platters and interfere with the heads, possibly destroying the drive at the same time (see Figure 14-5).

I expected to see drive failure within minutes of installing the now decapitated IBM drive. After locking the drive in its drive frame, I booted up the machine. I tried writing some data to the drive from my MP3 collection, around 3 GB in total. The drive worked extremely well. Watching the armature swing back and forth across the wildly spinning platters was fun and educational for me. The only irritating aspect of the drive was the noise level. A high-pitched scream emanated from the drive whenever it was powered up. I imagine a window would have cut down this noise substantially.

Three weeks later the drive was still working perfectly, with no cover and fully exposed. The test was over in my opinion, so I grabbed the IBM's armature and pushed it into the platters. Needless to say, the drive didn't like that too much. I tried accessing the drive again, and Windows gave me a read error proving that I really did kill the drive. Since then, the IBM has been entombed in Framed 8.0 for all to see, with its cables disconnected from the drive tray. It looks great in there and gives me inspiration to eventually mod my other drives with windows.

FIGURE 14-5: Exposed hard drive showing spindle and armature.

Many of the people who have done hard drive windows are having good luck with them. When I was building the mod, hard drive window mods were relatively new, so I needed to wait and see if there were any problems with this sort of madness before I cut into my good drives. The verdict is in and hard drive windows are becoming fairly common and functional. Seeing a drive working is much cooler than a plain LED showing drive access.

Modding the Power Supply

I had painted the power supply cover black at the same time as the optical drive covers, but the power supply now looked quite plain with all the open drives and exposed PCBs. When I was working inside the power supply, I noticed the two large vertical aluminum heatsinks and thought they looked rather nice. I removed the cover yet again for some modding. I cut a rectangular hole into the cover and made a slightly larger piece of clear acrylic fit into the opening from the inside of the cover. I drilled holes into the acrylic and the cover on each side for screws.

An idea hit me right then—why not drill four holes into the acrylic for switches and LEDs? Ever since I had first mounted the machine to the wall, I had been using the "resume after power failure" option in the BIOS to restart the machine via my UPS switch under the monitor stand. Before that I had to use a car key to start the machine with no switch headers. I jumped the two pins on the motherboard with the metal tip of a key, and then entered the BIOS. But I still had no regular power switch, reset, or LEDs for power or HDD access.

Using the original style cables from the front panel of the Inwin case, I began making a new harness for these items. I got some chrome surface-mounted LEDs and a pair of momentary switches and sat down for some soldering. I treated the whole harness to some heat-shrink tubing once it was complete and secured the parts to the acrylic. A small modification was necessary on the power supply cover to allow the harness to exit near the main power cables. You might say that switches don't really serve a purpose under the front acrylic cover, but while working on the machine they are quite handy (see Figure 14-6).

The new power supply cover looked great, but later in this chapter I will tell you about two more modifications I did to the power supply. I just kept refining it over and over until I was satisfied with the result. Sometimes you will get an idea long after you expected something to be finished, forcing you to pull a "completed" project apart once again. But that's what separates a true modder from the rest of the store-bought crowd.

Making a Card-Cooling Fan

It was time to tackle some of the miscellaneous details that still needed attention, such as the card-cooling fan brackets and cold cathode lights. The cooling fan I purchased was a clear blue LED 80-mm version with a Molex four-wire connector. The location of the fan was chosen to keep the AGP and PCI cards cool, and give the motherboard itself a little thermal relief. The cards were secured with thumbscrews, so I decided to make some brackets to mount the fan directly to the expansion card framework with them.

I started with some L-brackets from the hardware store, stainless steel and around $3/16"$ thick. They came with countersunk holes predrilled, which fit the fan screws perfectly. I straightened

FIGURE 14-6: Power supply with window and control switches.

them out with a big hammer and attached them to the fan. The assembly looked nice, and the additional holes that went unused looked cool as well. I added some heat-shrink and extensions to the wiring for a clean install. Little did I know that the wiring would need to be tapped into later for LEDs (see Figure 14-7).

FIGURE 14-7: Fan mounting brackets attached to fan and PCI card bay.

Lighting the Case

The cold cathode lights I bought were blue and came with separate inverters and expansion card brackets with switches and knobs for sound activation. I never use the sound activation feature, but I mounted the brackets in case I changed my mind. Most of my PCI slots remained unused. I disassembled the inverters and mounted each bare PCB under the bottom drive bays on both sides of the machine.

 Inverters produce enough current to kill you, so if you ever plan on opening an inverter, be sure you know what you are doing.

I modified the wiring that came with the CC lights slightly to fit my application better and added more heat-shrink to cover the adjustments to the wires. Since I needed to get the CC lights about four inches from the mounting board to allow the light to spread out better, some sort of standoff was in order. I found a bunch of brackets in my parts bin that I'd bought at an electronics surplus store years ago. These stainless steel pieces are angled at both ends and they also have an indentation that provides additional support to them. Both ends were threaded for screws, but one end of each needed to be drilled out to allow a larger wood screw to attach them to the mounting board. I found some matching screws in my parts bin to thread into the existing holes and some 1/4-inch aluminum spacers to provide a mounting surface for another feature I came up with.

 Chapter 4 contains information about various lighting methods, including cold cathode lights.

I work with plastic model kits on occasion, and I detail the kits with polystyrene. I love working with the material because it can be easily cut and formed. I used some polystyrene sheet from the local hobby store to make covers for the CC lights. Without them, the lights glare from this mod. I cut two sections, angled the corners for a bit of flair, and drilled the holes to match the CC light mounts. After attaching them I noticed that the white plastic allowed a small amount of light to pass through, making each cover glow blue like a modern car dashboard or wrist-watch backlight. I then began masking symbols on the covers. The left side represented my alias, ZeusEnergy and the right side my wife's favorite symbol, a sun. I painted the covers and removed the masks. The symbols glowed nicely and added to the overall theme of the case.

I cut another piece of polystyrene in a circular shape to cover the ugly bits of the card-cooling fan and then paintedthe newly cut polystyrene cover.

I used a compass to mark out the circles and cut them with a hobby knife (see Figure 14-8).

 Polystyrene is very easy to work with and is normally used for model railroad detailing. You can find many different types of this material—square, round, sheet, corrugated, and many others. Regular model glue or superglue can also be used on it, and the material lasts for years. Acrylic paint or vinyl dye also works well with this material.

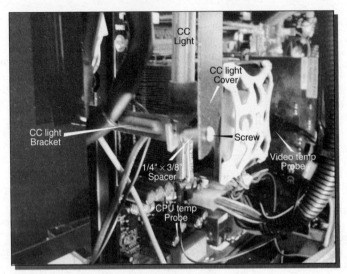

FIGURE 14-8: Cold cathode light mounting details.

I had no idea that the polystyrene would glow with a light behind it. It was an accidental discovery for the better. I have a feeling that more modders are going to start using polystyrene for its unique ability to conduct light.

Adding a Temperature Monitor

Temperature monitors can be fashioned from nearly any digital-readout display, be it in a Christmas gnome or part of a clock. For this mod, I found an inexpensive, dual-readout display on sale in a local electronics store for only $15. Once I got home, I began taking the screws out of its back, pausing only to test the temperature readouts to be sure that it wasn't faulty. This model has several very small screws, so it was essential to have jeweler's screwdrivers for the job. Some of the connectors were a bit fragile, so I needed to take care not to break any of them before the readout was reassembled. Other than that the device is very simple (see Figure 14-9).

You can get an additional remote sensor out of the unit by soldering two wires into the small PCB at the bottom and putting the sensor wherever you want. The sensor you would be trying to relocate is tiny. It looks like a resistor's grandmother, shriveled and sagging. This is the inside temperature thermistor. The leads can be wired either way. I tossed that old grandmother out and reached for the temperature sensor from my heatsink kit. It has a special thin-wire sensor that allows me to place it inside the CPU socket, up against the bottom of the core. This is the bottom reading device on my monitor, attached to the temperature monitor with another custom harness. It includes the original outside temperature lead, replaced with a normal PC thermistor probe. The sensor that goes into the CPU socket also has the original connectors soldered to this new harness, allowing a different style of sensor to be attached without tearing down the wiring.

Figure 14-9: Temperature probe mounted inside the mod.

To install the temperature monitor, I used the same brackets that I had left over from the cold cathode install. I mounted two of them to the back cover of the display by drilling holes in the plastic and attaching small screws through them into the threaded ends of the brackets. I drilled out the other ends so they would accept the wood screws for the mounting board. This solidly locates the device and stands it off the mounting board so much that all the cabling routed to the top half of the machine passes under it. This hides a substantial amount of cabling and keeps the look of the machine tight. Of course, it also matches the height of both CC lights, and the power supply is almost the same height too. There is truly a sense of three dimensions with the final product with the different levels of construction—the motherboard platform, the drive surfaces, and the power supply plane.

Plexiglas and Water

At this point, it was time to start working on the front Plexiglas panel and the water tubes. To install the acrylic panel, I needed to finish the water tubes first. This was more work than I had anticipated, but it was worth the time to create the effect.

Making Water Tubes

The plan was to get some clear tubing, cap the bottom end, and fill it with water. I would then mount a couple of tubes between the drive windows and the CC lights, acquire an air pump and some tubing, and watch the bubbles gently rise to the surface. They were designed to be very unique and purely for looks. I thought about using the water tubes as cooling reservoirs for a water-cooling circuit, but money is always an issue, and I didn't really need water-cooling for my setup.

These tubes were the hardest items to integrate with the mod. Water and PC components don't get along with each other well. Any water-filled object must be sealed and precautions taken before deciding to add such a whimsical, nonfunctional feature. The tubes need refilling twice a week, and they need to be cleaned about once a month to keep them clear. You have to really, truly love the idea if you plan on adding them to your project because babysitting water tubes is no fun if all you want is a low-maintenance PC. I really did want that look, so it was worth it to me to go to all the effort, even though I encountered a lot of problems.

Tip I have found similar mods that include water features since developing Framed 8.0, including side windows sandwiched together with a small space to provide a water layer between them. My main acrylic front panel could be made this way, and it would solve a lot of the problems I encountered, plus the bubbles would cover the whole machine.

The tubes I originally mounted were made from round nylon tubing with a 1-inch inside diameter. The tubing had originally come off a roll at the store, and the material seemed to have memory of the roll. It would coil back up as soon as you let it go, and it was a pain in the backside to get the tubes to stay straight. I used some angled aluminum and electrical tape to mount them temporarily until a better mounting solution presented itself. I spent the better part of three nights trying to work these tubes out. The result was great, and the "test" tubes were lit up nicely from the CC lights. I began concentrating on finalizing the pump, airlines, and AC power connection.

In a large department store's pet section, I found a dual-output high-pressure fish tank air pump for about $15. I purchased the air line and air rocks (the small stones at the ends of each air line that make the small bubbles) at the same time. I spent under $20 for everything I needed to make lots of bubbles. The pump came with a small tab to hang it, probably on a fish tank. I used that tab to secure the pump to the mounting board. I cut off the plug and most of the AC power cord and routed the cable into the power supply cover.

I soldered the connections to the switch inside the power supply; this way, I wouldn't need yet another electrical outlet for the air pump. Whenever the UPS is on, so are the water tubes. The airlines are nothing more than thin vinyl tubes meant for fish tanks. I routed them over the power supply cover because the lines are the same length, and the vinyl tubing reflects light from the cold cathodes—lending the machine just one more interesting detail. On a functional note, you might also want to keep each tube the same length so that the bubbles will be pushed from the tubes at an equal rate. I also mounted a pair of one-way valves to prevent the tubes from emptying into the air pump and leaking onto the CPU cooler (see Figure 14-10).

Once I got some new materials to work with, I began rebuilding the water tubes. The plugs that I fashioned from plastic fittings and end caps were sealed with automotive-grade RTV sealer. New aluminum parts and brackets were made to attach the tubes to the mounting board. Stainless steel clamps held the tubes into their respective brackets, and the tubes were refilled. After 15 minutes, I saw the first sign of trouble. There was water leaking directly into my CRT monitor. Framed 8.0 is mounted above my desk, with only two inches clearance between the bottom of the front cover and the top of the monitor. I immediately shut the monitor off and unplugged my whole system from the wall. I waited a day for the monitor to

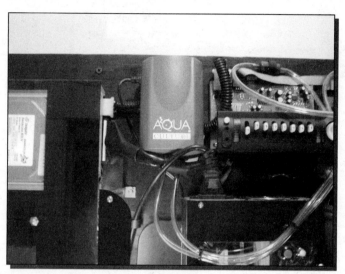

Figure 14-10: Air pump and plumbing.

dry out, and luckily for me it worked fine after that. I violently smashed those tubes to bits in a fit of rage. How dare they leak into my monitor? Back to the drawing board again.

I had seen a special kind of vase at a wedding once. It was about 2 feet tall, made from glass, and resembled the Eiffel tower. I started searching for "tower vase" online and within moments I had a solution to my dilemma. I ordered two 24-inch tall models from a very hospitable seller, and within a week they were delivered to my doorstep. Grand total was $30, including shipping. I had spent almost that much cash on the first tubes, plus about 10 hours of wasted time, and the old ones looked like crap compared to these beauties. However, I needed to make the front cover and its mounting subframe before these could be installed, since the outer edge of each stand needed support (see Figure 14-11).

Mounting the Front Panel

At the local DIY store, I found the perfect piece of acrylic measuring 36 inches × 30 inches. This piece had the same measurements I wanted for the front panel, so it was a bonus to find one precut to my specs. I decided to use some household drawer pulls as the actual fittings for the front panel. They are internally threaded, and you can find a wide selection of them at most hardware stores. I picked four spherical aluminum pulls for my project. These particular fasteners allow threaded studs to remain a part of the standoffs. Even without the spheres, the front acrylic panel was mounted easily without needing three people to hold and secure it.

The first order of business was to make the aluminum subframe and standoffs, using aluminum flat stock $3/16$ inch thick and $3/4$ inch wide. I cut four pieces 8 inches long, and bent over each end to form 90-degree bends. The bends created an elongated U- shaped part that served as a

FIGURE 14-11: Tower vases installed.

standoff. The distance between the bends was 6 inches. I used a 2 inch × 6–inch block of wood and a hammer to make the bends. If you have a heavy-duty bench vise, you can hammer them out even more easily. The upper standoffs mounted directly to the mounting board. I drilled holes in each piece for the screws to attach to the mounting board, and of course for the front cover studs at the outer end. You don't need to make these parts look fabulous, because they will be hidden behind the acrylic panel, and small errors in measurements can be adjusted by bending each bracket once it is attached.

The studs themselves were the original mounting screws for the drawer pulls, with a nut used to secure each one to its aluminum standoff mount. The lower standoff studs also secured the additional piece of aluminum that supported the outer edge of the water tube stands. This piece was 32 inches long and had four holes drilled into it—two for the studs and two for the outer water tube L-brackets. Make sure that your standoffs are mounted sideways with the flat portion facing into the machine because this helps stabilize the front cover and supports the weight of the water tubes better.

Two L-brackets secured each plywood stand for the water tubes to the mounting board on the inside, and an additional L-bracket was attached to the outer edge of each stand. I mounted the inner L-brackets in a way that allowed the wood stands to sit on top of them. I attached the outer brackets to the stands first and then drilled the aluminum bar to accept a small nut and bolt. The stands were 4 inches × 6 inches and made from the same material as the mounting board. With just three screws, the weight of each water tube was transferred to the mounting board and the lower standoffs. Two tower vases filled with water are heavy, and aluminum likes to flex. But the front cover and water tubes were quite secure and rigid once in place (see Figure 14-12).

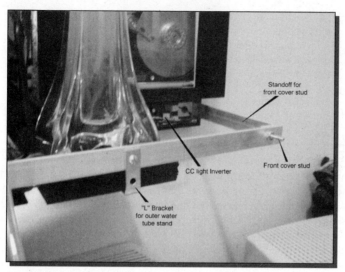

FIGURE 14-12: Sub-frame detail including aluminum mounting brackets.

After finishing the aluminum parts, I measured the threaded studs and took the dimensions for the four holes needed in the front cover. I drilled the holes with a standard carbide drill bit set, very slowly since standard drill bits can crack acrylic. I started with a smaller hole, and worked up to a larger size until the holes were slightly bigger than the studs. If I had drilled out the acrylic for the mounting holes before making the aluminum parts, then it would have been much more difficult to line everything up. It's much easier to get all the parts attached and modified if you stick to the right order. I was tempted to paint the cover before drilling the mounting holes, but if I had done that the window would have been slightly offset from the holes , ruining all the work I had done. Order was crucial at this stage because I could not go back after the painting.

I sprayed all the paint onto the back of the acrylic panel, thus making the panel reflective and seamless from the outside yet with depth in the painted sections. I applied the black first, masking off both the clear window area and they gray border before painting. I used spray cans of acrylic paint after the careful, tedious application of both masking tape and paper to hide everything but the black border.

Tip   Your paint needs to be applied in very light coats on acrylic. Use a light dusting for a first coat, and allow 10 minutes or more between each successive coat until light cannot pass through your color. Some of the lighter paint colors will naturally allow some light to pass through. Unless you apply several coats, darker colors are always easier. The gray border was done a few days later to let the black border dry completely first.

I used four coats on the gray portion, and some light still passes through it. The gray was sprayed over the back of the black border as well, adding to the reflective nature of the light inside the mod. There was a slight increase in projected light on the walls surrounding the machine after the gray paint was applied, since the black border wasn't absorbing the light anymore. A silver coat would increase this effect even more.

Chapter 6 contains instructions for painting and other methods of coloring the exterior.

Covering the Drives

Now that all the major components were installed, the image of the machine started to take shape. You could see the new tubes working, and the light transferred from the CC lights to both sides also moved, shadowing the bubbles ascending to the surface. I had another revelation. What if more acrylic panels were attached with small brass cap nuts over the drives? This would create windows to cover all the drives, painted from inside like the front panel and just as easy to remove. Soon, I had some ³/16-inch acrylic on my worktable, ready for modding.

Acrylic is easy to cut. Just score the material several times in the same spot using a utility knife, and snap the piece off. A T-square or metal artists ruler works well to keep the cut lines straight.

Scoring is just one way to cut acrylic. See Chapter 5 for a discussion of this method as well as other methods.

Once the two covers were cut, I installed some combination wood/threaded studs to the mounting board. Threading two nuts onto each stud and tightening them together was all it took to install these very handy fasteners. I then used a wrench on the top nut to drive them into the mounting board. I installed two of them in every space between the drives, eight in all. Lining the panels up to the drives, I could mark where the holes would go. I then drilled the holes in the acrylic to match the studs using the same techniques as for the front panel. That's one of the benefits of using acrylic. Marking it up for cutting and alignment is easy because you can see through it.

When it came time for painting the covers, the thought of adding gray borders similar to the front panel did come to mind. Thus, I decided that leaving room for this eventuality needed to be factored into the design. I have not added the gray as of yet, but someday I might, especially if I go to the trouble of windowing the hard drives. When the new panels were installed, they reflected the tubes and bubbles. I guess you could call it seeing bubbles "in stereo." (see Figure 14-13).

Adding Some Color

At some time during construction I was asked about coloring the water. I thought about the possibility, and of course I was curious to see what it would look like. One day at the grocery

FIGURE 14-13: Drive cover, painted and installed.

store, I found some green food coloring in a bottle. Only two drops, and the water was too dark for me. I emptied half the water and refilled the tubes. After that the color was fine, and the color remains even after half the tubes' water has evaporated. Just refill, no extra color needed. When you clean the tubes out just add one drop each. It works wonderfully.

Finishing Touches

Now it was time to add the finishing touches that would really make the case stand out as a personalized work of art. Custom paint and added lighting set off a project like this. I considered leaving Framed 8.0 the way it was, but after some manipulation in image-editing software I decided that these additions would be complementary.

Signing the Mod

I kept thinking about the front cover and how a symbol in the center would look. I had planned on sketching out a painted symbol from the beginning. It would look nice, and it could be big without taking up all the clear acrylic window space. What better way to adorn your creation, but with your own signature? Since my printer was out of ink, I was forced to draw out my symbol using a reversed version of it in an image-editing program. After that I needed to apply the paint, by hand, on a transparent object with the reversed tracing $3/16$ inch away from the surface. Tricky work.

Hand painting is much easier with paint pens. They are available in craft and art stores for about $3 each, and they make the work quite enjoyable. I picked up a black fine tip and gray medium tip pens, plus some felt pads to rest my hands on while painting the inside of the front panel.

Tip You need to be very careful when applying paint. If you paint yourself "into a corner," then you won't be able to finish your work until the wet paint dries. Start in one corner of the design and work your way to the opposite corner, turning the project as needed.

I did two full coats with the gray, and then bordered all the gray patches with a black outline. A major touchup after that gave me the effect and results I was looking for. The total time spent was around 3 hours. With the lights off in the office, the symbol is much less obvious. But when the switch is turned on, the symbol stands out yet looks matched to the hardware underneath it (see Figure 14-14).

Lighting the Insides

Some of the last things I added to the design were lights inside of the power supply and lights directed towards the motherboard from the card-cooling fan cover. I used ten 630 mcd green LEDs. Five of these wired in series resulted in a 12-volt load for direct connection to the 12-volt rail in the power supply. The other five were also wired in series and connected to the same wires as the fan. I made a new harness for the wires on this fan and reinstalled the whole thing. The reason I mounted the LEDs to the fan cover was to make them removable in one piece, integrated together, while the LEDs and wiring were hidden behind the cover. Two thumbscrews and one motherboard power connector were all that needed to be removed to access the expansion cards (see Figure 14-15).

Another notable feature on Framed 8.0 is the single LED used for the street-lamp-style light that illuminates the temperature monitor. I made a cable with a two-wire jumper pin

FIGURE 14-14: Symbol painted on the inside of the acrylic cover.

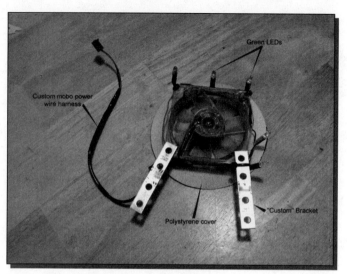

FIGURE 14-15: Fan bracket assembly with LEDs.

connector on one end and attached this lead to the motherboard's LAN connection LED header. The same type of LED was used inside this light as the ones for the power supply and motherboard lighting. The hood for the light was fashioned from the tip of a 12-volt car adapter intended for a phone. Rigid copper house wire was used inside the heat-shrink to support the wires and give the lamp the ability to be positioned easily. I used a rubber grommet and another two-pin connector inside the housing to complete the piece. With power applied to the machine, the LAN header always provides a constant signal unless the network wiring becomes unplugged. This gives me an easy way to tell if I have a good link to my network.

Conclusion

In the end, Framed 8.0 became more than just a modified computer. It is a functional work of art with many details, yet it's not overdone. I tried to keep a balance between good looks and good taste. The water tubes with the green food coloring are jewels that shine and the acrylic pieces add to the effect. Everything that was possible to display has been modified for viewing. Custom paint, wiring, cable management, and fasteners finish the whole project. And the results speak for themselves, due to planning and extensive attention to detail. What do I think of framed 8.0? It's off the hook! And it's only a PC bolted to a piece of plywood!

miniMAME

Russ "JediKnight0" Caslis

Anyone evenly vaguely the same age as me can remember far too many days of their youth "wasted" in the dark recesses of an arcade. I fondly remember the arcade at my local mall—it was called "Aladdin's Castle," and it had a long mirror-filled entryway lined with flashing lights like a carnival. Walking down that entryway, usually with my older brother, I could feel my heart beat faster as the indistinct sounds of explosions and alien death grew louder. I was never very good at all those games, but that excitement is something I won't ever forget.

Fast forward 20 years. Arcades are still cool but hard to find, and somehow they don't seem the same. The games are too complex—rows and rows of buttons that need to be pressed in some specific pattern to activate the 3-D gyro-death-spin-knockout-super-duper-punch. I had heard of people purchasing old rundown arcade cabinets with the classics like Pac-Man or Space Invaders, but I was married now, and my wife would never allow one of those huge cabinets into the house.

Then, I found out about a project called MAME—Multiple Arcade Machine Emulator. The program is an actual emulation of the complete chips inside the old (and not so old) arcade games. This program, when supplied with an appropriate ROM image from those old games, can faithfully represent the old arcade games. Everything, every little bug or trick, that was in the original game is there. The program is a marvel, but it has one problem—without the original control sticks and buttons, the games just don't feel right.

Walking through an office supply store shopping for office furniture a couple of weeks later, it occurred to me that one of those small three-drawer filing cabinets was about the same size as a 15-inch monitor. Hmmm . . . 15-inch monitor in a cabinet. . . like a smaller version of those sit-down arcade cabinets. Several months later, miniMAME (see Figure 15-1) was born.

Timeframe and Cost

This mod took approximately two months to build, but that was at a relatively slow pace. I built it several years ago, back when the competition between modders was less intense and such things as contests between

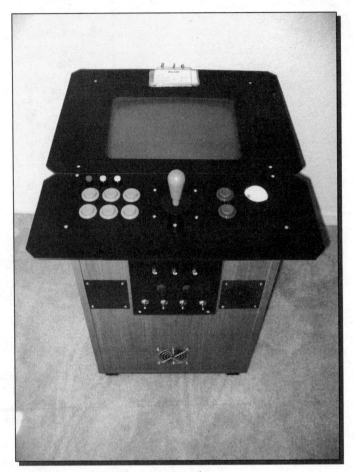

FIGURE 15-1: Completed miniMAME cabinet.

modders were very rare. It was built as a labor of love, not to show off to anyone so I took my time.

The cost was under $500, due to the fact that many components were leftover pieces from other projects. The monitor, the power supply, the hard drive, and the speakers were all excess equipment. All the other components, such as the cabinet itself and acrylic, the motherboard and CPU, memory, lights, and so on were all purchased new.

Tip   Since the system was built several years ago, you would think it could be built more cheaply now, wouldn't you? You would be wrong. Most of the components have stayed roughly the same price. Sure, for the same price a larger hard drive or faster processor could be purchased now. But because the components were already toward the lower end of the spectrum when I purchased them, they have not gone down significantly in price.

Required Parts and Tools

In many ways, this mod blended the creation of a computer and the creation of a piece of furniture. Therefore, I spent most of my time working with tools that would be just as important to building a table.

Parts

- Motherboard and CPU combo based on a Duron 1.1-Ghz processor ($80)
- Power supply ($35)
- AC-powered speakers (free, but should cost $20)
- 15-inch monitor (free, but should cost around $110)
- Dual green cold cathode lights ($15)
- Acrylic panels ($50)
- CompUSA "Crystal" trackball ($25)
- Lots of screws and brackets ($10)

Tools

- Hand drill with various-sized drill bits
- Dremel
- Hole saws (various sizes)
- Paint (ColorFleck paint and black acrylic paint)

Low-Cost Cabinet

The first piece I bought for the computer was the cabinet. Nearly all the three drawer file cabinets with two small drawers and one larger drawer were the same size. I just needed to find one with the right look. I settled on a nice cabinet with a light wood color and four wheels. The front wheels could turn and pivot, and the rear wheels just rolled without the ability to turn.

I quickly came up with the idea that I would use this cabinet backward. Thus, even though the cabinet had nonlocking wheels, the system would be largely stable. The player sitting in front of the system, really the back of the cabinet, might put force on the system when playing, but he or she would only be able to move the system forward or backward, not from side to side. In addition, the "new" back of the system would have the drawers open to provide access to the computer inside.

Basic Assembly

Since this was a rather cheap cabinet (less than $100), it came as a kit that required assembly. First, I assembled the cabinet itself almost exactly as described in the instructions except that I only put the middle set of rails for the drawers into the cabinet and I left the top off. Then, I assembled the middle drawer, but left the bottom out of the drawer and left the handle off. I saved all the remaining pieces, because I would need a few of them for the next few steps.

I purchased a few small hinges and a magnetic latching mechanism from a hardware store. I attached the two hinges to the bottom of the cabinet near the front and also the front panel for the large drawer. On the inside of the large drawer front panel I attached the metal plate for the latch, and attached the latch itself to the inside of the cabinet. Thus, the large drawer now acted like a door, hinged on the bottom.

I went about fixing up the other drawers next. Using some metal brackets purchased from the hardware store at the same time, I attached the front panel for the top drawer in its permanent position. The middle drawer was placed into its proper position by sliding it into the rails built into the side of the cabinet. Using some more metal brackets, I secured the middle drawer into its permanent position.

The basic file cabinet was built up. It looked . . . well, like a file cabinet with a few pieces missing.

Modding the Cabinet

It was time for a few modifications to the case, now that I knew what I had to work with. First, I removed all the drawers by unscrewing everything so I could work on them a little more easily.

For the large drawer, I used an 80-mm hole saw to cut a hole near the top of the panel in between the mounting holes for the handle. This hole would be the exhaust fan for the system. The inside of the hole was a little rough after using the hole saw because the drawer was just made up of particle board. I used a little medium-grade sandpaper to smooth it down and painted the inside of the hole with some black paint. After the paint dried I attached the handle and used some chrome molding with adhesive backing to accent the edges of the hole.

The middle drawer required a few test fittings. The basic idea behind the cabinet was to place everything for the system, including the monitor, inside the cabinet. I had previously noticed that the inside width of the cabinet was exactly the same width as an old 15-inch monitor I had left over from an old computer. When I placed the monitor into the cabinet with the screen facing up, the edges of the monitor were caught by the edges of the second drawer (why I avoided putting a bottom in the drawer). There was one problem though—the screen of the monitor stuck out about $1/2$ an inch above the sides of the cabinet. A bit of work with a sanding drum on my Dremel on the sides of the second drawer, and everything fit perfectly (see Figure 15-2).

For the top drawer, I used a scrap piece of wood to help extend the depth of the front of the drawer. This put some pressure on the monitor, holding it securely between the top drawer faceplate and the rear of the second drawer. Also, I attached a bit of black foam board on the

FIGURE 15-2: Middle drawer with missing bottom and sides sanded.

bottom of the drawer (see Figure 15-3). Thus, with the top drawer faceplate mounted in place using the brackets from earlier, the small space between the top and middle drawers was covered.

Finally, for both the top and middle drawer I attached a couple of rubber feet over the two holes that were designed to attach the handles.

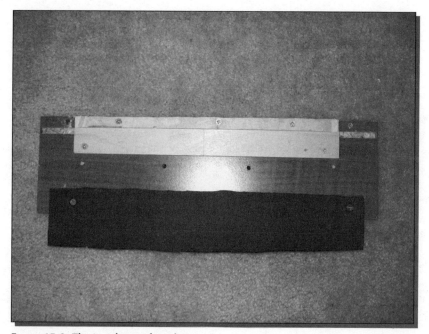

FIGURE 15-3: The top drawer faceplate.

Front Panel

The cabinet needed several more things to be a real arcade machine. I had to be able to do all the standard things like turn the system off and on, reset it if it locked up, and turn on the lighting effects (a marquee, of a sort). On top of that, what type of arcade system doesn't have speakers?

Speakers

I acquired a set of somewhat cheap, powered speakers. These speakers were nothing special, but did have a few controls on them. The controls included a power LED, a volume dial, which doubled as the power switch, and a knob for bass. I decided all these needed to be incorporated into the basic design.

I started by opening the case for the speakers and separating the pieces. One problem was obvious—the controls for volume and bass were integrated onto a large circuit board that would not easily fit inside the cabinet since the controls were mounted at a right angle to the board itself. If this board were attached to the front of the cabinet the way it was, it would block the path for a lot of cables at the very least, and it might not fit at all with the monitor mounted in the cabinet.

I carefully desoldered the power LED, the volume, and the bass dials from the circuit board. I then soldered them to a smaller piece of perf-board and ran wires from the original board to the new board (see Figure 15-4).

Cross-Reference   Soldering and unsoldering is covered in detail in Chapter 7.

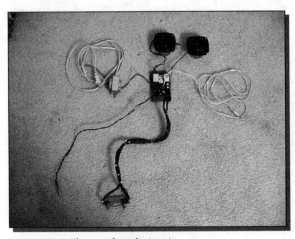

FIGURE 15-4: The speaker electronics.

To mount the speakers, I used an 80-mm hole saw to cut holes in the front of the case on either side of the location where the system controls would be. Once again, I sanded the inside of the holes and painted them black as well.

Also, I purchased a bit of metal mesh from an online retailer and cut out rectangular shapes than would fit over the round holes for the speakers. I carefully drilled holes in each corner for screws and painted these speaker covers hi-gloss black.

System Controls

The wood for the front of the system was far too thick to mount any switches on. Thus, I cutout a large hole in the front center of the system that I could cover with thinner material such as acrylic plastic (see Figure 15-5). I had to decide on what controls I needed so I could design the system control panel. Ultimately, I decided that I needed a number of controls: the speaker dials (volume and bass), some lights (speaker power, system power, and hard drive activity), and a few switches (computer power on, computer reset, cabinet power on, and lighting power).

I purchased a ¼-inch-thick piece of acrylic panel from a local glass shop that was already cut to the right dimensions for the front of the system. I also purchased a few matching switches, some momentary (such as computer power on and reset) and some nonmomentary (the other functions). I also purchased some nice chrome LED holders.

I proceeded with drilling the necessary holes for all the switches in the acrylic panel, and then painted the back side with black paint. This is where I learned that acrylic panels can be sensitive to the type of paint that is used—the first paint I used caused a spider-web pattern to appear in the acrylic. I experimented until I found a paint that would work—acrylic spray paint.

FIGURE 15-5: Front of the cabinet with holes cut out for control panel and speakers.

Specific details and techniques for painting are covered in Chapter 6.

I mounted the control panel to the front via four screws through the acrylic and wood. I also mounted the speakers, the speaker mesh, the front panel controls for the speakers, the speaker electronics, and the speaker power supply. Using one of the chrome LED holders, I mounted the power LED for the speakers to the front panel.

Cooling

I already planned to have the rear exhaust fan in the system, but wood is a wonderful insulator so I knew one fan wouldn't be enough. Most of the components for this mod, including the motherboard and power supply were going to be mounted against the floor of the cabinet. So the cooling solution was simple—just a direct path for the air from the front to the back.

I cut another 80-mm hole in the center bottom of the case for an air intake. Once again, I sanded the edges and painted them black. This would provide the path for air to take from the front of the case to the rear.

Starting Assembly

At this point, all the major alterations were made to the cabinet already, so I could start mounting components in it. This also helped reduce the amount of space I was using as a staging area for the mod, which certainly was a welcome change for my wife. Strange how some people just don't see the value of living surrounded by electronics components and tools. . . .

Computer Parts

The computing needs for this system were relatively minimal. I just needed something halfway decent—something approximately 1 GHz with over 256 MB of memory and a basic video card. The solution was a cheap CPU plus motherboard combo purchased from a local computer store. It lacked integrated video, but I had a spare ATI Rage video card so this wasn't a problem. Similarly, the power needs were basic. I had a spare 350-watt power supply that served the purpose nicely.

Mounting these components was a different matter. There were no mounting holes in the cabinet, of course. I used a drill to make holes slightly smaller than the threaded parts of standard motherboard standoffs. Then, I carefully but forcefully screwed the standoffs into the case and attached the motherboard on top of it. I attached the power supply near the back of the system using some additional brackets purchased at a hardware store.

Also at this time, I made some extension wires for the power LED and hard drive activity LED and attached one end to the motherboard, while attaching the other end through the front

FIGURE **15-6: Completed front control panel and speakers.**

control panel. I used the same type of chrome LED holders as I used for the speaker power LED with these LEDs (see Figure 15-6).

The two momentary switches I had previously purchased were connected through some long extension cables to the motherboard power-on and reset connections.

For the cooling side of things, in addition to a cheap heatsink/fan combo on top of the motherboard I attached an intake fan behind the hole in the front cabinet. Nothing special here, just a cheap black 80-mm fan on the inside and a standard chrome fan grill on the front that was attached to one of the motherboard fan headers. For the rear door of the case, I attached a clear fan with random flashing blue LEDs in the hub and a chrome grill. I made sure that the wires to the fan were long enough so the fan could still run even while the door was fully open.

Power

The system needed to be plugged into the wall somehow to get power, but I had a serious problem. There were at least three different components that needed their own AC power source—the computer, the monitor, and the speakers. I suppose I could have opened up the power supply and soldered long wires to carry AC voltage to all the components from the plug already in the power supply, but frankly AC power scares me with that whole "chance of electrocution" thing.

Caution

Don't be ashamed of fearing electricity. The electricity in the walls of your home is great for lighting, warmth, and thousands of other tasks but it really feels bad flowing *through* your body. I accidentally grabbed the bare metal on a power plug that wasn't plugged in all the way once, and knocked the breath out of myself for a good 30 minutes. It could have been much worse....

So, I went a different way. I purchased a cheap power strip and opened that up. With a great deal of difficulty due to my somewhat low-wattage soldering iron, I was able to remove the editing switch in the power strip and solder in my own switch. That switch was of course attached to the power supply via some long wires so it could be mounted in the front control panel for the system.

Using a couple of screws, I mounted the power strip to the side of the cabinet and plugged the computer power supply into that as well as the power cord for the speakers (see Figure 15-7).

FIGURE 15-7: The basic cabinet with computer parts and power system installed.

FIGURE 15-8: Cold cathode throbber circuit.

On the rear door of the cabinet, I sanded down a small area that allowed the end of the power strip to exit the cabinet while the door was closed.

Lighting

No modern computer mod is complete without some sort of cool lighting effect, so how could this system one be? Showing off the internal components of the system would ruin the basic effect of having an arcade cabinet (ever see an acrylic arcade cabinet?), so what was I to do? I didn't have a space for a marquee of any sort to light up either.

The idea I came up with was to mount two green cold cathode lights on either side of the cabinet. Although they produced an eerie glow, even that was not enough for me. Using a circuit design I found on a modding site called Bit-Tech (www.bit-tech.net) for a cold cathode throbber, one light slowly dims while the other gets brighter and then they alternate back and forth (see Figure 15-8).

The circuit was built on a piece of perf-board and mounted to the inside of the cabinet, while the switch to turn the effect on or off was mounted in the front of the cabinet. The lights themselves were mounted on both sides of the cabinet near the top. My plan was that when the lights were covered by the top piece of acrylic panel, they would not be directly visible—all you would see would be the indirect glow.

Cross-Reference Chapter 8 discusses how to build simple circuits from circuit diagrams.

Control Pad

The control pad required the most work of any piece of this case. Not only did all the holes for the various components have to be properly drilled, but the components had to be mounted and the electronics necessary to interface these with the computer had to be installed. I spent well over two weeks spent on this component alone.

Preparation

Just like the other acrylic panel I purchased from a local glass shop, the panel for the control pad was already the right shape. Also as with the other panel, I started by cutting off the square edges at a 45-degree angle and sanding them smooth. I then got to work on the basic arrangements of components.

The actual controls needed to be a compromise between the custom controls that some games require and the general controls that could apply to many games. I had very little room to work with, so I decided right off the bat that this would be a single-player system. I needed a joystick, obviously, and since all games designed for 4-way joysticks would work with 8-way joysticks (but not the other way around), the decision to get an 8-way joystick was clear. I needed some fire buttons too, and since many "fighting" games required a set of six buttons it seemed logical to go with that many. I also wanted a trackball for those types of games, and a trackball could also double for a mouse when working on the system. For this I needed another two buttons to go along with the trackball as left and right mouse buttons. Finally, I needed a few extra buttons to do things like add a coin, start a single-player game, and exit from the system. These are all the controls that were mounted in the control panel.

Now, I had to decide on the basic layout of the controls. Most games would use the joystick, so that took center stage. One thing I've noticed with arcade games is that when I was first going to arcades, the joystick was on the right and the buttons were on the left. This made sense, since most people are right handed, and you would want to control a ship moving through a difficult area with your best hand, while your left hand would just mash fire buttons all day. But arcades swapped those controls a few years later, I believe to make people do worse at the games and spend more money. Because this was a system for me, I could design it the way I wanted. I set up an array of six buttons to the left of the joystick.

The trackball was also needed, but less often. Therefore, the trackball was mounted to the far right side, but still had its buttons beside it slightly to the left. Finally, the three other buttons (of a different design) were placed to the far left top of the control panel.

I just had to decide on the colors for the controls. The three top-mounted buttons were the easiest—red for exit, yellow for add coin, and white for start. The joystick and six matching buttons were purchased in green, and the two buttons for the trackball were purchased in blue to differentiate them from the standard buttons. The trackball itself would be whatever I could get cheaply that would work with the computer.

Real Arcade Controls

Real arcade style controls are expensive when compared with their computer and console counterparts, but nothing else feels quite like them. Real arcade controls are designed to be beaten, mashed, and generally abused by hundreds or thousands of kids, while home systems are far more fragile.

Buttons for arcade controls come in two main variations, the microswitch and the leaf design. The leaf design is generally accepted as the better-feeling button, but is harder to maintain because the mechanism beneath the button can get out of alignment resulting in a dead button. The microswitch-style buttons have a slightly stiffer feel than leaf buttons, but are less prone to dead button syndrome. Microswitch buttons also make a clicking sound every time they are pressed.

The arcade joysticks come in a number of varieties as well, but the most important consideration is to whether to get a 4-way or an 8-way joystick. Games that expect 4-direction movement, such as Pac-Man, can be played with an 8-direction joystick but give unpredictable behavior when the stick is pushed diagonally (often by accident). However, games designed for an 8-way joystick, such as Bezerk!, cannot be played successfully with a 4-way joystick. Thus, as a compromise, 8-way joysticks are usually best.

There are dozens of proprietary controls such as light guns, crossbows, throttles, and others. But most of these don't adapt well to most games, so are best left off a general-purpose cabinet.

Electronics

The electronics for the control panel were relatively simple, but time-consuming. When building a MAME cabinet, there are two basic choices for how to get the control signals into the computer: use a keyboard or a gamepad.

Using a keyboard is one nice option, since the controls in MAME are already set up to use keyboard controls. Simply rip apart a keyboard and hack into the control signals for the various keys to use your own switches instead of keyboard keys. But the problem is that keyboards have a little-seen weakness—when multiple keys are pressed, "ghosting" can occur. Ghosting means that some key presses can't be seen in some circumstances or, even worse, extra key presses are seen for keys that were never pressed. Also, using an additional keyboard when the system must act as a real computer can cause conflicts.

The other option is to use a gamepad or joystick and hack into it to use it as a substitute for the keyboard. The first downside is that you have to use additional software that catches the controls from the gamepad and sends out keyboard signals when a button is pressed. Second, there are a limited number of buttons on a gamepad and there may simply not be enough signals for the control scheme you want.

In my case, I was able to find a cheap gamepad that had enough switches, joypads, and gizmos to simulate the number of keys I needed. In addition, the gamepad came with software that would catch the input from the gamepad and send out key presses that were configurable.

Before going any further, I took some spare wire and soldered on the appropriate crimp-style connectors for the arcade buttons I had purchased. I soldered enough wires so that I had all the connectors I needed—two per switch—remembering that the joystick alone needed four switches. I also made sure that I had enough wire so that I could work comfortably on the system by making each wire about 3 to 4 feet long.

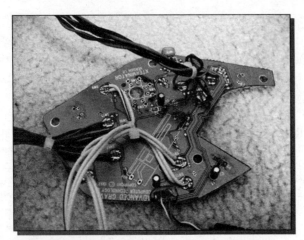

FIGURE 15-9: Electronics from a gamepad modified for arcade controls.

The next step was to open the gamepad up and expose the circuit board. I removed all the additional controls that I wouldn't be using, such as the throttle slider. At each contact point that had a button above it, there was an exposed area of metal. The wires from the previous step were soldered to these pads, and tie wrapped in a logical fashion (i.e., the joystick wires were tied together, the joystick button wires were tied together, etc.) Figure 15-9 shows the modified circuit board.

Special Consideration: The Trackball

I wanted something special and cheap for the trackball/mouse, and those two criteria usually don't go well together. Fortunately, I found exactly what I wanted—the Crystal trackball from CompUSA. This trackball plugs into a computer and acts like a mouse, but has one special feature. The ball itself is lighted green by a couple of LEDs underneath and turns red when any of the mouse buttons is pressed.

This was a nice feature, but it didn't fit my color scheme. I thought that I could replace the green LEDs with blue LEDs to match the arcade style buttons I had purchased for the mouse buttons, but blue LEDs require twice the voltage of green LEDs. Thus, when soldered in place the blue LEDs wouldn't even light up.

Not one to give up so easily, I used a trick. Each green LED had two separate connection points (for a total of two anodes and two cathodes when considering both green LEDs). I was able to cut the traces on a couple of those pads and use a bit of wire to jumper those pads together. Essentially, I created two total pads with ground on one pad and voltage on the other pad. Since these green LEDs each used 1.5 volts, combining them gave 3 volts total, which was exactly what the blue LEDs needed. I hooked up two blue LEDs in parallel.

Now, the trackball was normally blue, but would light up red when the buttons were pressed. However, I wasn't done yet. I removed the circuit board from its plastic enclosure and replaced the left and right buttons with more wires as I had done for the joystick.

FIGURE 15-10: Cutout in the cabinet for the trackball circuit board.

I just needed to figure out how to mount the trackball. Ultimately, I cut out a small section on the right side of the case so that the circuit board was held in place by the case on the front and right side, and by the monitor housing on the rear side. The cutout didn't go all the way through, but just enough so that there was a ledge I could rest the trackball on (see Figure 15-10). It was important to get the height right so that the trackball itself had roughly one third of its height above the surface of the control panel.

Cutting the Acrylic

The acrylic panel was going to be mounted slightly offset from the cabinet itself. Thus, the panel would overhang the cabinet on three sides. I carefully planned and measured all the locations for all the buttons, joystick, and trackball and marked the locations on the paper backing. Finding the exact size for the trackball was a bit of work, and required cutting a hole a little too small and slowly expanding it. In addition, the edges of the trackball cutout needed to be angled a bit.

Next, I took out my handle hole-saw set and got to work cutting out all the large holes. This was a slow and difficult process, because the hole saw had a tendency to melt the acrylic as I was cutting through it. If I went too fast, the holes would be uneven and chip when I finally cut through. In addition, the slightly melted acrylic disc would get stuck in the hole saw itself and required a bit of pushing and pulling to remove it.

Chapter 5 details various cutting and drilling methods, including how to use hole saws.

Once the large holes were cut, I drilled all the small holes for mounting the joystick itself. In addition, I drilled several holes all around the edges (except the top) for mounting the panel to the cabinet (see Figure 15-11). Once the cabinet mounting screws were in place, I wanted the surface to be flat. I used a triangular Dremel sanding bit to sand all the mounting holes to an inverted cone shape, so I could later use some flat-head screws to mount the panel.

Finishing Up

A clear control panel wasn't very interesting, so it had to be colored somehow. Some people use various graphics or patterns to make their panels more interesting, but I always thought that was a little too visually busy. The alternative was a flat color, which seemed too boring.

I came across this interesting paint called ColorFleck. Basically, this paint is a clear paint that contains particles that grab light and reflect the individual colors within it like a prism. I carefully removed the paper backing from the underside of the panel and painted it with this paint. After the paint was dry, I painted over that with a black acrylic paint. The paint was quite thin, and required at least five or six coats to block light from coming through.

Since the underside of the panel was painted, I turned the panel over and removed the protective paper from the top when the paint was dry. The result was a glossy smooth finish with a nice colorful surface that looked very professional (see Figure 15-12).

Painting the underside of an acrylic panel is a useful and easy way to get a professional-looking finish.

Figure 15-11: Test fitting the control panel on the cabinet.

FIGURE **15-12: ColorFleck paint shining in the sunlight.**

Finally, I went about mounting everything. I plugged the control pad into the gameport on the motherboard and mounted the electronics for the control panel to the inside of the cabinet with a screw. I mounted the buttons and joystick to the panel and attached them via the wires to the electronics. Then, I secured the whole panel on top of the cabinet with the countersunk screws.

The area with the trackball didn't look quite right because of the somewhat irregular sanding required to make the edges of the trackball hole. The solution was to cut out a ring of thin plastic, painted black, and glue it around the edge of the trackball hole.

Special Consideration: The Keyboard

Every so often, such as when installing updated emulators every few months, I would need to work on the system as a real computer. So, I needed to find a way to add a keyboard that wouldn't interfere with the normal system operation as a game system.

The solution was remarkably low tech. I inserted a couple of metal hooks into the exterior side panel of the cabinet and placed a mini-keyboard there. I routed the cord of the keyboard around the rear of the system so that it entered the cabinet via a small cutout in the rear door.

Final Assembly

At this point, the system was almost complete from a hardware perspective. Only the final pieces needed to be put in place and attached.

Mounting the Monitor

The edges of the monitor would likely be visible from the top of the system, even when the top acrylic panel was added. My solution was to paint the monitor.

Caution Monitors, even when unplugged, hold enough electrical charge to kill. Be careful when opening a monitor not to touch any of the high-voltage electronics.

I opened the monitor and removed the front faceplate. I painted this piece with flat black paint and, after the paint was dry, reattached it to the monitor. I also cut the power LED so that it wouldn't light up at all.

Finally, I plugged the power cord for the monitor into the internal power strip and the video cable into the video card,. I then carefully lowered the monitor into the cabinet. The monitor was permanently switched on. Whether the monitor was on or off would be controlled via power to the entire power strip and its switch mounted in the front of the cabinet.

Top Panel

The top acrylic panel was another thick piece of acrylic I purchased already cut to the right basic dimensions. I cut and sanded the sides at an angle just like the control panel and drilled and sanded down screw holes to accommodate the flat-head screws.

Painting this piece was also very similar to painting the control pad. The primary difference was that I needed to be able to see the monitor through the panel. So, before applying the ColorFleck and black paint to the underside, I attached a cutout in the shape of the monitor screen to the panel. Obviously, this required some test fits to make sure that I had the location right before I started the paint job. I had to apply the black paint much more thickly this time to make sure none of the light from the green cold cathode tubes made it through.

Another problem became clear as well. I was planning on running the MAME arcade emulator on this system, so I would map the controls to a good standard setup for that program. But I also wanted to potentially run other emulators as well, such as an emulator for all the game systems I used to have, including the Odyssey 2, the Atari 2600, and so on. All the emulators set up the joystick and button layout differently. How would I remember the various control setups?

The solution was to buy a bunch of plastic business card holders and some three-ring binders. I drilled a few holes in the top panel near the top and attached the business card holders to these by using the metal rings. I then printed out some diagrams of the button layouts I wanted and inserted them into the holders. Thus, I could simply flip to the right diagram whenever I ran the appropriate emulator.

Software

The software installation was relatively easy. After installing Windows, I installed the MAME32 emulator software and a number of arcade game ROMs. Everything was configured and ran perfectly.

Arcade game ROMs, even quite old ones, are copyrighted material and possession of them is illegal in most places unless you own an original copy of the ROM itself (at which point the electronic image is considered a backup). There are only a handful or legal to copy arcade ROMs available on the Internet. However, some sites such as `www.starroms.com` sell these ROMs for reasonable prices.

In addition to MAME32, I installed a number of other emulators for the other game systems I own. The most impressive of these emulators was MESS32 (Multiple Emulator Super System), an emulator that can simulate dozens of different home systems. I installed it plus a number of ROMs for games I still own, but would rather not pull out of storage.

Finally, I needed an interface to all these emulators. There are a number of these programs, called front ends, available. The one I liked and ended up using was called Party-On! and is available from `www.andrewburt.com/partyon`. I set up this program to automatically start after the system boots up. From its interface, I can select the specific game I want to play just by using the joystick and its buttons. The program has many nice features, including the ability to run different emulators and select which game to run from each emulator. Thus, I could run games from MAME32 or MESS32 directly without having to type anything.

Conclusion

This system was a blast to build, and it works wonderfully. It's a great way to blow off a little steam by playing my favorite games from my youth and get a little better at the ones I sucked at but never had enough quarters to improve my skill on.

Probably the best aspect of this system is being able to have a game system right in my living room that is self-contained and doesn't look out of place. Everyone who has come to my place, even the nontechnical people, instantly know what it is and are drawn to it. What more could I hope for?

Well, maybe if I could just beat Darth Vader's tie fighter on the "hard" setting. . . .

$3,000 Fish Tank

Daniel "Dan_Dude" Jonke

Why do it? That is the one question that just about everyone asks when they see this case. This case was built for one reason—because I wanted to. Building this case won't give you cooler temperatures, it won't be easier to work on, it'll be about as mobile as a grandfather clock, and it doesn't take a beating well. This case serves only one purpose: vanity. But it sure does a good job.

Although this chapter focuses on my own case specifically, the techniques and process described can be applied to any case design your mind can conjure up. Something to always keep in mind when doing a custom case is that the sky is the limit. If you don't like a specific feature, you can change it.

Timeframe and Cost

The raw materials for the case are relatively cheap. All the acrylic needed should only cost about $100. The ancillary stuff, however, can add up quickly if you've never worked with acrylic before. Glue, polish, sandpaper, saw blades, and other small pieces could easily total another $100. If you need to purchase tools for the project, the cost could balloon to over $1,000 to complete the case.

The time investment in any ground-up case project will be very large, and this is no exception. It took about nine months of planning, design, and construction to complete this case (about two hours a week). Bear in mind that a good portion of that time was spent teaching myself much of what I've written into this chapter. By reading this chapter you've already chopped two months off of the build time. If you decide to use my plans as they are, that's another three months of CAD time gone right there.

Tip   CAD stands for computer-aided design. Really, it's just a fancy word for using a computer to draw up very detailed and accurate plans before cutting anything. This allows the designer to work out potential problems without wasting materials and the time cutting parts.

Required Parts and Tools

You've got your plans for a killer case and the tools to bring it to life, but you're missing one more thing—the stuff to make a case out of. Following is a list of some obvious and some not so obvious things to have handy for the build.

- **Acrylic sheet**—This is what you end up making the case from. It's typically sold in 4 foot × 8 foot sheet form, and you can buy it in various thicknesses. I recommend $1/4$ inch because it's not overly expensive, but forms a very sturdy case. For drive bays it's easier to use $1/8$ inch so that standard case screws will go through it (price varies with quantity and type).

 Chapter 5 discusses the various types of acrylic sheet.

- **Sandpaper**—You need plenty of sandpaper in 220 grit (fine) and equal amounts of 400 and 600 grit if you decide to use them (less than $1 per sheet).

- **Solvent cement**—This is the technical name for what I refer to as "acrylic glue." It's a special chemical that actually melts the acrylic together and forms a bond as strong as the original pieces when it dries ($5).

- **Jeweler's rouge**—This is an abrasive you'll use with the buffing wheel to polish your acrylic. It's sold in sticks that look kind of like clay, and it has about the same consistency ($3 to $8).

- **Novus plastic polish**—You'll probably end up scratching something during the construction process, and this stuff will be your savior. You rub it in as if you were waxing a car, and the scratch disappears. It comes in three parts—you apply them in sequence #3 through #1 to polish out any marks ($15 for all three).

- **Windex**—To be more diplomatic I'll call it "multipurpose glass cleaner." When all is said and done, you'll want to clean all the fingerprints off the acrylic to enjoy its true beauty ($4).

- **Tools**—Later in the chapter I'll explain all the tools you could use to work on acrylic—and there are a lot—but for now I'll just cover the basics. Ideally, you'll want something large such as a table saw to cut out your initial pieces and something small such as a scroll saw to do detailed work. Most woodworking saws will work well with acrylic as long as they don't melt it. But if your patience outweighs your wallet, a single $40 jigsaw could be used to make this entire case. A set of files is a must to take out tooth marks and level out the pieces. You also may want a power sander to help out your forearms. And a syringe to apply the acrylic glue is a great thing to have.

A Little History

The design for this case went through several evolutions. It began way back in the summer of 2000 with some sketches for a more traditional acrylic case (see Figure 16-1).

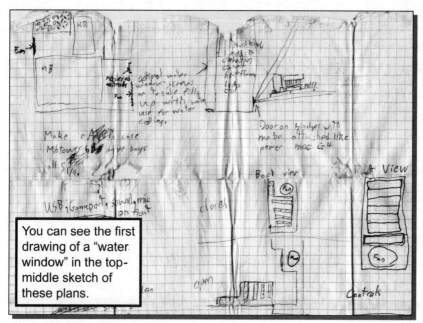

You can see the first drawing of a "water window" in the top-middle sketch of these plans.

FIGURE 16-1: The original drawings.

From looking at the original drawings you can see that I was first trying to emulate a standard midtower design. In fact, I drew a motherboard tray with the words "just like a Power Mac G4." But there was one cool idea I had—why not build one of the sides out into a thin box and fill it with water? I decided that the case had to be built, but real life got in the way at the time. I couldn't even afford the hardware to put inside the case, let alone the materials. So, I sat on the plans, and I eventually forgot about them entirely.

In the spring of 2002, a friend approached me about maybe building an acrylic case in shop class. I instantly remembered my previous doodlings, buried under a pile of papers on my desk. Looking at them I saw how vanilla the case was now. In the two years since the drawings, modding as an art form had evolved a lot and had seen many creative and unconventional case designs. I realized that as long as I was working from scratch, the parts could go anywhere I wanted.

I started doodling on a new sheet of graph paper and decided to try and think of all the things I disliked about traditional acrylic cases. I realized that the stuff you want to show off most is the circuitry—the motherboard and anything plugged into it. But looking at a case head on, you have drive bays obscuring your view. By far the ugliest thing in a PC is the power supply— the big box just doesn't have any appeal. But in a standard case it was right on top blocking your view down into the innards, dangling its hideous wires everywhere. So I started drawing some things out that addressed those flaws.

My epiphany came when I realized that the traditional computer box could be thought of con- ceptually as two boxes stacked one in front of the other, a box for the drives and a box for the motherboard. My idea was that I would separate those two boxes and stack them side by side to create a more square box. Then, I would place the power supply at the bottom of this box toward the back to keep it out of sight. With this design you would be able to view all the components of the case from a head-on and top-down perspective. The revised plans (see Figure 16-2) are much closer to the finished product.

Design

Now that you've read the boring back story its time to talk about the construction of this beast. The design itself took quite some time to figure out. But by spending the time on the computer, planning the smallest details and by knowing my own limits, I saved time in the long run by eliminating costly mistakes.

Down and Dirty with CAD

It's been my experience that paper is good for starting a case design and fleshing out ideas. But once you have a basic layout down, CAD can make your life much easier. Before constructing this case I drew it out in 3-D on the computer. You'll find that the more effort you put into making detailed and accurate plans, the better your case will turn out with less material wasted.

Tip

If you want the actual plans that I used to build my case so that you can steal some ideas or even if you just want to build an exact copy, all of the files are available for free online. Visit: www.vfdworld.com/3kfish tank.

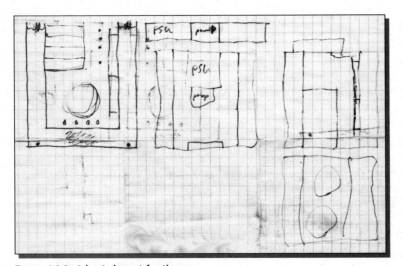

FIGURE 16-2: A basic layout for the case.

While it is common for people to just buy the parts they plan on using and measure the hole sizes and clearances off of them, it can lock you into a specific configuration for the life of the case. For this case I went online and downloaded the actual industry specifications for computer parts. It was more time-consuming, but it had the great benefit of allowing me to know that whatever motherboard I bought down the road would fit in the case without any modifications. Ditto for the graphics card, hard drive, and so on.

Another benefit of drawing the case in CAD is that you can begin to notice problems that aren't apparent in two dimensions. I was tempted to start cramming everything into a tiny space at first, but then it occurred to me that if every piece fit together tight like a jigsaw puzzle, it might not even be possible to insert them into the case. Parts not only need to fit in their final position, they need to have a clear path so that they can slide in and out of that position.

Can You Make It?

Remember what kind of detail you are capable of in construction. For example, I had been planning on sinking the power supply unit (PSU) into the bottom of the tank by building a small pit in the floor. Because the case has water in it, every piece needed to fit perfectly for a watertight seal. Making the pit in the floor would have tripled the number of edges that needed to be sealed, so I decided to just raise the PSU up so that I would have a single flat surface on the inner bottom of the case.

The final design (see Figure 16-3) was one that consisted of nine panels forming the outer case that enclosed the computer, and an inner removable support for drives made of five panels. Because the case was going to have water in it anyway, I knew it wouldn't hold up to any serious movement. Therefore, the drive support is not affixed to the case in any way. It's held in place only by gravity, and it hasn't had any problems.

Going From Screen to Saw

The computer-drawn plans will be accurate to 1/10,000 of an inch, but because the computer can't cut the acrylic for you and build the case, you're going to need some method of transferring

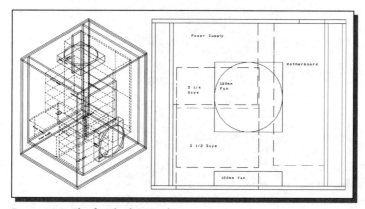

FIGURE 16-3: The finished CAD plans.

those measurements into a form you can use in construction. There are a few options for doing this.

- **Making a cut list**—The first thing that comes to mind for most people is a cut list. This is just a piece of paper with a list of all the needed parts, along with their dimensions and the locations/size of any cutouts or holes. For complex pieces a quick hand-drawn sketch might be attached, but nothing to scale. The advantages of using a cut list are the ease with which one can be made. All that's required is to sit down with a piece of paper and a pen. The downsides of using a cut list are numerous. If your measurements are incorrect, you won't know until you cut something and it doesn't fit. You must also make sure that the guides on tools you are using are accurate, or every piece you cut could end up being several fractions of an inch too small or too big. Though it may not sound like a big deal, if you plan on gluing your case together the pieces must fit exactly. I personally wouldn't recommend this method. There are better ones out there that will save you time and materials.

- **Making cutting templates**—A cutting template is a paper sketch of your piece, done to scale with all the cuts and dimensions laid out exactly where they will be on the finished product. After making a template you can simply tape it over your acrylic and use the lines to guide you as you cut (see Figure 16-4). Cutting templates can be made in a number of ways. If the part is small you may be able to fit a template on a standard 8.5 inch × 11–inch sheet of paper and print it out from your CAD software. Larger pieces can be

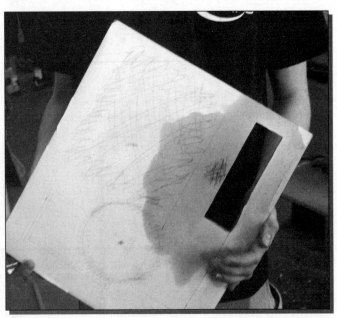

FIGURE 16-4: Template attached to a piece of acrylic that has already been cut.

done with a ruler and a pencil. Getting it accurate may take time but the results will be worth it. If you are really lucky, you might be able to find someone with a plotter you can use.

A plotter is a huge printer that draws with pens instead of ink. While far too expensive to purchase for the hobbyist (several thousand dollars and up), they are an indispensable tool for architects and engineers. I'd highly recommend going to a local high school, technical school, or community college and befriending the resident technology teacher. You'll find that they are just as enthusiastic about these kinds of projects as you are and can give you access to a plotter during off-hours.

- **Building a cardboard mockup**—Similar to a cutting template, a mockup is more sophisticated in that the pieces are cut out of cardboard or stiff paper, using either a cut list or templates. Then, the entire case can be assembled out of these pieces to be sure that everything fits, and you can use the cardboard pieces like the paper templates.

For my case I made cutting templates for all the pieces using a commercial plotter borrowed from my high school. This plotter was capable of drawing on sheets of up to 4 feet wide by unlimited length!

Not Just a Big Hammer

Having the right tools will make or break your case. With the right tools the actual construction process will be quick and painless, and the pieces will all have a tight fit with clean edges free of any marks. On the other hand, if you try and build a case from scratch using only a Dremel, it'll take forever and still look like crap. There is no such thing as a do-it-all when working from scratch; there are many tools suited for different tasks, and they should be used in concert to go from raw plastic to finished product.

Rough Cutting

Acrylic is usually sold in 4 foot × 8–foot sheets. The first task when starting a case is to cut out all the pieces you'll need from that sheet. You may be able to have your pieces cut for you by your plastic supplier. If they'll do it for free (many will), go for it. They probably can cut more accurately than you can. For my own case I had most of my pieces cut by the supplier at no charge (see Figure 16-5). The inner supports were done on a band saw. If you end up doing your own initial cutting, here are the tools that most people use.

- **Table saw**—The table saw is good for making the initial cuts to slice your acrylic sheets into the pieces that will eventually form your case. It is not terribly accurate and can only cut straight lines, so you should cut your pieces slightly bigger than you will need them. Table saws cost between $80 and $500, plus the cost for the blades.
- **Band saw**—This can be used in place of a table saw, although it has the advantage of being able to stop a cut in the middle of a piece. This allows you to notch out sections of

FIGURE 16-5: The acrylic pieces, fresh from the local plastic store and ready to be assembled into a case.

your panels. Band saws are available for between $100 and $400. Again, the cost of the blades adds to the total price.

Detail Cutting

After the initial cutting you can work on the smaller cuts such as holes for fans, drives, buttons, and lights. For that you need a smaller saw that can be controlled better to make a hole just the right size and in the right place. On my case all of the detail work was done with a scroll saw, and a drill press was used to make the starter holes, as well as the hole for the power button.

Cross-Reference   Chapter 5 contains information on using tools such as these for cutting your case.

- **Scroll saw**—The scroll saw is, in my opinion, the most useful tool for working with acrylic because it can do very detailed and accurate cuts. It can be used to make holes inside a piece without cutting in from a side, although you have to drill a starter hole in the piece then stick the scroll saw blade through it. Be sure to get one with variable speeds. If the blade is moving too fast the heat can melt the acrylic back into one piece behind the cut. It's not fun to finish cutting a complex piece and realize that it melted right back together. Scroll saws can be purchased for between $70 and $200.

- **Jigsaw**—The jigsaw can be used in place of a scroll saw, but it's hand-held, which makes it easier to use on large pieces. The disadvantage of a jigsaw is that the blade is larger than that of a scroll saw, which limits your ability to cut tight curves and increases friction, which it turn can cause the acrylic to melt as it is being cut, making for a very unattractive edge. Jigsaws cost between $30 and $200.

- **Rotary tool**—The definitive tool of modders everywhere, a rotary tool is just a hand-held motor with lots of little attachments that screw onto it. Using a carbide cutting bit you can make holes both big and small, but the cut is anything but straight, and long flat sections require a lot of filing to look good. These tools usually cost between $40 and $60.

- **Drill press**—Why not a hand drill? Because a drill press will allow you to get perfectly clean holes drilled at exactly perpendicular angles to the acrylic. This is important to ensure that mounting holes line up with hardware and also reduces the likelihood of a drill bit catching on the acrylic and cracking it. You need a drill to make starter holes if you are using a scroll saw or jigsaw, and you can also use it with a hole saw to get perfectly round holes for fans. Cheap drill presses are available for $100.

Edge Finishing

When all the pieces are cut, the really fun part begins. Every single edge you cut has to be made flat and smooth, not only for appearance's sake but also to ensure that the glue binds along the entire edge of the two panels. Having a good glue bond makes for a strong case, and a waterproof one as well. Unlike with the saws, you'll need to use a combination of the tools described here. There is no way of getting around the need for filing (see Figure 16-6) on all edges prior to polishing. However, you can get away without sanding if you go the flame polishing route.

Again, Chapter 5 contains useful information related to this section. Chapter 5 contains instructions on various methods of cleaning the edges of acrylic panels.

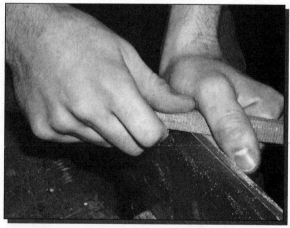

FIGURE 16-6: Filing isn't much fun, but it's an absolutely necessary step, and you will be doing a lot of it.

- **Hand files**—Even the best saw will leave a crummy finish on your cut pieces. By far the best way to smooth out tooth marks and level surfaces is with a hand file and a little elbow grease. Start with a coarse file and use progressively finer cuts to get your edge flat. For this mod, I taped the two side panels of identical size together before filing. By taping the panels together I was able to file the panels to the exact same size—and the time saved didn't hurt either. The price for hand files varies quite a bit, but you can get a decent multifile assortment for around $15.

- **Sanding block**—It's one of the simpler tools you'll use, just a wooden block with sandpaper stapled to it, but a sanding block is important. It further smoothes out the cut edges after filing has gotten them as smooth as it can. Yes it is a lot of work, but the smoother the finish, the better the glue will bond to the acrylic and the stronger your case will be. One pass with 220-grit paper should be adequate, but you will get better results if you do multiple passes with progressively higher grits (220, 400, 600). Sanding blocks cost less than $5.

- **Orbital palm sander**—All the finishing power of the sanding block, with none of the effort. What's not to like? Just be sure to use an orbital sander (the ones that vibrate) not a belt sander, which will probably end up melting your acrylic from the friction of the fast moving belt. These tools can be purchased for between $60 and $150.

- **Buffing wheel**—This is one of many tools you can use to give that final polish to your acrylic pieces. You mount it to either a drill or bench grinder and use jeweler's rouge to get an edge that, while a little hazy, is smooth to the touch and will form an excellent bond when glued. Buffing wheels cost around $5.

- **Torch**—An alternative to buffing your edges is to take a propane or butane torch and "flame" your edges. This will give you the best-looking edges with minimal effort but if you heat up the acrylic too much it can deform or develop bubbles within it that are impossible to remove. Also, don't be tempted to use a cheap cigarette lighter to do this. The rich-burning lighter will create soot that becomes imbedded into the melted plastic giving you a browned look on all your edges. Small torches are available for around $5.

Gluing

There's just one tool here and although you could get away without it, it will make life much easier.

- **Syringe**—Acrylic cement is water thin, and you need to use an extremely minute amount on each piece. Using a syringe is the preferred method of applying it. A thin-gauge metal needle will allow you to precisely control the amount of cement you apply and give you professional results. Syringes for acrylic glue cost around $4.

The Build

After all the preparation, it was finally time to build. I had the plans in front of me and a workshop full of tools with oodles of acrylic sitting in it waiting to be cut. I was out of excuses not to start building this thing. I just hoped I wouldn't screw up.

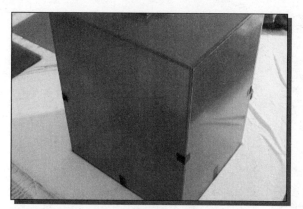

FIGURE 16-7: The pieces for the fish tankfish tank after being cut. Notice that the bottom panel is slightly oversized, because this allows the piece to be filed down to exactly the right size.

The first step was to take that big sheet of acrylic and rough cut the case panels out of it. When using a table saw, make sure the blade is intended for use with acrylic or it could take nasty chips out of your pieces that would take a very long time to file out. No matter what type of saw you are using, set up a cutting guide or fence to make the initial cuts as accurate as possible. Even though I would be filing later, the better the cut, the less time and sweat I would need to spend adjusting it with a hand file. What I ended up with was a set of pieces that fit together into the shape of a box (see Figure 16-7).

Cleaning Up Those Edges

I put the pieces in a vice and began filing them, being sure to keep the file flat and perpendicular to the acrylic face so that the edges would not be rounded. When using a flat file, you just push the file in a diagonal direction about 30 degrees off-center from the acrylic. I learned the hard way never to move at a direct right angle or the file will make terrible scratches. Keep filing until you can no longer see any marks left by the saw teeth.

Tip

A great trick I used is to pair up identical pieces. You should tape them together side by side and file each edge of the two pieces until both are even. This will ensure that they are the exact same size, and it will make the case very square because all the opposing sides will be identical.

When I had filed everything, it was time to break out the sander. At this point in the build, the sander was only needed to take off any sharp edges left by the filing that might have cut me while working (acrylic splinters exist and they do hurt). I used the 220-grit sandpaper, going over each edge until I couldn't see any marks left by the filing I had just done. You have to be very careful to keep the sanding block or sander level on the piece so that you don't accidentally round the edges. The initial edge prep will noticeably improve the quality of the pieces (see Figure 16-8).

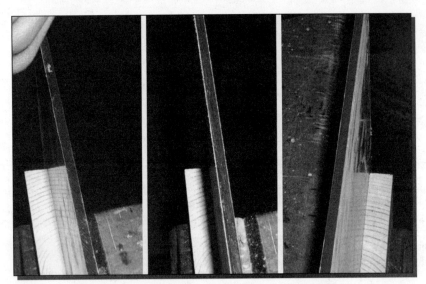

FIGURE 16-8: The same piece of acrylic as it went through initial edge prepping—fresh off the saw (left), filed flat (middle), and sanded smooth (right).

Good Thing I Drew Those Plans

Now I'd reached the part where I could begin to do the detail work. I attached my cutting templates and made all the necessary holes and cutouts in the pieces. The key to doing good-looking, accurate cuts is to go slow and watch what you're doing. A problem you may run into if you go too slow is the dreaded "melting acrylic" problem where the heat of cutting melts the acrylic as a saw goes through it. The pieces then cool and fuse into one piece again behind the blade. I learned this the first time I made a cutout for my drive bays and didn't realize it until I thought I was done. I had to cut out the piece all over again, going over every line to cutout the melted plastic that had formed back in place.

Experience taught me that this could be mitigated by using sharp blades that are tightened properly and a cutting lubricant. Just be careful and test any cutting oils on a scrap piece first because they may contain solvents that will damage the acrylic upon contact. It helps to have computer parts handy to check the fit for certain pieces. If you just cut a fan hole, stick a fan up against it and check how everything lines up. If you need to make an adjustment, you can do it now and still only have to file and sand once. After checking my pieces against the plans (and the parts if possible), I had to whip out the file and sandpaper all over again and clean up the edges. It wasn't fun, but the effort now made for a great looking case later on.

Making Things Pretty

Now the cutting was done for my case. It was time to make it sparkle and shine. I tried to polish everything until it was as shiny as possible. I started by looking over everything to find any nicks or chips that I might have missed the first time. If necessary I sanded them out. After that, I polished my edges using a buffing wheel. With a buffing wheel you just take the stick of rouge, rub it up against the spinning wheel, and get a dark coating onto it. Then, slowly run the pieces across the spinning wheel, not pressing to hard. Just let the fabric glide over the plastic, and after three to five passes, the edge should be visibly clear. Then, take a soft rag and wipe off the edge to clean off any rouge deposits. If you choose to flame polish your edges, start by setting the torch low, with just a tiny blue tip visible. Run the flame quickly over the acrylic edges just enough to melt the plastic in the edge into a gooey state, causing it to smooth out and cool with a perfectly smooth and clear finish. I used the buffing wheel for my case because after all the hard work I put into the pieces, I couldn't bear the thought of starting over because I melted one.

At this point I did another test fit of all the pieces, being certain that everything would line up perfectly now. Sadly the drive bays hadn't widened up as much as I'd hoped they would. So I got out the file and kept working until they were exactly 5.85 inches wide, as they should have been. With that out of the way, I breathed a sigh of relief. I was one step away from enjoying my most ambitious case ever.

Putting the Pieces Together

Now, all the pieces were cut, the edges were wineglass smooth, and I'd made sure that everything fit like a glove. It was time to start gluing. Solvent cement is a tricky product to use because it is very thin and runny. As it melts acrylic, if you get any on a surface that you don't want to glue, it will end up crazing the acrylic—making it all foggy on the surface and causing you to have to polish it out to a shine again. But if done properly, gluing will give you a case that is incredibly strong and looks fantastic.

Cross-Reference   Chapter 10 contains another perspective on using acrylic glue.

To ensure good results when gluing, I built a jig (see Figure 16-9). The jig I used for this was just two pieces of wood intersecting at a 90-degree angle, forming a V shape. As you can see,

FIGURE 16-9: The jig built to glue the case together.

the purpose of a jig is to provide a surface where you can clamp pieces into place before gluing them together. The jig will keep the pieces perfectly aligned while the glue sets. It can be made of any material, but the one I used was constructed of scrap wood.

Notice that the protective film was only peeled back enough to run a thin bead of cement with the syringe. I made sure to keep as much acrylic covered as possible so that if some cement dripped on the acrylic there wouldn't be any damage.

The glue sets very fast. I could have removed the pieces from the jig after a few hours, but I let them cure overnight to be safe.

The End?

When you finally glue that last piece and peel back the all the film for the first time there is a feeling quite unlike any other. You see before you a creation that is unique on the planet earth—born of your own imagination and birthed by your own hands. The hard work has paid off, and you have sitting before you a computer case ready for parts (see Figure 16-10). I noticed a nasty run of acrylic cement on the bottom-left corner, but thankfully I was able to polish it out.

You'll find that although major construction may have stopped on your case, it's never really finished. I'm always improving mine and adding little things here and there.

FIGURE 16-10: The case says hello to the world for the first time!

Retrospective

I finished my initial work on the case in June of 2003. As I sit here writing this now at 4:41 a.m., it is now May of 2004. For the past 11 months I've been using this case and computer everyday. It is not just a showpiece like so many custom cases; it's my daily driver. The great part about that is that I can look back and analyze what worked and what didn't work.

The look of the case has evolved significantly. It certainly looks much better then it did at first, but not all changes have been for appearances only. The following images contrast the way it looked the first time it was assembled with the way it looks now (see Figure 16-11).

Wires

I had hoped that by moving the power supply to the bottom I could hide the ugly wires. This didn't really work for me, so I sleeved every wire in the case with neon green wire sleeving to match the water. It was a lot of work, but totally worth it. Not only does it look great but it makes working with the case easier, because stray wires no longer get pinched in places they're not supposed to be. More then anything else this made the case much more attractive to look at. I wouldn't even consider doing an acrylic case without wire sleeving now.

DVD Window

I cut a window into the top of the DVD drive and lit the interior with green LEDs. This had always been part of my plan, and I was very happy with the way it turned out appearance-wise, but something I didn't anticipate was the hugely increased noise levels caused by removing a section of the cover. I now routinely open the case and place a paperback book on top of the

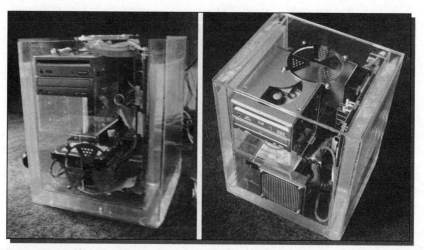

FIGURE 16-11: The case after its first assembly (right) versus the case in its current form (left).

DVD window when I want to watch a movie to quiet it down. It does the job nicely but I might think twice before doing this again. There were also unanticipated benefits to having the window. Now I can just look down into the drive to see what disk is in there. It's much more convenient then going to My Computer.

Gold Paint and Fan Covers

The gold paint for the DVD drive was always a part of the plan for the case. After cutting a hole in the drive for the window it would need a paint job anyway so I choose gold because it compliments the green water so well. When I saw how much better looking it made the drives, I began to notice how ugly the molded black plastic case fans looked in the case. I decided to fabricate aluminum boxes that would cover the outside frames of the fans and painted them gold to coordinate them with the drives. It turned out fantastic. The fans look a million times better then they did before.

Relocated Case Fan

You'll notice the case fan moved from the top of the case to the front of the case, and the radiation grill moved from the front to the top. This was purely the result of trial and error. I installed the fan in the top hole because I figured that the cooling would be most effective there, sucking all the hot air out the top of the case. When I began having heat problems I tried putting it into the hole in the bottom. and this brought case temps down 10˚C. I was going to keep the radiation grill where it was, but it's not very good at keeping things out of a fan. After the third time my toe got jammed in the intake, I put a regular fan grill on the front and moved the radiation grill up top. I like it better up there now anyway.

The fan filter was a necessity with the fan sucking in air down in front now and the case being on the floor. There were tremendous amounts of dust coming into the case. Besides the fact that it clogs up the heatsinks and can make things overhead, in an acrylic case, dust bunnies just look like crap.

Conclusion

This case is far from perfect, but it turned out pretty good. You've read this chapter now. Why are you still sitting here? Get out and build your own monster. Show it off online and get into a book yourself one day! And finally, a big thank you to Mr. Abbate for letting me use his shop to build this beast, and to Sara for keeping me sane while I built it.

UFOs Have Landed

Barry "Cold Dog" Collins

chapter 17

After modding a few stock cases, you might feel that you're ready to tackle something a little more challenging. You've gotten pretty good at cutting out windows and fan holes, added lighting and dabbled (hopefully with success) a little in the electronics part of things. But the prospect of building or modifying an unusual enclosure can and may seem a bit intimidating or beyond your abilities.

In this chapter, you'll see that it's not that difficult to create a completely custom PC enclosure. The key is keeping yourself in a creative frame of mind. If your brain fuzzes up at the first sign of a roadblock, then give it a day or two while you consider your options. Sometimes the answer is so simple you can overlook it. Other answers might include using better tools, consulting with members of an Internet case-modding forum, or consulting with a professional. Perhaps you'll need to farm out a particular task to a craftsman such as an auto/body painter or a sheet-metal worker. The important thing is to keep the project going in the right direction all the way to completion and not compromise your original concept.

Tip Lots of case-modding forums are available online, but a couple of the better ones are www.pheatonforums.com/forum and www.hardforum.com.

All concept or theme cases need a good germ of an idea. Pick a theme or a subject that interests you. That way you're enthusiasm toward the project should remain at a relatively high level during construction. My concept was to build a computer case similar to a flying saucer or a UFO like those that were seen in those great sci-fi B-movies of the 1950s (see Figure 17-1).

Timeframe and Cost

Overall, this computer cost around $1,100, mostly due to the computer components. By using computer equipment you already own, or by purchasing cheaper equipment, the cost will be much less for you. The case components only cost around $250. The hardware takes up the bulk of the cost. A quick rundown of the components and costs for this mod are:

FIGURE 17-1: The completed UFO PC mod.

- Motherboard ($150)
- Two hard drives ($200)
- CDRW drive ($50)
- Pentium 4 2.4GHZ ($180)
- 1-GB Kingston PC3500 ($225)
- CPU HSF and fan adapter ($25)
- 350-W power supply ($45)
- Rounded cables ($10)

Around 60 hours went into the fabrication and construction of this mod. Of course, if you follow the steps in this chapter, the time it takes you to complete a replica could be considerably less.

Required Parts and Tools

The parts list for this mod include all the usual parts one would expect. Besides the computer components, a good deal of acrylic and LEDs were used as well. The hardest to find parts are the main body parts themselves—a suitably sized wok and the plastic egg that formed the dome on the saucer.

Some of the power tools listed below aren't mandatory because there is usually more than one way to accomplish the objective. The cost for the tools involved varies greatly—average-quality tools cost much less than the professional-grade tools. In the end, both types of tools are good enough for modding.

Parts

- 14-inch wok ($10 on eBay, $25 shipped)
- Clear plastic bubble from egg-shaped toy container ($10)
- 2 sq. ft of $1/4$-inch white acrylic
- 2 sq. ft of $3/16$-inch white acrylic
- 1 sq. ft of $3/16$-inch tinted gray acrylic
- $1/2$ inch of 3.25-inch clear acrylic tube (about $15 for all the acrylic)
- Scraps of $1/16$-iinch aluminum plate (freebies)
- Noritake 2×24 parallel VFD ($10)
- Three red LED 80-mm fans ($20)
- Three custom alien fan grills ($30)
- Twelve 6-32 black thumbscrews ($10)
- Twelve or more $1/4$-inch 6-32 Phillip's-head screws ($5)
- 4-40 countersink screws w/nuts ($5)
- 2-56 socket head screws ($5)
- Four clear rubber "bumpers" (used on bottom of case) ($2)
- LED chaser kit w/ten 10-mm red LED's ($7)
- Silver auto door trim ($5)
- Red and green 8-mm LED ($10)
- Two momentary switches ($3)
- Auto cigarette lighter ($7)
- Miscellaneous construction materials (sandpaper, Novus, spiral wrap, and so on) ($30)

Tools

- 10-inch table saw w/80-tooth blade
- Jigsaw with plastic-cutting blade and 24-tpi blade
- Horizontal/vertical metal-cutting band saw w/24-tpi blade

- $^1/_2$-inch cordless drill
- Assorted drill bits
- Assorted plastic-cutting drill bits
- $^3/_4$-inch, $^7/_8$-inch, 2.5-inch and 3-inch hole saws
- Files (round, half-round, flat)
- Rotary tool
- Soldering iron and solder
- Electrician's scissors
- Tape measure, ruler
- Wet/dry sandpaper (various sizes from 100 grit to 2000 grit)
- Plumber's Goop ($4)
- JB Weld ($4)
- Novus #1 and #2 ($12)
- Shrink-wrap ($5-$15)

The Basic Form

You've seen those classic flying saucer shapes before haven't you? You know, kind of looks like a hubcap with a clear dome on top serving as a cockpit for the alien pilot? Well, what resembles this shape? How about a 14-inch kitchen wok? Hmmm . . . that should work, but it still needs a clear dome for the "cockpit." The top half of an Easter-egg-shaped toy spotted in a toy department should do nicely. Combined, the effect is quite convincing (see Figure 17-2).

Tip   It's important to use mockups and other aids like cardboard cutouts when you are trying to visualize the concept of what the finished project will look like. It will show you limitations as well as open doors for enhancements and improvements. The extra effort spent sizing up the situation will pay off down the road.

The first thing that needed to be done was to strip the wok down. Off came the wok handles and the lid knob. The wok handles were riveted on, so drilling through the rivets got rid of those. The lid knob was held in place by a screw, so that was easy enough to remove.

I needed to cut a hole in the very center of the lid for the clear plastic bubble to poke through. By measuring the largest diameter of the bubble, I was able to cut the hole so that it didn't exceed this dimension. In fact, I cut the hole a bit smaller so that the bubble didn't poke through too far and remained somewhat aesthetically balanced with the size of the wok. A properly sized bowl centered upside-down on the top of the lid and marked with a permanent marker gave a good line to follow for a jigsaw equipped with a 24-tpi (teeth per inch) metal-cutting blade. Clean up of the cut was done with a half round file and some sandpaper.

FIGURE 17-2: The basic elements combined.

 See Chapter 5 for a discussion on cutting through metal and other materials.

At this point, there was no need to worry too much about scratches and scrapes because the whole wok would be sanded inside and out later on. Some scraps of $^1/_{16}$-inch aluminum plate (see your local sheet metal guy—"fabricators" in the yellow pages) needed to be cut, drilled, bent, and fashioned to hold the bubble in place with some small screws. The screws made it easy to remove the bubble during the sanding process. Working with thin aluminum plate will be discussed in detail a little later.

To conserve space inside the wok, I trimmed off about an inch of the bottom of the bubble with a Dremel (rotary tool) equipped with a reinforced cutting wheel. After measuring with a tape measure and marking the measurement with a permanent marker, I marked a cutting line free hand about an inch up the base of the bubble. A Dremel tends to make a gooey mess cutting plastics, but it gets the job done and is indispensable on an odd shape such as this. Clean up of this rough edge with a file and some sandpaper followed by some polishing with some Novus #2 plastic polish got the bottom of the bubble back to looking smooth and "factory."

At this point, I built the enclosure. Whatever your project, it's a good idea to get the enclosure or box finished first (see Figure 17-3) and worry about where the components are going to go later. Of course, a little foresight will help you formulate where the components will fit as you go along. CAD drawings and sketches can be helpful if you're skilled at using it, but nothing beats working with the physical pieces. The enclosure would eventually be sanded, as well as having many more holes cut and drilled in it. This enclosure could and would look very different later on but the priority was to get it built first.

Installing the Motherboard

Perhaps the toughest part of this whole project was to get a motherboard mounted in the curvy bottom part of the wok. A very small motherboard will help, such as the Shuttle FB61 and will fit better than most. The good news is that at 185 mm × 254 mm (or 7.25 inches × 10 inches), the motherboard fit nicely, submerged inside the wok bottom far enough for a regular size heat sink/fan to clear the lid and actually rise up into the cockpit area. The bad news is that a full-sized video and sound card didn't fit (even with a riser card) but that wasn't too big of a deal—the motherboard has onboard sound and video. Motherboards with onboard sound and video are nice but their quality/performance is usually no match for decent video and sound cards.

To get the motherboard mounted, I used some more strips of $^1/_{16}$-inch aluminum plate. This was the same technique as I had used to hold the clear bubble to the lid. Thin strips of aluminum are quite bendable, yet rigid enough to give the motherboard good support. Some strips about $^3/_4$ inch to $^7/_8$ inch wide will do. There's not much science to making the pieces fit. Just place the motherboard in the bottom of the wok, grab a small strip of aluminum and bend and form as you go, one support at a time.

The strips of aluminum can be formed with your hands, but a vise will come in handy when you need a sharp angle. This is tedious work, and you may mess up a few times, but hang in

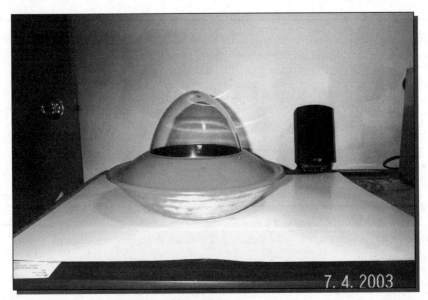

FIGURE 17-3: Looking much more like a UFO now. . . .

7. 4. 2003

FIGURE 17-4: Motherboard temporarily mounted in the wok bottom.

there until you get it right. Four supports, each one under a hole in each corner of the motherboard should be good enough (see Figure 17-4). Once each support was made, I drilled two holes in the bottom of the support to bolt or rivet it (the support) to the bottom of the wok. The top of the support was bent flat to accommodate a motherboard standoff. I also marked where the I/O cords (keyboard cord, mouse cord, etc.) would go. Placing the cutout area over the former location of one of the handles was a nice way of dealing with the holes left from the wok handles. The handle holes on the other side would be filled with JB Weld™ and sanded. JB Weld™ is a great epoxy type filler that you get purchase at your local hardware/home improvement store.

Sanding

You may have noticed in some of the previous pictures that the inside of the wok had a shiny appearance rather than the black surface that most woks have. The wok originally had a non-stick coating on it, but wet sanding with 100-grit and then 240-grit wet/dry sandpaper made short work of the nonstick surface. Luckily, the wok was made out of good old aluminum and not some type of pot metal alloy because aluminum carries a brighter (and longer lasting) luster than pot metal. I used 240-grit wet/dry sandpaper for the finish to give a sort of a brushed look—a little softer on the eyes (and a lot less labor intensive) than a polished look. Also, fingerprints and other debris wouldn't be so visible.

There's nothing fun about wet sanding a curvy surface like this. It has to be done mostly by hand. On the other hand, on a flat surface or a piece of plate, you could use a $1/4$-sheet palm sander or another small but powered sander. Powered sanders are real labor savers, so use one whenever you can. Use a little water with the wet/dry sandpaper, and progress will speed up. The water keeps the sandpaper from clogging up and lubricates the grit as it breaks away from the sandpaper. Wet/dry sandpaper can be found at your local auto-parts store and home hardware store. If you're looking for some higher-grit sandpaper (1,200 grit and up) to go the polishing route, your local Sears should have a wide variety. Be it metal or acrylic, with case modding, wet sanding is always the way to go.

Now was a good time to cut any and all remaining holes in the wok. That way the inner and outer shell (and the holes) could be sanded all at the same time. The plan was to install a couple of 80-mm intake fans and an LED chaser kit to go around the rim perimeter in the base of the "ship's hull." The fans used would be some 80-mm fans that had a built-in circular CCFL (cold cathode fluorescent light). The CCFLs would light up the inside of the wok to make it look kind of cool in a dark area such as dimly lit LAN party. I fitted, marked, and cut out fan holes with an appropriate hole saw. I decided upon ten 10-mm red LEDs for the chaser kit, so I spaced and drilled ten holes just a tad bigger than 10 mm around the rim of the wok. I also cut the slot for I/O cords mentioned above at this time. And then I sanded the remaining piece (see Figure 17-5).

See Chapter 5 for info both on using hole saws and how to properly sand.

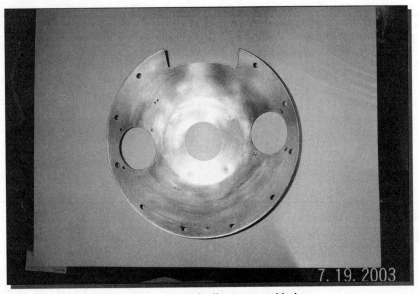

7. 19. 2003

FIGURE 17-5: The bottom of the UFO with all cutouts and holes.

Installing Chaser LEDs

As mentioned earlier, there would be a 10-LED chaser kit installed around the rim perimeter. The kit itself was made up of a 2.25 inch × 5-inch PCB (printed circuit board) and came with all the various electronic components that you install onto the PCB to get it up and running. These kits can be purchased from www.allelectronics.com (part #AEC). The chaser kit held 10 LEDs and a pot (potentiometer) that I later wired up from the PCB to the hull.

The LEDs were test fitted into the hull when a problem became clear—the LEDs in the holes seemed to poke out quite a bit. So, to remedy this, I trimmed each LED tip a little with a Dremel and filed, sanded and then polished them with some Novus #2 plastic polish until they didn't poke out quite so far (see Figure 17-6).

A small dollop of Plumber's Goop on the back of each LED and the aluminum held them in place against the hull. The Plumber's Goop is spread around on the back of the LED and the aluminum hull so that a little "bridge" is formed. No need to worry about the goop contacting the electronics because it has no conductive properties when dry. When the LEDs were wired up to the chaser kit, they would fire one after the other going in an eternal circle around the rim of the wok. The chaser kit's PCB board would be tucked away and hidden somewhere, most likely underneath the motherboard. Later, a potentiometer similar to the one that came with the kit but able to have a knob mounted to it was installed so that the speed of the chasing action could be sped up or slowed down from the front of the case.

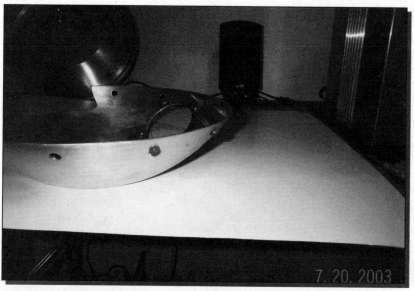

FIGURE 17-6: The modded LEDs test fitted into the bottom of the hull.

Not Enough Room

It became apparent that there was no way to get a complete system (hard drives, power supply, CD-ROM, etc.) within the confines of the wok. There just wasn't enough room. I needed a secondary enclosure. Some latitude should be allowed for custom cases, and a secondary enclosure might be a necessity at times. As long as the implementation is blended in with the theme of the primary enclosure, it may actually improve the visual impact of the final mod.

I considered mounting the UFO on top of a cube shape and a different but longer and squatty box shape (both made out of Plexiglas). In the end, a pedestal shape won out (see Figure 17-7). A pedestal is often used with a traditional work of art (such as a statue) to elevate it and to focus the eye on the statue itself. I applied the same principle to my mod.

Obviously, a large hole needed to be cut in the bottom of the wok, so out comes a $2^1/_2$-inch hole saw, and in short order, presto, we have a hole. I cut a matching hole in the top of the pedestal so that wiring and cabling could go back and forth. In this case, the pedestal's size would be large enough that a full-sized power supply, a CD-ROM drive, and a couple of hard drives would fit in it with a little room left over for a few extras. Here again, using a mockup allowed me to insert the actual components and move them around to make sure that there was enough room.

For the base (pedestal), I chose acrylic as the construction material. I used some $3/_{16}$-inch and $1/_4$-inch white acrylic to produce a faux marble look on the pedestal. However, because a VFD (vacuum fluorescent display) was going to be mounted somewhere in front, I used a single panel of transparent tinted gray acrylic as the front panel of the pedestal. This allowed the characters of the VFD (displaying system information) to be seen through the panel, while still being dark enough to hide the other contents inside.

FIGURE 17-7: Cardboard mockup of the pedestal for the UFO PC.

A table saw is invaluable for cutting up a sheet of acrylic. A fine-toothed or finishing blade (for example an 80-tooth blade, in a 10-inch table saw) works wonders. If you don't have a table saw or access to one, then you may have to wing it with a jigsaw or something else, in which case there will be much after-cut work involved getting the edges square and smooth. A table saw, operated properly, will give you nice square edges immediately and leave little clean up to do on the edges. So, try to get your pieces cut with a table saw even if you have to pay someone else to do it for you.

I used some aluminum tabs screwed to the panels to hold the acrylic box together (see Figure 17-8). In this situation, I preferred it to gluing because access to the contents (for maintenance or whatever) would be faster with screws. Also, unless you're really good at gluing, using screws is far less messy. To hold any box shape together, 16 tabs are needed—two in each corner, top, and bottom. So again, I cut some $^1/_{16}$-inch aluminum plate for the tabs and drilled some holes for screws to pass through. I bent the tabs in a vise at a 90-degree angle in preparation for attaching the acrylic panels.

Keep in mind, working with acrylic is not that much different than working with wood. You can use a lot of the same tools—for example, a jigsaw (with a special plastic cutting blade), a table saw, a band saw, assorted files, and sandpaper. When you need to drill holes, there's nothing better than using plastic-cutting drill bits—regular drill bits larger than about 1/8 inch can butcher the hole. Hole saws work as is, but you need to squirt a little water (a spray bottle works well) on the hole saw occasionally to keep it from heating up and melting the acrylic—(or just go slow). In certain situations, you can even use the reinforced cutting wheels of a rotary tool, but be prepared for a little extra clean up work because this will melt its way

7. 26. 2003

FIGURE 17-8: Tabs holding a couple of acrylic sheets in place. Note that the protective paper is still on the side acrylic panels.

through the acrylic. But always be on the lookout so that you don't scratch up the work. Tape the bottom of the jigsaw plate so that it doesn't scratch the acrylic. When using a vise, use some wood in the vise jaws to hold the piece. And by all means, leave the protective paper on as long as possible. If you do get scratches, they can be repaired, but a little caution is needed when working with acrylic.

Cross-Reference Chapter 10 contains info on fixing scratches in acrylic.

Acrylic, Sanding and Novus

An excellent Web site to get acrylic and acrylic products is www.usplastic.com. There you will find everything acrylic. They have sheets, rods, and tubes made of acrylic in clear and assorted colors and the tools for working with acrylic, including those hard-to-find drill bits made for drilling holes in plastic and acrylic. They also carry Novus #1, Novus #2, and Novus #3 (described next).

- **Novus #1:** A milky liquid used as a final polish. This has antistatic properties and works best when it is buffed by hand onto the surface. Apply with old, soft rags (washcloths, diapers, etc.) because paper towels can scratch the surface. Use it as a cleaner to remove dirt by rubbing lightly. Once the surface is clean, apply it with the pressure you would use with any other polish and keep buffing with a dry portion of the cloth till the surface becomes very slippery.

- **Novus #2:** A liquid paste with a very mild grit in it. This works on very fine scratches and should also be applied with soft rags. The depth of the scratch depends on the pressure you use. Follow with Novus #1.

- **Novus #3:** Made for heavy scratches that Novus #2 can't get out. Follow with Novus #2 and then Novus #1.

Frankly, I've never had much use for Novus #3. Fine-grit sandpaper can be substituted. As mentioned previously, Sears is a good source for high (superfine) grit sandpaper. 1,500- and 2,000-grit sandpaper will make dealing with acrylic scratches much easier.

So, how does one get rid of scratches on acrylic? Follow these steps:

1. Wet sand the scratch by hand with 2,000 grit, using circular motions until it disappears (depending on the depth of the scratch, you may need to start with a coarser grit). Rinse and dry the surface and hold it up to a light to see if it is gone. If not, repeat. Once the scratch is gone, the area where you wet sanded will be quite foggy.

2. Apply Novus #2 using a polishing motion in the foggy area using a clean, soft cloth. Keep the rag loaded with Novus #2 as you do this. This may take several applications, but keep at it till

the fogginess is completely gone and the surface is about as clear as it is going to get. Rinse off the excess Novus #2 with water and a clean, wet rag. Dry with another soft, clean rag. Again, hold it up to a light to check it. Repeat if necessary.

3. Finish up with Novus #1. Novus #1 seems to have glazing properties, and it is a good idea to buff it dry and to continue buffing with a dry portion of the cloth until the surface is quite slippery (unlike a normal glass cleaner, which leaves the surface ready as soon as the moisture is gone).

Also, use Novus for a "flameless" way to polish an acrylic edge:

1. Wet sand the edge with 240 or 400 grit to remove any cut marks from a table saw or other cutting tool. I personally like to wet sand by hand so that the edge becomes slightly rounded.

2. Finish the wet sanding with 2,000 grit. You can use a grit between 400 and 2,000 if you prefer (for example, 800 or 1,200) before the 2,000. The finer the grit of the sandpaper you finish with, the less elbow grease you will have to use with Novus #2 in the next step.

3. Polish the edge with Novus #2 until it is shiny. Rinse off the excess Novus #2 with water and dry the surface with a soft, dry rag. Finishing with Novus #1 is optional.

I rounded the corners of the top and bottom panels on the pedestal with a file so that they weren't so pointy and then sanded and polished them. Then, I cut the holes for the power supply in the rear panel and in the top panel for the power supply cabling to pass through (see Figure 17-9). A quick and easy mod, I replaced the stock 80-mm power supply fan with an 80-mm red LED fan. Some thumbscrews on the two side panels would allow for quick access into the insides should the need arise. Note that the two side panels were cut about a 1/16 inch short so that they could be easily removed and didn't become wedged against the other panels. The gap was hidden under the "roof" of the top panel.

On the front of the base on the tinted panel, I made a cutout for the CD-ROM drive. I also drilled holes for the power and reset buttons and the power and hard drive LEDs. A dab of Plumber's Goop on the back of the LEDs held them in place. Finally, I installed a novelty mod for someone with a bad habit—a cigarette lighter! (see Figure 17-10).

All that was left for the base was mounting two hard drives on the left side panel, the VFD, and the knob to control the speed of the LED chaser on the front tinted panel. Wiring won't be covered in detail here but suffice it to say one should leave enough space for ribbon cables, connectors, and power cables to allow all components to be hooked up or disconnected with a reasonable amount of ease. Some effort should be made to keep the wiring neat and/or hidden because wire management encompasses a complete other chapter.

Cross-Reference Chapter 3 contains detailed instructions on methods of wire management.

FIGURE 17-9: The back of the base with power supply installed.

FIGURE 17-10: The front of the base with CD-ROM and cigarette lighter installed.

Finishing Details

Back up top on the UFO, I cut some slivers to be used as ducts about $^1/_4$ inch wide off a piece of $3^1/_4$-inch clear acrylic tube using a vertical band saw (with metal-cutting blade) and glued them inside the old fan holes. Along with some custom fan grills, this added a nice touch to the fan holes. I threaded a small piece of 1-inch diameter acrylic rod with an 8-32 tap and bolted it to the bottom panel of the pedestal to lend support to the front of the power supply and take the stress off the back panel (see Figure 17-11).

On the back, I added some silver auto door trim around the I/O slot to neaten up that opening. Over on the other side panel, I fashioned some more $^1/_{16}$-inch aluminum plate to make a small hard drive bracket and fastened it to the side panel (see Figure 17-12). On the front, I installed the VFD along with the knob to control the chaser LED speed. Up on top, I completed the chaser wiring. Finally, I installed a 80-mm red LED fan on the 70-mm→80-mm heatsink adapter for the CPU and added another custom grill for the theme on top of that.

Conclusion

The UFO was now complete. Everything worked out as planned, from the "window" in which the motherboard was visable (see Figure 17-13) to the back of the mod where all the cables plugged in (see Figure 17-14). The mod has even made appearances at mod competitions such as the 2003 CPL (Cyber Professional League) contest.

FIGURE 17-11: Fan ducts and grills installed, and acrylic rod power supply support.

FIGURE **17-12:** Hard drive bracket installed on the side panel.

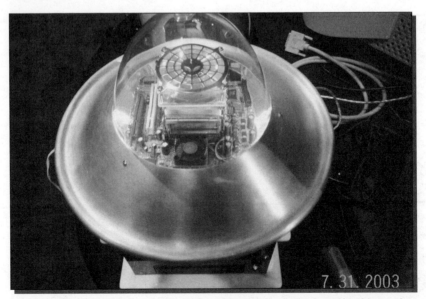

FIGURE **17-13:** The top UFO portion of the mod with the motherboard visible inside.

FIGURE 17-14: The back of the mod fully assembled.

Hopefully, this chapter has given you some ideas for your next project. As you saw with my UFO PC, I had some obstacles to overcome and needed to employ some creative thinking. But modding a unique enclosure or building one from scratch isn't all that hard when you break it down into a series of small jobs. As mentioned earlier, it's always a good idea to get the enclosure(s) built first and then move on to adding the computer components. If you get in a bind, don't be afraid to seek out some help—Internet case modding forums like www.pheatonforums.com are a great source of inspiration and ideas. Perhaps you may need to consult with a pro in a specialized trade. Whatever the situation, just don't get frustrated and give up. You'll be missing out on a lot of fun. Happy modding!

Millennium Falcon PC

Russ "JediKnight0" Caslis

started this mod the same way I start every mod—with an idea. I was looking for another project to work on and was visiting several different modding Web sites to see if inspiration hit me by looking at some other people's work. One interesting mod I discovered was some sort of a toy or model of a castle with a computer inside. I thought it was a good idea, and the modder did a good job of it with eerie green lighting, and so on. I just thought I might be able to do something a little more interesting—the Millennium Falcon from *Star Wars* (see Figure 18-1).

When I was a child, my hero was Han Solo. As such, one of my favorite toys was the Millennium Falcon for the action figures from Kenner. I loved that toy. It was huge—surely big enough to fit a computer inside. Plus the surface was actually very intricately detailed, which would save me a lot of work in making it look authentic. Since I had sold my collection of *Star Wars* toys years earlier while in college to support a bad habit (dating), first I had to find one.

Thanks to the magic of eBay, I found quite a few Millennium Falcon toys like the one I used to have. Most were in pretty bad shape, but my needs were simple. As long as all the external pieces were intact I could use any of them since the entire inside would be filled with computer components. The one I bought was yellowed from age, but that didn't matter since it was going to be painted anyway.

Timeframe and Cost

This mod was built over the space of about four months, although most of that time was spent just figuring out how to fit everything in the case. In addition, I also went through the trouble of videotaping the majority of the build-up, so I really only worked on it during daylight hours (with a few exceptions). If starting over now, the whole process would only take about a month (much less if I quite my day job).

FIGURE **18-1: The completed Millennium Falcon mod with custom wireless mouse.**

If you want to see the video of the build-up of this mod, along with a discussion of several of my other mods, head over to www.xkill.com. There, you can purchase a DVD with over 20 minutes of the Falcon build-up.

The cost of the mod was approximately $500 when you count the cost of all the parts, plus miscellaneous things like glue or paint. Overall, the when purchasing the parts separately the cost doesn't seem so bad—except when typing to explain the big ticket items (motherboard, hard drives, etc.) to your significant other.

Required Parts and Tools

To perform this project, I needed a number of tools and supplies. The following lists provide a general overview of some of the items I used. Of course, these lists are far from complete. They leave out simple items such as extra wire and solder, not to mention some blood, sweat, and tears.

Parts

- Kenner Millennium Falcon toy ($50 on eBay)
- Six laptop fans ($1.50 each)

- Mini-ITX motherboard and memory ($200)
- Blue EL wire ($10)
- 150-watt power supply for a shuttle PC ($40)
- Misc. electronics parts
    - 5-volt reed relay ($1)
    - 3-mm blue high-power LED ($1)
    - Two 5-mm white high-power LEDs ($1 each)
    - One 5-mm RGB LED ($2)
    - Perf-board ($2)
- Two laptop hard drives ($40 each)
- Clear transparency or thin acrylic sheet ($1 or $5)
- Female RJ45 network connector ($4)
- Female DB15 monitor connector and a separate monitor cable with male DB15 ($10)
- Female stereo audio connector and a separate audio cable with male audio connector ($10)
- Two PS2 extender cables ($6 each)
- USB extender cable ($8)
- Double-sticky foam tape ($4)

Tools

- Dremel with cutting wheels
- Hand drill with various size drill bits
- Enamel spray paint and bottle paint ($30)
- Soldering iron
- Screwdriver set
- High-strength epoxy ($4)
- Cans of compressed air ($5)
- Scissors
- Hot glue gun with glue sticks
- Modeling putty ($4)
- Flat toothpicks ($3)
- 600-grit sandpaper
- Medium hardness artist charcoal ($3)

First Steps

The first thing I did after gathering all the parts and tools was to open up the toy and see what I had to work with. Old toys are great. They depend on glue much less than current toys. Basically, I started by removing all the loose pieces such as the two landing gear and the top hatches. Then, I went after all the screws, being careful not to lose any. I separated the parts, unhooking any remaining latches. This allowed the top half to be removed, and I could then extract the extra parts such as the gun turret and cardboard wall from the inside of the toy.

At this point, I was able to identify what was going to be the most difficult part of this mod: fitting everything in. Front to back and side to side there is plenty of space. But the height is not consistent, the sides tapered off to just over an inch. Placement and types of components would be critical here.

Cleaning the Parts

Next, I needed to clean up the parts. I used the bathtub so I would have enough space to comfortably wash everything without running out of elbow room. I removed all the stickers that I could by hand, but there were still bits of 24-year-old adhesive that needed to be taken care of. Since I was going to be painting most of the parts, I just had to remove all the loose dirt. A simple 99¢ toothbrush worked pretty well for getting in all the little corners that my fingers couldn't reach. The toy, being so old, had a few imperfections where the plastic had been nicked or melted a little, but that was okay. This was one advantage of painting the toy, as the paint would help conceal any problems like this. Also, the Falcon is supposed to be a flying hunk of junk, so a few imperfections are to be expected.

I used only basic soap and water to clean the toy. While it may be tempting to use something stronger, it's a risk. Sometimes cleaning agents can actually melt plastic. I should know. I made that very mistake with this mod.

One part of the exterior had a bit of label adhesive that was really baked on. I couldn't get it to move with soap and water, so I tried another old favorite of mine—an adhesive remover called Goof Off. But I ignored both the directions and my common sense. I didn't try it on a part that would be hidden from view first and applied it directly to the outside of the toy. The plastic couldn't handle it and started to melt. As soon as I realized that the plastic was turning gooey, I ran the toy under lots of water to remove any trace of the adhesive remover. I then dried the toy off and let it sit for a few days to harden back up. The spot wasn't big, maybe less than half an inch in diameter, and it did harden back up. It wasn't real visible though the plastic was discolored even more. It could have been much worse.

 Cross-Reference Chapter 6 contains a discussion of "Goof Off" in the section discussion preparation for painting.

Gluing Parts Together

As with most toys or models turned into computers, I was really just interested in the basic shell of the toy. Opening doors and gizmos are really of little value to the computer itself and open up areas that could have short circuits or other problems. The Falcon had such an area—the removable ramp that the figures would use to walk into the ship.

I used epoxy to glue the removable door/walkway shut on the bottom of the toy (see Figure 18-2). Epoxy is great stuff—it's strong, it lasts a long time, it can be painted, and it works on many different types of surfaces. It generally comes in two parts that have to be mixed before use. I used a inch long nail (it's all that I had handy at the time) to mix the two parts of epoxy in equal amounts. Then, using the same nail, I moved a good deal of the epoxy onto the inside of the doorframe and placed the door there. The epoxy also has the side effect of plugging a lot of the holes where the door doesn't perfectly touch the exterior of the toy. After it's painted, the epoxy will help hide the fact that the toy wasn't one solid piece to begin with.

Caution

Epoxy is powerful stuff. Depending on the type, it can dry in as little as 30 seconds (although 5 minutes to 30 minutes is more common and easier to work with). Because of the gooey nature of the substance, it's very easy to accidentally get it on your hands or arms. Should this happen, wash the glue off immediately with a great deal of soap and water before it dries.

Also, the fumes from some epoxies can be dangerous, so make sure that no children or elderly (or cats) are around at the time. Good ventilation is a must.

Since I had the epoxy already out and mixed, I also worked on gluing the main laser cannon together. On the toy, this piece rotates around and makes clicking noises to simulate laser blasts. Due to a lack of space, I needed to glue everything in place. I cut the stalk piece that attaches the laser cannon to the toy right below where it enters the Falcon. I then epoxied the two halves of the cannon together, also gluing the stalk piece into the cannon. Later, after painting, I glued this assembly to the rest of the toy.

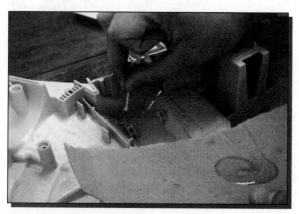

FIGURE 18-2: Gluing the walkway in place.

Making a Windowed Hard Drive

I then started on another major piece, the most dangerous one. I performed a hard-drive window mod, but to a laptop hard drive instead of a desktop hard drive (what most modders, when brave enough, attempt). This meant opening the hard drive and installing a window so that people could see the mechanism working. Needless to say, this would void the warranty and stood a significant chance of making the drive inoperable.

Tip

Making windowed hard drives is perfect for old hard drives that are too small to be useful anymore. Even something as small as 1 GB or less is perfect here.

If you use a small hard drive, you can place your Windows page file (i.e., the swap partition or file for UNIX lovers) on this drive. Should the drive ultimately die early because of the mod, no valuable data will be lost but there will be enough activity on the drive regularly so that people can see the mechanism work.

The first problem to deal with was dust. There is a myth that hard drives are airtight, so no dust can make it inside, but this is incorrect. All modern hard drives have a small hole with some type of filter to keep dust and contaminants out (see Figure 18-3). Unfortunately, I don't have a clean room in my apartment, so I just had to do my best and hope that

FIGURE 18-3: Laptop hard drive. Notice the small hole in the center—that's the air filter hole.

everything worked when put back together. In my case, I used my bathroom as a poor man's clean room.

I started a hot shower going with all the doors to the bathroom closed, leaving the fan off. After about 10 minutes or so, I shut the water off. This left the bathroom with slightly hot, slightly humid air. The humid air causes most of the dust in the air to fall to the floor and stay there.

After the room was humid enough, I opened the hard drive being careful not to lose any screws or get any components wet. I put all the components into a clear Tupperware container that could be sealed to keep the dust out. I left the top of the hard drive outside the container, because I needed to work on cutting that next.

After disassembling the hard drive, I decided where the window would go. Every hard drive is a little different. Some use the top cover and sometimes even a screw or two there as an additional stability point for the rotating platters. To be safe, I designed a pattern where the center spindle still had support. For this mod, the window only needed to be big enough so that the hard drive could be seen though the exposed circuits in the rear-left side of the hull of the Falcon. I traced the location where I needed the window to be on the top cover and cut it out using my Dremel, remembering to smooth the edges with a sanding wheel afterward. I also cut a small notch in the top of the cover where the additional wires for the internal light would go.

Tip   When cutting a window hole in the top of the drive, you probably want some protection for your hand, since the metal heats up while you are cutting it and can burn your hand.

Of course, the top cover was now completely covered in metal shavings and needed to be cleaned. I cleaned the top thoroughly with soap and water, then I shook all the excess water off. I used a can of compressed air (a lot of it) to remove any remaining water.

Tip   A single particle of dirt will ruin the entire hard drive, but the same can be said of a drop of water so I didn't skimp on the compressed air.

Next, I found some small connectors (both male and female) like the ones typically used for small fans. I soldered a couple of wires to the female connector and then soldered those same wires to a blue ultrabright 3-mm LED. I then made the cover for the window by cutting a piece of clear transparency film, like that used for overhead projectors, to shape then used tape to put it over the hole for the window. This method won't stand up to people pushing the window with their fingers, but was quicker and cheaper than using acrylic for the window.

I got the bathroom humid again, then took the hard drive out of the container that it was stored in. In an open area of the hard drive, I laid down a 2 mm thick bed of hot glue. Next, I laid the LED with the wires on it on that bed of glue and used more hot glue on top of the LED leads. Thus, the hot glue totally insulated the LED from any potential short circuits due to touching the metal drive casing and held it securely in place. Finally, I placed the top cover back on the hard drive, running the wires for the LED through the cutout I previously made. A little more hot glue around where the wires left the hard drive (see Figure 18-4) and all that was left was to interface the hard drive (and LED) to the system.

The LED needed a way to get power, so I hooked up the LED so that it would light up every time the hard drive was accessed (like the electrical arc that the Falcon was so famous for). Since this was a laptop hard drive and the motherboard used standard desktop hard drive cables, I needed an adapter for the hard drive. Laptop hard drives have one integrated connector that provides signaling and power on the same connector, while desktop drives have separate power and signal lines. Small adapters can be purchased at most computer stores.

Using a multimeter, I could see that between pin 39 on the adapter and the positive power connector the voltage rose to 5 volts every time there was drive activity and dropped to 0 volts when there was no drive activity. I calculated the value of the resistor I needed to light the LED without burning it out, then soldered both the resistor and the male connector from earlier to the adapter card.

Tip

See Chapter 7 for a discussion on how to solder successfully.

FIGURE **18-4: Windowed hard drive. Note the wires for the internal LED lighting at the top right.**

At this point, I plugged the hard drive and adapter into another computer and watched in glee as the hard drive spun up and the head moved over the platter's surface, accompanied by a beautiful blue light.

Inner Space

To fit the computer components inside the toy, I needed to remove as much of the extra plastic as I could from the inside of the case, while not harming the overall structural integrity. I also needed to make the holes for all the external ports such as video, keyboard, mouse, and power. This sounds simpler than it actually was. First, I made all the major cuts. On the bottom half of the toy, I cut out the support strut for the right landing gear, the support brace for the front landing gear, and the battery compartment (with it's internal ribbing). I took the spare piece of plastic that covered the escape compartment inside the toy and roughly cut it down to the size of the external battery compartment door. On the top sections of the toy, I cut out the bottom of the rear-left electronics hole (the part that you can see the inner workings of the Falcon through) and the exhaust port on the rear top of the toy.

The engine bay was a little more work. On the toy itself, the engine bay was separated into three compartments with a plastic wall in between. I used a cutting disc to remove most of the plastic there, making it one large section, then used a sanding wheel to remove the rest of the plastic so I was left with one large area.

Next, I had to figure out what computer ports would be available on the outside of the computer and cut holes for all those. Leaving off the detailed piece on the front of the Falcon's left side gave me a nice flat surface to mount most of the ports. I made cutouts for the following ports: VGA, single USB port, two PS/2 ports, audio port, and network cable (see Figure 18-5). I purchased connectors for all those ports and simply carved the holes using my Dremel, a hand drill, and a small hobby knife. The network adapter was a little tricky, because there wasn't enough space to mount it on the flat piece, so I had to cut a square hole slightly back from the flat area.

The cutout for the fake circuitry required some special attention. After removing the plastic circuitry that was there, I had several holes left in the side of the panels due to the way that the plastic was formed. Using a bit of modeling putty, I built up the area where those holes were left (Figure 18-6). After letting that dry for a day, I was able to sand the holes putty smooth and added a bit of epoxy on the backside for extra strength.

There were a few holes that still needed to be made, so I broke out my hand drill. I started by drilling out holes for the PS2 keyboard and mouse connectors as well as the audio connector cable. Then, I measured and drilled holes in the engine bay where the EL wire would crisscross to create the engine lighting effect. Also, I drilled one LED-sized hole in the top cockpit section of the Falcon.

Another particularly difficult situation was the cockpit, where I needed to place the controls. The existing plastic there was too brittle to work with and quickly disintegrated when I tried to work on it. Instead, I used a spare piece of wood and fabricated an entirely new panel. I cut a rough triangle just big enough to fit in the cockpit, then sanded it down a little at a time till it

FIGURE 18-5: Ports available on the case

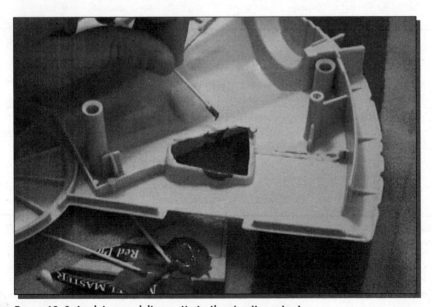

FIGURE 18-6: Applying modeling putty to the circuitry cutout.

fit in the cockpit perfectly. Next, I drilled five holes in it—two holes for screws to attach it to the toy and three holes for switches (power, reset, and engine bay lights). I painted this piece black after getting the spacing right.

Painting

It was time for the most time-consuming aspect of the entire mod—painting. The hardest part was not rushing the painting job. I was tempted to just hurry and get it done but I knew that when a mod is rushed disaster is sure to follow.

Cross-Reference Chapter 6 contains detailed instructions on how to paint.

I started by giving another quick bath to all the components. Nothing special here, basically the same as the last time I washed the toy—a lot of warm water, a little soap, and some quick work with a toothbrush. Of course, after the bath I let the pieces dry for a good 24 hours in a dust-free area before continuing.

Next, I applied the base coats of paint using enamel model spray paint, and a lot of it. For almost all mods, it's usually best to use paint intended for cars because of the durability and the easy availability. But this toy had plastic that was similar to that of styrene plastic model kits. This allowed me to use the smaller (and therefore cheaper) enamel model spray paint. I didn't even need to use primer first because this paint is formulated to stick to plastic.

Tip I wish there was a good way to tell exactly what type of plastic you are working with, but there isn't any way other than experience. Sure, the chemical compositions are surely different, but no modder has the equipment to figure that one out. Remember to test any new paint or glue on a section that won't be visible, and you should be fine.

I painted all the externally visible pieces in flat white paint, remembering to use many thin coats of paint—somewhere around eight coats of paint per piece. There are two things that cannot be stressed enough: do not paint too much in a single coat, and use lots of coats. If I used too much paint in a single pass, the paint would drip and look horrible. If I didn't use enough coats, the underlying plastic would be visible and most likely the paint would scratch off eventually. After each coat, I let it dry a minimum of five hours—longer if the weather was a little cold.

Following that, I was ready for the small details. Using toothpicks and several bottles of paint, I painted the details on the toy. Unfortunately, this toy wasn't 100 percent correct in relation to the real model used for the movies, but I did the best I could. All these details took some time. This process was aided by some mood music. I played the *Star Wars* soundtracks to get in the appropriate mood.

But the Falcon (whenever it's seen in the movies) is not a brand new, factory fresh ship. She's been around the block a few times, and I had to find a way to be true to that fact. I decided to add a few laser blasts on the toy. Since I didn't have any powerful lasers handy, I used the closest thing I had—my soldering iron. I heated up the soldering iron and literally poked a few holes in the toy (see Figure 18-7).

Another method for creating burn marks is to use charcoal. I bought some artists' charcoal and started drawing some lines on the exterior of the toy. I made sure to get lots of charcoal down in the recesses and holes on the toy. Using both my fingers and a small (dry and clean) paint brush, I gently blended the charcoal to give the case a nice dirty look. I also made some more laser burns on the surface by literally drawing them on using the charcoal. Finally, I used some charcoal in the laser blasts I had made earlier with the soldering iron to complete the effect.

Tip I had to be careful not to let any wind blow on the toy at this point, or I'd lose a good portion of all the extra charcoal I had on the toy.

After all that, I used some Dullcote clear lacquer to seal the dirt particles to the toy. It gave the paint a harder surface, making the paint less likely to chip or peel, and it glues all the charcoal to the surface of the toy. I used four heavy coats of Dullcote to seal everything and waited a few days till it dried.

FIGURE **18-7: Soldering-iron-induced burn marks, with charcoal accents.**

Preparing the Pieces

At this point, I had all the raw materials before me. I just had a few more items to fabricate before I could start assembling everything.

Fixing the Cables and Wires

I needed to start dealing with the power supply. There was no good way to make the side of the power supply accessible from the outside of the toy, so I needed to move the power connector to the outside of the toy somehow. I opened the power supply and lengthened the cables between the connector for the power cord and the power supply itself, enabling the connector to go on the outside of the Falcon. Ultimately, there were three wires (this makes sense, there are three connectors in a power plug). I made sure to cover all connections with heat-shrink tubing or liquid electrical tape (see Figure 18-8). I didn't want anything shorting out and causing a fire.

I made a place to mount the power plug by cutting out a matching hole in the center of the piece of plastic that used to be the escape hatch from inside the toy. After cutting the piece to fit the front of the former battery compartment area, I used a generous amount of epoxy to secure it in place on the bottom half of the toy.

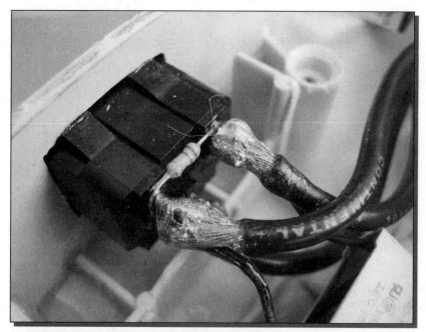

FIGURE 18-8: Inside of the power plug after moving it to the new panel. Note that the connections have been covered in clear liquid electrical tape to prevent any potential shorting out.

I decided to work on the control panel next (see Figure 18-9). I needed to have three switches on the control panel—power on/off, reset, and a toggle switch for the engine bay lights. I used some blue EL wire for the engines. I bought this EL wire from an auto-parts store rather than a computer store, since I was going to need the cigarette lighter adapter later. I cut off the end with the cigarette lighter adapter and soldered a Molex connector onto the inverter with a switch in the middle, which I placed into the control panel. I also attached connectors for the motherboard reset and power headers to switches I installed in the control panel.

Cross-Reference

Chapter 4 contains information on various lighting methods, including EL wire. That chapter also contains instructions for adapting auto parts for computer use, such as this EL wire kit.

Next, I started preparing the cables for the outside ports. Some were simple, such as the PS2 connectors. With those, I just bought a simple extender cable and coiled up the excess wire inside the case. Some cables were more difficult, such as the video cable. Because I needed such a short video cable I was forced to make my own from an extra monitor cable and a connector. For this cable, I cut an existing video cable down to the right length, then soldered on a new connector. This meant mapping out all 16 wires in that connector using a multimeter to make sure that I had connected pin 1 to pin 1, and so on. Soldering 16 small wires like that was certainly nontrivial, but in the end everything worked out okay. After I finished, I tested every pin using my multimeter just to make sure that there were no electrical shorts before plugging a monitor into it.

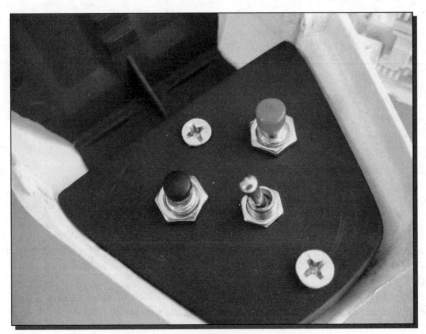

FIGURE 18-9: Cockpit control panel, painted and mounted.

Exhaust Vents

Previously, I cut out all the ports on the back cover for the exhaust vents. After finishing all the painting and weathering on this piece, I added fans. The first problem was with the general look of the exhaust ports—air should flow into the toy from the front landing gear bay and should be exhausted through the exhaust ports. But the laptop fans I had purchased had labels on the exhaust side (as do most fans) that ruined the effect. Ultimately, I just used a bit of black paint directly over the label to make everything look good.

Caution

Removing the labels on fans may seem like a good idea, but it's not. With most fans, directly underneath the label is the center spindle of the fan and a bit of lubricant. When you remove the label, the lubricant escapes and gets all over the fan and your fingers.

Next, I took a piece of perf-board, soldered on a female Molex power connector, and soldered on the fans, making sure to both get the polarity of the fans correct and measure the length of the wires I needed to make sure that they could reach. One elegant solution I used was to attach some male connectors to the perf-board and attach the corresponding female connectors to the fans. Thus, any fan can be disconnected from the system and replaced without any soldering, if it should fail in the future. Finally, I used some hot glue to glue all the laptop fans over the holes in the top cover, being certain to center them. I also hot glued the circuit board I had just made and plugged all the fans into that circuit board (see Figure 18-10).

FIGURE **18-10:** Fans attached to access cover and small circuit board.

Activity Lights

The Millennium Falcon actually has headlights (visible in *The Empire Strikes Back* during the asteroid belt scene). I mounted two white LEDs up front as headlights and had them flash when there was hard drive activity to further complete the *Star Wars* theme. On the front of the toy there were three round indentations on each forward strut, so I simply drilled out the middle one from both sides in for mounting LEDs.

The problem was that motherboards only have enough power for one LED for hard drive activity, not two. But there were a couple of different solutions to that problem using a little electronics knowledge. For example, I was able to build a small circuit based on a reed relay to control the LEDs. Basically, the circuit used the 5-volt power line and switches that went on and off based on another signal such as the original signal from the hard drive header on the motherboard. A reed relay has four connections on it: two coil connections, a common power connection, and a normally open connection. I simply attached the two wires from the motherboard HD header to the coil connections, 5 volt power to the common connection and the LEDs (with a proper resistor) to the normally open connection. When the hard drive is accessed, the connection inside the reed relay closes and the two LEDs should light up.

But even with that, I still encountered problems. This circuit worked great on some motherboards, but not on the specific mini-ITX motherboard I used. Luckily, there was another way. I used connections to IDE pin 39 and the positive power connector on the laptop to desktop IDE converter to control the signal, just as I had done earlier with the drive light inside the other hard drive. Using that instead of the HD header on the motherboard allowed the LEDs to work just as they should.

Cross-Reference Chapter 9 contains an alternate method of integrating multiple hard drive activity lights.

Putting It All Together

The first very important step in assembling the pieces was the placing of the landing gear. The weight of the entire computer would rest on these, so I used some high-strength epoxy and generously applied it to the toy where the landing gears attached to it. I was sure to use plenty of epoxy, and I worked a single gear at a time to make sure that no mishaps occurred. I made sure that every place a landing gear surface touched the toy that is not visible from the outside got a healthy serving of epoxy. After a few minutes, the epoxy began to set, but I let it dry for a full 24 hours just to be sure. I then moved on to the next landing gear, then the final gear. Assuming that the gluing was done well, the rest of the plastic should break and tear before the epoxy would ever come undone.

I laid out the two biggest components in the bottom of the toy—the motherboard and the power supply. The motherboard was held in place securely by the two plastic posts in the center of the toy and the back wall of the engine bay (ports facing away from the cockpit, toward the side with the cutouts for the ports). The power supply actually rested on the center landing gear, which gave the power supply extra support (good since it's the heaviest piece in the whole mod). I put the power connector through the hole previously made in the left side of the toy and attached the connector back to the power supply. Then, I closed the power supply up and attached the power supply to the toy by using double-stick foam tape on the underside of the power supply. The foam tape worked better and was stronger than you would probably think. Also, it's not as if it was possible to drill a hole in the case for some mounting screws without ruining the outside of the case.

Every ship has running lights, so I decided to use an interesting LED for the running light on top of the Falcon's cockpit. I found a special LED that, in one LED, could display the primary colors (red, green, blue) in sequence with a simple fading motion between them. I attached a standard motherboard header connection to this LED, mounted it in the top of the cockpit, and attached it to the motherboard power LED header.

The engine bay was the next area I tackled. As stated earlier, I had picked up an EL wire kit from an auto-parts store. I threaded the EL wire itself back and forth through the holes in the engine bay, being especially careful around the corners since the EL wire isn't really supposed to bend as much as I had to bend it to get the engine bay covered. I then attached the EL wire to the inverter that was placed beneath the motherboard in the secret compartment of the Falcon toy. The inverter was already connected to a switch in the cockpit and the power supply from earlier.

Mounting the windowed hard drive was the next bit of difficulty. The hard drive was able to sit at the right height merely by sitting on top of the support for the left landing gear, but it needed to sit so far forward that wasn't stable. Using the cigarette lighter adapter plastic from the EL wire kit, I was able to cut the top and bottom off the adapter so that when placed directly ahead of the landing gear support, the adapter has the same height. I epoxied the adapter in place, which would give the hard drive a stable platform to rest on.

While waiting for the epoxy to dry, I attached all the other cables. I attached the video cable simply by plugging one end into the motherboard and use mounting screws to attach it to the outside of the case. The PS2 cables and USB cable were similar, I just had to hot glue the cables to the inside of the Falcon and attach the other end to the motherboard. The network cable was a little more difficult, though not too hard. I had to strip the end off a network cable and attach the wires in the right place in the female RJ-45 connector.

Finally, when the epoxy was dry on the hard drive support, I attached the windowed hard drive on top of the two supports and test-fitted the top of the Falcon on. After getting the hard drive in the right position, I removed the top of the Falcon and used some more double-stick foam tape on both supports to hold the drive (and laptop to desktop drive adapter) in place and plugged it into the motherboard. I attached the remaining hard drive on top of the power sup-ply towards the center of the mod with more tape and attached the laptop to desktop drive adapter to the front headlights. Finally, I plugged this hard drive into the motherboard, and put the top of the Falcon together with the bottom securing the halves together with the original screws.

One final problem left—the OS installation. Because of space limitations, this system had no CD-ROM drive. But that wasn't a difficult problem to solve because the case was easy to work in due to the removable cover. I temporarily attached a CD-ROM drive by removing the cable from the windowed hard drive and leaving the nonwindowed hard drive attached to the system. After the installation of the OS, I just removed the CD-ROM and plugged the cable for the second hard drive back into the system. I then reconfigured the OS so that the secondary drive contained the page file for the OS.

Tip While not rocket science, moving or adjusting the Windows page file isn't the easiest thing to do unless you know where to look. For a more detailed discussion of how and why to adjust the page file, check out www.theeldergeek.com/paging_file.htm.

Mousing Around

This mod performed admirably for months. It got some attention in magazines and TV, but it received a few negative remarks as well. The negative remarks mostly focused on two areas—the lack of a CD-ROM drive and the fact that it didn't have a modified mouse. Adding a CD-ROM drive would require a complete redesign, but a custom mouse was certainly an option.

Many months later on another trip to a toy store, I came across the Playskool X-wing fighter toy. It was a little large, but its fuselage was almost the same width as a mouse. And the toy was on sale for only a little over $10. A few dollars later, I was on my way to a local computer store. When I left the computer store, I was now another $40 poorer but owned a laptop wireless optical mouse.

I took the toy apart and removed all the components inside that allowed the wings to separate. I then used some epoxy to glue the wings together in the non-X configuration. My Dremel got a bit of a workout as well, as I cut a square hole in the bottom of the nose for the optical sensor the mouse. I replaced the button near the top that activated the folding wings with flat piece of plastic with a couple holes drilled in it for the left and right mouse buttons.

I took apart the mouse and removed the circuit board from the plastic. I unsoldered and replaced the connectors for the batteries with an external battery holder purchased from a local electronics store. I unsoldered the left and right mouse buttons and soldered in place new switches attached to a bit of wire. I also unsoldered another switch for the reconnect to base station function from the mouse and attached it to another switch, again with a bit of wire in between. Finally, I connected a toggle switch in between the battery holder.

Painting the toy required a bit of patience. One problem I had was with the four laser cannons. They were made from a special rubbery plastic that I had problems getting paint to stick to. I ended up just using masking tape to cover these while I painted the rest of the toy. The rest of the painting went uneventfully—a base coat of white, some red and yellow detail painting, some charcoal weathering effects, and sealed with a coat of Dullcote lacquer.

Finally, I put the pieces of the mouse back together. I placed the mouse circuit board and optical lens in the nose of the toy and secured them in place with some hot glue. I attached the battery toggle and reconnect buttons through the rear of the toy, and secured the left and right mouse buttons through the top of the toy (see Figure 18-11). I screwed the two halves of the toy together. The battery compartment could be accessed for battery replacement through the lift-up front canopy of the X-wing mouse.

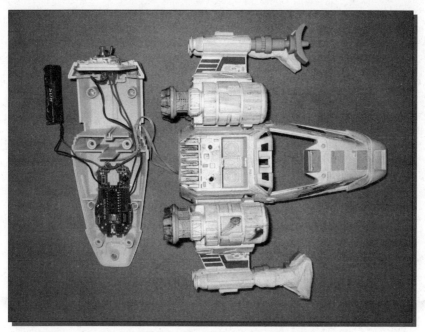

FIGURE **18-11: The pieces of the X-wing mouse during assembly.**

One final step—the mouse receiver needed to be installed. I disassembled the Falcon and installed a USB extension cable from the motherboard to the back of the cockpit. I cut a small hole in the seat in the cockpit so that the end of the wireless receiver could be poked through. This was needed because the receiver also had a wakeup button that would occasionally need to be accessed. I then reassembled the Falcon.

Conclusion

The completed mod (see Figure 18-12) was certainly fun to create and is quite an eye-catcher. The Falcon has received its fair share of attention from magazines, Web sites, and has even been featured on TechTV. Certainly, you could ask for nothing more of a case mod except for functioning well as a computer (which it does).

If this mod was to be recreated, there are a lot of steps that could be simplified or expanded even more. Things to try include:

- Forget using the EL wire for the engine bay. Just paint it instead.
- Don't do a hard drive window mod, just add more randomly blinking LEDs.
- Action figures. There are lots of *Star Wars* figures available; perhaps add a pilot?
- Add sound effects using a voice-recording circuit and tie it to the power-on button.

FIGURE 18-12: Completed Millennium Falcon mod with wireless mouse.

- Add a wireless Ethernet card to the computer.

- Don't use the landing gear. Instead attach a coat hanger (probably several) to the side of a desk or entertainment unit and hang the Falcon on the hook through the front landing gear bay. It would look just like the Falcon stuck on the back of the Star Destroyer in *The Empire Strikes Back*.

So . . . anyone inspired to create some science fiction case mods?

Aircraft Carrier PC

Russ "JediKnight0" Caslis

"Mommy, Mommy, can you buy me this?"

Every time I hear some child saying that as I roam around a toy store, I smile. One of the many advantages of being an adult is the ability to go anywhere I want, such as a toy store, and buy anything I want without anyone else to answer to.

The following project started as an impulse. I never planned to create it. I was walking around a toy store waiting for my wife to rummage through the latest selection of Barbie paraphernalia to find something suitable for her plastic friends when I saw it—a toy of the aircraft carrier *Enterprise*. As with most toys, the dimensions were way off and the accessories (two metal die-cast aircraft and a helicopter) were junk, but in the depths of the toy I could see another fun mini-ITX mod.

I promptly picked up the box, walked over to my wife, and said firmly, "Honey, can you buy me this?"

This is how the journey began—the journey that would transform a simple toy into a full-featured computer mod (see Figure 19-1) with everything from a DVD-ROM to a memory-card reader and lots of blinking lights.

Timeframe and Costs

This mod was built over a three to four month period, and I worked on it at least three or four hours through the work week and often for whole weekends. However, this mod was created at the same time as another mod so the timeframe could have been sped up a little, but not by much. Because this mod requires so much paint, in so many layers, it necessarily took a long time since paint only dries so fast.

As for cost, this mod cost less than $400 in new parts. But many parts were recycled from leftover hardware on other projects, so the numbers are a little off. In addition, VIA Technologies, the makers of the wonderful mini-ITX motherboard used in this mod, provided the motherboard for free as a sponsor. When buying all new parts, the cost of this most could easily be around $700 or more.

FIGURE 19-1: The completed aircraft carrier PC with modded mouse and keyboard.

Tip Finding a sponsor for your modding is something nearly every modder dreams of, but it's a somewhat rare occurrence. The best way is to build up a new nice mods (almost like an art portfolio) first. Then, contact companies that could provide parts for your next mod and point them at your past work as an example of what you can do. Make it worth their while somehow— provide free advertising or at least a detailed work log for their Web site.

Required Parts and Tools

The parts and tools list for this mod are actually pretty simple. Beyond the basic computer components such as motherboard, hard drive, and so on, the mod just required a few model kits, a bunch of LEDs, and the main toy itself. The tools are all basic modding stuff, a Dremel, a drill, and lots of paint.

Parts

- Aircraft carrier toy ($20)
- F14 fighter plane model kits (2 × $10)
- HO scale model tractors ($5)

- Mini-ITX motherboard ($200)
- Laptop hard drive with desktop adapter ($10)
- Laptop DVD-ROM with desktop adapter ($10)
- Small form factor power supply ($45)
- USB memory card reader/writer ($15)
- Digital voice recorder with speaker ($15)
- Lots of LEDs and a few integrated circuits ($20)
- Switches ($5)
- Acrylic panel and tubes ($20)

Tools

- Masking tape ($5)
- Paint (various color spray paints and bottle paints) ($40)
- Glue (both epoxy and model glue) ($10)
- Hobby knife ($8)
- Multimeter ($15)
- Drill ($50)
- Did I mention paint?

All Hands on Deck

Looking over this truly massive toy (see Figure 19-2), where was I going to start? Well, the first step was to take everything apart so that I knew what I had to work with. The toy itself was held together with a lot of screws in the bottom, but once they were removed everything came apart nicely because the toy maker did not use any glue.

Once the parts were all laid out before me, I started with the simple pieces, while my mind developed a plan for the overall look of the mod. It's usually a good idea to give yourself some time to work over the plan while you keep the mod moving by working on the simple pieces.

Command and Control

I decided to start with the command tower. The tower consisted of four parts—two antennas, a top piece, and the bottom piece. The command center and antennas were held in place merely by pressure, while the top and bottom pieces were held together with two screws. I separated the parts out and got to work.

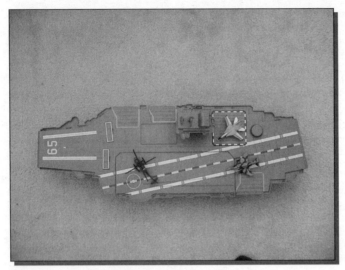

FIGURE 19-2: The toy in its original form.

For the top piece, I decided that I needed to add some detail. There were not nearly enough antennas, even for a rough approximation. I bought some HO scale model railroad telephone poles and started attaching them to the top by drilling small holes in the top and using a bit of epoxy to glue them in place. I tried to be creative with this. I cut three of the poles down so that they were just long sticks and attached them at various angles from the top. I cut another pole down so that it had only one horizontal bar, while I left another pole with all three horizontal bars. On yet another pole, I bent the horizontal bars slightly and epoxied another short piece perpendicular to the horizontal bars to simulate some sort of a disk antenna. In the end, I added six new antennas.

In Chapter 10, there is a discussion about kit—bashing-using model parts to add details to a case. The telephone poles turned antennas are one example of a kit-bashing.

The bottom of the command center also needed a little help. First, the plastic was very smooth and slippery. I've had issues getting paint (even with primer) to adhere to plastic like this, so I used some 400-grit sandpaper to rough it up a little before I continued. While I was doing this, I noticed that the toy maker had put detailing only on the long sides of the command tower. I used some sheet styrene plastic (available in sheets at most hobby stores for less than $5) to cut some basic shapes to roughly the same scale. I glued those shapes to the bare sides with epoxy to give it at least some detail.

Before doing anything else, I had to think about the basic electronics for the mod. It was obvious that I had to have a power and reset switch, but I also decided that I wanted working runway lights. Since those lights would probably be annoying at times, I needed a switch to turn them off. Finally, I needed a power light to let me know when the computer was on (as if the sound wasn't going to be enough). I decided a red blinking LED would make for a good power light. All the switches and the power light were excellent candidates for the command center.

The switches for power and reset were easy enough. I just drilled a couple of holes on opposite sides of the command center for momentary push-button switches and then ran the wires down through a hole I drilled in the bottom of the command center. The red blinking LED was also simple to install. I purchased the LED and attached it to a Molex connector with the appropriate resistor soldered in place. I then drilled another hole, mounted the LED, and the blinking LED was done. Similarly, the switch for the runway lights was easy. All I needed was one Molex connector wired straight to another connector but with one lead interrupted by the switch. To save space, I wired the blinking LED and the switch off the same Molex connector to reduce the number of connectors in and out of the command tower (see Figure 19-3).

Be careful when using blinking LEDs. Since LEDs are diodes, anything else in serial on the same circuit will blink on and off as well.

Before I could finish mounting the LED and switches, I needed to paint the tower. This was the simplest paint job on the entire mod. All I needed to do was paint the tower pieces with some automotive primer. Then, I used different color bottle paints to add some details to the tower, some dry-transfer letters to label the switch locations, and some Dullcote clear lacquer to seal it all in. The only real problem I had was the main antenna mast. I tried every type of paint known to man, but nothing would stick to its smooth waxy surface. I tried model paints,

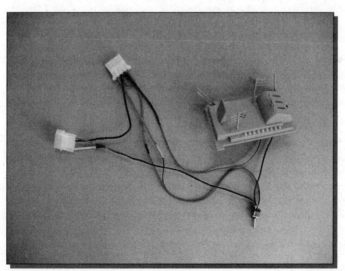

FIGURE 19-3: Runway light switch and Molex connectors attached to command center roof with extra antennas.

automotive paint, primer, self-etching primer, Krylon Fusion plastic paint, vinyl dye, plus others. Nothing would stick, even after using sandpaper to rough up the surface. Ultimately, since the plastic itself was already a shade of gray, I left it alone.

Tip On the bright side, getting the failed paint attempts off the main antenna mast wasn't too hard. I simply had to soak the piece in paint thinner for 24 hours, and roughly clean it with a toothbrush and some soap and water.

After all the paints were dry, I installed the LED and the switches. I decided not to use the original screws to put the pieces back together. Because I was going to permanently attach the tower to the case, using screws would make opening the tower back up impossible. The two tower pieces are held together securely enough without them.

The Hull

The main hull and deck are, of course, where the majority of the work was performed. In general, the work proceeded in two stages (not counting assembly)—plan the components with respect to location and function and perform all modifications to the case itself. Sounds much easier than it actually was, of course.

The planning of the hull was actually a gradual thing. I knew I would be using a mini-ITX motherboard and a small power supply because of the dimensions. But other items came later in the process, as I saw room and opportunity for enhancement. One significant problem with the planning stage was that despite the size of the toy, there were few areas that were flat enough on the hull to add all the ports I needed.

There were quite a lot of modifications to the basic structure of the bottom hull. I tried to keep from removing any of the support columns that housed screws that held the top and bottom of the carrier together, and only had to remove two of them.

One difficult section was the DVD-ROM drive I decided to add. For the front faceplate of the drive, where the disc would be ejected from, I needed a flat section that was quite long. The only place that would work was also the only place where the motherboard would fit. I measured the height of the DVD-ROM drive and the motherboard, and found I had enough space if I stacked them on top of one another.

The problems were not over though. The hull of the ship is rounded at the bottom. I ended up having to fabricate a shelf for the DVD-ROM to sit on that would raise it above the curved section of the hull, then also an additional shelf on top of that for the motherboard. This was accomplished through the use of flat acrylic sheet and acrylic tubes cut to the appropriate height (see Figure 19-4). After the shelves were built, I cut a hole in the hull to the exact dimensions of the DVD-ROM faceplate and glued the shelf into place using epoxy.

Tip I could have used any material for the shelves beside acrylic panel—it's just what I had handy around the house. In addition, gluing plastic to acrylic is relatively easy, while gluing plastic to metal is a little more difficult.

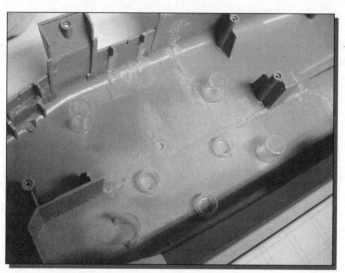

FIGURE 19-4: Acrylic tube risers glued to the hull, which has already had a lot of extra plastic removed.

The memory card reader writer also presented problems. After opening the device up and cutting the faceplate off so I could mount it in against the hull, I had a similar problem—no flat areas to mount it. I ended up cutting a hole for the reader/writer near the front of the ship and used lots of strong tape to hold the faceplate in place, slightly bent, until the glue could hold the pieces together.

Tip

Using the right glue for the right job is essential. In most cases, I like to use epoxy because it's a good strong general-purpose glue. But in instances like this I use regular model glue because it works well on plastic and actually melts the pieces together to make them act as a single piece. It doesn't work with as many materials as epoxy does though.

I also needed a place on the hull to mount all the connectors such as the power plug, video out, audio out, USB and FireWire ports, and so on. I ended up splitting these up because I didn't have enough flat sections to mount these holes while leaving enough space for cables to attach on the outside. Most of the connectors fit on a rear section of the ship around the back, but I had to mount the USB and FireWire ports up front. This was difficult due to the curvature of the hull, but I was able to bend the mounting bracket for those ports just enough that the ports were accessible from the outside through holes I carved using a drill and a sharp hobby knife.

When this was done, I painted the bottom hull with primer. I then masked off all but the bottom couple of inches and painted the water line red. I used some dry-transfer letters to place the name of the ship, *Enterprise*, on the back of the ship and covered everything in several coats of clear lacquer.

The Deck

By far, the majority of work on this mod was on the flight deck. I decided that the flight deck needed to have the following features:

- Working runway lights with the center light sequencing down the runway
- A separate circuit that would play the national anthem from an included speaker
- A removable panel to show the computer inside
- A working hard drive activity light built into an aircraft on the deck

The first thing I did was figure out what cuts were needed to accomplish these tasks. I started with drilling a couple of holes to attach leads for a hard drive activity light up front (more on this later). Then, I measured and drilled holes for white runway marking lights and center sequencing lights (over 22 holes for those alone). I already had a removable piece to access the computer inside the mod—it was molded into the toy as part of a storage area. I also cut a hole for the command center wires to run through.

The next thing I needed was paint, and a lot of it. I painted the catapults that aircraft are launched from with a dark gray surface and white marking lines. I did the same for the elevator, except with white and red warning lines around the edges. I painted the deck pieces gray around the edges, with dark gray for the main deck and white and yellow lines for the runways (see Figure 19-5). I also painted additional warning lines in yellow. At the end, I covered everything in clear lacquer.

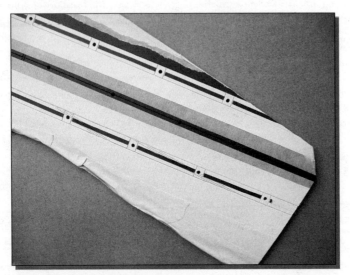

FIGURE 19-5: Part of the runway during the complicated masking used to create the runway lines. Note that the holes for the LEDs have already been drilled.

The preceding brief synopsis makes the process of masking and painting sound simple, but it isn't. A great deal of time is spent doing the masking and waiting for paint to dry. See Chapter 6 for a discussion of painting, including masking technique.

After all the paint was dry, I got to work on some of the electronics. There were two main areas to focus on—the runways lighting system and the sound system.

I started by sanding each LED used for the runway so that the light was more evenly spread, since ultrabrite LEDs have a narrow field of light. I used some hot glue to hold these all in the holes I previously drilled for them. The outside lights were easy enough because they just required a constant power source. The sequencing lights down the middle were more difficult. For these, I built a circuit that would light one LED at a time in a sequential pattern and connected the LEDs to that circuit.

This whole process was complicated by the fact that two thirds of the LEDs were on the removable panel that makes the computer accessible. I used a bit of network cable as the wiring harness to carry the signals to that panel. Thus, the panel can be removed (even while the lights are running) without affecting the rest of the mod.

The removable portion of the deck isn't big enough to actually do any work inside the computer such as adding more memory, so why did I want a removable piece? One problem that I've encountered with intricate mods like this one is that "normal" people don't believe a computer is really inside; they think it's all some sort of a trick. With a removable panel, I can quickly show them that the mod really *is* a computer.

While the removable panel in this mod wasn't for the purpose of making the computer itself upgradable, that would still be possible by removing the entire deck, which was secured using screws and not glue. No matter what your mod is, you should always have a way to disassemble it if you need to without permanently damaging it. Never use just glue to close up a mod because you won't be able to work on it ever again.

The sound system was a cool addition. I found a complete 20-second digital voice recorder/player circuits at an electronics chain store for $20 dollars. I replaced the switches and adapted it to work with a 12-volt power source rather than the 9-volt battery source it had originally required (see Figure 19-6). Next, I recorded 20 seconds of the U.S. national anthem and mounted it to the underside of the deck of the carrier. Through holes I drilled in the deck for the record and play buttons, the mod could now play some audio.

After all this, I decided to take a break from the mod for a couple of weeks and work on another, often forgotten part of a mod—the peripherals.

Tugboat Mouse

One of the most attention-getting details of this mod is the custom themed mouse that goes with it. I designed a tugboat mouse to go along with the marine transportation theme. The steps to create something like this may seem complex, but actually they're really simple.

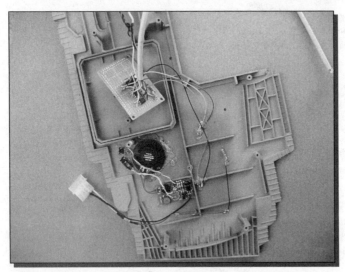

FIGURE 19-6: The sound recorder and the circuit for the runway lights are attached to the underside of the deck. Also visible are some of the runway LEDs hot glued in place.

The most important step of creating the tugboat mouse was finding the right platform to start from. I spent some time wandering around a couple of toy stores (a nice place to hang out, if you ask me). I ended up finding a police hovercraft toy that was vaguely the same size and shape as a mouse. This was my starting point.

Test Fitting

First, I opened the toy and removed all the electronics and other plastic pieces including a couple of large retractable turbines (see Figure 19-7). These turbines had to go for two reasons— they didn't really fit the theme, and they were made of the same terrible waxy plastic as the main antenna that experience had taught me wouldn't hold paint. I also removed all the waxy plastic pieces from the rest of the toy. Ultimately, I had two useful pieces left—the top and the bottom halves of the toy.

The bottom plastic had a lot of support structures embedded in it. Using my Dremel, I removed them all so that I had a flat surface in the bottom of the toy, while leaving as many of the screw mounting structures in place as possible. I then glued the battery compartment cover in place using epoxy to make the bottom piece as complete as possible. I covered the wheel holes with styrene plastic that was also glued in place with epoxy. Once that glue had dried, I used modeling putty to fill the remaining gaps and sanded it smooth.

Tip

As stated previously, remember to find a way to close up your modded pieces without permanently shutting them in case you need to work on them again. For the mouse, that's why I left a number of the screw holes in place—they provided a nonpermanent way to keep the mouse closed.

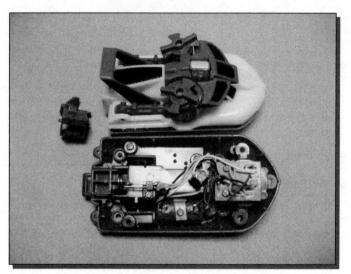

FIGURE 19-7: The toy tugboat during the disassembly process.

Next, I disassembled a cheap optical mouse I had purchased. Because I used a full-sized optical mouse, the main electronics board was too wide to fit inside the bottom of the toy, and I had to make some alterations. If I had purchased a laptop optical mouse, all the electronics would have fit, but that thought didn't cross my mind until after I was done assembling the mouse.

Electronics Alterations

The main circuit board for the optical mouse was too wide and long for the shell of the tugboat, so I needed to make a few changes. Circuit boards are actually simple devices—they consist of nothing more than a nonconductive material with pieces of conductive metal run across their surfaces (called "traces") that connect devices mounted on their surface (such as chips, LEDs, etc.). In other words, a trace is nothing more than a form of wire. As such, I could replace the traces with actual pieces of wire without affecting the functions of the mouse. Using wires allowed me to make the circuit board thinner by moving the traces vertically instead of horizontally.

First, I followed the traces for the mouse buttons on the circuit board back closer to the center of the circuit board. Using my Dremel, I cut off the entire section of the circuit board where the switches had been. I then took a couple of spare microswitches I had saved from a previous project and, using some wire, soldered the switches to the connection points I had followed earlier.

The second alteration was far more difficult. The circuit board itself was too wide to fit in the tugboat shell, so I had to make it slimmer. Once again following the traces on the circuit board, I could see that both sides had three long runs of traces across the board. One trace at a time, one side at a time, I soldered wires from the beginning of a trace to the end point of that trace on the circuit board. I then used a sanding wheel on the Dremel to grind away both the circuit board and the trace. I did this six times, and this finally made the board thin enough to fit inside the tugboat shell.

Finally, using the 5-volt power and ground connections from the USB header on the circuit board I soldered red/white/blue LEDs in a triangular pattern together. I used some resistors to dim the LEDs from their full brightness to a level that was more pleasing to the eye.

See Chapter 4 for a discussion about lighting, including how to use LEDs with the proper resistors.

Finishing the Basic Shape

Since there were a number of pieces missing from the original toy, the remaining shell had a number of holes in it. Using some sheet styrene plastic, I was able to cover these holes completely and make the top half complete again.

With this toy, after the waxy plastic pieces were removed there were four major holes in the top half. There were open areas over the windows in the front of the boat, one on each side of the center, and one large area in the back. I cut some 1 mm thick styrene plastic to cover each of these areas and used Testors model glue to glue it in place. After the glue had dried for 24 hours, I sanded each of these areas until the new plastic blended in with the existing plastic. Before the sanding, I used some modeling putty to help fill a few of the small holes between the two plastics.

Using a drill, I drilled five small LED-sized holes in the top. Near the front of the boat, I drilled three holes in a triangular pattern to accommodate the LEDs I had added to the circuit board earlier. I also drilled two holes in the rear of the top to accommodate the new left and right mouse buttons.

Finally, I cut holes in the bottom of the boat for the optical sensor for the mouse. I roughly mimicked the same shape as the existing hole on the bottom of the original mouse. I also cut a small circle out of the plastic piece I had added to the rear of the top piece of the mouse for the USB cord.

Painting the Mouse

At this point, I could paint the mouse parts. I gave the top piece a coat of primer much the same as the majority of the aircraft carrier itself. I painted the bottom piece with primer followed by a coat of red paint.

The plastic bottom for the mouse was already red plastic, so I could have left it that color rather than painting it. But I had closed up the holes for the wheels in the original toy with some white plastic and orange hobby putty, so by painting it the entire surface I made it a consistent color. In addition, I find painted surfaces have a more professional look and feel to them.

I painted several details such as the windows and the rear ribbed section of the top piece by hand with varying shades of black or gray to give a little more depth to the mouse pieces. Finally, I covered both the top and bottom pieces of the mouse with several coats of clear matte lacquer to seal the paint and give it some additional hardness.

Custom Mouse Cable

One very easy and cool mod I did to the mouse was to create a custom mouse cable. All I had to do for this mod was to use masking take to cover up alternating sections of the USB cable, making sure to get the masking tape straight so that the two sides of the tape meet up perfectly when the tape meets up with itself. I also masked off the connectors on both ends of the cable completely.

I used some red vinyl dye to paint the exposed sections of the cable. I hung the cable from something high so I could paint all sides of the cable at the same time. After the vinyl dye was dry, I examined the cable for any spots I missed and repainted a couple of small areas.

 Chapter 6 includes detailed info on using vinyl dye, such as using it on computer cables.

Finally, I waited another 12 hours or so and removed the masking tape. There were a couple small areas where the dye had seeped under the tape, but I simply used a hobby knife to scrape away a little of the dye and everything looked good. I was left with a cool custom cable that is reminiscent of a warning tether.

Final Details

Everything was coming together nicely now. I placed the main circuit board and lens for the optical mouse in the bottom section and secured them in place using hot glue (see Figure 19-8). I also secured the switches and the red/white/blue triangle of lights using hot glue.

I cut off the bottom metal leads from a couple of 5-mm LEDs and painted the LEDs white. Then I painted the bottom ring on the LEDs red and epoxied them to the sides of the top of the mouse in the location where the twin turbines used to sit. I figured that these round shapes looked like some sort of covered radar array or similar technology.

Finally, using three screw holes left in the bottom of the mouse I secured the top half of the mouse with the bottom half. I peeled the Teflon feet off the original mouse and stuck them on the tugboat mouse. Finally, I plugged in the mouse and tested it out (see Figure 19-9). Success!

First Attempts Sometimes Fail

Not every attempt at a mod will go perfectly. The cute little tugboat mouse I created was actually my second attempt. My first attempt didn't go so well.

At first, I bought a cheap ball mouse with the idea of painting it gray and red like the aircraft carrier. I wanted to create a missile bay on the back of the mouse by placing rows of red, white,

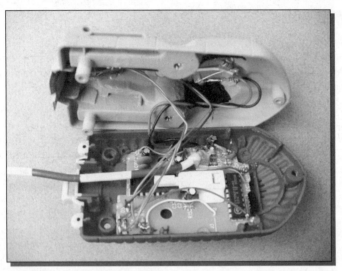

FIGURE 19-8: The mouse just before closing. All the electronics are mounted in their final locations.

and blue LEDs there. I bought some LEDs and a nonoptical mouse (to save money). Then, I started modding my new mouse.

I used my Dremel to etch some lines in the top of the mouse so that it would look like hull plating. I measured and drilled holes for the LEDs. I vinyl dyed the bottom red and the top gray, and after

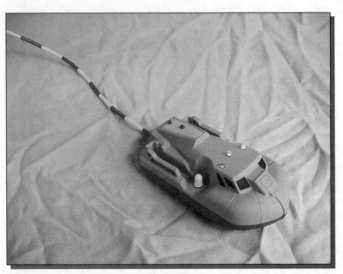

FIGURE 19-9: Complete modded mouse.

the gray dried I masked it off and painted the etched lines black. I removed the masking tape and it looked horrible. I had used too much gray vinyl dye and hadn't waited long enough for it to dry, so sections of gray color pealed right up. In addition, the masking wasn't perfect and the black seeped through so the edges had spider-web-like lines where there should have been solid gray.

Upset but stubborn, I went back to the computer store and bought another cheap mouse. This time I found a really cheap optical mouse (less than $7). I brought it home and commenced with the same measuring, drilling, and etching. I carefully vinyl dyed it, making sure to not put too much on. But this time the vinyl dye didn't hold either. It turns out the plastic was already painted a silver color and wouldn't hold the dye. I probably could have sanded the whole thing and salvaged it, but I was even more upset and angry at myself now.

A final trip to the computer store and another mouse purchase later, I was finally able to get something that looked OK and took the vinyl dye. I continued the mod and came up with my first ever modded mouse (see Figure 19-10).

I even took this mouse to work with me to show off to my coworkers. They were somewhat impressed, but not stunned. In addition, the LEDs bothered me because they were too bright. I couldn't really use the mouse because every time I took my hand off the mouse, the blinding color of the LEDs would grab my attention.

A few days later I came up with the idea of actually replacing the shell for the mouse. On the bright side, the second mouse purchase supplied the optical mouse electronics that I used in the tugboat mouse, and the first mouse supplied the nice white cable that became the custom mouse cord. So even in this set of modding errors, important lessons were learned.

FIGURE 19-10: Original functional modded mouse.

Keyboard Mod

I was well on my way to creating the aircraft carrier PC and had a pretty cool one-of-a-kind mouse. I felt I needed to have a keyboard to match.

I decided to do a simple keyboard mod. Nothing too fancy, just a paint job and some LED replacements. At the same time, I used the same technique I had used on the mouse cable for the keyboard cable.

I started by buying a cheap USB keyboard from a local computer store. Nothing too fancy, just the simplest and cheapest one I could find. It happened to have an additional row of multimedia keys, but honestly the mod would have been easier without them.

Disassembling the Keyboard

When I got the keyboard home, the first thing I did was take a picture of the keys (see Figure 19-11). I knew that I needed to disassemble the keyboard, so it was vital I knew where all the keys went. Taking pictures of the keyboard was a quick and easy way to make sure that I didn't forget the location of any of the keys.

Tip Whenever you are going to have to reassemble something you disassemble as part of a mod, you should make sure you have some "map" available to for reassembly. In this case, I used a photograph, which works in most cases. Otherwise, a sketch will work.

FIGURE 19-11: Unmodified keyboard as a reference for key locations.

I started by flipping the keyboard over and removing all the screws. After the screws were gone, the keyboard was held together by several plastic clips on the inside of the keyboard, but a little pressure and tugging with my fingernails and the top just came apart without anything breaking.

I continued taking the keyboard apart, including storing all the separate rubber nubs that go under every key and the circuit board that housed the three keyboard lights. After the keyboard was separated into dozens of pieces, I took all the plastic pieces and washed them in soap and water and allowed them to dry overnight after drying them with a towel first.

Tip Plastic pieces, such as this keyboard, usually have oils still left on them from the production process. These oils interfere when trying to paint the plastic, so it's best to clean the plastic with a mild soap before painting. Just remember to dry the pieces with a soft towel when done or you may end up with water spots (which also interfere with paint adhesion).

Painting the Keyboard

I took all pieces that needed to be painted and separated them. For this keyboard, I wanted the top to be gray (it was white) and the bottom to be red (it was also white). One problem I had was that the multimedia keys were molded in gray plastic, but the top of the keyboard was going to be painted gray leaving no contrast between the keyboard and those keys. Thus, I decided to paint the keys white.

Using the appropriate color vinyl dye, I painted each piece. The gray keys were a difficult thing to paint, since using vinyl dye to dye a darker plastic a lighter color can be an error-prone process. I went slowly but evenly and ended up using about four coats on those keys, as opposed to just two coats on the other pieces. The extra coats of vinyl dye only added about an hour to the overall time it took to paint the keys, but there was the extra danger during the first few minutes of drying time that a spec of dirt (or a flying insect) might decide to ruin the pieces.

While I waited a few days for the dye to completely dry, I started working on the electronics for the keyboard.

Replacing the LEDs

Standard green LEDs for the keyboard lights (num lock, caps lock, and scroll lock) just don't look right in this type of mod, so I replaced them with the more patriotic colors red, white, and blue.

I carefully desoldered the existing LEDs from the circuit board inside the keyboard. Before soldering the new LEDs in place, I attached the USB cable attached to the circuit board to another computer so that it had power, and quickly touched each LED to the mounting holes for the old LEDs so that I could find right polarity for each LED. I then soldered them to the circuit board, keeping in mind how the circuit board would be mounted in the keyboard. I wanted to be looking at red, white, and blue LEDs in that order (not reversed).

One problem that I encountered with the keyboard was bleeding from one color to another. With the keyboard fully assembled, I had a problem that when one LED was lit, the LED space next to it was also lit up the same color only dimmer. In the keyboard there was a solid clear plastic piece that mounted over the LEDs, and this was spreading the light in ways I didn't want.

I cut the clear plastic into three pieces, and painted the ends of the clear plastic with black paint. I then used some pieces of styrene plastic to glue the clear plastic back together into one piece the right size. This solved the problem of light bleeding through.

Putting it Together

Before the final assembly of the keyboard, I vinyl dyed the keyboard cable the same way I dyed the mouse cable. I now had all the pieces, so I started assembling everything.

I started by using the picture I took earlier to put all the keys back into the keyboard in the right order. Then, I mounted the electronics and the other plastic pieces I had in the appropriate spots and screwed them into place. In the bottom half of the keyboard, I attached the circuit board into place, then I turned the top of keyboard upside down and replaced all those small rubber nubs into the hole on each key, being careful not to lose any. Finally, I attached the two keyboard halves and screwed everything together (see Figure 19-12).

After all that work, I plugged the keyboard into another computer and verified that it worked. I found one key not working, so I had to open the keyboard back up and I found one rubber nub out of place. I moved it back into place, closed the keyboard again, and tested again. Success!

FIGURE 19-12: Complete modded keyboard.

Naval Aviators

The aircraft carrier toy came with some toy planes, but the toys were poor quality die-cast metal and didn't really help the mod stand out from the crowd.

I visited a local hobby store and found some model kits of F-14 fighters in 1/144 scale, about the right size for an oversized and out of proportion model like the aircraft carrier. Each plane was about three inches long, and as an added bonus F-14s are one type of plane that are actually stationed on the real *Enterprise* aircraft carrier.

I got a couple of kits. One plane was going to be just for looks on the flight deck, but the other plane I wanted as the hard drive activity light. I started by building the easier plane, the one without any electronics.

Basic Plane Build-Up

I started separating all the plastic pieces from the plastic tree they are attached to using a sharp hobby knife (see Figure 19-13). Then, roughly following the instruction sheet, I used model glue to glue most of the model kit together. The idea was to figure out what pieces were primarily the same color, and glue them together before painting them. For this simple model, there were three major colors used: black for the engine nozzles and tires, silver for the landing gear, and light battleship gray for the main body. All the main body pieces, including the wings and nosecone, were glued together first and allowed to dry overnight. Since I was working on the nonfunctioning plane first, I glued the wings in their swept-back storage position.

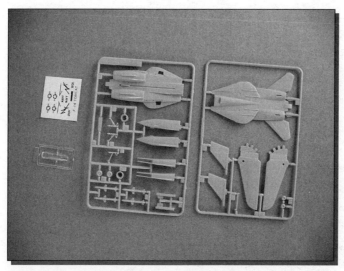

FIGURE 19-13: Model plane as a collection of plastic parts.

Tip

When you're going to paint something, it's a good idea to combine all the pieces that are going to be the same color because the paint will help to conceal any seams between the pieces. This helps the illusion that the two pieces were actually one piece to begin with.

These were cheap model kits, and had some quality issues. For example, when gluing the top and bottom halves together, the pieces didn't line up very well. I used some modeling putty to fill the holes and sand the pieces down. This was difficult to do since the sections I was trying to sand were only a few millimeters long, but it was worth the effort. After the sanding, I cleaned the pieces off with water and allowed them to dry. Then, I moved on to the painting.

The basic painting of the main shapes was done using spray paints because this allowed an even coat that would be impossible by hand. Using light battleship gray, I painted the basic air-plane shape. I also used black spray paint to paint the engine nozzles black, and silver spray paint to paint the landing gear.

After those coats were dry, I used small bottle paints to paint the details. Using black, I painted the inside of the clear canopy window and the tires. Using several different shades of gray, I painted the engine inlets and the area around the canopy gray. I even painted the canopy lines on the outside of the clear plastic canopy I had previously painted black.

Then I applied the water-slide decals that came with the model kit. I cut the decals out using some scissors and dropped the cutout in a shallow glass of water. After 10 seconds or so, I removed the decals and placed them (with paper backing) on the model near the final location for the decal. I gently slid the decal off the paper and onto the model and moved it to its final position. I removed any extra water with a napkin and let the decals dry overnight.

Finally, I used some Dullcote (clear flat lacquer spray paint with a matte appearance) to finish off the model. I used a few somewhat heavy coats to seal the underlying paint and decals. After

Figure 19-14: Basic plane completed.

that dried, I used a small amount of epoxy glue to glue the plastic canopy in place on the model. The easy plane was done (see Figure 19-14).

Advanced Plane Build-Up

I needed to make at least one of the F-14s light up, so I decided I would put lights in the engines and cockpit of one of them and have it be the hard drive activity light. I came up with the idea that if I used a couple of solid metal pieces as the power leads (like the pins from an LED), I could make the plane removable. What good is a toy with small planes if you can't remove the planes and play with them?

Adding the lights to the other plane proved to be somewhat difficult. Besides the small spaces I had to work in, the main section of the plane was best painted as one piece. If I painted the halves of the plane as separate pieces, the seams that I used putty to fill in the other plane would be clearly visible. I ended up building the electronics into the main body of the plane and glued everything shut. I used just enough wire that the lights could move around slightly, which allowed me to cover the lights with masking tape prior to painting (see Figure 19-15). After the painting, I was able to remove the tape and glue the final pieces (the engine nozzles and the cockpit) over the lights and get a professional result.

No Component Untouched

There was still a fair amount of work until all the components would work together nicely. I had all the components now, but several would not fit without a few more mods.

FIGURE 19-15: Some of the wires and LEDs inside the advanced plane.

Since the back of the motherboard with all the ports was going to be hidden in the depths of the mod, I needed to build extension cables for all the ports that were going to be accessible from the outside. Most cables were pretty easy to build by simply taking a prebuilt cable, cutting off one end, and soldering on a new connector. Cables like the audio cable only have three connections to worry about, but the VGA cable was a real pain with its 15 small wires.

All these port relocations included having to relocate the plug for the power supply. To do that, I had to open the power supply to move both the external power plug connector and the motherboard connector so that they exited the power supply housing at the top rather than the side (because the space was so tight inside the hull). I used some electrical tape to prevent the wires from rubbing holes in themselves against the side of the power supply and shorting out. While not an overly difficult move, anytime I have to work on something with huge capacitors and many volts of electricity I get a little nervous. Luckily nothing bad happened here.

Caution

It deserves to be said again—those big capacitors in the power supply store an electrical change even when the power supply in unplugged. The capacitors will be happy to release all their energy on anything even somewhat conductive that touches them—a piece of metal, a soldering iron, or even you! Be extremely careful when working inside a power supply.

Every computer needs cooling, and even though the mini-ITX motherboards run cool, the heat generated by the other components needed a way to escape. On the toy there were some removable pieces that seemed perfect for the task. I cut out the center of a couple of these and replaced the center of one with a couple of laptop cooling fans, while placing some extra metal mesh I had in the other piece. I placed these two pieces at opposite ends of the mod and positioned the fans as an exhaust. The idea was that cool air enters through the mesh, flows over the components, and gets pulled out through the rear.

The motherboard itself was held in place by mounting screws on an acrylic panel cut to the basic shape as the motherboard. I later positioned this acrylic panel on top of the acrylic tube risers so that it would sit above the DVD-ROM drive.

There was also one more detail for the hull that needed to be dealt with—the rear. In the original toy, there was a horrible looking piece of plastic that covered the back of the toy. To add insult to injury, the plastic was the same type of waxy plastic that gave me so much grief with the main antenna mast. I ended up cutting another piece of acrylic and actually bending it using my oven and one side of my toaster as a mold for the piece. When it was done, I painted it gray and printed out some computer logos (FireWire symbol, USB symbol, VIA logo, etc.) on clear transparency that I placed in front of the acrylic panel.

Finally, I realized that the deck of the aircraft carrier would be a little plain without something more on it. The control tower and a couple planes were not enough. I bought some HO scale model railroad tractors at a hobby store and proceed to sculpt away pieces that looked too much like farm equipment. After adding a few left over missiles from the model planes and a few coats of paint, they looked like machines used to load and refuel planes. Everything was now ready.

Assembly

After all this work, the final assembly actually turned out to be easier than I thought it would. I had already measured all the cables during their initial creation. All that was left to do was to put everything in its final location, glue it down, and plug it in.

The DVD-ROM slid into position along with its laptop to desktop converter and cable easily. Then the motherboard was placed over the DVD-ROM using the acrylic risers. I glued and screwed into place the memory card reader and FireWire ports. I placed the power supply into position and secured it with some foam tape. I placed the hard drive in the back of the system. I secured all the cables to the holes in the hull and the back of the motherboard. Everything was ready (see Figure 19-16).

The final step was to place the deck on the carrier and use the remaining screw holes to secure it. Once that was done, I glued the aircraft and support vehicles into place on the deck.

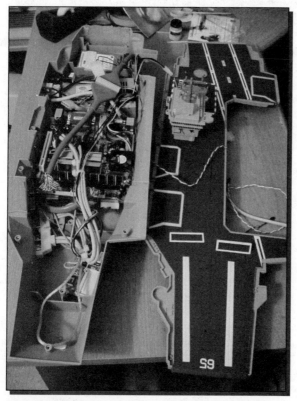

FIGURE 19-16: The computer assembled and waiting for the deck to be attached.

I applied power and installed Windows XP on the system. It worked wonderfully, including the modified keyboard and mouse.

Conclusion

The final outcome of the mod was very pleasing, and I'm proud to say that it's something that I created. When I first saw the toy, the mod that now sits in front of me is exactly what I envisioned. To me, that's a great measure of how a mod turned out. If I imagined something and created exactly what I saw in my mind, then the mod was a success.

This mod has been featured in multiple magazines and also on TV, so it's gotten its fair share of attention for a computer mod. I've received emails from some of the people that have worked on the actual aircraft carrier itself who have approved of the mod. That was also a great validation of its success.

In looking over everything now, there are a lot of areas that could use some more modding. Maybe the back of the ship where I placed the company logos could incorporate a place to store the mouse. Maybe the sound circuit should be tied into the computer start-up sequence somehow. Maybe there should be more detail on top of the deck. All these are areas that could be improved . . . Are you the person to do it?

Appendices

part

Overclocking

It's no secret that computers get old quickly. What was a top-of-the-line model yesterday is often superceded by the next great thing without any warning. While this typically means good things (that $300 processor you wanted last month is now only $200), you might be quite upset that you paid the full amount, while your best friend just paid two thirds of what you did for the same thing. If you don't have money to upgrade constantly, overclocking is a way you can increase your computer's performance for relatively little money.

Overclocking is the process of running some components at speeds faster than that at which they were originally certified to run (see Figure A-1). Overclocking generally involves the CPU, but memory and video cards are also good candidates for this.

But overclocking isn't for everyone. Overclockers gamble that they can get some extra performance for free, and sometimes they lose. Many CPUs have been damaged by attempted overclocking and the arcane tricks used to get there. But it's that lure of something for nothing that drives many down this path.

While overclocking is certainly not the focus of this book, no serious discussion of modding can take place without at least a passing reference to the subject. Many of the standard modding techniques are designed around increasing cooling, and increased cooling is the cornerstone of overclocking.

Caution | Overclocking any component in your system will void the warranty on the part. Thus, be prepared to absorb the cost yourself if a component (or multiple components) become damaged during the process. Returning a dead and formerly overclocked part to the manufacturer is not an option.

Why It Works

All the components in a computer system are controlled by a clock that determines how quickly they work and the speed at which they interact. For devices to run correctly and remain stable, they must draw their speed from the system clock and a multiplier/divider that regulates a particular device's speed relative to the other devices in the system. Thus, increasing that system clock rate will affect all the other components in the system.

FIGURE A-1: Pentium 4 rated at 3 GHz running at 3.4 GHz.

Components that run at higher speeds cost more to make and purchase. However, sometimes components rated for a slower speed are fully capable of running at higher speeds than what they are sold as.

Why is this? It just makes economic sense. Processors are fabricated in large sheets referred to as wafers. The individual processors on this wafer are then tested at different speeds to determine their top stable speed. Not all processors from the same batch will be stable at the same speed. Thus, processors are marked and sold at the top speed they can run at based on the results of this test.

A couple of factors work in favor of the overclocker. First, the tests that manufacturers perform are generally quite conservative in their outcome. Sometimes manufacturers take the top stable speed and lower it one notch "just to be safe" to make sure they don't get many returns or complaints. Also, these tests are performed at standard voltage levels. By increasing the voltage to a component you can often get the component to remain stable at higher speeds with the trade-off being increased heat generation. Finally, due to contractual limits a manufacturer sometimes has to supply a given number of processors at a given speed. So, if they have to provide one hundred 3-GHz processors and one hundred 2.8-Ghz processors, but over one hundred fifty processors test fine at 3 GHz, fifty 3-Ghz processors are marked down to 2.8 GHz and sold along with the fifty that could only do 2.8 GHz.

The problem is that unscrupulous retailers could easily repackage a slower part as a faster part just by falsely telling the user what multiplier the processor was supposed to be set at. The solution from the processor manufacturers was to lock the multipliers, therefore stopping the illegal activity of selling improperly clocked processors. With a locked multiplier, it's impossible to overclock the processor without affecting all the other components in the system. For any serious overclocking, the other components would be stressed so much that the computer would almost certainly not even boot.

As a direct result of this, some motherboard manufacturers have added complex manipulations of the multipliers/dividers to help keep the other components in the system within rated tolerances even when the processor is overclocked. This opens up the possibility of overclocking again, even if it's more much more complex than if users could simply set their own processor multipliers.

When Things Go Wrong

There are dangers to this whole process. Overclocking is by definition pushing components past their rated specifications. By doing so, you void the warranties. Also, there is increased wear and tear on the component, and it may fail much earlier than a nonoverclocked component. Because of the issues with multipliers/dividers and multiplier locking, other components in the system besides the focus of the overclocking will often inadvertently be overclocked as well. You end up with the entire system's stability being determined by the weakest link, whatever that may be.

If your particular motherboard cannot set the PCI and AGP bus speed independently of the main processor, all your cards must be capable of overclocking as well. Even if the PCI and AGP bus speed can be set independently, your front-side bus cannot due to multiplier locking. This means your motherboard's Northbridge chip must be able to overclock as well. There are dozens of things that can cause problems when trying to overclock your processor.

How It's Done

Entire books could be written about the art and science of overclocking. The specifics of what works and what doesn't changes with each generation of chips from the various manufacturers such as Intel and AMD. But the general idea remains the same—messing around with all the cryptically named options in the BIOS.

Tip There are just as many online forums that focus on overclocking as there are forums for modding. One place that has good discussions about both is www.hardforums.com.

In this section you'll learn about some of the basics. The three most common areas of overclocking are the CPU, system memory, and the video card.

CPU

For overclocking a processor, you must understand the relationship between the front-side bus (FSB) frequency and the CPU multiplier. For example, a 3-GHz Pentium 4 processor uses a 200-MHz FSB with a 15× clock multiplier, giving a total frequency of 3,000 MHz

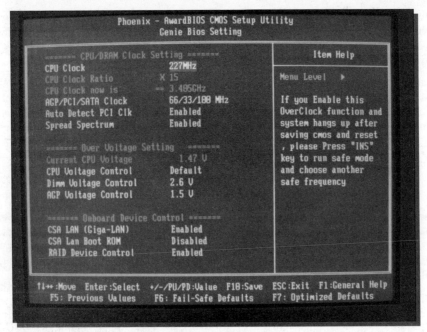

FIGURE A-2: Pentium 4 processor with overclocked FSB.

(200 × 15 = 3,000). Now, if the FSB were increased to 227-MHz, the overall processor frequency would increase to 3,405 MHz—a 13.5 percent increase in performance (see Figure A-2). Similarly, if the CPU multiplier were changed you could overclock the CPU without affecting the FSB. However, the CPU multiplier is usually autodetected by the BIOS and cannot be altered. Generally, the FSB can be changed in many BIOS setups.

Tip Modern Pentium 4 CPUs appear to have an 800-MHz FSB, but that number comes from using a trick called "quad-pumping" that feeds four instructions per clock cycle. Therefore, the actual speed of the FSB is 200 MHz.

Another parameter that can often be changed to help overclocking ability is the CPU core voltage. When it's overclocked, adjusting the CPU's voltage up a little will lead to higher temperatures but can also help the CPU to remain stable when running. Of course, if the increased heat is not removed adequately, the CPU will actually become less stable and can easily be damaged. Thus, always add voltage in small steps, and after making voltage changes watch the CPU temperature closely both when the system is under stress and when it is idle.

Figuring out the optimal setup for a system takes quite a bit of time and patience. The easy way to overclock your processor is to simple bump up the FSB speed a bit at a time until the system becomes unstable when running benchmarks or demos. Then, reduce the FSB speed slightly and things should work smoothly—(as long as you keep an eye on the temperatures of your CPU and your case).

Tip To keep an eye on your CPU temperature, you can purchase a temperature probe designed for computers. Any mod supply store should have a couple of different types, usually integrated with a fan controller. Simple probes cost under $20, while more elaborate fan controllers with probes can easier cost over $80.

Tip Another way to monitor temperatures inside the CPU and case is by using the built-in temperature monitors supplied on many motherboards. For this, you can either view the temperatures via the BIOS screens or use a Windows-based application such as "Motherboard Monitor," available for free from www.3degs.net.

Memory

The main memory in a computer has a huge impact on the general performance of the system. Since the processor must go to memory for virtually all data and instructions, if the memory is substantially slower than the processor, then the system is wasting time waiting for the memory. Fortunately, memory can be overclocked as well.

Overclocking memory is accomplished through tweaking the various memory timing options available in the system BIOS (see Figure A-3). These options can be pretty complex, and the process of finding the right settings is largely a matter of trial and error. Generally, you start the

```
           Phoenix - AwardBIOS CMOS Setup Utility
                  Advanced Chipset Features

   DRAM Timing Selectable    Manual          Item Help
   CAS Latency Time          2.5
   Active to Precharge Delay 7          Menu Level   ►
   DRAM RAS# to CAS# Delay   3
   DRAM RAS# Precharge       3
   Memory Frequency For      DDR400
   System BandWidth          MPS2
   System BIOS Cacheable     Enabled
   Video  BIOS Cacheable     Disabled
   Delay Prior to Thermal     8 Min
   AGP Aperture Size (MB)    128
   DRAM Data Integrity Mode  Non-ECC




 ↑↓←→:Move  Enter:Select  +/-/PU/PD:Value  F10:Save  ESC:Exit  F1:General Help
     F5: Previous Values   F6: Fail-Safe Defaults   F7: Optimized Defaults
```

FIGURE A-3: **Various memory timing options. Not all motherboards have these options, and sometimes these options are referred to by different names.**

process by finding the specifications for the memory modules you have from the manufacturer's Web site and slowly adjusting the values down until your system becomes unstable. At this point, increase the values slightly until your system is stable again.

Keep in mind the overall frequency the memory is designed to run at. This frequency is affected by the FSB speed, so increasing the FSB will also increase the speed of the memory. If you overclock the FSB, you may want to decrease the overall speed of the memory in the BIOS because the FSB overclocking will increase the speed of the memory. For example, if you overclock the FSB from 200 MHz to 227 MHz, then memory running at 200 MHz would also increase to 227 MHz. However, if you underclock the memory to 160 MHz, then the overclocking brings the speed of the memory to 187 MHz, which may suit your memory's performance capabilities better.

Be careful with any memory timing settings because they will heavily influence how stable your system will run. With all memory settings the lowest value is the fastest but has the most chance of being unstable. By selecting a higher value, you will increase system stability by slowing the memory down, which creates fewer errors. Some common memory timing parameters and their functions are:

- **CAS latency**—The number of clock cycles between the receipt of a read command and the point when the RAM chip actually starts reading. Obviously, lower numbers will result in less of a delay when memory is being read. Memory is basically a table with many rows and columns, and the CAS delay is invoked every time the column changes.

- **Active to precharge**—This timing controls how long after activation the access cycle should be started again. This influences row activation time, which is taken into account when memory has hit the last column in a specific row or when an entirely different memory location is requested.

- **RAS to CAS delay**—The timing between column access strobe and row access strobe signals. This is used when memory is written, read, or refreshed.

- **Precharge to active**—The length of the delay between the precharge and activation commands. This affects row activation time, which is taken into account when memory has hit the last column in a specific row or when an entirely different memory location is requested.

- **Active to CMD**—The length of the delay between the time when a memory bank is activated and when a read/write command is sent to that bank. This comes into play when the memory locations are not accessed in a sequential manner.

- **DRAM command rate**—Controls how long the memory controller latches on and asserts the command bus. The lower the value, the faster the memory controller can send commands out.

Also, just as with the processor there are often voltage options for the memory modules. The standard voltage specification for DDR memory is 2.6 volts. But be aware that increased voltage, while sometimes increasing the likelihood of being able to overclock memory, leads to increased heat. Be sure to have good cooling in the general area of the memory modules, especially if overclocking

Tip You can purchase memory heat spreaders from many modding Web sites. These are basically metal coverings for the memory modules that are supposed to act as a sort of heatsink for the memory. Their effectiveness is often debated, but they do look cool!

Video Card

Overclocking a video card is a bit more specific to the exact make and model of the video card. Basically, a specific piece of software is installed that tweaks parameters in either the BIOS of the video card or the system registry to allow the card to overclock. Modern video cards feature processors just as complex, if not more so, than the main CPU in the system itself and generate almost as much heat, so be sure your cooling solution is up to the job.

When overclocking a video card, there are two parameters that can be overclocked—the main graphics processing unit (GPU) or the on-board memory. Once again, the card manufacturers sometimes repackage higher-performing cards as lower-performing cards so that they have enough cards available at the various price points. If you are lucky enough, you may have one of these underclocked cards.

In addition to the usual tricks the manufacturers perform to make sure that you don't get something for nothing, video card manufacturers sometimes employ an extra trick. Sometimes these lower-model cards have a special video BIOS installed that actually disable parts of the chips such as the "pipelines" between memory and the GPU to make the card underperform. Sometimes these cards can be reflashed with the higher-performing card's video BIOS to reenable these features, but that is very specific to the exact video card you have.

The best way to overclock a video card is to use the built-in overclocking options that sometimes come with the video card drivers themselves, or use any of dozens of video overclocking tools such as RivaTuner.

Tip RivaTuner is an overclocking program for both NVIDIA and ATI-based video cards. It can be downloaded from `www.guru3d.com/rivatuner`.

Modding to the Rescue

If you have a processor that simply won't run past its rated speed no matter what tricks you try, there is not a lot that modding can do to help you directly. But if the processor is simply flaky—it runs for a while then causes errors of some sort—modding can help.

One basic problem with overclocking is heat generation. Overclocking generates much more heat than the component was probably designed to deal with. But as you have seen throughout this book many, many mods exist for solving heat-related problems.

Open up the case by cutting a few holes and adding fans. Replace existing fans with better quality fans. Add a better heatsink on top of the processor. Move on to extreme cooling—use a water-cooling kit to run water over your processor to remove heat. You can even, for short periods, use liquid nitrogen to cool your processor to a temperature lower than your freezer! All of these mods will help pull a little bit extra speed from that processor, luck permitting.

A lesson in Knowing Your Limits

It can't be emphasized enough here—know how far you are willing to go before proceeding with any extreme overclocking or extreme cooling.

- Many of the cooling methods can be quite dangerous. An improper water-cooling setup will damage every component that water can touch, and could even cause electrocution. Liquid nitrogen can literally freeze and shatter parts right off your body. Be careful.

- Overclocking itself, even without the ill effects of cooling gone wrong, can still ruin multiple components in your system at the same time. Be prepared for the risk of losing it all.

Only experiment with parts that you can afford to lose, just as with all mods.

Wrapping Up

In the end, it's your choice. The payoff can be great. The downside can also be just as great. Whether or not you should try overclocking also depends on the point of the system. If it's a mega-game-playing PC, and you have an occasional crash related to overclocking instability, then you can probably accept that. However, if you work on long video-editing projects with deadlines and 20+ hour times for segments of video to finish rendering, then a crash during the 19th hour that forces a complete rerender probably isn't worth the risk. Figure out your risk tolerance, and you're already ahead of the game.

Resource	Description
Think Geek (www.thinkgeek.com)	Toys for geeks, and some limited modding supplies.
Dome Stickers.com (www.domestickers.com)	If you are "old school" and want one of those traditional unlighted case badges, this is the place to go. Besides a good collection of case badges, they sell do-it-yourself kits.

Online Computer Parts Stores

These stores do not specialize in supplies for the modding community but in those for the computer enthusiast in general. However, without cheap and reliable sources of equipment modders would have nothing to mod.

Resource	Description
Newegg (www.newegg.com)	A great selection of merchandise for reasonable prices.
Zip Zoom Fly (www.zipzoomfly.com)	Another source of cheap components, and a decent selection.
Computer Geeks (www.compgeeks.com)	Good prices as well, and the occasional great deal.
LSDiodes (www.lsdiodes.com)	Modders go through ultrabrite LEDs like popcorn, but they are expensive at around $2 per LED. But not here. Limited selection, but prices that are typically a quarter of those at most sites.
All Electronics Corp (www.allelectronics.com)	A great source of electronics components online, with an excellent catalog.
B.G. Micro (www.bgmicro.com)	A good source of electronics components online, including the occasional great deal on large VFD displays.
eBay (www.ebay.com)	Like it or not, this is the 500 pound gorilla of online auction sites and can be just the place to get some components cheap.

Noncomputer Suppliers

Modders, by definition, think outside the box. Therefore, they shouldn't and can't limit themselves to just stores or sites that specialize in computer parts. Here are some sites that carry tools and supplies that are not typically thought of as being related to computers.

Resource	Description
TAP Plastics (www.tapplastics.com)	If you want something acrylic, or tools relating to plastic, this is the place. If they don't carry it or can't get it, there is a 99 percent chance it doesn't exist.
Sears (www.sears.com)	A general department store, widely respected due to their "Craftsmen" line of tools with lifetime warranties.
The Home Depot (www.homedepot.com)	A large home improvement store chain with many of the raw materials or tools needed for modding.
Lowe's (www.lowes.com)	Another large home improvement store chain.
Dremel (www.dremel.com)	Home of every modder's best friend, the Dremel rotary tool. Visit the Web site to view all the different attachments they make.

Exotic Links

These links are important for specific mods mentioned in this book. While limited in scope, they are certainly important and contain valuable info often found nowhere else on the net.

Resource	Description	Specific mods
VFD World (www.vfdworld.com)	Home of the famous VFD Thinger, a great program for controlling VFD (and some LCD) displays. The site and the program are maintained by a great modder as well.	Used for the Scientist mod in Chapter 12. This site is maintained by the modder who created the $3,000 FishTank mod in Chapter 16.
Multiple Arcade Machine Emulator (www.mame.net)	Perhaps the most ambitious emulation project ever, this site contains the software you will need to build you own arcade emulator.	Used for the miniMAME mod in Chapter 15.
Happ Controls (www.happcontrols.com)	A good source of real arcade components such as joysticks, buttons, and trackballs. Also note the real price tag, but the quality of components can't be beat.	Also used for "miniMAME" mod in Chapter 15.

Resource	Description	Specific mods
I-Appliance BBS (www.linux-hacker.net/ cgi-bin/UltraBoard/ UltraBoard.pl)	A great source of information about Internet appliances and various other fascinating and unique moddable hardware.	Source of some info for Picture Frame PC in Chapter 13.
Virgin Webplayer info (www.webplayer. 0catch.com)	One of the better collections of Webplayer info on the Web. WARNING: Use a pop-up blocker before going to this site.	Extensively used for the Picture Frame PC in Chapter 13.
Select Products (www.selectproducts .com)	One source of grille metal, such as that used to cover speakers and other components. Finding a high-quality source of small quantities of grille metal can be difficult.	Used in both miniMAME (Chapter 15) and Aircraft Carrier PC (Chapter 19)
The LED Museum (http:// ledmuseum.home.att .net)	Everything you ever wanted to know about LEDs and much, much more. You will be amazed that so much can be written on this topic.	LEDs are covered in Chapter 4 and used in almost every single mod.

Index